THREE DEMONSTRATIONS AND A FUNERAL

& OTHER ESSAYS

CSLI Lecture Notes Number 231

THREE DEMONSTRATIONS AND A FUNERAL

&

OTHER ESSAYS

MARÍA DE PONTE, KEPA KORTA
AND JOHN PERRY

CSLI
PUBLICATIONS
Center for the Study of
Language and Information
Stanford, California

Copyright © 2025
CSLI Publications
Center for the Study of Language and Information
Leland Stanford Junior University
Printed in the United States
29 28 27 26 25   1 2 3 4 5

Names: de Ponte, Maria, | Korta, Kepa, | Perry, John 1943- .
Title: Three Demonstrations and a Funeral and Other Essays - Maria de Ponte, Kepa Korta, John Perry.
Description: Stanford, Calif. : CSLI Publications, 2025. | Series: CSLI Lecture Notes Number 231 | Includes bibliographical references and index. | Summary: "The papers collected here are the best sample of one of the most original theories in the philosophy of language and communication (Critical Pragmatics). They present the development of the theory from its intial sprout from Perry's critical Referentialism, with "Three Demonstrations and a Funeral" (2006) as its first visible result. to a critical clarification of its tenets in "Critical Pragmatics: Nince Misconception" (2011), this is the most important book on "Critical Pragmatics," as it was conceived, developed and applied by its creators" — Provided by publisher.
Identifiers: LCCN 2024045411 (print) | LCCN 2024045412 (ebook)
      | ISBN 9781881526933 (paperback) | ISBN 9781881526001 (ebook)
| LCC P26.G635 C66 2018 (print) | DDC 415–dc23
Subjects: LCSH: Pragmatics. | Semantics.
Classification: Classifications: P99.4.P72 I35 2025 (print) | LCC P99.4.P72 (ebook)
      — DDC 425.01/836–dc23/eng/20241026
LC record available at `https://lccn.loc.gov/2024045411`
LC ebook record available at `https://lccn.loc.gov/2024045412`

CIP

∞ The acid-free paper used in this book meets the minimum requirements of the American National Standard for Information Sciences—Permanence of Paper for Printed Library Materials, ANSI Z39.48-1984.

CSLI Publications is located on the campus of Stanford University.

Visit our web site at
`http://cslipublications.stanford.edu/`
for comments on this and other titles, as well as for changes
and corrections by the author and publisher.

It is wonderful to have all seventeen of these papers (previously dispersed across myriad journals and books) together in a single volume, amply demonstrating the explanatory power and depth of the Critical Pragmatics paradigm. The volume will be an indispensable reference for anyone wanting to understand how linguistic communication works.
—*Robyn Carston (University College London)*

Maria de Ponte, Kepa Korta and John Perry's Three Demonstrations and a Funeral and other Essays does not just bring together a set of individually important contributions to issues at the intersection of semantics and pragmatics. Taken together, the papers offer a compelling picture of what we say and do with our utterances, thereby demonstrating the fruitfulness of the theoretical framework originating in Perry's Reference and Reflexivity (2001). It should be read by any philosophers interested in language, mind and action.
—*Stacie Friend (University of Edinburgh)*

The papers in this volume sharpen Critical Pragmatics, focusing critically on approaches that postulate some form of pragmatic intrusion, and expand it, applying it to a variety of issues, including fictional names, the passage of time, Frege's notion of identity and the notion of luck. The last paper contains an extremely well-articulated defense of the theory from a series of pervasive (and incomprehensible, one might add) misconceptions. Having all these papers in a single volume will be an inestimable tool for anyone interested in critical pragmatics and, more generally, for anyone interested in reference, communication, and the semantics and pragmatics of referential devices.
—*Genoveva Martí (University of Barcelona)*

Started with the collaboration between John Perry and Kepa Korta, this kaleidoscopic selection of papers is enriched in its last part with the intrusion of a third element, Maria de Ponte, who brings new subjects into focus, such as the topic of luck and of fictional entities. Most of the papers mix a high analytic endeavor with the levity of multifarious examples that help clarify the most irksome conceptual points. Even the old fashioned Fregean themes find a new illumination, following the idea that the late Frege's suggestion to consider truth values as the referent of a sentence obliged many philosophers to make a long detour to reach a new interpretation of what he suggested in the introduction of his Ideography. And, eventually, readers will find, not so hidden inside the selection of papers, new insight on the original topic from which all started: the essential demonstratives.

—*Carlo Penco (University of Genoa)*

John Perry's reflexive-referential theory, as expounded (inter alia) in his masterpiece Reference and Reflexivity, applies tools from action theory to issues in the philosophy of language and communication. Pragmatics as a discipline evolved from a new conception of language as action put forward by philosophers such as John Austin, Paul Grice and Peter Strawson (not to mention Wittgenstein). The affinities between these different approaches are obvious and open up an interesting research program: explore the potential of Perry's reflexive-referential theory to illuminate and hopefully resolve pending issues in pragmatics. Carrying out this research program was the aim of Korta's and Perry's first joint book, Critical Pragmatics, and it remains the aim of this major collection of papers where de Ponte, Korta and Perry attempt to arbitrate the current debates on the semantics/pragmatics distinction, the minimalism/contextualism debate, etc. The book offers new insights on key issues and is a must read for philosophers and linguists working in that area.

—*François Recanati (Collége de France)*

Contents

Foreword   ix
Introduction   xi
Permissions   xix

1. Three Demonstrations and A Funeral   1
  KORTA AND PERRY

2 Radical Minimalism, Moderate Contextualism   25
  KORTA AND PERRY

3 How to Say Things with Words   43
  KORTA AND PERRY

4 The Pragmatic Circle   63
  KORTA AND PERRY

5 Reference: A New Paradigm   75
  KORTA AND PERRY

6 Intentions to Refer   87
  KORTA AND PERRY

7 What is Said   107
  KORTA AND PERRY

8 Highlights of *Critical Pragmatics*: Reference and the Contents of the Utterance   123
  KORTA AND PERRY

9 Squaring the Circle   143
    KORTA AND PERRY

10 Full but not Saturated: The Myth of Mandatory Primary Pragmatic Processes   155
    KORTA AND PERRY

11 New Thoughts about Old Facts: On Prior's Root Canal   173
    DE PONTE AND KORTA

12 Truth without Reference: The Use of Fictional Names   191
    DE PONTE, KORTA AND PERRY

13 Utterance and Context   211
    DE PONTE, KORTA AND PERRY

14 Four Puzzling Paragraphs. Frege on "≡" and "="   225
    DE PONTE, KORTA AND PERRY

15 Language and Luck   245
    DE PONTE, KORTA AND PERRY

16 Philosophy of Language and Action Theory   265
    DE PONTE, KORTA AND PERRY

17 Critical Pragmatics: Nine Misconceptions   287
    DE PONTE, KORTA AND PERRY

References   307
Index   319

Foreword

MARÍA DE PONTE, KEPA KORTA AND JOHN PERRY

This book is a result, not only of the collaboration of the three authors, but of two universities—the University of the Basque Country and Stanford University. In 1986, the late Jesus Mari Larrazabal and John Etchemendy met at a conference. They started talking about Etchemendy's Basque heritage, which was evident to Larrazabal from his name. Then they discussed logic and philosophy and found they had a lot in common in addition to being Basque. They became friends and Etchemendy visited the University of the Basque Country. Soon John and Nancy Etchemendy brought John and Frenchie Perry with them on a visit to Donostia, and they met Kepa Korta, then finishing up his doctoral dissertation directed by Larrazabal. On his next trip, Perry was awarded an honorary doctorate. Years later, María de Ponte started working with Kepa Korta as a postdoctoral researcher and met John Perry at a workshop on Semantics, Pragmatics and Rhetoric (SPR), organized by the ILCLI. So, as of now, all three authors of this book are connected with the University of the Basque Country; Korta and de Ponte are professors there, and Perry has an honorary doctorate.

Korta began a series of visits to CSLI at Stanford, and the bond with Perry grew stronger; also, over the years a number of Larrazabal's and Korta's students have visited Stanford. And María de Ponte made an extended visit with Korta in 2015 and 2016. This would eventually be the first of many. So, it is appropriate that CSLI Publications, led by our common hero and friend Dikran Karagueuzian, is publishing the book.

In addition to colleagues, family, and friends we owe a great deal to the two universities and especially to Jesus Mari Larrazabal and John Etchemendy for getting the collaboration between the universities, their institutes —ILCLI and CSLI—, and their philosophy departments off to a great start.

Introduction

María de Ponte, Kepa Korta and John Perry

After the first edition of *Reference and Reflexivity* in 2001, John Perry asked his friend Kepa Korta to help him explore whether the semantical theory developed there, which he called "Reflexive-Referential Theory" as well as "Critical Referentialism," had any interesting applications to pragmatics.[1]

The key idea of Critical Referentialism is that truth and falsity are, fundamentally, properties of utterances—events that occur at a place and a time in circumstances. Fundamental conditions of truth are *reflexive*, in that the truth-conditions of an utterance are conditions *on* the utterance *itself*. For example, an utterance u of "Putin once sold shoes in New Zealand" is true if and only if the person referred to by the speaker's utterance of "Putin" in u had at the time of u, the property referred to by the speaker's use of "once sold shoes in New Zealand."[2] These are the *reflexive* truth-conditions of u. But these are not the only truth-conditions u has.

We get further truth-conditions by filling in some facts about the utterance, and asking *what else* has to be the case for u to be true, *given* those facts. For example, given that u was uttered in March 2024 by Mary, u is true if and only if the person referred to by Mary's utterance of "Putin" in u had, at some time earlier than March, 2024, the property referred to by Mary's use of "once sold shoes in New Zealand." If we take all the relevant facts as

---

[1] For reasons that, we hope, get clearly explained through the book, it may sound a bit weird that we use proper names to refer to ourselves, as we do in this introduction, but we did not find a better way. Also, as we explicitly say in some of the papers, since they are all co-authored, there really is no referent for our uses of "I." However, we find the first-person singular too effective, in particular for presenting examples. So we do not give it up.

[2] "Multiple reports have suggested Putin was sent by the KGB to New Zealand, corroborated through New Zealand eyewitness accounts and government records. This has never been confirmed by Russian security services." *Wikipedia* entry on Putin.

given—that Mary was the speaker of *u*, that she was referring to Vladimir Putin and that she used "once sold shoes in New Zealand" for the property of selling shoes in New Zealand, and that *u* occurred in March 2024, what else has to be the case is that Vladimir Putin sold shoes in New Zealand at some time before March 2024. These are the *referential* truth-conditions of *u*. They can be captured by a singular proposition that could be expressed by different people at different places and times.

The referential truth-conditions are what we usually focus on, often taken to be *the* content of the utterance, having the status of *the* proposition expressed. But Perry argued that the reflexive truth-conditions are also truth-conditions and contents of the utterance, as are the truth-conditions considered in the last paragraph, corresponding to *what else* has to be the case for truth when only some of the relevant facts of reference are given. At some point we started calling them "hybrid truth-conditions."

These additional contents of utterances, Perry argued, are useful for dealing with traditional problems in semantics. Frege asks how "Hesperus is a planet" and "Phosphorus is a planet" (not quite his example) can have different "cognitive significance"; that is, how one can believe an utterance of the first but not of the second, when they have the same truth-conditions, since they attribute the same property to the same thing. But although they may have the same referential truth-conditions, they have different hybrid truth-conditions, taking the reference of "is a planet" as given but not the reference of "Hesperus" and/or "Phosphorus." Truth of the first utterance requires that the planet referred to, Venus, be named "Hesperus" but not that it be named "Phosphorus," and the opposite for the second utterance. Perry thought these ideas would have important applications for pragmatics, but he needed a better grasp of the main theories.

So he turned to his friend Kepa Korta, who knew—Perry thought—considerably more about pragmatics. They wrote several papers between 2006 and 2011, including the first seven papers of this volume, building the framework that they would later call "Critical Pragmatics." In 2011, the same year that Perry finished the second edition of his book *Reference and Reflexivity*, their joint book *Critical Pragmatics* was published, giving a systematic development of a semantic/pragmatic theory and applying it to a number of classical issues in the philosophy of language and to more recent issues in debates in semantics and pragmatics.

In their first joint paper, "Three Demonstrations and A Funeral" (Chapter 1), Korta and Perry considered a famous case from H. P. Grice:

> A is standing by an obviously immobilized car and is approached by B. The following exchange takes place:

A: I am out of petrol
B: There is a garage around the corner (Grice, 1967a [1989], 32)

It is hard to see what is going on if we simply focus on what A and B said. According to Grice's very plausible and very influential theory, with which most readers will already be familiar, we need to distinguish between what is said and what is *implicated*. A says that A is out of petrol at the time of the utterance. She doesn't ask about garages in the vicinity. She doesn't *imply* this either, in the sense in which "implies" means something like "logically entails." What she does is *implicate* that she would appreciate information about where she could get some petrol. That means, basically, that B, given a modicum of common sense, will realize that the most plausible explanation for A saying what she did in the way she did in the situation she was in, was to elicit such information from B. B's reply doesn't imply that the garage around the corner sells gas, but again it implicates it.

It seems that what A says is a matter of semantics, that is, basically the truth-conditions of her utterance. What she implicates seems to be a matter of pragmatics, how we use language to do things. This seemed, at first, to fit the standard view of how semantics and pragmatics were related: It is the job of semantics to determine what is said. Then pragmatics takes over, and tells us what is further implicated. But it was soon realized that Grice's theory challenged this picture. If a person mumbles, we may rely on implicatures, on what they are trying to do, to figure out what they said. Dealing with Grice's insights led to divisions among philosophers of language and linguists.

We discuss Chapter 1 here, not to spare the reader the task of reading it, but rather to motivate them to do so. In the rest of the paper, Korta and Perry use their incipient framework to explain Grice's theory and what it implies and doesn't imply about the relation of semantics and pragmatics, to begin building the framework of Critical Pragmatics. We now offer a bit of information about the essays that came next.

Chapter 2, "Radical Minimalism, Moderate Contextualism," is the long version of "Varieties of Minimalist Semantics," a contribution to a symposium on Herman Capellen and Ernie Lepore's book, *Insensitive Semantics* (2005), held by *Philosophy and Phenomenological Research*. Due to space limits, Korta and Perry had to cut from that earlier version the parts where they present their moderate position regarding what came to be known as "contextualism," but they later incorporated them in the paper here included, originally published in a volume edited by Gerhard Preyer and Georg Peter.

The origin of Chapter 3, "How to Say Things with Words," was an invitation by Savas Tsohatzidis to participate in a volume on the work of John Searle. That is why we focus on a discussion of the applicability of our pluralistic theory of contents to Searle's speech-act theoretic notion of propositional content. We argue that Searle's theory requires not only a level of referential content, neutral among speech acts with different illocutionary forces, but the whole variety of reflexive and hybrid contents to reflect the variety of satisfaction-conditions established by those illocutionary forces.

Chapter 4, "The Pragmatic Circle," addresses an issue in the boundaries between semantics and pragmatics or, as we prefer to say, between *near-* and *far-side* pragmatics (Korta and Perry, 2006b). For some decades, what is said by a speaker uttering a sentence has been considered to be largely a matter of semantics, with some pragmatic *intrusion*, consisting basically in certain facts needed to resolve reference of context-sensitive expressions. Despite significant disagreements on the amount of pragmatic intrusion into what is said, the fact that pragmatic facts involving Gricean planning and reasoning are admitted to intervene into the determination of the proposition expressed create the problem that Levinson (2000) called "Grice's Circle": If pragmatic processes are needed to determine what is said, and the determination of what is said is needed to pragmatic processes to take off, we face a vicious circle. We claim, in this chapter, that our approach has the tools to solve—or dissolve—the problem.

Chapter 5, "Reference: A New Paradigm," focuses on the use of referential devices in communicative settings, with an emphasis on the role of indexicals and demonstratives. On our view, indexicals and demonstratives are not a sort of hybrid of the two paradigmatic tools for referring and denoting—names and definite descriptions. Rather, taken as devices of role-coordination, they offer a new paradigm, according to which the speaker's aim is not only to designate an object, but to offer the hearer a way to identify the object that accords with her communicative plan. Indexicals and demonstratives exploit utterance-based roles. Names and descriptions are role-coordination devices too.

In Chapter 6, "Intentions to Refer," the attention moves to the intentions that accompany the use of referential devices by the speakers in communicative acts. On our view, the intentions involved in acts of reference are Gricean intentions of certain kinds—*grammatical, directing, target, path,* and *auxiliary*—, which, together with the speaker's goals and beliefs, conform a structured referential plan. In this chapter, we develop the motives for the theory, explain how it works, and apply it to a number of examples.

Chapter 7, "What is Said," discusses a central dilemma in the referentialist/descriptivist debate concerning the best way to characterize what is said by a speaker's utterance containing a name, an indexical or a demonstrative. On the one hand, Kaplan's arguments, for instance, favor a singular proposition as the best candidate for what is said. On the other hand, Grice's theory of implicatures seems to require some general proposition; a proposition that contains an identifying condition of an object rather than the object itself. Based on a discussion of the semantics and pragmatics of indirect speech reports, we argue that Critical Pragmatics offers a simple, natural and elegant way out of the dilemma.

Chapter 8, entitled "Highlights of *Critical Pragmatics*: Reference and the Contents of Utterances," is, of course, a *Précis* of our 2011 monograph, after a kind invitation from the editor-in-chief of *Intercultural Pragmatics*. We give a short general overview of the whole theory and we focus a bit more extensively on two aspects of our theory as exposed there: On the one hand, we focus on our account of reference as action motivated by a complex Gricean intention or plan that exploits the cognitive fixes that the speaker has on an object and that she plans the hearer to have. On the other hand, we insist on the renounce to "mono-propositionalism" and the defense of a systematic variety of truth-conditions—or, more generally, satisfaction-conditions—for utterances and cognitive states like desires, beliefs and intentions.

The next two chapters deal with yet another novelty of our approach: the provision of purely semantic contents or truth-conditions—satisfaction-conditions—that do not need any sort of completion to become "fully propositional." In Chapter 9, "Squaring the Circle," we apply that idea to tackle "Grice's Circle" once again. In Chapter 10, "Full but not Saturated: The Myth of Mandatory Pragmatic Processes," we begin by arguing, once more, that the assumption that some pragmatic processes are needed in order to get a fully truth-evaluable proposition is false. Minimalists and contextualists all share that assumption when it comes, for example, to the provision of references for indexicals and demonstratives: Without those references, they claim, the utterance lacks complete truth-conditions. We show they are wrong. If primary pragmatic processes are mandatory, it is not due to reasons of completion.

By 2016, Critical Pragmatics was well-known among linguists and philosophers as a powerful alternative to the transmission model of human linguistic communication. Korta and Perry continued to work, and the duo became a trio when María de Ponte joined the team. de Ponte and Korta had been working together since 2009, and her collaboration with Perry was sparked by a common interest on Dummett—and their shared admiration for Korta. While thinking about the—yet to be written—paper on Dummett's views on time and truth, she co-authored the last seven papers in this collection. de Ponte had something both Perry and Korta liked, facility with logic and familiarity with philosophers like Prior, whose work on tense, predication and propositions is quite relevant to pragmatics and semantics; not to mention an innate capacity for procrastination shared and embraced by Korta and by Perry alike.[3] And she comes from Tenerife, in the Canary Islands, Hume's favorite island after Britain, which ought to count for something.

de Ponte and Korta co-authored "New Thoughts about Old Facts," (Chapter 11), where the focus moves from issues closely related to semantics and pragmatics, to issues on the epistemology and the metaphysics of time. They discuss Arthur Prior's famous paper "Thank Goodness that's Over" (1959) and argue against a widely shared interpretation that takes it to constitute a strong argument about the nature of time; in particular, an argument showing that a B-theory of time is false. They do not argue against A-theories, but they show that Prior's argument provides no support for them. Critical Pragmatics proves to be a useful framework to disentangle linguistic, epistemological and metaphysical threads. This paper was the continuation of a series of papers, where de Ponte and Korta applied Critical Pragmatics to problems of philosophy of time (2014, 2015).

Chapter 12, "Truth without Reference: The Use of Fictional Names," the first paper authored by the trio, elaborates, with some modifications, on Perry's account of fictional names, presented in Perry 2001 [2012]. Briefly put, it defends a view according to which fictional statements lack referential truth-conditions but possess notion-bound truth-conditions, that is, fictional notions like the notion of Sherlock Homes created by Conan Doyle in his fictional stories. There is no need, then, of postulating any sort of fictional (non-)entities to which proper names in fictional statements refer.

The aim of "Utterance and Context," Chapter 13, is to discuss the differences between two pairs of concepts: David Kaplan's and our notion of context, on the one hand, and his notion of sentence-in-context and our notion of utterance, on the other. A general difference between Kaplan's approach and ours is the use we make of those notions: Kaplan's goal is to build a logic of indexicals, and that is why he sacrifices utterances for sentences-in-context, defining contexts as the quadruple of agent, time, place and world. Our goal is to build an account of natural language and thought in communicative settings; a more inclusive notion of utterance becomes central. In this paper, we argue for the advantages of our view for such an account.

Chapter 14, "Four Puzzling Paragraphs. Frege on '≡' and '='," is largely an elaboration of some of the ideas defended by Perry on his book *Frege's Detour* (2019a). In that book, Perry makes a defense of Frege's earlier work, mostly in the *Begriffsschrift*, claiming that Frege had all the tools he needed

---

[3] Saying that Perry embraces (structured) procrastination is clearly an understatement. In 2011, Perry won the Ig Nobel prize in literature for an essay on structured procrastination. He later turned this essay into a book: *The Art of Procrastination: A Guide to Effective Dawdling, Lollygagging and Postponing* (2012). Perry's mastery of the subject has been crucial in turning Korta and de Ponte's clumsy procrastinating habits into structured and somehow productive ones.

to solve problems of identity and more general difficulties associated with singular terms. Frege's elimination of circumstances as the reference of sentences, and their substitution by truth-values, among other claims, sent philosophy into a long and largely unnecessary detour; one we can avoid, or at least conclude, with the adoption of a reflexive-referential account. In this chapter, we focus on Frege's treatment of identity, and his notion of identity of content, as introduced in the *Begriffsschrift*. We defend that there, Frege does not hold that identity is a relation between signs, and we discuss the type of problems Frege was concerned with, and how he did, or did not, solved them.

In Chapter 15, "Language and Luck," we put the reflexive-referential theory to work in a completely novel area for us—luck. We focus in the analysis of two sorts of cases: cases of lucky necessities and cases of linguistic luck. The first concerns assessments of luck associated to necessary facts, like the fact that I'm not Jack the Ripper. If I'm not Jack the Ripper, then it is a necessary truth that I'm not Jack the Ripper. Still, if upon opening your house door, your neighbor Bob says "you are lucky I am not Jack the Ripper," we would tend to think he is right—particularly if your house is in London, in the late nineteenth-century. Making use of the reflexive-referential theory, with a particular emphasis in the notion of "episodes," we give an account of these sorts of cases. We also consider cases of linguistic or, more precisely, communicative luck like the classic Loar (1976) example on what we call "referential convergence." Explaining these cases leads us to discuss Critical Referentialism, and some interesting differences between "notions" and Fregean senses.

In "Philosophy of Language and Action Theory," Chapter 16, we discuss the relation of these two fields in the history of the philosophy of language since the beginning of the twentieth-century. The origins of this discipline were closely related to logical and formal aspects of language, far from any interest in action theory. The conception of language as action inaugurated by Austin, Grice, and Strawson inspired new philosophical theories, like the Reflexive-Referential theory or Critical Pragmatics, to deal with classic puzzles in the philosophy of language like reference and cognitive significance. We defend the reflexive-referential account as an example of the beneficial impact of action theory on the philosophy of language.

Our last chapter, "Critical Pragmatics: Nine Misconceptions," was conceived for a workshop celebrated with occasion of the tenth anniversary of the publication of *Critical Pragmatics*. It was also almost 20 years since Korta and Perry's first joint publication (Chapter 1), so in this paper, rather than highlighting or extending on key aspects of the theory, we set out to discuss, explain and undo various misconceptions we have identified during the years; not only on Critical Pragmatics, but also on Critical Referentialism and on Perry's seminal theory on indexicals and demonstratives.

The account developed in *Critical Pragmatics* hasn't quite converted the majority of philosophers of language to our view, at least not yet. Give it time. But it has been used, adopted and extended by a number of brilliant philosophers and linguists, like Shannon Bain, Eduarda Calado, Lenny Clapp, Eros Corazza, Beñat Esnaola, Stacie Friend, Ekain Garmendia, Joana Garmendia, Chris Genovesi, Jenny Hung, Armando Lavalle Terrón, Genoveva Martí, Eleonora Orlando, Carlo Penco, Ernesto Perini Santos, Ana Clara Polakof, Richard Vallée, and Larraitz Zubeldia. And it has been discussed and criticized by a number of eminent philosophers, who have hopefully enjoyed it and who may have learned a thing or two from it. So we think making these papers available in this form will be useful. By publishing these papers, we will make our views available to more philosophers, linguists, and other interested in pragmatics. We hope the result will be more adherents of our view. But it may be more critics, finding flaws and oversimplifications in our views. That's philosophy, after all.

Permissions

Chapter 1. Kepa Korta and John Perry. 2006. "Three Demonstrations and A Funeral." *Mind and Language* 21/2: 166–86.

Chapter 2. Kepa Korta and John Perry. 2007. "Radical Minimalism, Moderate Contextualism." *Context-Sensitivity and Semantic Minimalism: Essays on Semantics and Pragmatics,* eds. Gerhard Preyer and Georg Peter, 94–111. Oxford: Oxford University Press.

Chapter 3. Kepa Korta and John Perry. 2007. "How to Say Things with Words." *John Searle's Philosophy of Language: Force, Meaning, and Thought,* ed. Savas L. Tsohatzidis, 169–189. Cambridge: Cambridge University Press.

Chapter 4. Kepa Korta and John Perry. 2008. "The Pragmatic Circle." *Synthese* 165/3: 347–357.

Chapter 5. Kepa Korta and John Perry. 2009. "Reference: A New Paradigm." *Meaning, Content and Argument,* eds. Jesus M. Larrazabal and Larraitz Zubeldia, 73–88. Bilbao: UPV-EHU.

Chapter 6. Kepa Korta and John Perry. 2010. "Intentions to Refer." *Meaning and context,* eds. Luca Baptista and Erich Rast, 161–186. Bern: Peter Lang.

Chapter 7. Kepa Korta and John Perry. 2010. "What is Said." *Context-Dependence, Perspective and Relativity,* eds. François Recanati, Isidora Stojanovic, and Neftalí Villanueva, 51–67. Berlin: Mouton De Gruyter.

Chapter 8. Kepa Korta and John Perry. 2013. "Highlights of *Critical Pragmatics*: Reference and the Contents of the Utterance." *Intercultural Pragmatics* 10/1: 161–182.

Chapter 9. Kepa Korta and John Perry. 2013. "Squaring the Circle." *Perspectives in Pragmatics and Philosophy,* eds. Alessandro Capone, Franco Lo Piparo, and Marco Carapezza, 291–302. Springer.

Chapter 10. Kepa Korta and John Perry. 2017. "Full but not Saturated: The Myth of Mandatory Primary Pragmatic Processes." *Meaning, Context, and Methodology,* eds. Sarah-Jane Conrad and Klaus Petrus, 31–49. Mouton de Gruyter.

Chapter 11. María de Ponte and Kepa Korta. 2017. "New Thoughts about Old Facts: On Prior's Root Canal." *Reference and Representation and Thought and Language,* eds. María de Ponte and Kepa Korta, 163–178. Oxford: Oxford University Press.

Chapter 12. María de Ponte, Kepa Korta and John Perry. 2020. "Truth without Reference: The Use of Fictional Names." *Topoi* 39: 389–99.

Chapter 13. María de Ponte, Kepa Korta and John Perry. 2020. "Utterance and Context." *The Architecture of Context and Context-Sensitivity,* eds. Tadeusz Ciecierski and Pawel Grabarczyk, 15–28. Springer.

Chapter 14. María de Ponte, Kepa Korta and John Perry. 2021. "Four Puzzling Paragraphs. Frege on "≡" and "="." *Semiotica* 240: 75–95.

Chapter 15. María de Ponte, Kepa Korta and John Perry. 2023. "Language and Luck." *Linguistic Luck. Essays in Anti-Luck Semantics*, eds. Abrol Fairweather and Carlos Montemayor, 15–35. Oxford: Oxford University Press.

Chapter 16. María de Ponte, Kepa Korta and John Perry. 2023. "Philosophy of Language and Action Theory." *The Cambridge Handbook of Language in Context*, ed. Jesús Romero-Trillo, 95–115. Cambridge: Cambridge University Press.

Chapter 17. María de Ponte, Kepa Korta and John Perry. "Critical Pragmatics: Nine Misconceptions." *Topoi* 42: 913–923.

1

Three Demonstrations and A Funeral

KEPA KORTA AND JOHN PERRY

1 A Dilemma about What is Said

Consider Grice's classic example of the motorist who has run out of petrol—long considered a paradigm of Gricean implicature:

> Example Ia
>
> *A* is standing by an obviously immobilized car and is approached by *B*. The following exchange takes place:
> *A*: I am out of petrol
> *B*: There is a garage around the corner (Grice, 1967a [1989], 32).[1]

According to Grice, B *says* that there is a garage around the corner, and *implicates* that it is or at least may be open and selling petrol. The implicature is an instance of Gricean meaning; that is, *B* intends to get *A* to believe that the garage may be open, and to do so as a result of believing that *B* intends him to believe this. We see the contrast between *what is said* and *what is implicated* as a central part of Grice's theory. Essential to this central part is an account of the reasoning involved; how the speaker *plans* and the hearer *interprets* the speaker's intentional act of uttering.

Grice provides this formula for understanding such implicatures:

> He has said that *p*; there is no reason to suppose that he is not observing the maxims, or at least the Cooperative Principle; he could not be doing this unless he thought that *q*; he knows (and knows that I know that he knows) that I can see that the supposition that he thinks that *q* is required; he has done nothing to stop me thinking that *q*; he intends to think, or is at least

---

[1] All page references to Grice's work are from Grice, 1989.

> willing to allow me to think, that *q;* and so he has implicated that *q*. (Grice, 1967a [1989], 31).

It seems then that to understand implicatures, one first must grasp what is said. Then one finds the implicates, by asking what further communicative intentions a helpful conversational partner would have for saying *that*.

This picture seems to fit well with a certain view about the "semantics-pragmatics interface." It is the job of semantics to determine what is said. Then pragmatics takes over, and tells us what is further implicated.

The picture also seems to fit well with a view of semantics as computing truth-conditions of utterances compositionally according to the types of expressions used in the utterances and the ways they are combined. This part of planning and interpreting utterances does not involve the open-ended, pragmatic processes typically involved in figuring out how to have a certain effect in a particular situation, or figuring out what someone intended to do. Beyond the intention to speak a certain language, it all depends on rules connected with types by that language, not on the facts of a particular utterance.

Unfortunately, this picture doesn't seem to fit well with the combination of both views. Semantics, conceived as computing in this way, does not get us all the way to what is said. The rules associated by English with the sentence "I am out of petrol," get us to a truth-condition for utterances of it: such an utterance will be true if its speaker is out of petrol at the time of the utterance. But this is not what is said. *A* hasn't said anything about his utterance. The proposition that he expresses, what he says, is that he is out of petrol at *t*, where *t* is the time of the utterance. What he said could be true, after all, even if he didn't bother to say it. To get from the output of semantics so conceived, to what is said, we need two facts about this particular utterance, who said it, and when.

As Grice said, concerning an utterance of "He was in the grip of a vice,"

> Given a knowledge of the English language, but no knowledge of the circumstances of the utterance, one would know something about what the speaker had said, on the assumption that he was speaking standard English, and speaking literally. One would know that he had said, about some particular male person or animal *x*, that at the time of utterance (whatever that was), either (1) *x* was unable to rid himself of a certain kind of bad character trait or (2) some part of *x*'s person was caught in a certain kind of tool or instrument (approximate account, of course). (Grice, 1967a [1989], 25).

The additional knowledge needed largely concerns the speaker's intentions: to whom did the speaker refer with "he," and what meaning did the speaker intend to convey with "vice." It seems that semantics, conceived narrowly as what we know when we know the rules of a language, gets us only part way to what is said, the input of pragmatics.

We seem to have here a fundamental dilemma for the Gricean picture, which has shaped discussion of "the semantics-pragmatics interface" from the 1960's until the present. Do we stick to the narrow conception of semantics? Then pragmatics has to take over before we get to what is said. Or do we stick to the conception of semantics as giving us what is said? Then we must abandon the conception of semantics as computing according to rules of language associated with types.

Still, things don't seem so bad. It's pretty automatic to see who the speaker is and what time it is. Particularly if one is the speaker. Whenever I say something, I am the speaker, and the time is, as I would put it then, *now*. Perhaps an ever so slightly augmented conception of semantics as computing according to rules, that allows for the virtually mechanical application of the rules for "I" and "now" to the particular facts of an utterance, can be accepted.

Grice's own thinking was along these lines, but went further. He regarded what is said as determined by the conventional rules, plus the facts about which meanings of ambiguous terms and phrases were in play, plus the facts that determined the referents of indexicals and demonstratives, plus, perhaps, known facts about the designations of definite descriptions.[2] There is no way that these facts can be gathered under the narrow conception of semantics. If we consider semantics to be the science that tells us what is said, Grice let the nose of the pragmatic camel intrude under the tent of semantics.

Subsequently, a number of pragmatists have argued that the factors listed won't always get us to what is said, at least in one fairly robust sense of that phrase. We need to deal with hidden indexicals, unarticulated constituents, and enrichments of various kinds. In the light of this, debate has focused on how much more of the camel needs to be let in. In Recanati's terminology (Recanati, 2004), those on the literalist side don't want to go beyond Grice, even as it has become clear that the factors listed above won't get us to what is said. Those on the contextualist side want to let as much of the camel in as is required, and some suspect that the camel of pragmatics will pretty much take up the tent, leaving precious little for semantics, conceived as the computation of meaning according to rules, to do.

We argue the dilemma is false. We don't let any of the camel under the tent. We advocate sticking to the narrow conception of semantics, and

---

[2] Grice prefers to remain agnostic on this point:

> This brief indication of my use of *say* leaves it open whether a man who says (today) *Harold Wilson is a great man* and another who says (also today) *The British Prime Minister is a great man* would, if each knew that the two singular terms had the same reference, have said the same thing (Grice, 1967a [1989], 25).

accepting that what it delivers, as Grice pointed out in the quotation above, does not determine what the speaker says, nor enable the hearer to identify it fully. Still, we claim, the output of semantics is all that is needed as the input into pragmatics.

The key to our view is a distinction between description of what is said, and determination and knowledge of what is said. Gricean pragmatics requires a description of what is said, and this semantics narrowly conceived can provide, with no intrusion from pragmatics. Semantics can provide a description of what is said by an utterance, even though semantics, by itself, does not fully determine, but only constrains, what is said. Possession of the description of what is said provided by semantics will often not count as knowing what is said, and may not even enable one to express what is said. Nevertheless, we argue, it is adequate for the needs of pragmatics. In §§2–7 we use Grice's example to explain why we think that semantics, narrowly conceived, supplies what is needed for the pragmatic reasoning, and explain some terminology and ideas. In §§8–10 we look at examples of our own construction, concerning demonstratives ("Three Demonstrations"), domains of quantification (of people at "A Funeral"), and names, to illustrate how descriptions of what is said provided by semantics interact with pragmatic reasoning about speaker intentions to secure the understanding of what is said and what is implicated. In the last section we return to the nature of the saying/implicating distinction.

2 Gricean Reasoning

Grice is interested in the implicature of B's remark, that the garage around the corner is probably open, or at least has someone around that can be roused, and might have petrol. But let's think for a minute about B's interpretation of A's opening remark. A's opening remark sets the stage for B's reply, since B is trying to be helpful to A. It is natural to take A's opening remark as implicating that he would like some help in finding petrol for his car.

Let's suppose that in fact A is Harold Wilson.[3] According to the theories of names and indexicals that are now widely accepted, A would have then expressed the same proposition in this scenario, the singular proposition individuated by Harold Wilson and the property of being out of petrol.[4]

---

[3] We pick Harold Wilson, British Prime Minister from 1964 to 1970 and from 1974 to 1976, because Grice talks about "Harold Wilson" and "the Prime Minister" (see previous note).

[4] Grice himself was sympathetic to this in the case of demonstratives. To understand what is said by an utterance containing a demonstrative referring to x, he thought it necessary to *know the identity of x* (Grice 1967a [1989], 25).

Example Ib

> A: Harold Wilson is out of petrol.
> B: There is a garage around the corner.

In scenario Ib there is no motivation for *B*'s remark. What does the proximity of a garage to the participants in the conversation have to do with Harold Wilson's being out of petrol?

Let's look again at Grice's formula for understanding such implicatures:

> He has said that p; there is no reason to suppose that he is not observing the maxims, or at least the Cooperative Principle; he could not be doing this unless he thought that q; he knows (and knows that I know that he knows) that I can see that the supposition that he thinks that q is required; he has done nothing to stop me thinking that q; he intends me to think, or is at least willing to allow me to think, that q; and so he has implicated that q (Grice, 1967a [1989], 31).

So in Ia *B* thinks:

> This fellow I am talking to says that *he* is out of petrol... he would not be doing this unless he thought that *I* could help him...

Here the phrase "that *he* is out of petrol," designates the proposition that *A* expressed with "I am out of petrol." The that-clause is, as we shall say, a *propositional description*. As Grice realized, it is not just the proposition described (*that P*) that is important, but the way it is described (that *P*). It is this particular description, not the proposition that it describes, that is crucial to *A*'s reasoning. Here are some other descriptions of the same proposition:

> What that man just said.
> That Harold Wilson is out of petrol.

Although each of these describes the same proposition as "that *he* is out of petrol," they would not play an equivalent role in the hearer's reasoning about what is implicated. This raises the question, then, of which descriptions of what is said are appropriate to reasoning about implicatures, and how one arrives at them, on the basis of the expressions one hears the speaker use.

3 Interpreting Utterances and Other Actions

Grice considers both saying and implicating as special cases of meaning. The speaker seeks to induce or reinforce beliefs in the hearer by getting the hearer to recognize that very intention. The hearer's job, then, is to interpret action, in the sense of figuring out the intentions with which it is done.

Descriptions like "what that man said" do not contain a sentence that the hearer could use to *express* what is said, in contrast to descriptions like "that Harold Wilson is out of petrol," or "that he is out of petrol" that do contain such sentences. We'll call these *expressive descriptions of what is said.* In Grice's schema, the hearer's reasoning takes off from a thought of the form "*A* said that *S.*" "*A*" will be how the hearer thinks of the speaker; in the petrol case, something like "this fellow I'm talking to," or "the fellow standing before me." "*S,*" it seems, will be a sentence that, from the hearer's perspective, expresses the very same proposition that the speaker expressed with the sentence he used. In the petrol case, this will be something like, "He is out of petrol," which, in the context, expresses the same proposition *A* expressed with "I am out of petrol." Grice's formulation implies or at least strongly suggests that the hearer's reasoning begins with an *expressive description* of what is said.[5]

We want to note that in the general case of interpreting action, arriving at something analogous to an expressive description seldom plays any role. Suppose that you are watching Beckham executing a corner kick. What you see is someone approaching a ball and moving his body, legs, and right foot in a certain way, and the ball leaving the ground, and so forth. You interpret what you see as action, and will usually not find it too hard to figure out the intention behind it, what Beckham is trying to do. Most clearly, he is trying to put the ball in the goal or in a position where a teammate can put it in the goal. Perhaps you can confidently go further: he was trying to get it in front of the goal, about six feet high, so that Ronaldo could head it in.

One thing you will probably not do, in interpreting Beckham's corner kick, is to try to figure out how you could have moved your body and your legs and so forth, so as to do the same thing, achieve the same result, from where you are sitting, that Beckham achieves, or tries to achieve, from the corner. To do so would be rather silly. Among other things, even if you could kick the ball from the stands to the perfect place for Beckham's teammate to head it into the goal, something that would be even harder than what Beckham is trying to do, it would not count as a goal, since the rules of soccer do not permit fans to assist in scoring goals.

It is a feature of language and communication that something like an expressive hearer's representation often seems possible. Language is such a powerful instrument that we assume that at least in a very wide set of circumstances, if there is a way for *A* to say that *P* in his circumstances, then there

---

[5] We think this applies to Grice's picture whether understood as a processing model or as a rational reconstruction.

must be a way for B to say that P in his circumstances. B may well take advantage of this way of saying what A said to report what A said, should he be called on to do so. Nevertheless, we don't think such representations are essential to pragmatic reasoning.

Let's call descriptions like "what he said," *non-sentential* descriptions of what is said. There is an important class of category between non-sentential and expressive descriptions, which we'll call *utterance-bound* descriptions of what is said. These descriptions are sentential, but the words used in the sentences identify some of the factors in what is said only indirectly, in terms of the utterance itself, or, more usually, some elements of the utterance, such as the speaker. Some examples:

> He said that whomever he was talking about was a fool.
>
> Whoever wrote this said that he or she was very depressed at the time they wrote it.
>
> She said that Mabel invited everyone in whatever group they were talking about to the party.
>
> Jim said that it was raining somewhere or other—wherever he was talking about.
>
> Fred said, of whomever he was using the name "John" to refer to, that he talked too much in department meetings—but there are three Johns in the department, so I don't know exactly what he said.

These descriptions, unlike "what is said," employ sentences that provide some information about the content of what was said. But they do not express what was said. They can be used when the person doing the describing does not know what was said. In each case, the ignorance resulted from lack of knowledge of the speaker's or writer's situation. The intentions of the speaker are a key item of ignorance.

Our key claim in this paper is that semantics, conceived as a science of the meanings of types of expressions, can provide utterance-bound descriptions of what is said, that provide the input for pragmatic processing. Semantics has the job of allowing the hearer to describe what is said, but it does not have the job of providing an expressive description of what was said, as opposed to an utterance-bound description.

4 Saying and Describing What is Said

Following Grice, we regard saying as an activity that paradigmatically involves a speaker's intention to get the hearer to believe that the world meets certain conditions, by recognizing the speaker's intention to do so. Philosophers keep track of these conditions with abstract objects for which they use the term "proposition"—a term that is used in related, but somewhat different ways, by some other pragmatists. Propositions are canonically described with the phrase "that S," where S is a declarative sentence.

If I say, "Elizabeth enjoys raising dogs," I have said that Elizabeth enjoys raising dogs. If, however, I say, "Perhaps Elizabeth enjoys raising dogs," or "If Elizabeth enjoys raising dogs, it is because they are better behaved than most of her children," I haven't actually said that Elizabeth enjoys raising dogs. I have, in the terminology we will use, *expressed the proposition* that Elizabeth enjoys raising dogs. My intention is not to get my hearer to believe, but to consider, the proposition that Elizabeth enjoys raising dogs, by recognizing my intention to have him do so.

The resources a speaker has to say something, or more generally to express a proposition, include, but are not limited to, the conventions of language. The speaker may rely on generally known facts, customs, and default expectations—what Searle calls "the background" (Searle, 1980). He may rely on particular facts about the linguistic and non-linguistic context, and shared beliefs, about it. Uttering words with the intention of expressing a certain proposition P is neither necessary nor sufficient for doing so. For example, if I intend to say that Jesus Mari knows Latin, and I say, "Jesus Christ knows Latin," I will not have said that Jesus Mari knows Latin, even if my hearers all rightly interpret my intention, and I will have said that Jesus Christ knows Latin, even though no one thinks I intended to do so.

There is an old tradition that holds that a speaker must know what proposition he expresses in order to say it, and that a hearer must know what proposition the speaker has said, in order to understand what is said. This old tradition, which is an important part of the background for the view we reject, is neither very clear, nor obviously correct. Suppose, KK comes up behind JP and puts his hands over JP's eyes and says, "I have a surprise." JP has no idea who is doing this. He says, "You have just broken my glasses." It seems that JP understands what has been said, even though he does not know that KK is the referent of "I." And it seems that he has said that KK has broken his glasses, even though he does not know that KK is the referent of his use of "you."

To maintain the principle, in the light of examples like this, one must adopt a relatively weak condition of knowing what proposition is expressed by an utterance. JP knows, in this case, that "I" refers to the speaker of the utterance. Thus he can identify what is said by KK as, "that the speaker of this utterance has a surprise for me." Of course KK has not said anything about his own utterance. JP's description is correct if we take it as meaning that there is a certain person who uttered the remark, and that what that person said, the proposition he expressed, is that he has a surprise. Does this count as knowing what is said? Of course, JP could go further, given that he realizes that the speaker is the person with his hands over his eyes: "the person with his hands over my eyes has said that he has a surprise for me, and I said that he has broken my glasses."

Now suppose JP finds a note, in fact written by Mark Twain, in an old book he finds at his cabin. The note says, "I am sick of all these frog stories people are sending me." He has no idea who wrote the note or when. He can say, "The author of this note was sick of all the frog stories people were sending him around the time he wrote this note. And I'm sure he was right. He was sick of getting frog stories. Who wouldn't be?" Does JP know what proposition the author of the note expressed? Or what proposition he expressed, when he registered his faith in the note-writer's sincerity? Only if one adopts a weak condition for knowing what proposition was expressed.

We do *not* intend to develop an account of one's knowledge about which proposition is expressed by an utterance, either one's own or someone else's. But we do want to emphasize the point that understanding what one says, or what someone else says, in a way that enables one to formulate responses, come to opinions about the truth of the utterance, and seek to know more about it, does not, *in general*, require very much. The Mark Twain example shows that, for certain purposes, a merely utterance-bound or *reflexive* conception of the proposition expressed by an utterance suffices. By "reflexive," we mean a way of identifying the truth-conditions of an utterance in terms of the utterance itself, and the meaning of the expressions it uses, without recourse to more facts about it.

In thinking about these matters, it is important to distinguish facts about reference and truth-conditions, from psychological facts about speakers and hearers. When JP says to KK, "you broke my glasses," he refers to KK, and says something that is true iff KK has broken his glasses. KK is the *referent* of JP's use of the indexical "you." It is quite a separate issue whether JP has in his own mind linked the condition for being the referent of his use of "you" with any notion he has of KK or anyone else. Even if JP is quite sure, for example, that FR is the culprit, he has not said that FR broke his glasses, but that KK did.

There are, then, a number of ways that a hearer might have to describe what a speaker has said. One important dimension along which these descriptions vary is degree of reflexivity, of dependence on the utterance itself. When JP finds Twain's note, he can identify what it says only reflexively, in terms of the author of that very note. Being able to describe what the note said, in this reflexive way, may enable him to find out more about the author, and arrive at less utterance-bound ways of describing what is said.

First JP has the note dated by a scientist, and examines carefully the niche in the cabin in which it was found. He becomes certain that the note was written in 1878, stuck in the niche, and never removed, and so must have been written by someone residing in the cabin in 1878. He can now provide a less utterance-bound, but still not expressive, description of what the note says:

> In this note, one of the residents of this cabin in 1878 says that he or she is sick of all the frog stories they are being sent.

After more research, leading to a study of Mark Twain's time in Calaveras County and his feelings about frogs, JP can report.

> In this note, Mark Twain said that he was sick of all the frog stories he was being sent in 1878.

This description of the proposition Twain expressed is not utterance-bound at all; neither the author nor the year are identified in terms of the note.[6] At this point JP might say confidently that he knows *what the note said* or *what the author of the note said.*

One might think that the less utterance-bound a hearer's description of what a speaker has said is, the better it will be for determining the implicatures the speaker intends to convey. This is not so, as we shall see when we return to Ia. But first we will develop a somewhat systematic way of approaching descriptions of what is said.

5 Reflexive Truth-Conditions

In Perry, 2001 [2012], a distinction is made between *referential* and *reflexive truth-conditions of an utterance.* The idea is very simple; one looks at the truth-conditions of an utterance without fixing various contextual values, merely constraining them in terms of the utterance and whatever circumstances are taken as given. This generates a variety of truth-conditions, to all of which a competent language user may have access in various situations,

---

[6] Actually we believe it is important to distinguish between the note and the utterance, which was Twain's intentional act in authoring the note (see Perry, 2001 [2012], 45–47), but we ignore this for the purposes of this essay.

and which can be used, we shall claim, in explaining the "cognitive significance" of utterances, including the ability to trigger Gricean inferences.

The basic idea is that one can identify the truth-conditions of an utterance more or less reflexively, depending on how much one knows about the utterance. This is captured by the schema:

> Given ...., what the speaker of **u** said is true iff -------

We use bold face roman to indicate which things are the subject matter of the proposition, the things it is about. For example,

> that **Schwarzenegger** governs **California**

and,

> that **Schwarzenegger** governs **the most populous state in the USA**

designate the same proposition, the one which in a possible worlds framework would be modeled with the set of worlds in which Schwarzenegger governs California, including worlds in which California is not the most populous. On the other hand;

> that **Schwarzenegger** governs *the most populous state in* **the USA**

is about Schwarzenegger and the USA, saying he governs whichever state is most populous. The set of worlds that model this proposition would include some in which Schwarzenegger governs California, some in which he governs Nebraska, and so on.

Where **u** is a slightly simplified version of Mark Twain's note, and using "be" as a way of speaking tenselessly:

> (i) Given that **u** is in English, and uses the sentence "I am sick of frogs," what the speaker of **u** says is true iff:
>
> (A) *the speaker of* **u** be sick of frogs at *the time* **u** *be written*
>
> (ii) Given all of that, plus the fact that Mark Twain wrote **u**, what the speaker of **u** says is true iff:
>
> (B) **Mark Twain** be sick of frogs at *the time* **u** *be written*.
>
> (iii) Given all of that, plus the fact that **u** be written in 1878, what the speaker of **u** says is true iff:

(C) **Mark Twain** be sick of frogs in **1878.**

(A) is about **u**, (B) is about **u** and Mark Twain, and (C) is about Mark Twain and 1878, and not about **u** at all.

Thus, the conception that a hearer has available of what a speaker of an utterance has said depends on how much the hearer knows about the utterance. The reflexive truth-conditions, such as we have in (A) and (B), are not the same as what is said. Mark Twain did not say anything about his own note. (A) and (B) are utterance-bound ways of getting at the truth-conditions of the note. When we get to (C), however, the truth-conditions correspond to the proposition expressed. They are no longer conditions on the utterance, as in (A) and (B), but on the subject matter, the things out in the world that Twain was talking about, which exist independently of the utterance.[7]

With this under our belts, we return to Ia.

6 Back to Ia

Here is our reconstruction of B's reasoning:

1. "The utterance I am hearing, **u**, is an utterance by someone of 'I am out of petrol'." (This B knows through hearing **u** and recognizing its basic phonological properties.)
2. "Given that **u** is in English, it is true iff *the speaker of* **u** is out of petrol at *the time of* **u**." (B recognizes the language as English, and he knows the meaning of the sentence.)
3. "Given all of that, and that the speaker is the person I am now looking at, it expresses the proposition that *the person I am looking at* is out of petrol **now**." (B turns and sees that the speaker is someone in his shop—as opposed, say, to someone on the radio—and therefore that the time of the utterance is present.)
4. "Given that, and the fact that the person I am talking to is Harold Wilson, and it is now noon June 18, 1962, it expresses the proposition that **Harold Wilson** is out of petrol **at noon June 18, 1962**." (B recognizes that the person talking to him is the Prime Minister, and looks at the clock and the calendar.)

Thoughts 1 and 2 do not contain enough information to motivate B's helpful reply. *Neither does step 4.* It is thought 3 that puts B in a position to recognize the implicature, that A would like to know where he can get some petrol.

---

[7] One may well doubt that Twain said something about 1878, by using the present tense when he wrote in 1878, but we will oversimplify these issues for the purpose of this essay.

To recognize the implicature, *B* needs to ask under what conditions it is, as we shall say, "Conversationally appropriate." (We use this phrase as a way of not taking a position, in this essay, about whether Grice's theory of conversational maxims, or some improved version of them, or some relatively radical departure from them, such as proposed by relevance theorists, is the best account of the constraints involved.) So instead of the schema,

> *Given..., u is true iff---*

we have:

> *Given..., u is Conversationally-appropriate only if---*

Notice that being conversationally appropriate is, unlike truth, a relational concept. The remark is to be relevant to a particular conversation, in this case the one *A* is initiating with *B*. It is conceivable that a single statement could be part of two conversations, with different implicatures for each. Imagine Harold Wilson saying "I'm out of petrol," on the phone to a reporter who has asked him about running for election, while simultaneously glancing meaningfully towards the petrol can in a way his subordinate cannot mistake.

If we simply take what is said as given, we won't get any significant results. Let *P* be the proposition that **Harold Wilson** be out of petrol at **noon June 18, 1962**. This proposition could be expressed by indefinitely many sentences in various situations. From the fact that an utterance expresses this proposition, that this is what the speaker says, nothing follows about what the speaker implicates; that is, from just knowing this about the utterance, one cannot reasonably draw any conclusions about what else the speaker might be intending the hearer of his remark to come to believe by recognition of his intentions.

In the petrol case, *A* means to convey that he would like *B* to provide some information about where he can get petrol. What is given will be such facts as that the speaker of **u** is talking to *B*, that he is a stranger, initiating a conversation, that he doesn't seem to be telling a joke or recounting a story, and so forth. Also what is given will be what *A* said. The key point is that the description of what is said will have to *interact* with the other factors, if any implicature is to be generated. *B*'s thinking will be something like this:

> Given that **u** is in English, etc., and that the speaker of **u** is this fellow, and this fellow isn't telling a joke or a long story about his miserable life, and that **u** is true iff he is out of petrol now, **u** makes conversational sense only if this fellow would like me to provide some information about where he can get petrol now.

If we substitute the description of what *A* said from (4), we get something that makes no sense:

> Given that **u** is in English, etc., and that the speaker of **u** is this fellow, and this fellow isn't telling a joke or a long story about his miserable life, and that **u** is true iff Harold Wilson is out of petrol at noon June 18, 1962, **u** makes conversational sense only if this fellow would like me to provide some information about where he can get petrol now.

This way of looking at things leads to the following conclusion: In order to figure out the implicatures of a remark, the hearer needs to arrive at a description of what is said that allows him to figure out what else the speaker must intend to convey, for the speaker to suppose that the remark is conversationally appropriate.

This means that Grice's schema requires too little of the hearer. *B*'s reasoning could not have gotten off the ground if he merely had the description "the speaker of **u** said that Harold Wilson be out of petrol at noon June 18, 1962."

However, Grice's schema also requires too much, as we shall see in the next section.

7   Grice's Example

Now we look at *B*'s reply to *A;*

> *B*: There is a garage around the corner.

In arriving at an understanding of what *B* means, *A* will have to arrive at an understanding of what *B* said that interacts with other facts about the conversation:

> Given that the utterance is in English etc., that this man directed it at me, it is true iff there is a garage around some corner salient to the two of us.

> Given all of that, and that he knows I am out of petrol and am seeking information about where I can get some, the remark is conversationally appropriate only if he believes that the garage probably sells petrol and probably is open, or at least there is someone there who can be roused to sell the petrol.

Suppose that *B*, being English, muttered his remark in such a way that it sounded to *A* like,

> There is a garage mumble.

A would still be able to describe what *B* said, although he would not be able to *say* it in his own words:

> Given the utterance is in English etc., that this man directed it at me, etc. it is true iff there is a garage at some place to which the words I heard as "mumble" refer.

This understanding of *B*'s remark, though an utterance-bounded description, should suffice for *A* to figure out the implicature, that *B* believes the garage in question probably sells petrol, etc. He can then ask for more details about where the garage is.

We see, then, that Grice's schema requires both too much as well as too little. It requires too much in that to figure out the implicature, the hearer need not have a sentence "*S*" with which he can think:

> *B* said that *S*.

He merely needs to have a description:

> Given..., *B*'s utterance is true iff so-and-so

such that the information in "..." and the conditions in "so-and-so" interact so as to have implications about the conditions under which the utterance is conversationally appropriate.

8 Three Demonstrations

Aside, perhaps, from the first-person pronoun, resolution of the reference of indexicals and demonstratives requires knowledge of speaker intentions.[8] Knowledge of these intentions is not some sort of special process of intention discovery that belongs on the semantics side of the semantics-pragmatics divide. It is a part of the general job of pragmatics, which is to work out what is said and what is implicated, based on the constraints on what is said delivered by semantics, by working out the speaker's intentions.

This point is shown by the fact that the appropriate description of what is said, for the purpose of deriving implicatures, is not simply a matter of semantics. The "resolution of indexicals and demonstratives" is simply part of the process of figuring out what the speaker is trying to do.

---

[8] See Perry, 2001 [2012], §4.4 for discussion.

Return to the Grice example. How did *B* know that he should think of what *A* said in terms of "this fellow is out of petrol," rather than "Harold Wilson is out of petrol?" Clearly because this description of what *A* said meshed with other facts to identify an implicature that made conversational sense of the conversation. We illustrate this further with three examples that involve interpreting demonstratives.

Suppose JP says to KK, while KK is driving along the narrow and picturesque streets of Donostia,

(1) He is going to drive his car into yours.

JP is, let us imagine, referring to FR, a famous philosopher, who is careening down the street in the opposite direction. There is a pretty clear implicature that KK would do well to engage in evasive maneuvers, to avoid getting hit. But how is KK supposed to figure this out?

If we analyze the case in terms of reflexive truth-conditions, it seems that we can construct a reasonable account. The reflexive truth-conditions of JP's utterance are derived by instantiation from:

(2) An utterance *u* of (1) is true iff $\exists x, y$ the speaker of *u* refers to *x* with "he" and addresses *y* with "you" and *x* is going to drive *x*'s car into *y*'s car.

Let's call JP's utterance of (1), "**u**." Then we have by instantiation,

(3) **u** is true iff $\exists x, y$ the speaker of **u** refers to *x* with "he" and *y* with "you" and *x* is going to drive *x*'s car into *y*'s car.

In this case there are a number of "modes of presentation" that KK has of FR:

i) *The person to whom the speaker of* **u** *is referring with the use of "he."* This is based on hearing the utterance and knowing English.

ii) *The person to whom my passenger is referring with the use of "he."* This is based on the above, plus KK's perception that his passenger is the speaker of **u**.

iii) *The person the passenger of my car is staring at, bug-eyed, as he screams at me.* This is based on the above, plus common-sense, plus further observation of the passenger.

iv) *The person driving that car that is now to my right but is cutting across the street so it will soon be on my left.* This is based on the above, plus observing the scene to which the passenger was directing his gaze.

v) *The famous philosopher FR.* This is based on the above, plus recognizing the driver of the car as the famous philosopher FR.

It's clear in this case that the speaker intends for the hearer to think of the referent of "he" as in iv). Until the hearer gets to mode of presentation iv), he is not in a position to do much about the fact that FR is careening towards him. To take proper evasive action, it is unnecessary, and perhaps counterproductive, to recognize JP's referent as the famous philosopher FR. KK might become awestruck to be on the same street at FR and freeze. Similarly, the speaker intends the hearer to think of himself as the referent of "you."

We note that it is natural to appeal to considerations of conversational relevance to explain the special status of mode of presentation iv). The speaker has every reason to believe that the hearer will put in the cognitive effort to arrive at this description of what is said, as until he gets to this point, he has no way of acting on the information he has been given. The speaker expects that the hearer's efforts to resolve the demonstrative "he" will be guided by the principle of conversational relevance, however. When the resolution fits in with other factors so as to generate a clear implicature—that is at level iv)—the efforts at resolution should cease and efforts at evasion should begin.

Now let us alter the example slightly. KK is organizing a talk later in the afternoon, where RC is to be the featured speaker. However, RC has not yet arrived in Donostia as far as KK knows and KK is a little worried about whether she will show. RC is driving down the street, but it is a somewhat wider street, and she is driving carefully and soberly. JP recognizes RC and says,

(4) She is driving toward the Aula Magna now.

In this case, in order to arrive at a relevant representation of the proposition expressed, KK needs to go further:

i) *The person to whom the speaker of* **u** *is referring with the use of "she."*
ii) *The person to whom my passenger is referring with the use of "she."*
iii) *The person at whom the passenger of my car is looking.*
iv) *The person driving the car that is approaching on my left.*
v) *The famous pragmatist RC.*

KK must get all the way to v) before he becomes a representation of what is said that is reasonably relevant given that it implicates:

RC will be on time.

Finally suppose that KK and JP are driving along a wide boulevard with no traffic problems. KK has asked JP for suggestions about whom to invite for an upcoming conference.

> JP: He is rather unreliable, doesn't have much to say, and always takes a long time to say it.
> KK: Next.

Here KK need not resolve the demonstrative reference beyond the very early levels, that is, beyond an utterance-bound description of what JP says: JP's remark is true iff the person he refers to with "he" has a number of undesirable characteristics. JP implicates that he believes KK will not want to invite this person.

In these three demonstrations KK understands what JP intends to convey, even if in two of them he doesn't arrive at an expressive description of what is said by JP. He only needs a description of what JP said that interacts with other factors so that they produce the intended implicature. One always has *some* utterance-bound description of what is said to get started, based on semantics, even if one does not know very much at all about the utterance.

To sum up, the description that a hearer needs to have of what the speaker says in order to figure out implicatures varies from case to case, and need not, and in some cases should not, be the sort of utterance-independent characterization that goes with the most full and objective understanding of what is said. All that semantics needs to provide, in order to provide a hook for the pragmatic reasoning, is a description of what is said in terms of the reflexive truth-conditions of the utterance. And, as we have tried to show, semantics does provide such a descriptive proposition, and not only an "incomplete logical form," "semantic skeleton," "semantic template," "propositional schema," "sub-proposition" or "incomplete proposition," as proponents of (one version of) the linguistic underdeterminacy thesis maintain. Semantics does provide a full truth-evaluable proposition, albeit a reflexive one, answering to an utterance-bound description of what is said.

9 A Funeral

In this section we look at an example involving the domain of a quantifier phrase.

X has died. X was an associate of both KK and JM. KK doesn't much want to go to the funeral. JM says, (utterance **u**) "Everyone should be there!!!" JM is thinking of the domain of Basque philosophers who are in Donostia at the time.

To know what JM has said, KK should identify the domain JM was thinking about as the domain of Basque philosophers in Donostia at the time. Some pragmatists think this is a matter of "saturation of hidden indexicals," others that it is a matter of identifying an unarticulated constituent, others see it as a case of enrichment. We won't take a stand on this. Our point is that KK need not arrive at an utterance-independent description of this domain to grasp JM's implicature.

KK reasons:

i) **u** is true iff ∃ D, such that D is the domain that the speaker of **u** is implicitly referring to & everyone in D should be at the funeral. (Knowledge of English)

ii) Given that JM is the speaker of **u**, **u** is true iff ∃ D, such that D is the domain that JM is implicitly referring to & everyone in D should be at the funeral.

iii) Given that JM is authoritative, ∃ D, such that D is the domain that JM is implicitly referring to & everyone in D should be at the funeral.

iv) Given that JM is being relevant, ∃ D, such that D is the domain that JM is implicitly referring to & everyone in D should be at the funeral and *I am a member* of D.

v) I'll go to the funeral.

Here KK's reasoning has completely avoided the cognitive burden of figuring out that JM was implicitly referring to Basque philosophers who were in Donostia at the time. Given his deference to JM's opinions on such matters, this would have been an unrewarding inferential detour, a long way of getting to the conclusion that he ought to go to the funeral.

In this case, KK's reasoning stays near the level of reflexive truth-conditions. It may be that the force of JM's words would be lost if he went further than this. That is, the only mode of presentation of *Basque philosophers who are now in Donostia* that would play an effective role in KK's reasoning, and issue in the conclusion that he ought to go to the funeral, is *Domain of people such that JM has said that they should all be at the funeral.*

This example shows that the hearer's understanding of what is said that best serves the purposes of the speaker may not constitute the sort of understanding that counts as "knowing what was said." What is important about the domain, as far as KK is concerned, is not which domain it is, but that it is a domain KK belongs to, and which JM takes to be such that all members of it should attend the funeral. KK may not know exactly what JM said, but he knows exactly what he meant to implicate.

The determination of quantifier domains has been widely discussed as to whether it should count as the result of either *saturation, completion* or *expansion* in the process of getting from the "incomplete logical form" or "non-truth-evaluable propositional radical" provided by the conventional meaning of the sentence uttered to the expressive description of what is said.[9] We argue here that such an expressive description is not needed, in the first place, for the inference of the relevant implicature. In this case, what semantics needs to deliver is an utterance bound-description of what is said of the sort we imagined KK starting his reasoning with in step i); a description that constitutes a complete truth-evaluable proposition, albeit a reflexive one, available as the input of pragmatic processes.

10 Names

Now we move to a case in which two parties to a conversation understand the proposition expressed by a third in a completely knowledgeable and expressive way. To figure out the conversational intentions of the speaker, however, they must use pragmatic reasoning to get to *more* utterance-bound descriptions of what has been said.

Here is the situation. GM and KK are both at a conference. JP has wanted them to meet each other for a long time, and has told each about the other, and their common philosophical interests and tastes. He realizes that although they are talking to each other, neither knows who the other one is. He walks up and says, "KK is talking to GM." Both GM and KK can identify exactly what JP has said. His intention is to introduce them, to get each to know the name of the other.

Pragmatic reasoning, guided by the search for conversational appropriateness, is required to understand what JP is trying to convey. GM is intended to think "KK is the very person is talking to me." KK is intended to think "My goodness gracious, I am talking to GM." In this example, the thinkers arrive at the useful description of what has been said by starting with a completely utterance-independent description—that KK is talking to GM—and then reasoning back to a more relevant but less objective description.

---

[9] See Bach, 1994a, 2000; Carston, 2002, §2.7; Korta, 1997 and Stanley and Szabo, 2000 for discussion.

11 Conclusions

Above we quoted remarks of Grice which make it sound as if knowing what is said is a necessary first step in figuring out implicatures. He also said,

> ...the implicature is not carried by what is said, but only by the saying of what is said, or by "putting it that way" (Grice, 1967a [1989], 39).

So it is not simply *what* the speaker says, but how he says it, that is crucial. But given this, the hearer must not simply arrive at some way or another of describing what is said, but one that connects with circumstances and conversational maxims, as illustrated by all of our examples.

The process of finding implicatures need not begin with the identification of what is said. It can begin with a possibly quite lean description that is the output of a pristine semantic module, which deals with no specific facts about the utterance except the types of expressions involved. The description can be replete with quantified clauses, quantifying over the speaker of the utterance, the time of the utterance, the conversation of which the utterance is a part, various defaults, unarticulated constituents, values of hidden indexicals, and the like. All of these factors are brought in by the meanings of the expressions used, but their values are not determined by the meanings of those expressions. The description describes what is said by an utterance in terms of the truth-conditions of the utterance, but does not provide the proposition expressed. Semantics does not *determine* what is said, and knowledge of semantics does not allow us to *know* what is said, whether it is us or someone else that says it. To know that, we need to know, in addition, a lot about intentions, our own if we are the speaker, the speaker's if we are not, and other facts about the context of the utterance.

Most, if not all, positions in the debate of contemporary pragmatics on the concept of what is said share two basic inter-related assumptions linked to linguistic underdetermination: (i) that knowing the conventional meaning of the sentence uttered does not, usually, determine a full-fledged truth-evaluable proposition and, therefore, (ii) that pragmatic processes are required to get at a full or complete proposition that would then serve (or not, depending on which position you defend) as the *input* for the inference of implicatures. As we saw, the second assumption seems attributable to Grice. He requires on the part of the hearer at least an expressive description of what has been said, and this is not fixed by the conventional meaning of the utterance. But he never claims anything similar to (i). On the contrary, as we noted above, in discussing the case of an utterance of "He was in the grip of a vice," he notes that what knowledge of the English language by itself delivers, would fall far short of a full identification of what is said. We disagree with Grice himself, then, only about point (ii).

This disagreement is within a larger agreement about the importance of the distinction between what is said and what is implicated. The distinction remains important even if both what is said and what is implicated are determined in part by factors that go beyond what is provided by semantics, and for the identification of which the hearer must use pragmatic reasoning.

All action has a structure; one achieves a result *by* achieving another result, in certain circumstances. Our repertoire of basic actions, of basic ways we can move our bodies and their parts, combined with knowledge of what the results will be in various circumstances, allow us to plan and execute a great many actions with a relatively limited number of movements.

In language, we make noises and thereby utter words and thereby say things and thereby produce all sorts of changes in people's minds and thereby bring about a lot of other stuff. At each stage, different sorts of circumstances are exploited to obtain results: facts about mouths, facts about air, facts about ears, facts about linguistic cultures and phones, facts about conventions, facts about the way people's minds are organized.

The difference between saying and implicating corresponds to a major break between the sorts of circumstances on which one relies to achieve one's ends. What we say depends largely on the sounds we utter, the language we speak, its conventional meanings, and contextual factors tied to our own minds—what we are looking at, thinking of, and the like. The changes we produce in how others act depends on quite different circumstances, about how they will react to learning that the world is as we say it is, or at least learning that we think it is this way, or want them to think so. It is a miracle that we can fairly reliably say what we intend to by making noises. And it is a miracle we can get people to do things by saying things. But they are different miracles.

Pragmatics is not a module that takes what is said as input and produces implicatures as output. It is rather bringing to bear all that we know about the world and hearers in it in order to plan linguistic actions that will have the results we desire, and bringing all that we know about the world and the speakers in it to interpret speech. If semantics is conceived as the study of non-natural, conventional meanings of expressions and structures, it is an important part of pragmatics. If semantics is conceived as the study of all meaning, natural and non-natural, as the study of how parts of the world, including but not limited to the intentional acts of humans, can provide information about other parts, then pragmatics is a part of semantics.

But, to return to our main theme, the dilemma pragmatics and semantics have lived with for at least forty years is false. A pristine semantics determines constraints on the truth-conditions of utterances, and understanding of semantics allows us to describe the truth-conditions of utterances, and so what is said, in terms of these constraints. That is all Gricean pragmatics needs from semantics.[10]

---

[10] Thanks to Kent Bach, David Israel, Jesus M. Larrazabal, Ken Taylor, and the two *Mind & Language* referees for their helpful comments and corrections. The first author's work has been partially supported by a grant of the University of the Basque Country (9/UPV 00109.109-14449/2002) and the Diamond XX Philosophy Institute. The second author thanks the Center for Advanced Study, Oslo, Norway, the Stanford Humanities Center, the Stanford Philosophy Department, and the Diamond XX Philosophy Institute for support.

2

Radical Minimalism, Moderate Contextualism

KEPA KORTA AND JOHN PERRY

1 Introduction

Cappelen and Lepore's (hereafter, "CL") book *Insensitive Semantics* faces issues involved in reconceptualizing the nature of and boundaries between semantics and pragmatics in the light of the phenomenon often called "pragmatic intrusion." The received theory might have been expressed this way. Semantics determines *what is said*; that is, the proposition that is expressed by an utterance is determined by the conventional meanings of the words used and compositional rules for combining words. Pragmatics takes as its input what is said, and taking into consideration facts about the particular utterance (and possibly some other conventions), determines what has been conveyed and what speech acts have been performed, largely by considering the communicative and other perlocutionary intentions of the speaker.

The classic picture of pragmatic intrusion is that we often need to reason about the intentions of the speaker in order to determine what is said; semantics doesn't get us the whole way. Authors like Bach (1994a), Carston (1988, 2002), Recanati (1989, 2004), Sperber and Wilson (1986), and others point to a variety of cases: comparative adjectives, quantifier expressions, weather reports, etc.

CL seek to develop a concept of semantics that does not countenance pragmatic intrusion. They alter the received picture by disengaging the "output" of semantics, the "semantic content," from the intuitive concept of "what is said." The semantic content can be determined without regard to intrusive pragmatic elements. Pragmatics plays a role in getting us to what is said, but since what is said is beyond the border of semantics, it isn't intrusion. Thus their "semantic minimalism." But CL have further ambitions about the concept of what is said; they want not only to demote it from the role of being the terminus of semantics, but also to undermine the idea that it is an important, central, and robust concept of pragmatics. Thus their "speech act pluralism."

We are sympathetic to the project of keeping semantics free of pragmatic intrusion, but we pursue a somewhat different strategy, that we see as both more radical than that of CL, and closer to their motivating ideas. On the issue of what is said, however, we differ; we think what is said, or some theoretical explication of it, has a central and honorable role to play in pragmatics.

This essay began as a contribution to a symposium on *Insensitive Semantics* for *Philosophy and Phenomenological Research* [Korta and Perry, 2007c]. In order to meet the page limits, the second part of our case, concerning pragmatic pluralism, had to be cut. At the invitation of Gerhard Preyer, we include the entire original paper here, with such changes as the passage of time and the accumulation of wisdom have dictated.

2   Terminological Preliminaries

First, there is the "content" of an utterance, more commonly called "the proposition expressed." The question is how much pragmatics is involved in determining it. Literalists say none. Contextualists say a lot. Moderates say something in between. But this concept of semantic content is basically a conflation of two quite different concepts. We'll call these *locutionary content* and *semantic contribution*.

Locutionary content is rooted in such common locutions as "what X said," and "what X said by uttering (saying, writing, signing) so and so." They surface in Austin, Grice, and the "new theory of reference." There the *theoretical* concept of *the proposition expressed* is motivated by intuitions mined with the help of these common-sense concepts. This is most explicit in Kaplan's *Demonstratives* (1989a), in the crucial Peter–Paul argument (pp. 512–13).

Our working definition of "locutionary content" is the conditions the truth of an utterance of a declarative sentence puts on the objects it is about. This is called "referential content" in Perry, 2001 [2012]. The locutionary content is, we think, *normally* what is said, but not in those cases for which Grice used "make as if to say" instead of "say." There are also other cases, such as informative identity statements, where we might not identify what is said with the locutionary content. Thus we agree with CL and others that "what is said" is a rather complicated concept, but we find more order in this complexity than they do.

The second root of the concept of content is "semantic contribution." Meaning is commonly assumed to be a property of simple and complex expressions that derives from conventions that pertain to the meaning of simple expressions, found in a lexicon, and conventions about modes of combination. This is what the semantic component of model-theoretic or other formal analyses of languages assign to expressions. It is also what philosophers and cognitive scientists take to be a central aspect of knowledge of language, of "semantic competence."

"Content" is a semi-technical expression. The philosophy of language has been heavily influenced by Kaplan's use, where paradigmatic content primarily is assigned to utterances, or uses of declarative sentences, or, as officially in his formal development, pairs of such sentences and contexts, where contexts are quadruples of agent, location, time, and world (Kaplan, 1989a). Declarative sentences are the model, and the content is taken to be a proposition that incorporates the truth-conditions of an utterance, use, or sentence in context. We will reserve the use of "content" for utterances, uses, and sentences in context, and "meaning" for types of expressions, following Kaplan, whose approximation of meaning is called "character." So, in Kaplan's system, the content of a sentence in context is a function of the character of the sentence and the context. We'll use the term "semantic contribution" for the property of sentences that CL seem to be after.

In our terms, CL maintain that the semantic contribution of a sentence is not as tightly linked to the locutionary content of an utterance of the sentence as might be thought. Locutionary content is a concept that belongs to pragmatics, semantic contribution belongs to semantics. With this we agree. Thus there are two questions instead of one:

> How much pragmatics is involved in determining the locutionary content of an utterance?
>
> How much pragmatics is involved in determining the semantic contribution of a sentence used in a standard way in an utterance?

We are contextualists with regard to the first question, and minimalists as regards the second, and so in broad agreement with CL. We are more moderate than they on the first question, which we pursue in sections 5 and 6. We start with the second, where our complaint is that CL are not minimalist enough. But, before that, a remark on the epistemology of language.

3 A Note on Epistemology

The word "pragmatics" brings to mind two sorts of facts that are connected with particular utterances. First are narrow contextual facts: the speaker, audience, time, and place of the utterance. Second are matters of the intentions of the speaker (and perhaps relevant mental states of other participants in the conversation). The paradigms of such intentions are the sort that Grice emphasized in his study of implicature: intentions to convey something beyond, or in place of, what is literally said. But in fact the discovery of intentions is involved at every stage of understanding utterances.

Herman says to Ernie, "I am tired." Ernie learns that Herman is tired. Knowledge of different kinds is involved here. First, there is the knowledge Ernie has as a semantically competent user of English. We take this to be the knowledge of the meanings of the words of English and how to interpret the modes of combination one finds in complex English expressions. This, *and this alone*, seems to us to be semantic, at least from a *minimalist* perspective. And this does *not* depend on anything about the utterance; Ernie's knowledge of the semantics of the English sentence "I am tired" was in place before Herman said anything, and the same knowledge would be involved in his understanding of anyone's utterance, or Ernie's own production of such an utterance.

Then there is perception of the public factors involved in Herman's utterance. Ernie hears the words Herman uses, and recognizes them as sounds that could be used as words of English. He also sees that Herman is the speaker.

Then there are Herman's intentions. If, as we assume, Ernie knows no Norwegian, he might briefly entertain the possibility that the sounds he hears are being used as Norwegian words. But why would Herman say something in Norwegian to Ernie? So he concludes Herman is speaking English, a fact about Herman's intentions in producing the noises he does. Notice that Ernie's knowledge of the semantics of "I am tired" will likely play a role here. If Herman emits some sounds which sound like "Albuquerque is probably pregnant," his knowledge of Herman's likely intentions and the semantics of "Albuquerque is probably pregnant" would instead argue for the utterance not being in English.

Having established that Herman intends to be speaking English, another layer of thinking about intentions comes up with the word "tired." Probably Herman realizes he is not an automobile, and means to use "tired" in the sense in which people who would like to nap are tired. There is the issue of exactly what Herman counts as "tired." Consistent with English he might mean to say that he is tired as opposed to being full of vim and vigor, or that he is dead-tired, barely able to lift a pencil. More intentions. Then, finally, there is the question of what Herman is trying to convey, to implicate, by saying what he does. That he needs a coke? That he needs a nap? That he needs a vacation? That battling with the absurdity of life and language has driven him to a deep and unshakeable ennui? More intentions.

Our point is that the understanding of particular utterances requires a great deal of knowledge in addition to semantic knowledge, properly so-called, and knowledge of intentions saturates every aspect of understanding in every transaction. The picture that semantic knowledge, in any reasonable sense, gets us very far by itself is untenable. In particular, the idea that simply by knowing the meanings of English expressions and modes of composition we can get to the locutionary content, and only after that, in figuring out implicatures, to what we need to discover and reason about intentions, is certainly false.

4 Minimalisms

In Kaplan's theory, philosophical arguments about what is said guide the choice for what the content of an utterance is taken to be, suggesting that content is *what is said,* in a fairly robust and intuition-rich sense of that phrase, which, in the limited sort of cases Kaplan considers, is or is very close to locutionary content in our sense. Character is semantic contribution. Content is determined by character and context. This gives us two possible, Kaplan-inspired, minimalisms:

(i) Minimal semantic contribution should be like Kaplan's *content*; it is determined by character *plus* context (agent, location, time, world).
(ii) Minimal semantic contribution should be like Kaplan's *character*; it is the same for every utterance of a sentence.

Minimalism (i) seems to be a non-starter. In Kaplan's system, *content* is what *varies* from utterance to utterance, even though the semantics—everything Kaplan's theory tells us about the sentence, everything in the lexicon and the compositional rules—stays the same. Minimalism (ii), on the other hand, seems quite promising; it identifies minimal semantics with exactly the sort of facts that semantic theories like Kaplan's provide, and the usual meaning of "semantics," namely, the meaning of expressions as determined by the conventions of the language to which they belong.

CL explain their basic idea as follows:

> The idea motivating Semantic Minimalism is simple and obvious: The semantic content of a sentence S is the content that all utterances of S share. It is the content that all utterances of S express no matter how different their contexts of utterance are. It is also the content that can be grasped and reported by someone who is ignorant about the relevant characteristics of the context in which an utterance of S took place. (p. 143)

CL emphasize their broad agreement with Kaplan, so this use of "content" is rather odd; for Kaplan the content is what *changes* with context; the character remains the same and is what is grasped by someone ignorant of context. If the *contents* of all utterances of a sentence S were the same, their truth-value would also be the same: a bullet no one wants to bite. At this point one might suppose that minimalism (ii) fits everything in the basic idea so well that this use of "content" must just come to "contribution." Thus we would have:

> There is a *semantic* contribution that all utterances of a sentence S make to contents of the utterances, which is the same for all utterances whatever the context and is what someone who is ignorant of the relevant characteristics of the context grasps.

However, having given us this basic idea of semantic minimalism, CL almost immediately replace it with another conception; they call it an "elaboration," but it is really nothing of the sort. It is a move from something prima-facie coherent like (ii) to something prima-facie incoherent like (i). They list seven theses of what we shall call CL Semantic Minimalism. The heart of the matter is their thesis 5, which gives us our next concept of minimalism:

(iii) CL minimalism (pp. 144–145)

In order to fix or determine the proposition semantically expressed by an utterance of a sentence S, follow steps (a)–(e):

a) Specify the meaning (or semantic value) of every expression in S (doing so in accordance with your favorite semantic theory…).
b) Specify all the relevant compositional meanings rules for English (doing so also in accordance with your favorite semantic theory…).
c) Disambiguate every ambiguous/polysemous expression in S.
d) Precisify every vague expression in S.
e) Fix the semantic value of every context sensitive expression in S.

What are clauses (c) through (e) doing in an exposition of semantic *minimalism*, a description of the "content" that all utterances of a sentence *share*? The clauses (c), (d), and (e) all pertain to factors that *differentiate* the content of English sentences as used by different people at different times, or with different intentions about which meanings of ambiguous expressions they wish to employ, and the standards of precisification for vague expressions. Something has gone awry, and the basic idea of semantic minimalism has slipped away.

5 KP Minimalism

We will propose two forms of minimalism that are more in accord with CL's basic idea—more pure—than CL minimalism. We will call them "Kosher and Pure minimalisms" or "KP minimalisms" for short.

Both forms of KP minimalism result from eliminating parts of CL minimalism. The first form eliminates (d) and (e); the second form eliminates (c) as well.

For this purpose we use the concept Content$_M$ from Perry, 2001 [2012]. In general, the content of an utterance is what the world has to be like for the utterance to be true, taking certain things about the utterance as fixed. Let **u** be an utterance of "I am tired" in English, the meanings of the words and the mode of composition involved are given, but not the speaker, time, etc. The Content$_M$ of **u** is:

(1) That the speaker of **u** is tired at the time of **u**.

(1) is what we call a *reflexive* content of *u*, since it puts conditions on *u* itself. Content$_M$ gets at the vision behind CL's basic idea: it is what all utterances of the same sentence have *in common*.

Of course, two utterances, **u** and **u'** of "I am tired" by different people will not have the same *content*, reflexive or locutionary, and they may differ in *truth-value*. This difference is reflected in the difference between (1) and (2):

(2) That the speaker of **u'** is tired at the time of **u'**.

Suppose you find a note **n** that reads "I am tired." You don't know who wrote it, or when, but you assume it is written in English. On the CL account you *do not* grasp the semantic contribution of the sentence, for you do not have the information necessary, on their theory, to grasp "the proposition semantically expressed." But of course you do, and you can report it:

Note **n** is true iff the person who wrote it was tired at the time he wrote it.

Suppose Tom wrote the note at noon Wednesday. If you knew that you could say,

Note **n** is true iff Tom was tired Wednesday.

The proposition that Tom was tired Wednesday is what we call the locutionary content of the note; the Content$_C$ or the referential content in Perry, 2001

[2012]. It is what is required of the world for the note to be true given *not only* that it was written in English, *but also* that it was written by Tom on Wednesday. With the sentence "Tom was tired Wednesday" you can actually *express* the proposition Tom expressed with the note. Without that information you cannot *express* that proposition, but you can give an *utterance-bound* or *reflexive* characterization of it.

The requirement that to grasp the *semantic* content of an utterance you need to know the contextual facts, so that you can *express* the locutionary content, as opposed to merely providing an utterance-bound description of it, is unmotivated by CL's basic idea, and by the general truth-conditional and compositional approach to semantics.

If one looks at a formal theory, such as Kaplan's in "Logic of Demonstratives," the compositional clauses work at the level of utterance-bound meaning; that is, they quantify over contexts, and thus contextual factors. One can grasp the contribution that parts make to wholes, on Kaplan's account, without having any idea who made the utterance and when (or what the context of a sentence-context pair is).

Consider, for example, a note:

(3) Because I ran a marathon yesterday, I am too tired to fix the car today, so I'd better wait until tomorrow, so you can't use it to go to the store until then.

We can grasp the utterance-bound truth-conditions of (3) if we grasp the utterance-bound truth-conditions of the parts; we don't need to know who said it, and when, and to whom.

This is not a point that simply pertains to indexicals. Suppose the note is "I'll fix the car soon." What does the speaker mean by "soon"? It is a vague expression. CL would claim that we don't grasp the semantic "content" unless we can fix what counts as "soon." But surely we do grasp the utterance-bound truth-conditions:

> The note is true iff the author of the note fixed the car he is referring to within the length of time that counted as upper bound of what counted as "soon" according to his intentions.

Suppose you get an email from Gretchen that says, "David has made an amazing discovery." There are a lot of Davids. You don't know which one Gretchen is referring to with her use of "David": David Kaplan, David Hills, David Israel? You respond, "David Who?" Your response can be understood precisely because you *do* grasp utterance-bound truth-conditions of the email:

This email is true if the David the author it was referring to with "David" has made a great discovery.

By recognizing the fact that the *common* semantic contribution of sentences of English is at the level of utterance-bound truth-conditions, we can provide a conception of semantic contribution and semantic content that is much more in accord with CL's basic idea:

> KP-1
> The semantic contribution of an English sentence is determined by the meanings of the expression in the sentence in English and the English rules for modes of combination, plus a disambiguation of any ambiguous expressions. The semantic content of an utterance of the sentence is the reflexive truth-conditions of the utterance, where contextual factors, the reference of nambiguous[1] names, and standards of precisification are not fixed but quantified over.

We also propose a more radical rendering of semantic minimalism, limited to (a) and (b) on CL's list.

> KP-2
> The semantic contributions of an English sentence is determined by the meanings of the expression in the sentence in English and the English rules for modes of combination. The semantic content of an utterance of the sentence is the reflexive truth-conditions of the utterance, where contextual factors, the meanings of ambiguous expressions, the reference of nambiguous names, and standards of precisification are not fixed but quantified over.

This is the conception of semantic contribution needed by the working epistemologist of language or cognitive scientist. Consider Grice's example (1967a [1989]) "He was in the grip of a vice." What does someone know, who hears this sentence uttered, and recognizes the expressions, based merely on his knowledge of the meanings of words and the grammar of English? We suggest, following Grice rather closely, something like this:

> This utterance is true iff the speaker is using "in the grip of a vice" to mean "has a particularly bad habit or moral failing," if the person the speaker uses "he" to refer to has a particularly bad habit or moral failing, or if the speaker is using "in the grip of a vice" to mean "held by a clamping vise" and the person he is referring to is held by a clamping vise.

---

[1] "Nambiguous" is Perry's neologism for names with multiple bearers. This phenomenon is quite different from ordinary lexical ambiguity. See Perry, 2001 [2012], Ch. 6.

The material to the right of the "iff" provides us with an utterance-bound truth-condition. This is a complicated proposition that is ultimately about the utterance itself. This proposition fits very well with CL's basic idea, for it is what a semantically competent speaker of English grasps simply in terms of that semantic competence, with no additional knowledge of the intentions of the speaker beyond that of speaking English.

Perhaps we need to emphasize that utterance-bound contents are *not* our candidates for what is said, or *the* proposition expressed, or locutionary content. The utterance-bound content of an utterance **u** of "I am tired" is the proposition that the speaker of **u** is tired. This is certainly *not* what is said. The speaker was not *saying* something about his or her own utterance, but about him or herself.

We believe that once either of these truly—radically—minimalist conceptions of semantics is adopted, many of CL's arguments against the presence of pragmatically or contextually determined elements in locutionary content, such as unarticulated constituents, lose whatever force they may have had. But for now we turn to CL's "Speech Act Pluralism."

6 Pluralism and Contextualism

Both minimalists and contextualists must face the question:

> How much pragmatics is involved in determining the locutionary content of an utterance? (For the moment, you can take "locutionary content" just as our technical term for "what is said").

Once CL have separated locutionary content from the output of semantics, they are free to agree with contextualists: a lot of pragmatics is involved in getting to what is said.

This is not their only coincidence with contextualism. They share with many contextualists the assumption that for the generation of implicatures it is necessary to have what we called an expressive description of a certain proposition, not what is said, but the (enriched) explicature (in Carston's terminology) or the contextually shaped what-is-said (in CL's terminology, pp. 179–81). We argue elsewhere[2] that this is a mistake; one can reason about the likely intentions of a speaker on the basis of a very utterance-bound description of what he has said.[3]

---

[2] See Chapter 1 of the present volume.

[3] It is true that relevance theorists admit mutual adjustments of explicatures and implicatures, so the former need not be determined *before* the latter. Our point, anyway, is that the expressive description of the proposition need not be determined either *before* or *after* the determination of

But what is most surprising and puzzling to us is that, concerning what is said, now distinguished from both the semantic content and the enriched explicature, CL defend a contextualism virtually without limits. That is, they appear to deny that the utility of what is said, or theoretical concepts based on our intuitions about what is said, play a significant role in shaping the enterprise of semantics and pragmatics.

In our view CL's "Speech Act Pluralism" is the collection of three different theses that we will call "content pluralism," "the relativity of what is said," and "pragmatic indiscernibility." The first we accept; the second leads to a theoretical pessimism we don't want to share; the third we reject; it goes directly against Grice's fundamental distinction between what is said and implicatures, and, ironically, combined with the second, threatens to undermine any motivation for CL's version of semantic minimalism. Let's consider them one by one.

6.1 Content Pluralism

Content pluralism concerns the quantity of contents of an utterance; it claims that any utterance has a variety of them. We have already argued for the existence, for any utterance, of at least a minimal content corresponding to the semantic contribution of the sentence uttered, a locutionary content which can be considered for our current purposes more or less as what is said, and a bunch of more or less utterance-bound or reflexive contents somehow "in between." Each of these contents is available for the hearer when understanding an utterance. We (theoreticians) can represent them as different propositions, with different truth-conditions. Contrary to what is common usage among philosophers and linguists, then, it is misleading to talk of *the* content of an utterance—or equivalently about *the* truth-conditions of an utterance. We think there is a plurality of contents, of sets of truth-conditions, of an utterance. We agree with CL on this point. We are pluralist on contents.

However, assuming that any of these contents can equally be considered *as said* is an error too, and so also that they can be called "the proposition expressed," where that bit of technical terminology is introduced, as is common, in terms of the intuitive concept of what is said.

As we pointed out, we do not ordinarily consider the utterance-bound truth-conditions of an assertion as what is said or even part of what is said. If OJ's utterance **u** is of "I am innocent," he has not said that there is a unique speaker of **u** and that person is innocent. He hasn't said anything about **u** at all. Someone who heard **u**, but didn't hear who said it, would know its

---

implicatures; an utterance-bound description will often do either as the input for an inference or as the result of mutual adjustment. Thanks to one of the referees for raising this point.

utterance-bound truth-conditions, but not what was said. Probably, he could figure out who said it, and thus what was said, if he knew enough about the trial he was attending.

Another sort of pluralism that must be acknowledged has to do with the plurality of *descriptions* or other designations available for any particular proposition. If one takes propositions to be abstract objects, then, like any objects, there will be innumerable ways of designating them. There is a special, perhaps canonical, way of designating propositions in (philosophical) English: embed a sentence that expresses the proposition from the speaker's context in a that-clause. Among the innumerable ways of designating propositions will be ordinary ways open to competent language users:

> that OJ is innocent
> What OJ just said
> Whatever OJ just said (I didn't hear him clearly)

as well as ways that are used by theorists, in the context of a certain way of modeling propositions:

> $\{w \mid OJ \text{ is innocent in } w\}$, that is, the set of possible worlds in which OJ is innocent;
> $<< \lambda x[x \text{ is innocent}]>, OJ>$, that is, the ordered pair consisting of the property of being innocent and OJ

The plurality of descriptions of what OJ said, does not, of course, imply a plurality of things OJ said.

Finally, we ordinarily count the subject-matter-preserving entailments and near-entailments of what a person said as among the things they said. So OJ said he was innocent, then he said that he wasn't guilty; that he didn't do the deed; and so forth. If he said he wore shoes and socks and a coat that day, then he said he wore shoes and he said that he wore socks and a coat.

Another complication, and the primary reason we think it is worth developing a semi-technical concept, *locutionary content*, as an explication of what is said, is that the latter concept has a heavy *forensic* aspect, that is tied to its daily use in not only describing utterances but assigning responsibility for their effects, but isn't helpful for theoretical purposes.

Consider a variation of one of CL's examples. Suppose L and C are with some worshipful graduate students in the philosophy lounge. Looking at famous philosopher X, affectionately called "that moronic clown" by C and L, L says, somewhat carelessly since others are listening, "That moronic clown just published another book." Our concept of locutionary content (still in development) would zero in on the proposition L believed, and intended to communicate to C, namely, that X just published another book. Something like Donnellan's concept of referential uses of descriptions would help get to that content. We wouldn't want the moronic attributes, real, or imagined, or merely ascribed affectionately with some sort of pretence, to be part of the locutionary content. But suppose one of the graduate students spreads the word that L thinks X is a moron. Called to account by L, the student says, "But that's what you said." We would have at least great sympathy with the student's claim. L was responsible for the effects of his careless utterance. This forensic aspect of what is said is partly responsible for the sense that what is said is so contextually relative as to be theoretically useless.

The concept of what is said that partly motivated the "new theory of reference" comes close to what Perry calls the "referential content" of an utterance. It is the proposition that captures the requirements the truth of an utterance places on the objects referred to. In a wide variety of cases, preserving these requirements with a different form of words will count as "saying the same thing." And in a wide variety of cases, the counterfactual possibilities to which an utterance directs our attention will involve those objects and requirements, and not other requirements involved in referring to them in the actual world. So "Aristotle might not have been named 'Aristotle'" and "I might not be speaking, or might not even exist" make perfectly good sense.

But in some cases, it is clear that the information one intends to communicate is not the referential content, but something that involves the conditions of actual world reference. If K says to a confused P, "Donostia *is* San Sebastian," he intends to convey that "Donostia" is another name, or perhaps one should say, the real name, of the Basque city of San Sebastian. He does not merely intend to honor that city with an attribution of self-identity. In such cases, the ordinary use of what is said may track the information conveyed, rather than the referential content.[4]

These complications with the ordinary use of "what is said" do not imply that it cannot be the basis of a robust and useful theoretical concept; and of course it has been just this, in at least two quite different traditions, Gricean pragmatics and the new theory of reference of Donellan, Kripke, Kaplan, and others. The considerations raised by CL fall far short of showing otherwise.

6.2 The Relativity of What is Said

CL jump from content pluralism plus the observation that it is sometimes difficult to determine what is said and the claim that there are a lot of descriptions or reports, indefinitely many, about what is said, to the

---

[4] See Perry, 2001 [2012], 132 ff.

conclusion that no one description or report is more correct than any other, and therefore, any of them counts as said by the utterance. The "first thesis of Speech Act Pluralism" is:

> No one thing is said (or asserted, or claimed, or...) by any utterance: rather, indefinitely many propositions are said, asserted, claimed, stated, etc. (p. 199).

There is no compelling argument for this conclusion. While it is sometimes difficult to determine exactly what is said, for reasons just surveyed, it is often very easy to identify what is said; as easy as it is *to say the same thing*. Take one of CL's examples. OJ uttered:

> (4) At 11:05 p.m. I put on a white shirt, a blue Yohji Yamamoto suit, dark socks, and my brown Bruno Magli shoes.

Knowing English, the identity of the speaker, and the day of the utterance, there is no difficulty in identifying what was said. JP can do it and can also say the same thing uttering (referring with "he" to OJ, and talking about the same day):

> (5) At 23:05 he put on a white shirt, a blue Yohji Yamamoto suit, dark socks, and his brown Bruno Magli shoes.

KK could also say it uttering:

> (6) Gaueko 11k eta 5ean, alkandora zuria jantzi zuen, eta Yohji Yamamoto traje bat, galtzerdi ilunak eta bere Bruno Magli zapata marroiak.

This is one of the most amazing properties of linguistic action. It is possible for different people, OJ, JP, and KK for instance, to say the same things, in different places, in different contexts, in different languages. CL should accept that these three utterances express the same proposition, and constitute no argument for the relativity of what is said. They would also agree, we think, that one can correctly report what OJ said uttering:

> (7) OJ said that at 11:05 p.m. (the day of the offense) he put on a white shirt, a blue Yohji Yamamoto suit, dark socks, and his brown Bruno Magli shoes.

But one could also report it as

(8) OJ said that at shortly after 11:00 p.m. (the day of the offense) he put on a shirt, a Yohji Yamamoto suit, socks, and his Bruno Magli shoes—he mentioned the colors, but I don't remember them.

The that-clause does not provide a *canonical* description, for the sentence that follows the "that" does not express the proposition in question. It does identify some of the constituents of the proposition (OJ, suit, socks, Bruno Magli shoes) and delimits accurately if incompletely the others (the colors of the suit, socks, and shoes, and the exact time). Similarly with

(9) OJ said that he put on his clothes—I don't remember which—at 11:00 p.m.—more or less.

Finally, one can just say,

(10) What OJ said

to designate the proposition in question.

This plurality of descriptions in no way implies the existence of a plurality of propositions *said* by OJ's original utterance. All of them are true descriptions of what OJ said, although only (7) is a canonical, *expressive description*. (8)–(10) are less and less informative and do not claim to express the same proposition OJ did—(10) is of course sub-sentential, so doesn't express a proposition at all.[5]

Even when there is some relativity to context in what is said, there is not the radical sort of relativity required to undermine the utility of what is said as a basis for theoretical work. As we noted, if L says "That moronic clown just wrote another book," forensic issues may introduce a certain amount of relativity. Those issues aside, whether one wants to maintain that L said that X just wrote another book, which, assuming X is not both a moron and a clown, would require a Donnellan-like treatment of descriptions, or rather maintain that L managed to convey the information that X just wrote another book to C, not by saying it, but by saying something else, obviously false or without truth-value, and thereby implicating that X just wrote another book, would depend on one's overall theory. But theorists, in debating this, would be using and developing what is said as a central theoretical concept, not abandoning it.

---

[5] Sometimes by making sub-sentential utterances speakers do express full propositions (see Carston, 2002, 152–7), but this is not the case with (10).

6.3 Pragmatic Indiscernibility

CL go further than content pluralism and the relativity of what is said. They claim that, given some facts that should be mutually known, the following would also be true descriptions of what OJ said:

(11) He said that he dressed up in some really fancy clothes late in the evening.
(12) He said that he changed his clothes right after 11 p.m.
(13) He said that he stopped exposing himself to the neighbors right after 11 p.m.
(14) He said that he gave the sign at 11:05.

All of these examples are naturally regarded as falling into one or both of two categories. They may be what one might call incremental implications of what OJ said. That is, what OJ said, together with certain assumptions, as for example that Bruno Magli shoes and Yohji Yamamoto suite are pretty posh duds, implies that he dressed up in fancy clothes. Or they may be regarded as implicatures: why else would OJ tell us of these brands, if he didn't want to impress us with what a fancy dresser he was?

Most authors would consider (11)–(14), in the right context, as reports of putative implicatures—stronger or weaker, following Sperber and Wilson's (1986) distinction—of OJ's sayings. They could only be considered as reports of what he said, as CL do, if one ignores the Gricean distinction between what is said and what is implicated by an utterance. And this is what CL do. Contrary to what they seem to assume when defending (their version of) semantic minimalism,[6] CL just end up erasing the Gricean theoretical distinction between what is said and what is implicated by an utterance:

> There is no fundamental theoretical divide between sayings and implicatures. They are both on the side of speech act content. Whatever mechanisms might generate implicatures are also all used to generate what speakers say. (p. 204)

This is really puzzling. CL's greatest enemies, confessed radical contextualists such as relevance theorists for instance, do admit that the same kind of pragmatic processes are involved in the derivation of both

---

[6] Here for instance: "we agree with her [Carston] that you need a contextually shaped content to generate implicatures in all of the cases she discusses... What's needed in order to derive the implicature in these cases is a contextually shaped content, i.e., a contextually shaped what-is-said" (p. 180).

what-is-said (explicatures, in their terminology) and implicatures;[7] but neither they nor other radical contextualists like Recanati, Searle, or Travis are ready to blur the distinction between what-is-said and implicatures. CL are. And thus, they go not only against what everybody else accepts in pragmatics nowadays (this we don't consider bad in itself; we sympathize with defenders of unpopular causes), but they go also, we are afraid, against their own version of semantic minimalism.

7 Semantic Minimalism Defeated

Consider the following premises, both quoted from CL:

(a) "There is no fundamental theoretical divide between sayings and implicatures" (p. 204).
(b) "One of the many propositions asserted by an utterance [i.e. one of the sayings] is the semantic content of the utterance (the proposition semantically expressed)" (p. 200).

Ergo—one can be led to conclude:

(c) There is no fundamental theoretical divide between the proposition semantically expressed, sayings and implicatures.

So we are asked to believe that, on the one hand, there is a minimal proposition called the "semantically expressed proposition," that results from the sentence's conventional semantic meaning plus pragmatic processes of reference fixing, disambiguation, and precisification, that plays a crucial role in a theory of understanding and communication. On the other hand, this proposition is only one, among indefinitely many others. What is so important about it? It isn't what is said. Even if it were, it would only be one of indefinitely many "sayings." Why are the factors, specific to the utterance, that resolve ambiguities, the reference of demonstratives and names, worthy of elevation into the well-guarded realm of semantics, while other utterance specific factors are not? The relativity of what is said seems to undermine any story that would account for what is special about their "semantic content."

---

[7] Recanati (2004) makes a distinction between primary and secondary pragmatic processes in order to distinguish the (non-inferential) pragmatic processes involved in getting at "what is said" and pragmatic processes involved in the inference of implicatures. Relevance theorists think that the same kind of (inferential) pragmatic processes are involved in the derivation of both explicatures and implicatures. [See Chapter 10 for discussion.]

8 Conclusion

Our main contentions, then, are as follows:

- We agree with CL in a minimalist conception of semantics. Semantics is the study of the conventional meanings of types of expressions and modes of combination.
- We disagree that the suitable conception of semantic contribution, given the minimalist perspective, is their conception of semantic content, which incorporates into semantics not only the objective contextual facts that resolve the reference of indexicals, but also a number of factors that depend on the intentions of the speaker and perhaps also other mental facts about the participants in the conversation in questions: the resolution of demonstratives, the reference of names, and precisification of vague terms.
- We instead maintain that, insofar as semantics needs to reason about contents (propositions) rather than merely about meanings (or characters), the appropriate vehicle is the utterance-bound content, which quantifies over contextual and intentional factors.
- That said, we do not maintain that such minimal semantic contents are what is said, and we claim that determination of what is said inevitably depends on factors typically inferred by pragmatic methods. Here we agree with CL.
- We disagree, however, with their skepticism about the theoretical usefulness of what is said. We are confident that a theoretically useful concept of what is said, explicated as locutionary content, can be developed that will play more or less the roles contemplated by both Grice and the new theorists of reference.
- We do not claim to have provided such a concept here, but only to have made some progress towards developing it.[8]

---

[8] The first author thanks the University of the Basque Country (9/UPV 00I09.I09-14 449/2002) and the Diamond XX Philosophy Institute for support. The second author thanks Stanford University and the Diamond XX Philosopher Institute for support. Both authors thank the editors and the anonymous referees for their valuable comments and suggestions.

3

How to Say Things with Words

KEPA KORTA AND JOHN PERRY

1 Introduction

You really do not need us to tell you how to *say* things with words, any more than you (or your ancestors) needed J. L. Austin or his student John Searle to tell you how to *do* things with words. Austin's *How to Do Things with Words* (1961) and Searle's *Speech Acts* (1969) offered a theory to explain how we do things that go *beyond saying*: that is, how we perform illocutionary and perlocutionary acts in and by saying things.

In this essay, we develop Austin's concept of a locutionary act, using the "reflexive-referential theory" of meaning and cognitive significance as developed in Perry's *Reference and Reflexivity* (2001 [2012]).[1] We distinguish the locutionary content of an act both from what a speaker says and what a speaker intends to say. These three concepts often coincide, but keeping them separate is important in reconstructing the plans of speakers and the inferences of hearers, for those cases in which the concepts diverge are often of great theoretical interest.

Our plan is as follows. In section 2 we give an overview of our reasons for distinguishing locutionary content from what is said. In section 3 we explain locutionary content in the context of speakers' plans. In section 4 we look at a number of examples to show how locutionary content can diverge from what is said. In section 5 we compare our concepts to Austin's, and consider Searle's misgivings about locutionary acts. (We should emphasize that, although there are some differences between our concept of a locutionary act and Austin's, and although we disagree with Searle's rejection of locutionary acts, we see our concept of locutionary content as a friendly amendment to the basic ideas of the Austin–Searle theory of speech acts.)

---

[1] See the appendix for a brief introduction to this theory.

9 Locutionary Content versus "What is Said"

Pragmatics and the philosophy of language have put a number of pressures on the concept of what is said by (the speaker of) an utterance. First, David Kaplan and others grounded the concept of "the proposition expressed" in intuitions about what is said, to support arguments that the contribution names, indexicals, and demonstratives make to the proposition expressed is the object referred to, rather than some identifying condition that the referent meets.[2]

Kaplan distinguishes between the character and content of a sentence in a context. The character of the sentence, together with the context, determines the content; semantics spells this out. Since the content of a sentence is the proposition expressed, which is explained in terms of what is said, it creates a second pressure: *what is said* is (more or less) equated with what semantics provides.

A third pressure comes from Grice's (1967a [1989]) distinction between what is said and what is implicated by an utterance. In the standard case, the hearer takes what is said as the starting point in inferring implicatures. So what is said has another role to fill, serving as the starting point of Gricean reasoning about implicatures.

These combined roles for "what is said" give rise to what we will call the "classic" picture of the relation between semantics and pragmatics. Semantics provides what is said as the input to pragmatics. In both speech act theory and Gricean pragmatics, as originally developed, pragmatics is focused on what is done with language *beyond saying*.

We do not think the ordinary concept of saying is quite up to meeting all of these pressures, and that this has obscured some issues about the interface between semantics and pragmatics. There are (at least) the following two difficulties.

On the one hand, as we argued in "Three demonstrations and a funeral" (Chapter 1), it is not always the *referential* content of an utterance that provides the input to Gricean reasoning about implicatures. Often it is some kind of *utterance-bound* or *reflexive* content. In section 5 we extend this point to speech act theory. Information that is required to determine the illocutionary force of an utterance is sometimes lost at the level of referential content, but available at the level of reflexive content.

On the other hand, and this is our main point in this essay, it is necessary to distinguish between acts of saying and locutionary acts. Our locutionary content is, like the classical picture of "what is said," a form of referential content, and is intended to give grounding to the ubiquitous concept of "the

---

[2] See the Peter–Paul argument in Kaplan, 1989a, 512 ff.

proposition expressed." The problem is that the ordinary concept of saying is shaped by the everyday needs of folk psychology and folk linguistics, and does not quite carve phenomena at their theoretical joints, in the following ways.

First, saying is naturally taken to be an illocutionary act, of the same species as asserting, with perhaps somewhat weaker connotations. A speaker is committed to the truth of what she says. But propositions are expressed in the antecedents and consequents of conditionals, as disjuncts, and in many other cases without being asserted.

Second, the concept of saying is to a certain extent a *forensic* concept. One is responsible for the way one's remarks are taken by reasonably competent listeners. But locutionary content is not sensitive to the actual and hypothetical mental states of the audience.

Finally, what we take as having been said is sensitive to the information that the speaker is trying to convey. Intuitively, Joana does not say the same thing when she says "I am Joana," as she does when she says "Joana is Joana" or "I am I." An utterance of "I am I" would not commit her to having the name "Joana," but this might be the main information she is trying to convey when she says "I am Joana." Locutionary content does not have this sensitivity to the information the speaker is trying to convey to sort this out. Our theory is quite sensitive to such matters, but we do not handle this by stretching the concept of what is said to cover all needs, but replace it, for theoretical purposes, with a number of other concepts.

These three differences we illustrate and discuss by going through a number of examples in section 4.

10 Locutionary Acts and Locutionary Content

The central concept in our approach is that of a *speaker's plan*. This is a natural outgrowth of the Austin–Searle concept of language as action, and of Grice's concept of speaker's meaning. Paradigmatically, a speaker utters a sentence with the intention of producing an utterance with certain truth-conditions, and thereby achieving further results, such as conveying information to a hearer, and perhaps thereby getting the hearer to do something. So, for example, Kepa might say the words "I'm hungry" with the intention of uttering the English sentence "I'm hungry," so that his utterance is true if and only if he, the speaker, is hungry, and so informing John that he is hungry, implicating that he'd like to break off work to go to lunch, and eliciting John's response as to whether that seems like a good idea.

We take an *act* to be a specific occurrence, an *action* to be a type of act. In analyzing any species of action, one takes certain actions that can be performed at will, at least in circumstances taken as normal for the analysis, as basic.[3] These actions are *executions*; usually they can be thought of as bodily movements. By executing movements, the agent brings about results, depending on the circumstances. These actions, what the agent brings about, are *accomplishments*. Accomplishments can be thought of as nested, each action being *a way of* bringing about further accomplishments in wider and wider circumstances. We use "accomplishment" in such a way that accomplishments need not be intended. By moving his arms in certain ways, in certain circumstances, John may pick up the coffee cup; by doing that he may spill the coffee on his lap; by doing that he may burn himself. Kepa may say, using "accomplish" in the way we have in mind, "My, look at what you have accomplished."

For our purposes, we assume that we are dealing with competent speakers who can utter (speak, type, write, or sign) meaningful words, phrases, and sentences of English at will, as a part of a plan that marshals the requisite intentions to perform locutionary acts. This involves:

(1) Producing grammatical phrases of English, by speaking, writing, typing, signing, or other means;
(2) Doing so with appropriate intentions that resolve:
   a. which words, of those consistent with the sounds uttered (or letters typed), are being used;
   b. which meanings of those permitted by the conventions of English for the words and phrases being used, are being employed;
   c. which of the syntactic forms consistent with the order of words, intonations, etc. are being employed;
   d. nambiguities; that is, issues about the reference of names which various persons, things, or places share;
   e. the primary reference of demonstratives and other deictic words and issues relevant to the reference of indexicals;
   f. anaphoric relations;
   g. the values of various other parameters that are determined by the speaker's intentions.
(3) Having (possibly quite minimal) beliefs about the facts that resolve the semantic values of indexicals;
(4) Having the intention of producing an utterance that will have certain reflexive truth-conditions, and of thereby producing an utterance with certain referential truth-conditions, in accord with the beliefs in (3);

---

[3] See Goldman,1970, and Israel, Perry, and Tutiya, 1993.

(5) Having (possibly quite minimal) intentions to accomplish other results by producing his utterance: conveying implicatures, performing illocutionary and perlocutionary acts, and the like;
(6) Accomplishing other results by doing all of this: conveying implicatures, performing illocutionary and perlocutionary acts, and the like.

In determining the locutionary content, the speaker's intentions (1) and (2) are determinative; actual and possible misunderstandings, however easily the speaker could have foreseen and prevented them, are not relevant. Thus the intended reflexive truth-conditions will be what the speaker intends them to be, so long as the meanings and structures the speaker intends are allowed by the conventions of English. The speaker's beliefs in (3) are *not* determinative for locutionary content, however. The *intended* locutionary content will be the referential content of his utterance *given* his beliefs in (3). But the *actual* locutionary content will be determined by the facts, not by the speaker's beliefs about them.

Suppose, for example, that John is in the philosophy lounge, but thinks that he is in the CSLI lounge. "Kepa is supposed to meet me here," he says. He intends to use "here" indexically rather that deictically, and intends the range of "here" to mean the room he is in, not, say, the campus he is at or the nation in which he resides. These intentions are determinative. The locutionary content of his utterance is that Kepa was to meet him in the philosophy lounge, the actual referent of his use of "here." The intended locutionary content, however, is that Kepa was to meet him in the CSLI lounge, the place he thought would be the referent of his use of "here."

11 "Locuted" but not Said: Some Examples

Grice's main distinction in his analysis of utterance meaning is between what is said and what is implicated. Grice also remarked that there are implicatures in cases in which the speaker says nothing, but only "makes as if to say." Irony is a case in point. Let us assume that X, with whom John has been on close terms until now, has betrayed a delicate secret of John's to an academic rival. John and Kepa both know this and they both see X passing by. John utters:

(4.1) He is a fine friend[4]

---

[4] We will use citations such as "(4.1)" to refer to sentence types and also to hypothesized utterances involving those types; context should make it clear which.

Mere reflexive content will not do:

(4.1.1) That ***the person that* John *is referring to by his use of "he"*** is a fine friend (the reflexive content of (4.1)).

Kepa must go through sentence meaning to the locutionary content of (3).

(4.1.2) **X** is a fine friend (the referential content, and hence the locutionary content, of (4.1)).

Independently of what John might intend to communicate—typically, the opposite, or something implying the opposite, of (4.1.2)—and how the understanding process exactly works, it seems clear that for Kepa to take the utterance as ironic he has to identify the referent of "he" and the property of "being a fine friend," i.e. the locutionary content. Without identifying X and the property ascribed to him in the locutionary content of John's utterance, and as the X that has betrayed John's confidence in him, Kepa will not grasp John's utterance as ironic, and will miss the point. John may be *making as if to say* (Grice, 1967a [1989]), *pretending* (Clark and Gerrig, 1984) or *echoing* (Sperber and Wilson, 1986) a proposition, but definitely he is not saying it; he is not committing himself in any way to the truth of the locutionary content. However, this content has a role to play in the understanding of John's ironic utterance.

However the difference between saying and just making as if to say should be characterized, it seems clear that, when a speaker is being ironic, she refers to objects and predicates properties so as to provide content for her utterance that the hearer is intended to grasp. From the perspective of the speaker, this content plays a role in her utterance plan; from the perspective of the addressee, it plays a role in understanding the utterance. This content does not count as what she said because, possibly among other things, she is overtly not committed to its truth, and she expects the hearer to understand that she is not so committed, but it is a content anyway: a content that is locuted but not said.

In the case of many logical operators and other sentence embedding constructions, propositions are locuted but not said, as Frege pointed out, and Geach reminded a generation of ordinary language philosophers.[5] When someone says, "If Hillary is elected, Bill will enjoy his return to the White House," she does not say either that Hillary will be elected, or that Bill will

---

[5] Frege, 1879; Geach, 1965.

return to the White House. These seem to us sufficient reasons for keeping a place for locutionary content in a theory of utterance content.

(4.2) John is turning red

In a discussion with alumni about politics on campus, Kepa says, "John is turning red." He means that JP's face is turning red, perhaps from anger, or eating a hot chili pepper. The alumni take him to say that JP is becoming a communist. Kepa should have seen that people were likely to interpret his remark that way. Later he may protest, "I didn't say that." John might retort, "You didn't mean to say it, but you did, and I had to do a lot of explaining." Perhaps this retort is not correct. But the fact that the issue is debatable suggests that our ordinary concept of what is said is to some extent responsive to uptake on the part of the audience. What is said seems to have both illocutionary and perlocutionary aspects. In contrast, our concept of locutionary content will not depend on effects on the listener.

(4.3) Flying planes can be dangerous

Kepa produces the sounds necessary to say "Flying planes can be dangerous" [(1)].[6] He intends to be producing a token of "planes," not of "plains" [(2a)]. He intends to be using "plane" with the sense of airplane, not flat surface [(2b)]. He intends to use "Flying planes" as a verb phrase, rather than a noun phrase [(2c)]. These intentions are all determinative for the locutionary act.

They might not be determinative for what is said. Suppose Kepa and John are flying kites on a hill near the airport with some other folks. People have been discussing the dangers that birds, power lines, electrical storms, and other phenomena pose for kite flyers. Kepa has not really been paying attention, but is daydreaming about being a pilot. He utters, "Flying planes can be dangerous," somewhat loudly, to remind himself of the reasons for forgoing his dreams. Everyone takes him to have used "flying planes" as a noun phrase, and to have added a warning to the list generated by the conversation about the dangers of flying kites on the hill. Any semantically competent listener who had been listening to the conversation would have taken Kepa that way, and Kepa himself would have realized this if he had not been daydreaming.

When Kepa realizes how he has been taken he can surely protest, "I didn't *mean* to say that." But it is at least arguable that he *did* say it. Our ordinary concept of saying has a forensic element; Kepa would be responsible if a member of the group, frightened by his observation, quit flying kites. A

---

[6] Bracketed items refer to the list of elements of a speaker's plan given in section 3.

discussion of whether he *did* say what he meant to, or said what he did not mean to, would likely devolve into a discussion about his responsibility for the effects of his remarks on others. But, to repeat, with respect to our theoretically defined concept of locutionary content, there is no room for debate. There are no "uptake" conditions, no forensic dimension, to consider.

(4.4) Aristotle enjoyed philosophy

Graduate students are discussing the life and times of Jackie Kennedy and Aristotle Onassis in the lounge. John comes in, and hears a debate about whether Aristotle Onassis enjoyed philosophy. What he hears is a loud assertion: "Aristotle despised philosophy and philosophers." He thinks the conversation is about the philosopher, and says, "That is the stupidest thing I have ever heard. Aristotle enjoyed philosophy." His intention in using the name "Aristotle" is to refer to the philosopher, and this is determinative for the locutionary content [(2d)]. The locutionary content of John's remark is a true proposition about the ancient philosopher. But it is at least not totally clear that this is what he has said.

One might object at this point that we are abusing the concept of reference. We are assuming that one could consistently say that John *locuted* (for we will now allow ourselves this verb) truly that one fellow liked philosophy, while, in the very same act, *saying* falsely that another fellow did. But surely he referred to one or the other, or perhaps neither, but not both.

Two points are in order here. First, the reflexive-referential theory sees propositions as abstract objects that are used to *classify* events of certain types (cognitive states and utterances, paradigmatically) by conditions of truth (or other relevant forms of success)—used explicitly by theorists such as ourselves, and implicitly in the practice of those who have mastered the propositional attitudes and similar constructions. We do not see propositions as denizens of a third realm to which some quasi-causal relation relates us, but as devices by which we can classify events along different dimensions of similarity and difference. Different propositions can be used to classify the same act, relative to different frameworks for associating success-conditions of various sorts.

A normal assertive utterance will express a belief on the part of the speaker, it will have a locutionary content, it will count as saying something, it will be taken a certain way by listeners. When things go right, the same proposition will get at the truth-conditions of the belief, of the locutionary act, of the saying, and of the resulting beliefs. But not when things go wrong. John's assertion expressed his belief that the philosopher enjoyed philosophy, locuted the same thing, but conveyed something different.

There are two quite intelligible routes from John's utterance of "Aristotle" to potential referents. One proceeds through his own system of mental files, back through centuries of commentary, to an ancient Greek philosopher. The other proceeds through the ongoing use of "Aristotle" in the conversation of which his remark is a part, back through the minds of the other participants, to decades of commentary in various supermarket tabloids, to the shipping magnate. While our ordinary concepts of reference and "what is said" are keyed to the successful cases, our theoretical concepts need to be more flexible. In a case like this, one choice of referents is suitable for understanding the utterance as the production of a person with John's beliefs; another is more suitable for understanding the effects of his utterance on the other conversants.

An analogy from the philosophy of action may be helpful by way of our second point. Indeed, given the Austin–Searle perspective of language use as a type of action, it is more than a mere analogy. We can classify the results of action propositionally, as is done with the concept of accomplishment explained above. By spilling his coffee in his lap, John accomplished a number of different things. He dampened his pants: that is, brought it about that his pants were damp. He wasted the coffee: that is, brought it about that his coffee was wasted. And he brought it about that Kepa was amused. And so on. Each of these accomplishments is used to characterize the act given various circumstances and connections.

We can also characterize acts by accomplishments they were intended to have, or would have had in various counterfactual conditions. John wanted to bring it about that he got a drink of coffee; he might have brought it about that he had a seriously burned lap, or that Kepa laughed so hard he had a stroke.

Our practice of saying, and our concepts for classifying what we do in speaking, have the feature that, when things go right, a great number of different aspects of the act will be classifiable by the same proposition: the conditions under which the belief that motivates the utterance is true, the conditions under which the intended locutionary content is true, the conditions under which the locutionary content is true, the conditions under which what is said is true, and the conditions under which the beliefs that the utterance leads the audience to adopt or consider are true. This gives rise to the picture of a single proposition that is passed along, from a speaker's belief, to his utterance, to the mind of his audience. But the picture breaks down when things do not go right, and we need different propositions to classify different aspects of the act, relative to different circumstances and interests.

(4.5) You are late

Here is the situation. Kepa and John were supposed to meet at 10:30 at their office at CSLI. It is 10:35. Kepa hears the door handle turn, and hears the door begin to open. He looks toward the door and sees the shoulder of the person who is coming in, whom he takes to be John. He utters the words, "You are late."

Kepa's plan is as follows. He intends to produce a certain string of sounds that count as a token of the English sentence "You are late" [(1), (2a)]. He intends to produce these sounds as words and phrases with certain of the meanings permitted by English: "you" as a the second-person singular pronoun, which refers to the person the speaker addresses; "are late" as a verb phrase that is truly predicated of a person if that person, at the time of the utterance, is late for an event, which event being determined by the speaker's intentions [(2b)]. He intends to be referring with "you" to the person entering the room, whom he is addressing [(2e)], and he intends to predicate being late for the meeting they had scheduled, which is the event he has in mind [(2g)]. So he intends to produce an utterance **u** that has the reflexive truth-conditions:

(4.5.1) That *the person the speaker of* **(4.1)** *is addressing* is late for *the event that the speaker of* **(4.1)** *has in mind*.

Given that Kepa is the speaker and the event he has in mind is the appointment, the incremental truth-conditions are:

(4.5.2) That *the person* **Kepa** *is addressing* is late for **Kepa's 10:30 appointment with John** [truth-conditions with speaker and (2g) parameters fixed].

Kepa takes it that the person he is addressing is John [(3)], and so intends to produce an utterance with these referential truth-conditions:

(4.5.3) That **John** is late for **the 10:30 meeting between Kepa and John**.

This is the *intended locutionary content*. If Kepa had been right about whom he was addressing, it would also be the locutionary content. But given that it is not John, but Tomasz, whose shoulder Kepa sees, the actual locutionary content of his act is

(4.5.4) That **Tomasz** is late for **the 10:30 meeting between Kepa and John**.

In this case, Kepa produced an utterance with the reflexive content that he intended, but not with the locutionary content he intended. The locutionary content depends on the actual features of context relevant to indexical features of language.

We need to use the concept of the speaker's plan to approach concepts like "intended referent" or "speaker's referent" with the needed delicacy. Did Kepa refer to the person he intended to refer to? Yes, because he referred to the person he was addressing, just as he intended? Or no, because he referred to Tomasz, when he meant to refer to John? The answer is that Kepa intended to refer to whomever was playing a certain role vis-à-vis the utterance, and in this he succeeded, and he intended by doing that to refer to John, and in this he failed. Because his belief was false, his utterance did not have the locutionary content he intended it to have.

The conventions of English permit one to use "is late" to predicate being late for an appointment or other event, which need not be articulated, and it is in this way that Kepa intended to use the phrase [(2g)]. The conventions also permit one to predicate the property of arriving later than one usually arrives. Perhaps, independently of appointments, John usually shows up by eight, and is in the office before Kepa arrives after his train trip from the city. John might take Kepa to have used "late" in this sense and to convey not criticism in hopes of producing chagrin, but curiosity in hopes of obtaining information about what happened to get John off to a late start on this particular day.

For the locutionary act, however, Kepa's intentions in the matter are determinative. Even if John understands Kepa to have used "are late" in the second way, it does not matter. Even if any fair-minded observer would have taken Kepa to have used them in that sense, it does not matter for the locutionary content.

(4.6) I am Joana

With identity statements what is said seldom coincides with locutionary content. When Joana says (4.6) to John, the locutionary content of her utterance is:

(4.6.1) That **Joana** is **Joana**.

If this were what she said, she would have said the same thing by saying

(4.7) Joana is Joana

or

(4.8) I am I.

But only those with intuitions twisted by theoretical commitments would suppose that this is correct. So what is going on?

There are many people in the world who share the name "Joana," a number of whom Joana knows, and uses the name to refer to. The issue of which Joana she refers to is settled by her intention [(2d)]. In this case, of course, she refers to herself. So Joana intends to produce an utterance (4.6) with the reflexive content

(4.6.2) That *the speaker of* **(4.6)** is *the person the speaker of* **(4.6)** *is referring to with the name "Joana."*

Joana realizes that she is the speaker, and that she intends to use "Joana" to refer to herself, and so intends, by producing an utterance with (4.6.2) as its reflexive truth-conditions, to produce one with (4.6.1) as its referential truth-conditions. She succeeds in this, and so (4.6.1) is the locutionary content of her remark.

But our ordinary concept of "what is said" is responsive to the information the speaker is attempting to convey, which may be lost at the level of referential content. In this case, Joana might be trying to convey that her name is "Joana." This would be likely if she were talking to someone for a while, whom she did not have any reason to believe had ever heard of Joana Garmendia, but had obtained a concept of her, and would like to know her name. The relevant information might be identified as the truth-conditions with the context and the meanings, other than the referent of "Joana," fixed:

(4.6.3) That I am *the person with the name "Joana" to whom the speaker of* **(4.6)** *intends to refer*.

Or perhaps Joana's interlocutor has been waiting for Joana Garmendia to show up to give a talk, but does not recognize her. Then the information she manages to convey is that the person he is looking at, and whose utterance (4.6) he hears, is Joana. She conveys this information by conveying the truth-conditions of her utterance with the meanings fixed, including that of "Joana," but the context allowed to vary, so what the interlocutor grasps is:

(4.6.4) That *the speaker of* **(4.6)** is **Joana**.

Since the interlocutor identifies (4.6) as "the utterance I am hearing," and the speaker of it as "the woman in front of me," he learns that the person he has been waiting for is now in front of him, something he would not have learned had Joana said (4.7) or (4.8).

12 Locutionary vs. Propositional Content

Our concept of a locutionary act is intended to be similar to Austin's. His definition was: "The utterance of certain noises, the utterance of certain words in a certain construction, and the utterance of them with a certain 'meaning' in the favorite philosophical sense of that word, i.e. with a certain sense and with a certain reference" (Austin, 1961, 94). According to Austin, locutionary acts are what saying consists in, when taken in its full general sense. They are the acts *of* saying something in contrast with the acts performed *in* saying something. We formulate it as the difference between the act of "locuting" something (with a certain content, in our favored sense of the word) and the act of "saying" it (telling it, asking it) to someone. How faithful to Austin this is depends on just what he had in mind, which has been a matter of debate (cf. Searle, 1968; Strawson, 1973; Forguson, 1973, for an early discussion).[7]

Surprisingly, Searle rejected Austin's distinction between locutionary acts and acts of (illocutionary) saying, arguing that "it cannot be completely general, in the sense of marking off two mutually exclusive classes of acts"

---

[7] Our locutionary content would probably be closer to Strawson's B-meaning, but we are not interested in exegetical issues here.

(Searle, 1968, 407).[8] From our point of view, this would mean that the same act could be an instance of two different actions, locuting and saying, and would not constitute a problem. Setting this argument aside, it seems that Searle followed Austin's lead, and offered a concept of locutionary act under a different label: the *propositional* act.

So, in order to clarify our concept of locutionary content, a comparison with Searle's propositional content will help. In (5.1)–(5.5) Kepa is talking to John; John is the speaker in (5.3), Kepa in the others, and all occur on Monday, May 14, 2006.

(5.1) Will I finish the paper by tomorrow?
(5.2) I will finish the paper by tomorrow.
(5.3) Kepa, finish the paper by tomorrow!
(5.4) (I hope) to finish the paper by tomorrow.
(5.5) If I finish the paper by tomorrow, (John will be pleased).

According to Searle, the same propositional content is expressed by the unbracketed parts of all of these utterances.

Within the reflexive-referential theory, there is more than one candidate for this content. For each utterance except (5.3) we can identify a reflexive content:

(5.x.1) **That** *the speaker of* **(5.x)** finish *the paper referred to by the speaker of* **(5.x)** *before the day after* **(5.x)** *is uttered.*

But this will not do. First of all, since the reflexive truth-conditions are conditions on the utterance itself, the reflexive truth-conditions for each utterance are different. Second, a proposition of this sort will not do for (5.3), where John is the speaker. So it seems our candidate for the common propositional content must be the referential content:

(5.x.2) That **Kepa** finishes **the paper by May 15, 2006.**

That seems to work for all of the utterances. They are all about a person and his finishing a certain paper by a particular date. They use this content in different ways but all locute or express it. It fits well our intuitions that, on Wednesday, May 16, Kepa could express it by uttering:

(5.6) I finished the paper by yesterday,

---

[8] Searle does not distinguish between meaning and content, and this makes him sound quite a literalist, i.e. as defending that sentence meaning determines utterance content. That would contrast with his better-known contextualist views as exposed in Searle, 1980, for example.

or John by addressing Kepa,

(5.7) You finished the paper by yesterday (as you promised).

It seems, then, that our locutionary content is just another label for Searle's propositional content. But there are some points where Searle's propositional content diverges from our locutionary content.

First of all, according to Searle's original view, there would be no difference in the propositional content of utterances (5.1)–(5.5) on the one hand, and (5.8), on the other:

(5.8) I promise to finish the paper by tomorrow.

Thus, the content of the (sub-)utterance of "I promise" would vanish from the content of (5.8) because its meaning, he thought, determines the illocutionary force and that is what we are trying to contrast the proposition with.

On our view the locutionary content of the subordinate clause in (5.8) is the proposition (5.x.2), but the whole of (5.8) has a more complex locutionary content:

(5.8.1) That **Kepa** promises at **the time of (5.8)** to bring it about that **Kepa** finishes **the paper** before **the day after the time of (5.8)**.

However, Searle changed his view on this point in his later essay, "How performatives work" (1989), where the propositional content does include the content of the "performative verb" and its subject, so this is a moot point.

There is a second and more important difference between propositional content and locutionary content, however. An important concept in Searle's theory is the concept of the propositional content conditions of a speech act. Some of these conditions are determined, according to the theory, by the illocutionary point. The commissive illocutionary point, for instance, establishes that the propositional content of a speech act with that point—e.g. a promise—must represent a future act of the speaker. The directive illocutionary point, in contrast, determines that the propositional content of a speech act with that point—e.g. a request—must represent a future act by the addressee.

We think that the locutionary content (or Searle's propositional content) is not the content that could satisfy the "propositional content" conditions of the speech act. Recall our basic picture: a speaker plans to produce an utterance with certain reflexive truth-conditions, and intends to thereby produce an utterance with certain referential truth-conditions, i.e. locutionary content. The level of reflexive content is crucial, because many of the effects that a speaker will intend his utterance to have will depend on the hearer's recognition of the reflexive content. This was illustrated by the discussion of identity statements in section 4. Joana's plan for conveying the various bits of information she wants to convey involves the hearer hearing the utterance and grasping its reflexive contents. The hearer can combine this content with what he already knows, and infer the information she is trying to convey. In one case, this was the name of the person he is talking to; in another, it was the whereabouts of someone whom he already had a "file" on, namely, that Joana is the person talking to him.

We call the constituents of the locutionary content, the places, things and people that are constituents of the proposition expressed, the *subject matter* of the utterance. So Joana is the subject matter of her utterance, "I am Joana." Often, the elements of the subject matter play a role in the utterance situation. Indexicals, of course, are the most explicit means of conveying this information. When Joana says "I am Joana," she conveys not only the trivial locutionary content, but the important fact that the person in the subject matter of the locutionary content is also playing the role of the speaker of the utterance itself. When John says to Kepa, "You must finish the paper," Kepa is an element of the subject matter, the paper-finisher, but also a part of the utterance situation, the addressee. This information is conveyed by "you." This sort of information is lost at the level of locutionary content. If the speaker does not get the reflexive content right, even if the locutionary content is grasped, important information will be lost.

We agree with Searle that the illocutionary point of an utterance is not part of the locutionary content or propositional content. It is a fact about the utterance that it is important for the listener to grasp, but it is not part of the proposition expressed. And we agree that certain illocutionary points (and forces) of utterances put conditions on the content. But it is up to the reflexive content, not the locutionary content, to satisfy these conditions.

It is in grasping the reflexive content that the hearer understands the intended relationships between the speaker and the utterance, including the time of the utterance and the addressee.

Consider again

(5.2) I will finish the paper by tomorrow.

and now compare it with

(5.9) Kepa finishes the paper by May 15, 2006.

Both of these utterances could arguably be uttered as commissives: that is, with that intended illocutionary point on the same locutionary content. But (5.9) puts a greater cognitive burden on the listener. To understand (5.9) as a commissive, the hearer has to have at least the information that the speaker is Kepa and the time of utterance is prior to May 15, for one can only commit to future actions, and one can only commit *oneself*. (5.6), on the other hand, cannot be understood as a commissive. The reflexive content of (5.2) imposes the right utterance roles on the finisher of the paper and the time of finishing; the reflexive content of (5.9) is *consistent* with them having the right roles in the utterance, and the reflexive content of (5.6) is *inconsistent* with them playing the appropriate roles; the finishing has to be in the *past*. Similar remarks apply to (5.3), uttered as a directive.

Searle's theory of speech acts poses two different tasks for the concept of propositional contents. On the one hand, it represents the basic content on which the diverse illocutionary forces operate. On the other hand, it is the content that meets the conditions imposed by certain illocutionary points and forces. But, as we argued for the case of the ordinary concept of what is said, these two tasks cannot be accomplished by a single content. The locutionary or referential content of an utterance can be taken as that basic shared content of different speech acts but, instead of locutionary content, reflexive content is needed to serve as the content fulfilling Searle's "propositional content conditions." The theory of speech acts, as well as the theory of implicatures as we showed in "Three demonstrations and a funeral" (Chapter 1), and the theory of meaning, content, and communication in general, would benefit if they adopted a pluralistic view of utterance content in terms of locutionary and reflexive contents such as the one we sketch here. They all are too demanding on a single content, whatever it is called: "what is said," "propositional content," "proposition expressed," or "truth-conditions of an utterance."

13 Conclusion

The main focus of this essay is the development of the concept of locutionary content, as a theoretical concept that is better suited than the ordinary concept of *what is said* for some of the theoretical purposes to which the latter has been put, especially that of grounding the concept of *the proposition expressed by an utterance*.

What does this tell us about how to say things with words? The important lesson, we believe, is that the intentions involved in saying something are not simply a matter of choosing a proposition to serve as locutionary content, and hoping that the uptake circumstances are such that one manages to convey the information one wishes; instead one has to focus on the reflexive truth-conditions of the utterance one plans to produce, for only at this level can much of the crucial information, necessary to producing the intended cognitive and noncognitive effects, including the grasping of the intended illocutionary force, be found. The reflexive-referential theory allows us to incorporate this point of view into a theory that ties the pragmatics of an utterance closely to the semantics of an utterance, conceived (more or less) traditionally as a matter of its truth-conditions.

Appendix: The Reflexive-Referential Theory

The reflexive-referential theory of meaning and content (RRT) has the following basic tenets and uses the following notation:

1. The basic subject matter of semantics and pragmatics are the *contents* of utterances, where utterances are taken to be intentional acts, at least typically involving the use of language. Utterances are assumed to occur at a time, in a place, and to have a speaker.
2. The paradigm is the use of a declarative sentence. For such utterances, the contents of utterances are *propositions*. Propositions are abstract objects that are assigned *truth-conditions*. Propositions are conceived as classificatory tools rather than denizens of a third realm. Theorists use propositions to classify utterances by the conditions under which the utterances are true. This use of propositions is a development of a capacity of ordinary speakers, who classify not only utterances but also other cognitive states and activities by their truth-conditions, typically, in English, with the use of "that"-clauses.
3. We adopt a notation for propositions that is compatible with a number of different theories of what propositions are, and choices of abstract objects to model them. The proposition that **Elwood** lives in **Dallas** can be thought of as the set of worlds in which Elwood lives in Dallas, or the function that yields truth for worlds in which he does and falsity for worlds in which he does not, or as a sequence of the relation of living, Elwood and Dallas, or in a number of other ways.

    Now suppose that Elwood is in fact the shortest podiatrist. The proposition that **the shortest podiatrist** lives in **Dallas** will be the same proposition as that **Elwood** lives in **Dallas**. The roman bold-face in our language for specifying propositions indicates that the constituents of the proposition are the objects designated (named or described) by the bold-face term, rather than any identifying condition that may be associated with that term.

On the other hand, the proposition that ***the shortest podiatrist*** lives in **Dallas** does not have Elwood as a constituent, but the identifying condition of being the shortest podiatrist; this is what is indicated by the boldface italic. This proposition will be true in worlds in which, whoever the shortest podiatrist is, he or she lives in Dallas. The proposition that ***the shortest podiatrist*** lives in ***the city in which*** **John F. Kennedy *was shot*** is true in a world in which whoever the shortest podiatrist is, he or she lives in whatever city Kennedy was shot in. This will be the same proposition as that ***the shortest podiatrist*** lives in ***the city in which*** **the thirty-fifth President *was shot*.** The boldface roman indicates that Kennedy himself, the person described by "the thirty-fifth President," is a constituent of the condition that identifies the city. On the other hand, the proposition that ***the shortest podiatrist*** lives in ***the city in which the thirty-fifth President was shot*** is true in worlds in which whoever is the shortest podiatrist lives in the same city in which whoever was the thirty-fifth President was shot.

4. RRT assigns *contents* to utterances based on the idea of *relative truth-conditions*: given certain facts, what *else* has to be the case for the utterance to be true? We illustrate the idea with an example. Let **u** be an utterance of "You are irritating David," by Kepa, addressed to John, and expressing the proposition that **John** is getting on **David Israel**'s nerves.

   a. Given that u is uttered by Kepa in English, and given the meanings of the words, etc., and that Kepa is addressing John, and that Kepa is using "irritate" with its meaning of "get on the nerves of," and that Kepa is using "David" to refer to David Israel, **u** is true iff **John** is getting on the nerves of **David Israel**.

   The proposition that **John** is getting on the nerves of **David Israel** is called, at various times, the *referential* content of **u**, the *official content* of **u**, and the content of **u** with the facts of meaning and context fixed and nambiguities resolved, notated "Content$_C$." ("Nambiguity" is the phenomenon of more than one person, place or thing having the same name.)

   b. Given *only* that **u** is uttered in English, and given the meanings of the words, but none of the other facts listed above, **u** is true iff there are x, y, and z such that x is the speaker of **u**, x is addressing y, x is exploiting a convention that assigns "David" as a name of z to refer to z, and either (i) x is using "irritate" with its meaning of "get on the nerves of" and y is getting on z's nerves, or (ii) x is using "irritate" with its meaning of "cause inflammation" and y is causing the inflammation of some part of z.

The proposition identified by the sentence to the right of the "iff" is what the RRT calls *a* reflexive content of **u**. The word "reflexive" honors the fact that the proposition in question has **u** itself as a constituent; it gives us the truth-conditions for **u** in terms of conditions on **u** itself.

   c. Given everything in (b), plus the fact that the speaker of **u** is using "irritate" to mean "get on the nerves of," and is using "David" to refer to David Israel, **u** is true iff there are x, and y such that x is the speaker of **u**, x is addressing y, and y is getting on David's nerves. This is also a reflexive content; it is what we call *indexical content* or Content$_M$—content with the meanings fixed and ambiguities resolved, but not the contextual facts.

   d. Given everything in (b), plus the fact that Kepa is the speaker, he is speaking to John, and is using "irritate" to mean "get on the nerves of," **u** is true iff there is a z such that Kepa is using "David" to refer to z and John is getting on z's nerves. Here the context is given, and the meanings that are being exploited, but the nambiguity is not resolved. Notice that the proposition expressed by the sentence to the right of the "iff" is not reflexive in our official sense; its constituents are Kepa and John, and do not include the utterance. However, it is not fully referential either, since it involves an identifying condition of David, and not David himself. Sometimes such contents, which no longer have the utterance itself as a constituent, are called "incremental," and the referential content is called "fully incremental."

5. The official or referential content is what is ordinarily taken as the proposition expressed, or *what is said*; that is the basis of the account of locutionary content in this essay. But the other contents are available to describe the various communicative intentions and uptakes that occur, as is also illustrated by examples in the essay.[9]

---

[9] We are grateful to Savas L. Tsohatzidis for inviting us to collaborate in this volume, for his enormous patience with our delays, and for his helpful comments and corrections. We would also like to thank Joana Garmendia and Genoveva Martí for comments and criticisms, and the Center for the Study of Language and Information (CSLI) and the Institute for Logic, Cognition, Language, and Information (ILCLI) for support.

4

The Pragmatic Circle

KEPA KORTA AND JOHN PERRY

1 Introduction

According to our view, which we call "Critical Pragmatics," utterances are the subject matter of pragmatics. Utterances are intentional acts of speaking, writing or signing, usually for the purpose of communication, and usually in service of further goals, such as developing a plan, persuading someone to do something, teaching, learning, passing the time, or whatever. The utterance is an act by the speaker, which the listener interprets, by divining the intentions behind it and the results that will ensue from it, using many tools that are used for interpreting all sorts of actions, and some that are specific to language. Pragmatics, the study of utterances as ways of doing things, is central and critical to the study of language.

In saying that utterances are the basic subject matter, we do not mean to imply that for certain purposes abstracting from many of the properties of utterances to construct models that focus on other properties of utterances may be useful. This is typically done in formal approaches to semantics. For example, Kaplan uses sentences in context rather than utterances in his "Demonstratives" (1989a). A "sentence in context" is an abstract object, consisting of a sentence type and a context, where a context is a quadruple consisting of an agent, time, location and possible world. Unless the abstract theory constructed from these elements could be applied, by taking the sentence, agent, time, location and world of a sentence in context to be the sentence used in an utterance by a speaker at a time in a location in the world of the theorist, and testing the predictions of the model as to truth and reference against the properties of the utterance, the formal theory would be of little value to understanding natural language.

2 Near-side and Far-side Pragmatics

In the classical conception of pragmatics, due mainly to Grice, Austin, and Searle, the natural dividing line between semantics and pragmatics is based on the intuitive concept of *what is said*. Setting subtleties aside, Grice's picture is that what the speaker says is determined by the semantics of the sentence he uses, and then pragmatics takes over, to figure out the best explanation for his saying what he did, in light of the conversational principles. We call this "far-side" pragmatics, that is, pragmatics on the far-side of what is said. Austin's *locutionary act* and Searle's *propositional content*, subtleties aside, strip the concept of what is said of its illocutionary force to arrive at a conception of what meaning and reference give us, that is, the proposition expressed, whether asserted, commanded, or queried; speech act theory takes over to tell us what is done, in various circumstances, in virtue of this (purified) act of saying. (A number of terms are used for the content of this purified act of saying. Recanati still uses "what is said;" Cappelen and Lepore use the term "semantic content;" relevance theorists use the term "explicature." First as a neutral place-holder, then later as a technical term, we will use the term "locutionary content.")

This is oversimplified, however, for as Grice points out, we don't get to what is said without resolving ambiguities, and the reference of proper names, indexicals and demonstratives. Cappelen and Lepore add resolution of standards of precision to the list. These are issues on the "near-side" of what is said, and insofar as pragmatics is needed to resolve them, we must also consider "near-side" pragmatics.

"Literalism" is Recanati's term for a family of pragmatic theories that hold that what is literally referred to and literally said depends wholly, or very largely, on semantics, with no supplementation, or only minimal supplementation, by pragmatic considerations. Pure literalism seems clearly to apply only to small parts of natural language, like mathematics, where issues of tense and indexicality, for example, are not relevant. Such issues seem to dictate a somewhat more liberal literalism that allows that objective facts about the utterance, like the speaker, and the time and place it occurs, may be needed to determine issues of truth and reference. Arguably, resolving issues of indexicality and tense only require such objective facts, and not discovery of the speaker's intentions.

If, however, we are to incorporate the whole list of issues that arise on the near-side, given one paragraph back, we seem to be forced to a weaker form of literalism, advocated by Cappelen and Lepore, and called "minimalism." Semantic content depends on resolving reference, ambiguity, and issues of precision—but that's it.

Three questions arise. First, is everything needed on the list, or must it be expanded? Second, in order to resolve the issues on the list, whether expanded or not, we need to employ Gricean reasoning, which aims at discovering speaker's intentions? Third, can we employ Gricean reasoning on the near-side? We'll consider the second and third questions, and return to the first.

To resolve issues involving some indexicals, such as "I" and (perhaps) "today," Gricean reasoning is not needed. For such indexicals, the meaning of the expression and the objective facts about the utterance suffice. But in resolving other issues, even those on the unexpanded list, pragmatic considerations, in the sense of considerations about the speaker's intentions above and beyond merely speaking English, will enter in. For example, if Julius is talking about someone named "Aristotle" in his seminar on Greek philosophy, we will take him to be talking about the philosopher and not Aristotle Onassis. This does not seem to be an objective, perceivable fact about his utterance, like the time and place and speaker. It seems to involve his intentions—not merely his intention to speak English, but to use the name "Aristotle" to refer to one person rather than another. Our inference that this is what he intends to do seems easily explained, within the Gricean framework, by considerations of relevance. Similarly, we resolve anaphors, demonstratives, and ambiguities and vagueness by appeal to what makes sense in the conversation. (Indeed, we may use such considerations to determine which words we actually heard, and which syntactic structures are being employed.)

But does it make sense to use Gricean pragmatics on the near-side? Classical Gricean pragmatics, aimed at computing implicatures, is usually conceived as dealing with far-side pragmatics. It involves reasoning about why what was said, was said. Near-side pragmatics, on the other hand, is pragmatics in the service of determining, together with the semantical properties of the words used, what was said. But this raises the specter of "the pragmatic circle." If pragmatics seeks explanations for why someone said what they did, how can there be near-side pragmatics? Gricean reasoning seems to require what is said to get started. But then if Gricean reasoning is needed to get to what is said, we have a circle.

3   Recanati's Spectrum

Perhaps the best way to explain our approach to this problem is to start with François Recanati's recent book *Literal Meaning* (2004). Recanati's scheme for sorting out the issues involved in current debates about semantics and pragmatics has been deservedly influential. He sees the range of positions as having two poles, literalism and contextualism:

> [The literalist holds that] we may legitimately ascribe truth-conditional content to natural language sentences, quite independently of what the speaker who utters this sentence means... [Contextualism] holds that speech acts are the primary bearers of content. Only in the context of a speech act does a sentence express a determinate content. (3)

Recanati goes on to distinguish a number of intermediate positions. The minimalist position is essentially the one we described above, where what semantics provides is supplemented by a short list of other factors to get to "semantic content"; this is the position of Cappelen and Lepore, in their book *Insensitive Semantics* (2005).

Recanati and relevance theorists are far over to the contextualist side. Both camps call on Grice. Literalists use Grice's ideas to create a sort of shock-absorber between our intuitions about what someone says and what their theories deliver as semantic content; the intuitions are supposed to confuse semantic content with conversational implicatures. The contextualists see (broadly) Gricean reasoning about speakers' intentions involved throughout the process of interpretation.

In discussing Perry's "Critical Referentialism" or "reflexive-referential theory" developed in Perry (2001 [2012]), Recanati sketches an approach that seems to us to be quite plausible, capable of resolving the pragmatic circle, and promises to do justice to both literalist and contextualist insights and theoretical ambitions. He is discussing an utterance of the sentence "I am French." On the reflexive-referential view, an utterance u of this sentence by Recanati has the singular proposition that Recanati is French as its *referential* content. Its reflexive content would be the proposition that u is uttered by someone who is French—reflexive because it is a proposition about the utterance *itself*. (For more about the reflexive-referential theory, see the appendix to Chapter 3.) Recanati says:

> ...the reflexive proposition is determined *before* the process of saturation takes place. The reflexive proposition can't be determined unless the sentence is tokened, but no substantial knowledge of the context of utterance is required to determine it. Thus an utterance u of the sentence "I am French" expresses the reflexive proposition that *the utterer of u is French*. That it does not presuppose saturation is precisely what makes the reflexive proposition useful, since in most cases saturation proceeds by appeal to speaker's meaning...
>
> The reflexive proposition is admittedly distinct from that which the speaker asserts...but why is this an objection? [The reflexive proposition] comes as close as one can get to capturing, in propositional format, the information provided by the utterance in virtue solely of the linguistic meaning of the sentence "I am French." (65–66)

This is pretty much the approach we hold. One caveat:[1] We do not hold that an utterance *u* of "I am French" *expresses* the proposition that the utterer of *u* is French. We describe that proposition as giving the reflexive truth-conditions of *u*, or being the reflexive content of *u* (with meaning fixed). These truth-conditions are available to any competent speaker, and, need to be appealed to in understanding both the generation and the comprehension of the utterance. But we do not claim or think it is what is said or is the proposition expressed.[2]

What we propose is a) that the reflexive content, with meaning fixed, is the content provided by semantics, in the sense in which a literalist wants such a thing for theoretical purposes, that is, constructing a compositional, truth-conditional theory of meaning; b) while the reflexive content is not *what is said*, it provides a description of what is said, that serves the purpose of allowing Gricean reasoning about why something, meeting the description, was said. In this way, we avoid the pragmatic circle.

4 Avoiding the Pragmatic Circle

Consider a simple example:

(1) I'll take that one (said by a man in a supermarket line to the clerk).

Let's suppose the clerk's attention was distracted by the clerk at the next register as the customer uttered (1), so he was looking behind his back and could not see that the customer was pointing to a pack of Marlboros. The clerk hears the utterance and knows how English works. As he turns back to the customer, he thinks of utterance (1) as "the utterance I just heard" or something along those lines. The clerk knows, simply on the basis of hearing the utterance, recognizing the words, and grasping the semantics of English:

(2) The utterance I just heard is true if the person who uttered it is referring to some item, and that person is using "will take" to mean *would like to purchase* or to mean *will pick it up and walk off with it*, and that person would like to purchase that thing (if that's what they meant), or intends to pick it up and walk off with it (if that's what they meant).

---

[1] Or perhaps quibble. As long as "the proposition expressed" is introduced, as by Kaplan, 1989a, in terms of "what is said," it shouldn't be taken to be the reflexive content. But of course "the proposition expressed" is a technical term, which could be given other meanings.

[2] For the alternative view that something like this minimal reflexive content should be taken as *what is said*, see Stojanovic, 2007.

The proposition the clerk grasps, solely on the basis of semantics and perception of the utterance, as its truth-conditions, is the (or more precisely *a*) reflexive content of the utterance (1), which might be put like this:

(3) $\exists x, y, R$, x uttered (1) & x referred to y with "that one" & x meant R with "will take" & $R(x, y)$ & R = *would like to purchase* $\vee$ R = *will pick up and walk off with*.

Now (3) is not by any stretch of the imagination what the speaker (1) *said*. The speaker of (1) wasn't talking about his own utterance, and the possible references and meanings of the words he used. Still (3) does give conditions under which the utterance (1) is true, as determined by the semantic rules of English and the meanings of the words used.

(3) provides a starting point for pragmatic reasoning, both near-side and far-side. The clerk can ask himself, given the reflexive truth-conditions of (1), plus the fact that he heard it, what are the likely witnesses for the existential quantifiers in (3)? As we envisage the situation, the likely answers are:

(4) The likely speaker is the man in the front of the line, whom he is looking at when he turns back from talking to the other clerk; this man is looking at the row of pack of cigarettes displayed behind the counter, where people under eighteen can't get them;

(5) He probably meant *would like to purchase*, since that's what non-thieving people usually mean in the supermarket, and he's not wearing a mask or acting threatening in any way;

(6) He probably was referring to one of the packs of cigarettes, since that seems to be what he's looking at, and everything else in the store he could have just put in his cart without having to ask for it—but I don't know which pack.

Based on this reasoning, he arrives at:

(7) Given (4), (5) and (6), the utterance I just heard is true if the person who uttered it is referring to one of the packs of cigarettes behind the counter, and he would like to purchase it.

That is, what he has grasped, on the basis of semantics, more perception, and reasoning, is

(8) That ∃y, A used "that one" to refer to y, y is a pack of cigarettes, and A would like to purchase y.

Grasping (8) might naturally lead the clerk to say something like, "Which pack did you wanted?"

In this example, (3) is the minimal, literal output of semantics. It gives the conditions the utterance has to fulfill to be true, given the semantics of English. Arriving at (3) does not require resolution of reference, ambiguity and standards of precision. (3) can be generated compositionally. The need that authors like Cappelen and Lepore feel to include resolution of reference, ambiguity, and vagueness as part of the "semantic content" is not motivated by the needs of semantics nor by the needs of pragmatics. Perhaps it was motivated by the view that a proposition like (3) is unsuited to serve as the input to pragmatic reasoning, but in fact, it is not.

5 Content and Implicature

Notice that (8) is still not what would be taken, on ordinary referentialist principles, as what was said or the proposition expressed. That would instead be (9):

(9) That **A** would like to buy **B** (where **A** is the speaker, and **B** is the object the speaker pointed at and referred to).

Our clerk wouldn't ordinarily be taken to have grasped (9), since his only way of thinking of **B** is reflexive, or as we also say, *utterance-bound*:

- The pack of cigarettes that the speaker of **u** referred to;

or at least *speaker-bound:*

- The pack of cigarettes that this fellow referred to;

Our clerk clearly didn't need to grasp (9) in order to begin reasoning about pragmatic issues on the near-side; that's how the pragmatic circle is avoided. But notice that he also doesn't need to grasp (9) to begin pragmatic reasoning on the far side. That is, he doesn't need to ask himself a question of this form:

(10) Why did the speaker say that *S?*

He need only ask himself a question of the form:

(11) Why did the speaker produce an utterance u that is true iff $D(u)$?

That is, the clerk doesn't need to have in mind a sentence S that will *express* the proposition the speaker expressed with **u**; it suffices to have a sufficiently rich utterance-bound description D of the conditions under which **u** is true. Having gotten as far as (8) the clerk may reason:

(i) This fellow produced an utterance **u** that is true if and only if there is a pack of cigarettes that he referred to with "that," and he wants to purchase that pack of cigarettes.
(ii) He wasn't telling me that because he thought I had an abiding interest in his desires.
(iii) He probably wanted me to get the pack and put it on the counter.

It is this reasoning that motivates the clerk's question, "Which pack did you want?"

Suppose now that when the clerk turns around there are two people standing next to each other, either one of which might have been the speaker of **u.** So the clerk can't even make it to (8); he can't identify the speaker. Still, he is in a position to figure out the implicature (iii) and ask his question. When one of the possible speaker's points to a pack of cigarettes, it will answer both of his questions: who was the speaker, and which pack do they want me to put on the counter?

So what is said doesn't really serve either of the boundary fixing-functions Grice used it for. It isn't the output of semantics, and it isn't the input to far-side pragmatics. In both cases, what we need is the reflexive content with the meaning fixed; that is, the condition the utterance must satisfy to be true, given the facts the semantics provides: the facts about the meanings of the words used and their modes of composition in the language used.

6   Reflexive Content and Searle's Propositional Content

While J. L. Austin inaugurated speech act theory, its main developer and exponent after Austin's untimely death was his student John Searle. The concept of propositional content plays a central role in Searle's thinking, and, like what is said in Grice's scheme, sets the boundary between semantics and (far-side) pragmatics.

On Searle's view (1969), various speech acts may have various *illocutionary points,* but the same propositional content. The illocutionary point of a speech act may put conditions on the content of the speech act. A commissive, such as "I will go to the store," requires that a future act of the speaker be represented by the propositional content. The directive illocutionary point, in contrast, determines that the propositional content of a speech act with that point—the request, "Will you go to the store," for example—must represent a future act by the addressee.

Now consider my request to you, "Will you go to the store?" and your promise in response, "I will go to the store." It seems that these speech acts share the propositional content that you go to the store. But this shared propositional content doesn't specify any role you must have to the utterance, and of course this differs from utterance to utterance. What is needed, in addition to the shared propositional content, is the differing reflexive contents of the utterances. The reflexive content of the first requires that its addressee goes to the store by some (contextually determined) point after the utterance; the reflexive content of the second requires that its speaker do so.

It is in grasping the reflexive content that the hearer understands the intended relationships between the speaker and the utterance. The same point holds for the time of the utterance. Consider, "I will finish the paper by tomorrow," and "I did finish the paper by yesterday," the first said by you on Monday and the second on Wednesday. We want to recognize both the sameness of content; what is asserted Wednesday is just what was promised Monday. But the different illocutionary forces impose different conditions on the time of the utterances; the first has to occur before the time the paper's completion is promised, the last after the paper's completion is reported.

Searle's theory of speech acts poses two different tasks for the concept of propositional contents. On the one hand, it represents the basic content on which the diverse illocutionary forces operate. On the other hand, it is the content that meets the conditions imposed by certain illocutionary points and forces. But, as we argued for the multiple tasks Grice's theory imposes on the concept of what is said, these two tasks cannot be accomplished by a single content. The referential content of an utterance can be taken as that basic shared content of different speech acts but, instead of referential content, reflexive content is needed to serve as the content fulfilling Searle's "propositional content conditions." The theory of speech acts, as well as the theory of implicatures, requires adopting a pluralistic view of utterance content in terms of locutionary and reflexive contents as the one we sketch here. They all are too demanding on a single content, whatever it is called: "what is said," "propositional content," "proposition expressed" or "truth-conditions of an utterance."

7 Literalism and Contextualism

Let's end by returning to Recanati's contrast. Assuming everyone agrees to talk ultimately about utterances, we can put things like this. Literalists hold that our abstract semantical theories can ascribe truth-conditional content to the utterance of sentences just based on the meanings of the parts of the sentence and how they are put together. Contextualists hold that only speech acts or utterances express determinate contents, which depend on many aspects of context.

Either view seems clearly correct to us. Abstract semantics can provide reflexive truth-conditions for utterances. Such truth-conditions are not yet propositions, but conditions *on* utterances; such as condition plus an utterance gives us a proposition, the proposition that the utterance satisfies the conditions, what we call the reflexive or utterance-bound content. But the *referential* content of the utterance, the proposition usually taken to be the counterfactual truth-conditions, or the proposition expressed, or what is said, or the propositional content, or the locutionary content (our own favorite term, explained in Chapter 3 of this volume) depends not only on the semantic properties of the sentence used, but also on the contextual properties of the utterance.

So a critical pragmatist, one who takes utterances as central and critical to both pragmatics and semantics, and who acknowledges that with language we convey information about things in the world *by* putting conditions on our own utterances, can be both a literalist and a contextualist.

Saying this does not resolve all disputes about the role of various contextual elements in the truth-conditions of utterances, and in particular whether the list provided by Cappelen and Lepore needs to be extended to get from the reflexive content to the locutionary content.

Consider, for example, domain restrictions. Suppose Maude says "I invited everyone to the party," in a context in which she clearly conveys that she invited everyone in the neighborhood to the party. How should we think of this? If we confine ourselves to Cappelen and Lepore's list, the restricted domain doesn't make it into the locutionary content. Maude's utterance is true only if she has invited everyone in the universe to her party. Only farside pragmatics gets us to the proposition that she invited everyone in the neighborhood.

An alternative way of looking at it is that Maude's had no intention of saying or expressing anything false; she intended to utter something that was true if and only if she had invited everyone in the neighborhood to the party. Her plan is that her hearer's will recognize that she is talking about the neighborhood, and take her to be saying something about it, not that they will take her to have been literally expressing an obviously false proposition. In addition to the items of Cappelen and Lepore's list, we need to allow that speakers may intend to say things about various items that are contextually available, and that these intentions can be recognized for what they are without an unexpected circuit through obvious falsehood and far-side pragmatics.

Let Maude's utterance be **u**. Within our theory, the question at issue is whether the reflexive and referential contents of **u** are given by (12a-d) or by (13a-d). According to the first option, we have that

(12a) **u** is true iff $\exists x$ Speaker-of $(x, \mathbf{u})$ & $\forall y$ Invited-to-the-party (x, y)
(12b) Given that Maude is the speaker of **u**, **u** is true iff $\forall y$ Invited-to-the-party (Maude, y)

so the reflexive content is (12c) and the referential content (what the speaker says, or the explicature, the proposition expressed, the semantic content, locutionary content, or whatever one calls the input to far-side pragmatics) is (12d):

(12c) That $\exists x$ Speaker-of $(x, \mathbf{u})$ & $\forall y$ Invited-to-the-party (x, y)
(12d) That Maude invited everyone (in the world) to the party.

According to the second option,

(13a) **u** is true iff $\exists x$, $\exists D$ Speaker-of $(x, \mathbf{u})$ & Intended-domain $(\mathbf{u}, D)$ & $\forall y$ ($y \in D \rightarrow$ Invited-to-the-party (x, y)
(13b) Given that Maude is the speaker of **u** and the neighborhood is the intended domain of **u**, **u** is true iff Maude invited everyone in the neighborhood to the party.

so the reflexive content is (13c) and the referential content (what the speaker says, or the explicature, the proposition expressed, the semantic content, locutionary content, or whatever one calls the input to far-side pragmatics) (13d):

(13c) $\exists x$, $\exists D$ Speaker-of $(x, \mathbf{u})$ & Intended-domain $(\mathbf{u}, D)$ & $\forall y$ ($y \in D \rightarrow$ Invited-to-the- party (x, y)
(13d) That Maude invited everyone in the neighborhood to the party.

While both possibilities may be stated within our approach, it is not quite neutral. There is no doubt that from the materials provided by semantics alone, plus the identity of the speaker, (12) delivers a candidate for what Maude said (or the explicature, or the semantic content). The words "everyone," "invited," "party," "to," "the," and "I" give us all we need for (12a), and the only bit of contextual information that is needed to get to (12b) and

(12c), the identity of the speaker, a constitutive fact of the utterance, available to the hearer by perception in normal circumstances. So far-side pragmatics is not needed. Hence, this minimalist route is a way of avoiding the pragmatic circle. Hence, the pragmatic circle provides some motivation for the minimalist strategy.

It is hard to see any other motivation. To generate the right implicature from the proposition that Maude invited everyone in the world to the party, one needs to suppose that the speaker's plan is to say something blatantly false, and have the hearer infer from this that she must be trying to convey something else, and figure out what it is. To make it plausible that this is the speaker's plan, it does not suffice to note that there is a candidate that can be assembled from conventional meanings alone, with minimal, non-Gricean appeals to context, on the near side. There is an additional claim involved, that the speaker's plan was to make this proposition available as a premise in Gricean reasoning. The hearer has to smell a falsehood, and seek an explanation at the level of implicature, and this has to be the speaker's plan.

If, as critical referentialism supposes, another proposition is available for the input to Gricean reasoning, (13c), then this sole consideration for strategy (12) seems to lose any force. We need only suppose that the speaker intends to be talking about the people in the neighborhood, and thinks that the hearer, using Gricean reasoning, will figure this out. The hearer does not need to seek an explanation for the speaker saying something false, but merely seek a relevant candidate domain for the speaker to be talking about, and to intend to convey information about. As Recanati puts it,

> I concede to the minimalist that it is possible to *define* the (minimal) semantic content of the sentence as that which results from saturation alone; but I claim that this notion of content is an idle wheel in the overall theory of language and communication. (Recanati, 2006, 3)

So, our approach is not neutral between (12) and (13) in just this sense: Insofar as one finds it intuitively implausible that the speaker intends to put forward something blatantly false, one is provided an avenue for avoiding this claim, without running afoul of the pragmatic circle.[3]

---

[3] We are grateful to Isidora Stojanovic for her kind invitation to contribute to this volume, her infinite patience with our delays and her useful comments and criticisms.

5

Reference: A New Paradigm

KEPA KORTA AND JOHN PERRY

1 Introduction

Over the past fifty years, most discussions of reference by philosophers of language, although certainly not all, have been conducted in the following framework. (We use "designate" as a general term, and "reference" for cases Kaplan (1989a) would call "directly referential"; that is, cases in which the individual designated and not some description or identifying condition is contributed to the proposition expressed.)

1. Statements express propositions.
2. Whatever one's ultimate theory of them, propositions, can be usefully thought of as sets of possible worlds, those worlds in which the statement, with its meaning fixed in the actual world, is true.
3. Singular terms include proper names, definite descriptions, and pronouns. All of these, at least in paradigm circumstances, *designate* individuals: persons and other things.
4. Definite descriptions designate the individual they denote, that is the individual that uniquely fits the descriptive content. The descriptive content, rather than the individual described, is contributed to the proposition expressed; descriptions do not refer.
5. Names name; that is, their meaning consists of a convention directly assigning them to an individual, the "bearer" of the name. In thinking about names, the apparent fact that many people have the same name, can usually be left to one side (indeed, it is only an apparent fact, if one adopts Kaplan's theory of name individuation).

6. Context plays an essential role in the case of pronouns. Many are indexicals ("I," "you") or demonstratives ("this," "that") or demonstrative phrases ("that man"), or personal pronouns used demonstratively ("he" and "she"). In these cases, following Kaplan, a context should be considered as an abstract object, a quadruple of agent, time, location and world. The relevant concept of meaning is *character*; a function from expressions-in-context to contents; propositions in the case of statements (declarative sentences in context), individuals in the case of referential singular terms, and other suitable objects for other kinds of expressions.
7. A different sort of context plays a role in the case of anaphora, where context fixes the anaphoric links among pronouns and other singular terms. The whole issue is somewhat messy, and on the whole best left to linguists and logicians.

2 Two Paradigms

This set of assumptions involves two paradigms of reference, names and descriptions, and a sort of hybrid, indexicals (Perry, 2001[2012]). The issues can be organized around two questions (Martí, 1995):

- Does the singular term denote or name? This is a question about the "mechanism" of reference. Naming is the relation names, as standardly construed, have to their bearers; it is a matter of conventions, usually established, for people, by their families, and then passed on. Denotation is a matter of the meanings of the constituents of a complex expression, like a description or a possessive, providing an identifying condition, which the designated object has to fit.
- Does the singular term refer or describe? This question has to do with the propositional contribution. Terms that refer contribute the individual designated to the proposition expressed by statements that contain them, terms that describe.

For names and descriptions, the answers to these questions coincide. Names name and refer, while descriptions denote and describe:

	Name	Denote
Refer	Names	
Describe		Descriptions

Part of this coincidence is forced upon us: with names the mechanism of designation does not provide us with an identifying condition, so it's not easy to see how they could describe. On the other hand, descriptions could in theory refer, contributing the denoted individual. That this sometimes happens is one interpretation of Donnellan's (1966) distinction between attributive and referential uses of descriptions. If we give referential uses a "pragmatic" explanation, things seem to line up in a very natural way, and this perhaps explains why the distinction is often not appreciated.

Once we have made the distinction, however, it is natural to treat indexicals not as providing a new paradigm, but as sort of a mixture, picking up elements of the two paradigms. Indexicals denote and refer. The character of the word "I" does provide us with an identifying condition, relative to context: the individual designated is the agent of the context. Indexicals certainly do not name; the conventions of language associate these words with characters, not with individuals. On the other hand, as Kaplan convincingly argues, it is not the condition of being the agent that is contributed to the proposition expressed, but the individual designated. So we have:

	Name	Denote
Refer	Names	Indexicals
Describe		Descriptions

Given this analysis, the only thing truly new about indexicals is that they denote relative to context. The mechanism of designation for indexicals is basically that of descriptions, with the addition of this relativity; the propositional contribution is that of names.

3 Roles

On our view, the case of indexicals has more radical implications, however. They constitute a substantially different paradigm for reference, that should change the way we think of names and descriptions, and, ultimately, sentences. To appreciate the new paradigm, however, we digress for a bit and discuss roles.

A lot of our thinking is organized around roles. Key questions about an object of a certain kind are often organized around a set of characteristics and important relations things have to objects of that kind. Think of a realtor's summary description of house on the market. This will be a list of roles, relative to the house, and which objects play them: Address, # of rooms, square feet, type of heating, etc. In setting up tables or data bases, to handle information about objects of various kinds, we try to isolate key roles, so that the relevant information can be given by identifying the occupants of those roles. Kepa is giving a party! Then tell me the time, place, and type of party it is.

Three important operations are involved in roles: nesting, linking, and transferring.

Some examples of nesting. Riding your bike, you squeeze a brake lever; you thereby tighten the cable attached to the brake lever (that you squeeze); you thereby close the caliper attached to the cable (attached to the brake lever (that you squeeze)); you thereby slow the wheel inside the caliper (attached to the cable (attached to the brake lever (that you squeeze))); you thereby slow the bike, resting and rolling on the wheel (inside the caliper (attached to the cable (attached to the brake lever (that you squeeze))))). Roles allow us to keep track of things in a fairly easy way, suppressing variables and quantifiers that logical notation would require to express the same thing.

Linking comes in two types. The first involves one thing playing two different roles relative to the same object. In the present example, the same bike is both the bike ridden, and the bike braked. The link between the roles of being the bike one is on, and being the bike one slows by squeezing the brake lever by one's hand, is built into the architecture of bicycles, and a good idea it is! And, of course, the complex role-linking between being the lever squeezed and the bike brakes is architectural too; it falls out of the way brakes work.

The second kind of linking involves one thing playing the same or different roles, relative to different objects. If we have the same neighbor, one person plays the neighbor role relative to each of us. If my neighbor is your father, one person plays the neighbor role relative to me, and the father role relative to you.

Transferring involves the same object playing the same role, relative to different objects. We are riding bikes. You ask me how to slow down your bike. I squeeze the lever on my bike to show you. You learn that you can slow your bike by squeezing the lever on your bike.

When ways of nesting roles, and situations in which roles are linked, are architectural, as a result of the way Mother Nature or some other designer puts things together, the person who exploits them need not understand how they work. We are, as we say, attuned to the way things work, when we know what to do to get a certain desired result. I know that, by squeezing the lever I can reach, I can slow the bike I am on; doing the one is a way of doing the other. The linking and nesting are reflected in my knowing how to do things, not in my knowing why they work the way they do, or knowing how to describe it.

Moreover, the ways one has of doing things, may work over a wide range of intervening mechanisms. I hop on the bike and ride, counting on stopping by squeezing the lever. The connection could be by cable, or hydraulic, or, these days, wireless and involving micro-computers. I don't need to know to use it, although I would certainly need to repair it.

We plan, and interpret plans, in terms of roles. Typically objects come to our attention, in perception, through memory, through conversation. I see a pizza; I am accosted with a desire to eat it; I put it on a plate, and pick it up; I eat it. There is a sort of transcendental, or at least biological, linkage of roles at the bottom of all this; the roles of seer, desirer, plate-getter, and pizza eater, are all played by me. Then there is the fact that the same pizza gets seen, desired, put on the plate, and eaten. The (imperfect) guarantee is not purely architectural, but based on my know-how; I know how to put the same pizza I just saw and formed a desire for on a plate I just retrieved from the shelf (although I could have been fooled); I know how move so that the seen pizza will be the eaten pizza.

The way familiar and basic ways of acting work can only be understood against the background of familiar roles that objects play in our lives, and how we can, in virtue of the way our bodies work, the way environments are laid out, and the way artifacts are designed, count on them being nested and linked. When I type I know that the key pressed will affect the screen seen; when I drink I know that the glass seen will be the glass grasped; that the liquid in the glass that is grasped will be the liquid that ends up in my stomach.

4 Roles in Action

Acts (particulars) involve agents at times and locations moving their bodies and limbs in various ways. Actions (types) can be individuated in terms of the types of movements ("executions"), or the results the movements have in circumstances ("accomplishments"). We use the locutions "by" and "way of" to get at the various relations. Moving ones right forefinger downward is an action: a type of movement. Making an "h" appear on the screen is an action, an accomplishment. One way of making an "h" appear on the screen is moving one's forefinger down in the circumstance in which one's forefinger is perched over the "h" key of a properly functioning keyboard attached in the right way to a properly functioning computer. That is the way I just used; I made the "h" appear *by* moving my forefinger. There are other ways of doing the same thing. In different circumstances I could have moved my middle-finger, or hit the "h" key with a pencil, or said "Horatio" into the microphone of my voice-recognition system.

Movements affect—act upon—objects that play certain roles in the agent's life at the moment of action: the key over which his forefinger is perched; the bike to which the brake attached to the cable attached to the lever he is grasping is attached, and so forth. The results of the action depend on the properties of the object one acts upon. Moving your forefinger and thereby poking an "h" key attached to a computer has a quite different effect than moving your and thereby pushing a button that sets off a bomb.

So, intelligent action means moving in ways that take account of which object the movement acts upon, and its further properties; the role it plays in your life, and what properties it has.

5   Roles in Communication

We will focus on one fairly common communicative situation. The speaker has a bit of information about some object X; that X if F. X plays a role in the hearer's life, that puts him a position to act upon X in a helpful or useful way, and he would do so if he had the information that X if F in an appropriate form. So the speaker's job is to get it to him in that form.

So the speaker creates an utterance; he refers to X, and predicates being F of X. The utterance plays two roles; it is created by the speaker, and perceived by the hearer. And it creates two roles: being the object referred to by the speaker of the utterance, and being the object of which F-ness is predicated.

These roles are liked by the syntax of the sentence. The speaker has an additional linking project, however. He has to get the role of being the object referred to linked to the action-affording role the object is playing in the hearer's life.

To do this the speaker provides additional role-coordinating information. In the case of indexicals and demonstratives, this amounts to identifying a role that the object plays in the speaker's life, such that the hearer can identify the occupant as playing the relevant action-affording role in his own life.

When I say, "I'd like the salt," I identify an object that plays a certain role in my life (the role of self; that is, being the person I am identical with) and predicates a further property of that object (wanting the salt). I say it to you, across the table from me. I thereby create an object (my utterance) that plays a certain role in your life (you hear it). I thereby create a nested role that I play in your life: the speaker of the utterance you hear. I assume you will be able to link this role with another one I already play: "the person sitting across from me."

Since you know the meaning of "I" and the way English syntax works, you know that the speaker of the utterance is the person who, if it is true, wants some salt. So you learn that the person sitting across from you would like the salt. You know how to pass the salt to the person sitting across from you, so you pass it to me. If you are an agreeable sort of person, you pass it to me.

Indexicals are devices of role-coordination. The speaker identifies an object by a role it plays in her life, and then enables the hearer to identify the object by the role it plays in his life. Indexicals are appropriate, when the initial state of the hearer is such that knowing the role the object plays in the life of the speaker, will enable him to know the role it plays in his own life.

6 Establishing Reference versus Providing Information about Reference

An assumption of the traditional treatment of reference is that the job of the indexical or name is to establish reference. We modify that assumption. The job of a name or indexical is rather to enable role-based identification of the referent.

On our view, referring is easy. The speaker needs to have an object in mind, about which he intends to say something; typically, but not always, in order to communicate information (or misinformation) to a hearer. This point can be made in terms of what we call an "unhelpful pronoun."

You have been thinking about the world economic crisis, while everyone else is talking about football. Suddenly you burst out, "He is an idiot." The "he" is an unhelpful pronoun; no one has an idea to whom you are referring. The pronoun is completely unhelpful. Still, you have referred; your statement is true if the person you have in mind, of whom you intend to predicate the property of being an idiot, is an idiot.

Even in this case, an additional link is provided. The logical subject of your statement is the person that you intend to refer to. But you have not provided any help in identifying that person, as you would have by using an indexical or a demonstrative or a name.

If you attempt to provide information, you take a risk of getting it wrong. Suppose you think that Bush is an idiot, and he is whom you had in mind. You think that the man we all see on the television screen is Bush, so you say, "That man is an idiot." But it isn't Bush, but a Bush-impersonator. So you don't refer to the person you intended to refer to, and don't say what you intended to say. Your plan was to refer to the person you intended to refer to, Bush, by referring to the man you saw. You thought that one man played both roles, but you were wrong. When the speaker's plan works, the name or indexical will not establish reference, but provide an additional role played by the object to which reference has already been established.

7 Names as Role-Coordination Devices

Now consider a different scenario. The famous actress Julia Roberts sits at our table. I see she is looking around the table, presumably for the salt. You are well positioned to reach the salt and pass it to her; she sits directly across from you. I tell you, "Julia Roberts would like the salt." What do roles have to do with this?

Consider any sentence of the form, "X is so and so," where X is a singular term. The syntax of the sentence imposes a link between utterance relative roles: the person or object the speaker is designating, and the person or object about whom the speaker is predicating something; we can call the combined role "the logical subject." The particular term "X" will impose further links, if it is an indexical or a demonstrative. If the sentence is "I am so and so," the logical subject will also be the speaker; if it is "you are so and so," the logical subject will also be the addressee, and so forth.

Names are also a way of providing such information. When I say "Julia Roberts wants the salt," you learn that the person I intend to refer to bears the name "Julia Roberts."

Here the background situation is quite different than in the case where an indexical might be used. Everyone at our dinner party knows that the beautiful actress seated at our table is named "Julia Roberts." Of course she is not the only one; there are probably hundreds of people named Julia Roberts living in the United States alone. Still, in the situation, common sense and the added information that the intended logical subject is named "Julia Roberts" will enable my hearers to identify the person I am talking about in a manner that is linked to various roles she is playing in their lives, viz, the person they see sitting near them, and, in the case of those sitting near her, the person they can pass the salt to.

So a name, like an indexical, provides supplemental information that enables hearers to link the role of being the speaker's intended logical subject with various roles people are playing in their lives. Although names are not, like indexicals, associated by meaning with utterance-relative roles, they nevertheless provide tools with which speaker can coordinate roles.

So here my plan is as follows. My goal is to get you to pass the salt to the person sitting across from you. I assume you have the ability to pass the salt to the person across from you, and will do so if you know she wants it. So, my subgoal, get you to believe the person sitting across from you wants the salt. I assume you recognize her, and know her name is Julia Roberts. So, it will suffice to get you to believe that Julia Roberts wants the salt.

When I utter, "Julia Roberts wants the salt," I will create the roles of being the person referred to by the speaker of that utterance, and being the person the speaker asserts to want the salt; the syntax of my sentence links the roles. By using the name "Julia Roberts" I provide additional information about the role occupant, that allows you to identify her. Now you realize that one person occupies the roles of being the person asserted to want some salt, and being the person across from you.

The name serves as a role-coordination device; it provides the incremental information necessary to link the roles of being the person across from you and being the person of whom wanting the salt is asserted.

8 Pure Communication

Of course, often we communicate not with the goal of enabling a specific action, like passing the salt to someone who wants it, but simply to modify beliefs. I say, "Julia Roberts won an academy award." My goal is simply to change or reinforce your beliefs.

Here I assume that Julia Roberts already plays a role in your life. I assume that you have an idea or notion of Julia Roberts, an idea picked up by meeting her, or, more likely, seeing her in movies and perhaps reading and talking about her. My plan is that you will add the information, "has won an academy award" to your Julia-Roberts notion. To do this, you need to link the role of being the person who is the source of your notion, and the role of being the person who is the referent of my utterance. My utterance creates a new role for Julia Roberts to play: being the person I am referring to. I assume that by using her name, I provide information that will allow you to link the roles "being the hearing" and "being the person I think about with notion n," where n is your Julia Roberts notion.

In simple transmission of information about individuals, the speaker has a plan to get the hearer to think about the same individual she is thinking about. Our hypothesis is that names and indexicals are suited, by their meanings, to bring this about indifferent common cognitive situations.

In a paradigm case of communicating information about an individual, the speaker has a plan. It will be a plan for getting the hearer to believe a proposition about the individual in a certain way (or a constrained set of ways)—that is, by a role or roles that the person plays in the hearer's life.

Suppose you meet Elwood the philosopher at a cocktail party. You are talking about world events, cognitive science, and other subjects in a way that presuppose that your interlocutor is knowledgeable. In order to convey that he really doesn't know much about any of this, Elwood says, "I am just a philosopher." You learn that the person you are talking to is just a philosopher, and move to simpler (but more profound) topics.

If Elwood had said, "Elwood is a philosopher," that wouldn't have achieved his purpose, since you don't know his name yet. The indexical "I" was the appropriate role-linking device.

Suppose on the other hand you and Elwood are discussing the works of François Recanati. Recanati, whom you haven't met, happens to be at the party, over by the bar collecting yet another drink. Elwood says, "Recanati's earliest work was on performatives." His intention is to have an affect on your Recanati-notion; to get the role of being the source of that notion linked to being the person he is talking about. If he had pointed to Recanati, and said, "That man's earliest work was on performatives," he wouldn't have succeeded. You would have linked the role, "being the man Elwood is talking about" with the role, "being the man I see at the bar."

In the simple case of introducing oneself, the different role-linking strategies are both involved. Elwood says, "I am Elwood." What you learn is that the man you are talking to is named "Elwood." You link the roles of being the speaker and being the man the speaker is referring to in virtue of the meaning of "I." You are aware that a condition for referring to a person with the name "Elwood" is that the person have the name "Elwood." So you learn that Elwood's name is Elwood. It wouldn't have worked for him to say "I am I" or "Elwood is Elwood."

9   Roles, Descriptions and Anaphora

Definite descriptions are also devices of role-coordination. Descriptions, like names, do not (or at least need not) disclose a role the referent plays in the life of the speaker. But they provide the incremental information necessary to the hearer to link the object that plays the role of being referred to by the speaker, with roles the object does or may play in the hearer's life.

The situation is as before: I see Julia Roberts looking at the distant salt shaker; you are sitting across from her, and can reach the salt shaker. I am not much of a film fan, and I don't know the name "Julia Roberts." But I am aware that the lady sitting across from you is a movie star. So I say, "The movie star would like some salt."

This is an instance of what is sometimes called an "incomplete definite description." There are lots of movie stars, so how can "the movie star" pick out just one of them? If we think of the job of the description as providing incremental information, there is no problem. My hearer understands what is going on; what the overall point of my utterance is to get him to pass the salt to someone. Presumably it is someone whom I can see wants the salt and someone to whom he can pass the salt. The description is appropriate because there is only one movie star who is a candidate. The job of the description is to provide the additional information about the person I refer to, that will enable you to identify her, in terms of the role she plays in your life; being the person sitting across from you, to whom you can pass the salt.

A description might do its role-linking job, even though it does not denote the object referred to. In the uses we are thinking about, the definite description doesn't secure reference; that is done by the speaker's intentions. A description may be inaccurate, but still suffice to make the speaker's intentions clear.

Suppose that I say to you: "the best turn of the century actress wants the salt." You whisper "She's definitely not the best, but I'll pass her the salt." Let's assume that you are right; in fact, Juliette Binoche is the best turn of the century actress, not Julia Roberts. So my description denoted Juliette Binoche. Nevertheless, I referred to Julia Roberts. The error I made was not referring to the wrong person, but providing inaccurate information about her to assist you in interpreting my intentions. But, even with the inaccurate information, you were able to do so.

In your reply, you use the pronouns "she" and "her," anaphorically, to refer to Julia Roberts. I opened an anaphoric chain with my inaccurate description. Anaphors created linked roles, and the speaker provides just the information necessary to sort out which anaphoric chains he continues.

10 Conclusion

The paradigm of singular terms as role-coordinating devices suggests the following framework:

1. Statements express propositions. But we shouldn't assume that the proposition expressed is the only proposition associated with a statement.
2. Even if we accept that statements containing indexicals and names express *singular* propositions—with the individuals designated as constituents—while statements containing descriptions express *general* propositions—with identifying conditions as constituents—, there are other contents involved classifiable by other propositions. They may be about the role played by the individual or some other content that constitute the operative content of the statement.
3. Singular terms are role-coordinating devices. They don't establish reference but they provide information about the object referred to, that enables the hearer to link the role of being the object referred with various roles in his own life.
4. In the case of indexicals, the incremental information is a further role the referent plays in the speaker's life, such as being the speaker herself ("I"), the person the speaker addresses ("you"), and so on. Indexicals are appropriate when the hearer will realize that the object that plays this role in the speaker's life plays a role in his life.
5. Names and descriptions are not (necessarily) associated by their meaning with speaker-relative roles, but they provide incremental information that allows role-coordination.

6. The individual referred to by the use of a definite description do not always coincide with the individual denoted by it. The speaker can achieve successful reference, opening the chain for subsequent anaphoric references, even when she misdescribes the individual referred to.

In our view, this new paradigm of reference is faithful to the view of language as action, inherited from the work of Wittgenstein, Austin, and Grice, providing a coherent picture of how the parts of language study concerning reference fit together within a larger picture of human thought and action.

6

Intentions to Refer

KEPA KORTA AND JOHN PERRY

> "If something happened along the route and you had to leave your children with Bob Dole or Bill Clinton, I think you would probably leave them with Bob Dole."
>
> —Bob Dole, April 15, 1996, campaigning for President.[1]

> "I am not at all sure that I'd want to leave my children with someone who talks about himself in the third person."
>
> —Ellen Goodman in the *Boston Globe* for April 18, 1996.[2]

1 Introduction

If language is action (Austin, 1961; Grice, 1967a [1989]), referring to things is not something that words do, but something that people do by uttering words. According to this pragmatic view, then, a theory of reference should be grounded on an account of our acts of referring; that is, the part of communicative acts that consists in referring to individual things. In our view, referential plans involve a structure of beliefs about an object the speaker intends to talk about and of Gricean intentions to achieve various effects on the listener, in virtue of the listener's recognition of them. Among these, we distinguish the *grammatical, directing, target, path,* and *auxiliary* intentions, and call our analysis the GDTPA structure of referential plans. In this paper we develop the motives for the theory, explain how it works, and apply it to a number of examples. Communicative acts are explained in terms of the speaker's intentions or, better said, in terms of the speaker's communicative plan: a structure of her goals, beliefs and intentions that motivates her

---

[1] According to column by Ellen Goodman in *The Boston Globe* for April 18, 1996.
[2] Ibid.

communicative behavior. As parts of communicative acts, referential acts are subject to the same sort of analysis.

In this paper, we will argue that referential intentions are a complex type of Gricean intention. Referential acts exploit a speaker's cognitive fix on an object and aims to induce a hearer to have a cognitive fix on that object appropriate to the speaker's communicative goals. The GDTPA structure of referential plans (Korta and Perry, 2011) offers an account of the paradigmatic use of names, indexicals, demonstratives and (some uses) of definite descriptions as referential devices. In section 2, we present a brief historical summary of the semantic view of reference, in which we argue that there is a change in what is taken as the paradigmatic referential expression, going from proper names and definite descriptions to indexicals and demonstratives. In section 3, we introduce two of our basic theoretical tools: roles and cognitive fixes, before explaining, in section 4, how we understand the pragmatics of reference within a Gricean picture of language and communication. In section 5 we explain in some detail what we call the "GDTPA structure" of referential plans, giving various examples of paradigmatic uses of referential expressions. In section 6, we draw some conclusions.

An immediate consequence of the present picture is that understanding reference is not a matter of just identifying the object the speaker is referring to but identifying it in the manner intended, that is, with the *target* cognitive fix, that the speaker intends for the listener to have. Another consequence of the picture of language as action is that utterances, *qua* acts, have a variety of contents relative to different things that can be taken as given.

2 From Descriptions and Names to Indexicals: A Paradigm Shift in the Philosophy of Language

Singular reference has been intensely studied by philosophers during the twentieth century, and lively interest in the topic continues. The inquiry is usually regarded as a matter of semantics, the theory of meaning and truth. The key question is usually taken to be what contribution referring expressions make to the truth-conditions of the statements of which they are a part. The issue of how they fit into the speaker's plan to convey information, generate implicatures, and perform speech acts has not been center-stage.

The topic of reference has been dominated, since the beginning of the last century at least, by two paradigms, *naming* and *describing*. Due mostly to the work of Gottlob Frege (1892 [1997]) and Bertrand Russell (1905), there was a sort of consensus throughout the first half of the twentieth century. Definite descriptions refer by describing objects; ordinary proper names refer by abbreviating or being associated with descriptions. The consensus began to fall apart in the 50's and 60's, and a set of ideas Howard Wettstein (1991) dubbed "The New Theory of Reference" became widely accepted. Donnellan (1966, 1970, 1974), for example, argued that definite descriptions can be used to refer, that when they are so used they can refer to objects that do not fit the description, and that proper names do not need a backing of descriptions to pick out the object they refer to. Donnellan thought that both descriptions and names are used to make "statements" that are individuated by the particular objects they are about, so the same statements could have been made by other means that referred to the same objects in much different ways. Donnellan emphasized the role of the speaker's intentions in securing reference, but did not develop much structure for dealing with those intentions.

David Kaplan's work on indexicals and demonstratives added a third paradigm to the mix. In his monograph "Demonstratives" (1989a), he demonstrated that the techniques of formal logic, and in particular ideas from modal and intensional logic, could be applied to indexicals with illuminating results. Kaplan's work reinforced rejection of the thesis that reference required a backing of descriptions to pick out the object referred to, without relying on intuitions about proper names of the sort to which Donnellan and Kripke had appealed.

We think Kaplan's investigation of indexicals, and his concept of character, suggest a new paradigm for thinking about singular reference [see Chapter 5 of this volume]. They suggest the importance of what we call "utterance-relative roles." Our version of Kaplan's character rule for "I," for instance, is a generalization that quantifies over utterances: An English utterance of the word "I" refers to the speaker of that very utterance, that is, the person who plays the role *speaker of* relative to the utterance. The role provides an identifying condition of the referent, but one that is *utterance-bound*, which is not what classical description theorists had in mind. And even though an utterance of "I" refers rather than describes, no tag-like direct connection between the expression and the referent is involved. In the case of indexicals, utterance relative-roles are the key to understanding how things work. We think that utterance-relative roles are an important part of the story in *all* cases of reference. This is *not* to say that all kinds of singular terms are indexical. It is rather to say that something comes out very clearly in the case of indexicals, that is also very important, if more difficult to ferret out, in the cases of names, pronouns, and descriptions.

Finding this sort of inspiration in Kaplan's work requires a bit of reinterpretation. Kaplan (1989a) said he was *not* providing a theory of utterances, but a theory of "sentences-in-context." Utterances do not appear at all in his formal theory. But they often are mentioned in the informal remarks that motivate the theory, and it's clear that the contextual elements of agent, location, time and world, and the fundamental stipulation that the agent be in the location at the time in the world, are suggested by the utterance-relative roles of speaker, location, time and world, and the fact that the speaker of an utterance is in the location of the utterance at the time of the utterance. When he turns to developing a formal theory, Kaplan sets utterances aside because they don't fit well with his goal of developing the logic of indexicals. For one thing, utterances take time, so the premises of a spoken argument won't all occur at the same time, but for the purposes of logic we want them to occur all in the same context. For another, Kaplan wants to consider the content of context-sentence pairs in which no utterance of the sentence by the agent at the time occurs—hence the agent is not dubbed "the speaker."

From the point of view of pragmatics, however, utterances do not get in the way; they are central to the project. Gricean intentions are intentions to bring about changes in the hearer; they are intentions to produce concrete utterances, in order to have effects on the hearer. The meanings and contents of the concrete utterance contribute to the effect. At the heart of the conversational transaction is the hearer perceiving a concrete token or event, and reasoning about its cause, that is, about the intentions that led to its production. Properties of meaning and content are relevant to intention discovery, but so are many other properties, like being aware that the speaker is attempting to amuse by telling a philosophical joke rather than pronounce a serious and profound philosophical claim.

The concept of a pair of a Kaplanian context and sentence type makes intuitive sense if we think of it as a model for an utterance in which a speaker at the time and location of the context makes use of a sentence of the type. Much the same is true of other concepts important in the development of referentialism; by our lights at least, they fit better with a theory of utterances than with a theory of sentences and other formal objects. The intentions to which Donnellan appealed in his referential-attributive distinction, are intentions that lead to particular acts of using expressions. The causal and historical chains appealed to in the referentialist account of proper names, are best thought of as connecting acts and earlier events.

In what follows we develop an account of the meaning and use of singular reference within a theory of utterances, based on the concept of utterance-relative roles, and of the pragmatics of singular reference, based on the speaker's need to manage roles to produce the intended effect on his audience. For that purpose, first, we'll introduce a couple of useful basic concepts: roles and cognitive fixes.

3 Basic Concepts

3.1 Roles

We use the word "role" a lot in this paper. We will talk about utterance-relative roles, speaker-relative roles, epistemic roles, pragmatic roles and so forth. So we should say a little bit about what they are.

Roles are not an addition to a metaphysics that recognizes individuals of various sorts, properties, and relations. Rather they are a way of talking about and organizing information about important relations things have to one another. They provide a way of organizing information that comes natural to humans and is reflected in many ways in language.

Roles are, first of all, important relations. If we ask Elwood, "what roles do you play in your son's life?", we expect an answer like, "provider, mentor, friend, disciplinarian." If he said, "my bedroom is down the hall from his," we might suspect he was telling us that he played no role worth mentioning in his son's life.

Roles are often significant because they are involved in constraints, the laws, principles, rules, conventions and other regularities that provide the structure within which we perceive and plan.

Consider the following constraint:

(1) If an x-ray y of a human arm exhibits pattern ψ, *then the person of whose arm y was taken* has a broken arm.

The constraint makes the relation between an x-ray and a person, that the former was taken of the latter's arm, something of importance. It means that the x-ray can give us information about the person's arm. And of course (1) is simply one of a family of constraints that x-ray technologists learn, telling what kinds of break x-rays mean, for various bones, and much else. Within the practice of using x-rays in medicine, the relation of being the person of whom an x-ray was taken is critical. Similarly with being the speaker-of, in the realm of utterances. In these cases, we generalize across roles; it is the health of the patient—that is, the person the x-ray was taken of—that is disclosed by the x-ray. It is the state of mind of the speaker—that is, the speaker *of* the utterances—that is disclosed by its linguistic properties.

A list of key roles can provide a schema for characterizing salient facts about an object. Sometimes when we are dealing with a lot of facts about numerous inter-related objects, one object will take center stage for a period of time, during which we focus on which objects stand in various relations to it, or, as we say, play various roles relative to it. Elwood is interviewing Angus, asking him a series of one-word questions: Father? Mother? Birthplace?

Year of Birth? Angus can give one-word answers or one-phrase answers, specifying the objects that stand in those relations to him, or, as we say, play those roles in his life. Angus could start his answers with words like, "My father is...," and "My birthplace is...," but he really needn't mention himself at all. His place in the facts he is using language to state doesn't have to be indicated linguistically, because it is built into the situation. Angus's system of representation is asymmetrical; the objects that play the key relations to him get named, but he makes it into the propositions he asserts just by his role in the conversation.

As Elwood records the information he may also use an asymmetrical system of representation. Angus's name is written in on the top of a card, perhaps, on which words for the various important roles Elwood is to query him about are printed; Elwood fills them in, in response to Angus's answers. For another example, think of a party invitation. The invitation as a whole represents the party; on the invitation the objects (broadly speaking) that fill various roles relative to the party are linguistically identified: time-of, place-of, hosts-of, purpose-of, and so forth.

Handling relational information with roles is useful when one object is the focus of attention and thus a participant in all the relational facts being discussed, and where due to the situation, the way information is being obtained, communicated, or used, there is no need to re-identify him or her or it. During Angus's interview, he is the one Elwood is asking about. We know that all the information given on an invitation is for the same party, the party the invitation is an invitation for.

A particularly important example of organizing information by roles is our ordinary way of perceiving the world in those uncomplicated cases where neither communication, long-term memory, nor long-term intentions are involved; we'll call this "the natural stance." Here the perceiver/agent is the fixed object, the "index." We look out on the world and see objects to the left, to the right, above and below; we hear things to the left and to the right, near at hand and in the distance; we feel the heft of things we hold in our right or left hands, and the taste of things in our mouth.

Often the occupants of different roles are known to be the same, in virtue of the common index and the *architecture* of the situation. The stuff I put in my mouth is the stuff I taste in my mouth; the things I hold in front of me are the things I see in front of me. The car I slow by stepping on the brakes is the same one I steer by turning the wheel, and the same one I gather information about by looking through the windshield.[3]

---

[3] The paper is co-authored, hence there really is no referent for "I." However, we find the first-person singular too effective for presenting examples to give it up.

3.2 Cognitive Fixes

Humans are blessed with a rich variety of perceptual abilities, which allow them to find out things about objects that stand in certain relations to them; that is, play certain roles in their lives. I can find out the color and shape of the object I am looking at; I can discover the hardness and weight of the object I hold in my hand, and so forth. Such objects, we will say, play *direct epistemic roles* in our lives; that is, they are related to us, on a given occasion, in such a way that we can perceive them to have various properties.

Often the objects that play direct epistemic roles in our lives are also ones that play *direct pragmatic roles* in our lives. You see an apple; it looks like it is ripe, but perhaps it is overripe and mushy; you pick it up, and squeeze it a little to make sure it is firm; you put it in your mouth and bite off a piece and chew it; you taste it, and on the basis of what it tastes like, go ahead and swallow it or spit it out.

In thinking about this we find a concept and a term from Howard Wettstein useful: "cognitive fix." One's *cognitive fix* on an object is how one thinks of it, in a broad sense of "thinking." We like the phrase because it is rather vague, and not tied, like, say, "mode of presentation" to a particular theory. Still, we will gradually develop a theory of cognitive fixes, and tie Wettstein's term to our own theory. We think of cognitive fixes on an object as involving epistemic roles, pragmatic roles, or both. Cognitive fixes may be perceptual, in which case they will be expressed naturally with demonstrative phrases: "that man," "this computer." They may involve the roles the objects play in conversation, in which case they will be expressed naturally with the appropriate indexicals: "I," "you." Often a mere name seems to do the trick, both in thinking and speaking; we call these nominal cognitive fixes. Sometimes we think of things in terms of uniquely identifying conditions; we have a descriptive cognitive fix, and descriptions may be the appropriate expressions to use. We think of singular terms as devices for providing hearers with cognitive fixes on objects, that are appropriate for the communicative aims of the speaker.

Here the apple plays a number of roles in your life: the thing you see, the thing in front of you that you can pick up by moving in a certain way; the thing in your hands; the thing in your mouth; the thing providing certain taste sensations, and so forth. All of these roles are *linked*; that is, one thing plays all of them. The job of the agent's buffer is to keep track of all these linkages. But there may also be nested roles to keep track of. The apple may be the very one that your office-mate took out of her lunch bag before stepping away for a moment; by eating the apple, you will have an effect on her, perhaps making her angry. And perhaps she has the boss's ear, so the apple is the one that by eating you can anger your office-mate, cause bad things to be said about you to your boss, and get yourself fired.

Signs are objects that play a direct epistemic role in one's life, whose perceivable properties are related in reliable ways to the properties of other objects, to which it is related. You see the paw print along the trail; on the basis of the pattern and size of the print, you learn that it was caused by a fox. The fox plays a complex, indirect epistemic role in your life; it is the animal that caused the print you are perceiving, and hence the animal you learn about by examining the print.

Nature provides us with many signs; that is, certain events carry information about other objects (or about themselves at other times) in virtue of the way nature made them and the way the world works. Other objects carry information because of structures created by humans, which harness natural information for various purposes. A certain characteristic twitch at the end of your fishing rod tells you that there is, or may be, a fish on the hook tied to the end of the line that feeds into the rod. A ringing doorbell tells you that someone is on the porch.

In interpreting a sign, one basically asks what the rest of the world must be like, for the object perceived to be as it is, or for the event or state perceived to have occurred. As in the case of the effects of one's acts, one doesn't worry about everything; one has in mind certain structures, certain objects that are or might be related to the object seen, and certain ways the world works. I see a paw print of a certain shape and size; I know that given the way the world works there is some animal that made it, and that given the shape and size it was a fox. Interpreting signs is a manner of inferring what the rest of the world has to be like (or probably is like, or may be like), given various structures and constraints, for the sign to have occurred.

So, typically, the interpretation of a sign involves perceiving an object or event as having certain properties, and inferring from those properties what the rest of the world must be like. Paradigmatically, this means inferring that various other objects related to the sign in certain ways, have or lack various properties.

Now we are well equipped to introduce our view on referential acts, which we think fits well in a Gricean picture of reference.

4 Gricean Reference

Our terminology differs a bit from Grice's. He distinguishes between natural and non-natural meaning. What he calls non-natural meaning involves an agent doing something in order to change the beliefs, or otherwise affect the cognitions, of a hearer, in virtue of the hearer's recognizing the speaker's intention to affect this change. Language use is a case of non-natural meaning, but not the only case.

According to Grice, if we are talking about natural meaning, "X means that S" entails that S. This view of Grice's is connected with the use of "information" by Dretske and others, including one of the present authors in previous writings, to imply truth (Dretske, 1981 [2000]; Barwise and Perry, 1983 [1999]). We adopt a looser view in this paper. (We use "information" in the way Israel and Perry use "informational content" (Israel and Perry, 1990, 1991).) When a bird can see an unobstructed view of an object, it takes this as a sign that it can fly directly to the object. In the modern world, this leads many birds to their death, as they fly into windows and plate glass doors on the sides of buildings. We regard this as natural meaning; the bird is responding to a natural sign, but one that is not infallible. The importance of this may be mostly terminological; it allows us to use terms like "natural sign," "natural meaning" and "information" rather than circumlocutions. But natural meaning, in our weaker sense, is the natural concept to explain how the interpretation of phenomena as signs plays an important evolutionary role; as long as the tendencies involved in interpreting signs lead to good results in a sufficient proportion of cases, the trait of doing so will propagate.

Interpreting the intentions and other cognitions of other people is a natural, evolved ability of humans. From this point of view, there is nothing non-natural about this ability, and the development of language as an extension of it is also a part of nature. We draw approximately the same line as Grice, but we see it as a line between signs that are intentionally produced to be the signs of intentions, and other signs.

Now consider an example of Herb Clark's (1992, 1996). A person stands in line at the checkout counter of a grocery store. When his turn comes, he takes a sack of potatoes from his cart and puts them on the counter. The checker will take this as a sign that the shopper wants to purchase the item, and will proceed to ring it up with the expectation of getting paid. This act has at least some of the features of Gricean communication. The shopper wants the clerk to ring up the sack of potatoes. He probably has no great interest in why the clerk does so, but he at least implicitly expects that part of the motivation will be realizing that the shopper wants to buy them. If he doesn't want to buy them, but merely learn the price of the potatoes, he'll have to say something.

It is natural to find a reference-predication structure in this episode, even though no language is involved. The shopper conveys his intention about a certain item, the sack of potatoes. He conveys that he wishes to buy it. If he had held the sack up and asked, "How much?" he would have conveyed his desire to have the clerk tell him the cost of the item. The act of putting the sack of potatoes on the counter is a primitive act of reference. The fact that he put the sack on the counter shows that the desire he wishes to convey concerns the potatoes; the fact that he placed it on the counter and said nothing, conveys his desire to buy them. Different aspects of the shopper's act convey different aspects of the desire he wishes to convey.

Clark interprets the act of putting the potatoes on the counter as a demonstration. Perhaps cigarettes are not available for the shopper to put in his cart, but displayed behind the checker, who is not supposed to sell them to those under sixteen. The shopper could convey the same information about a pack of cigarettes that he did about the sack of potatoes by pointing to it. Or he could say, "That pack of Camels, please."

The examples have a common structure. The shopper has a desire about a certain item, to purchase it. He wants to convey to the clerk which item it is he wants to purchase. He does so by bringing it about that the item plays certain roles in the clerk's life. That is, he draws the clerk's attention to the item, in such a way that the clerk will realize it is the item the shopper wishes to buy, and will have a cognitive fix on the item that enables him to take the desired action towards the item: to ring it up. The act of reference is the act of getting the referent to play a certain role in the hearer's life, in such a way that the hearer realizes that it is the object that the shopper desires to buy, and has a cognitive fix on the item that permits him to do what the shopper wants him to do with it.

Now suppose that you are eating dinner with a group of people, and you want the salt, which you can't reach. You say to the person next to you, who can reach the shaker,

(2) I'd like some salt, please.

Here you are conveying to your hearer that a certain person would like the salt. The predicate "like some salt" conveys what the person, to whom you refer, would like. The word "I" conveys which person that is, but it does more than that. By producing your utterance, so that it is heard, you provide the hearer a succession of cognitive fixes on the referent, that is, the person of whom wanting the salt is being predicated. It is (i) the person who the speaker is referring to. Your choice of "I" indicates that that person is (ii) the speaker of the utterance. In this particular situation, the hearer can see who the speaker is: (iii) the person next to him. This puts him in a position to carry out the implicit request, and pass you the salt. Here again your intent is to identify the subject, the person who wants the salt, for the hearer in such a way that the hearer can fulfill your goal in speaking, and pass you the salt.

Suppose now that it is not you who wants the salt, but the woman sitting across from you and your hearer; she is looking at the salt shaker, but is too shy to say anything. You say,

(3) She'd like the salt,

with a glance across the table. Perhaps you nudge the hearer, so that he will turn towards you, and follow your eye gaze and subtle nod towards the woman. Again, you have a referential plan. You want to convey the belief that a certain person wants the salt. The speaker will understand your sentence, and realize that the person referred to by the utterance he hears wants the salt. Other things being equal, he will take it that that person is a female. He will follow your eye gaze and realize that the person you are referring to is the person seated across from you, someone he is in a position to pass the salt to.

These cases illustrate one of our basic theses. The pragmatic aspects of singular reference are largely a matter of role-management. We refer to objects in the ways that we do in order to provide our hearers with an *apt cognitive fix* on the people or things or places we want to convey beliefs or other attitudes about, that is, one enables them to take whatever further actions we would like them to carry out with respect to this object.

Suppose now the woman across from you is the movie star Julia Roberts. You say,

(4) Julia Roberts would like the salt.

Your neighbor hears the utterance, and has an initial fix on the person of whom wanting the salt is predicated: (i) the person the speaker of the utterance I hear refers to. He will realize that she is named "Julia Roberts," a person he already has a notion of, and can think of as: (ii) Julia Roberts. His is a notion that includes a conception of what she looks like. He will look around the table until he recognizes her. He will then have a cognitive fix on the person who needs the salt as: (iii) the person sitting diagonally across from him, and will pass her the salt. Again, your plan to get Julia Roberts the salt involved providing a path the hearer could take, from having a cognitive fix on the salt deprived person merely as the subject of the utterance he is hearing, to being the person across from him, an apt cognitive fix that enables him to get the salt to her.

Perhaps the person sitting next to you is a true intellectual, who never sees movies except documentaries; he has barely heard of Julia Roberts, and has no idea what she looks like. Then your plan will fail. Your plan puts a certain cognitive burden on the hearer; in order to follow the path you have in mind, he has to have a notion of Julia Roberts sufficiently detailed that he can recognize her. He may come to believe that Julia Roberts wants the salt, but can't go on from there.

Suppose Bob Dole is at the dinner too. Bob Dole, the Republican candidate for President of the USA in 1996, has a habit of referring to himself in the third person. He says to the person next to him,

(5) Bob Dole would like some salt.

This may not work; he isn't as well-known as he once was. If instead he had said "I'd like the salt," it would have worked. His choice of words puts an unnecessary cognitive burden on the hearer. It also sounds a bit pretentious—this is probably what Ellen Goodman was reacting to in our opening quote. His plan assumes that people will have a rich enough notion of Bob Dole to recognize him, and that's the sort of assumption most ordinary folk won't make, when there is a simpler way of getting the hearer to have the appropriate cognitive fix, by using the first person.

Perhaps it's 1996, and Bob Dole has been talking politics with you, who have been sitting next to him at a dinner party. As he leaves he says, "I hope you vote for me." To vote for someone, you have to know his or her name. He is putting the same cognitive burden you as in the case above. If he is cautious, and thinks the dinner conversation has made a good impression on you, he will say "I hope you vote for Bob Dole." Or, more likely, he will say, "I am Bob Dole. I hope you vote for me."

He clearly adds something to the conversation by saying "I am Bob Dole" that he wouldn't have added by merely saying "Bob Dole is Bob Dole," or "I am I." He assumes that the hearer has a notion of Bob Dole, rich enough to include the information that Dole is a candidate. He assumes that the hearer has a notion of the person he has been talking to, which includes that he is an intelligent and affable fellow. The effect Dole wishes to achieve is getting these notions merged, so that the hearer has a single notion that include being a candidate named "Bob Dole," being the person he is talking to, and being affable and intelligent. Dole's remark gives you two cognitive fixes on one person, as the person speaking to you, and as the person you think of as "Bob Dole."

Perhaps it hasn't occurred to Bob Dole that he hasn't been recognized, and he simply says "I hope you vote for me." Later you tell a friend about this puzzling remark. "I was talking to a man at dinner. When he left he said he wanted me to vote for him. I wonder what he is running for." "That man is running for President," he tells you. "He is Bob Dole." Your friend plans that you will recognize that the person he is referring to with "that man" is the very one whose behavior at dinner motivated your remark. He is building on a fix you already have on the man, in order to get the result that you merge your notion of the man you talked to, with your Bob Dole notion.

These cases all illustrate our basic thesis that reference involves role-management. The thesis has implications for the semantics of the kinds of expressions we use in singular reference: demonstratives and demonstrative phrases, indexicals, personal pronouns, names, and definite descriptions. The meanings of these expressions are what enables utterances of them to have the role-management uses that they do, and the semantics of these expressions must explain how that is.

5 The GDTPA Structure of Referential Plans

In our view, reference involves a complex of Gricean intentions (intentions aimed at being recognized by the hearer) or *plans*: structures of intentions and beliefs. We distinguish five aspects of such plans, which we call the grammatical, directing, target, path and auxiliary intentions, and refer to the whole as the GDTPA structure of referential plans.

In a paradigm case the speaker S will have a belief, which we'll call *the motivating belief*, with a certain content; she intends that the hearer H will come to have a belief with the same referential content, in virtue of recognizing S's intention to have H do so. This intention will be in the service of further intentions S has for H; inferences, or other actions, S wants H to perform, or refrain from performing.

When reference is involved, the motivating belief will be about (at least) one thing X; the belief's referential content will be a singular proposition about X, to the effect that X meets a certain condition. As part of instilling the belief in H, S intends to get H to think about X, to have a cognitive fix on X, and recognize S's intention to have H believe that X meets the condition. S will intend for H to think about X as the object that plays a role in H's own life, the *target role*, one that is suited to S's further intentions for H's actions and inferences. S intends to accomplish this by exploiting a role X plays in S's own life, the *exploited role*, through use of an expression whose meaning suits it for helping to identify this role. The expression will be part of a sentence, which identifies the condition X must meet for the utterance to be true. H will infer from the fact that X plays the exploited role in S's life, that X plays a role in H's own life, and will think of X in a way suited to thinking of objects that play that role.

In such a paradigm case, there will be a singular term E that is part of the sentence S utters, so that S intends to refer to X by uttering E. This intention will be part of a referential plan that involves the means of reference, and the effects of reference. This is a plan about E, X, the hearer H, an exploited role, and a target role.

Where the content of S's motivating belief for uttering "$F(E)$" is that $C(X)$:

- S believes that the sentence "...E..." predicates C of the object identified by E, and intends to assert of that object that it meets C (the grammatical intention);
- S believes that X plays the exploited role in S's life, and that the meaning of E makes uttering E a way of identifying the object that plays that role, and S intends, by uttering E, to get H to recognize that she intends to identify the object that plays that role (the directing intention);
- S believes that X plays the target role in H's life, and that by thinking of X in that way, and believing that X meets condition C, H will be likely to perform the further inferences and actions S has in mind, and S intends for H to recognize that S intends for him to think of X in that way (the target intention);
- S believes that H can infer from the fact that X plays the exploited role in S's life, that it plays the target role in H's life, and intends that H recognizes that S intends for H to make that inference (the path intention);

We call this the GDTPA structure of paradigm referential plans. It is also useful to note that S may think that by using E to identify X, certain further information will be conveyed to H about X; the intention to convey this information we call the *auxiliary intention*. We'll explain the GDTPA structure a bit more, and then apply it to a range of examples.

5.1 The Grammatical Intention

When we predicate a property of an object, or a relation between objects, or some more complex condition, in the usual way by uttering a declarative sentence, the various argument roles involved in the condition are grammatically specified. In English this is mainly done by word order; in other languages case markings carry the bulk of this information. The predicate "kills" expresses a relation between a killer, a thing killed, and a time of the killing. To understand S's utterances of such sentences as "Ruby killed Oswald," "Oswald was killed by Ruby" or phrases like "Ruby's killing of Oswald," "Oswald's killing by Ruby," "the fact that Ruby killed Oswald," H needs not only to recognize that it is killing, Ruby and Oswald who are involved in the belief that S wishes to impart, but the roles they play in the killing; the word order combined with the sort of construction used—active or passive—specifies that Ruby is the killer and Oswald the victim. We will take the intention on the speaker's part to convey this information, the *grammatical intention,* largely for granted here, without meaning to suggest it is unimportant, semantically trivial, or pragmatically insignificant.

5.2 The Directing Intention

In order to impart her motivating belief to *H* in an apt way, *S* has to refer to *X*. She might, as in Clark's case of the shopper and the clerk, do so by putting *X* directly in *H*'s line of vision, without saying anything. Or perhaps *X* is a person who stumbles out of a bar and falls at the feet of *S* and *H*. "Drunk," *S* says; there is no need to get *H* thinking about *X*, since he no doubt already is. But we'll focus on cases in which *S* refers, and uses language to do so.

Our thesis is that the meanings of expressions suit them for use in referring to things that play certain epistemic or pragmatic roles in one's life—that is, things on which one has one kind or other of cognitive fix. In choosing her referring expressions, *S*'s goal is not merely to refer to the object her motivating belief is about, but to refer in a way that is apt for bringing about the right sort of understanding on the part of *H*. And for aiming at that target *S* exploits her own cognitive fix or fixes on *X*. *S* may have choices here, for she may have (or think she has) different cognitive fixes on the same thing. The *directing intention* is the intention to refer to the object *S*'s motivating belief is about, by using an expression, or some other intention-indicating device, or a combination, that is associated, naturally or conventionally, with some cognitive fix one has on that object one's motivating belief is about. For example, *S* may use the word "I" to refer to herself; the word "I" is suited for that role by its meaning. *S* may use the word "that man" to refer to a man she sees; the phrase "that man" is suited by its meaning for referring to a man with that role in the speaker's life. *S* may use "you" to refer to the person she is talking to; the word "you" is suited by its meaning to refer to that person. These are directing intentions. In each case, *S* may have further intentions. She may, by using "you" and referring to the addressee, intend to refer to Elwood Fritchey, and by referring to Elwood Fritchey, intend to refer to the next Dean of the College. Those are not directing intentions.

Directing intentions are *determinative.* That is, the speaker has referred to whoever or whatever plays the role involved in her directing intention. The further intentions are not determinative. Suppose *S* thinks she is talking to Elwood Fritchey, but is instead talking to Elwood's twin Christopher. When she says "you" she has referred to Christopher, not Elwood.

To the question, "Does intention determine reference?" our theory says "Yes and No." Basically, the speaker has authority over which role she exploits. But she does not have authority over who or what actually plays that role; if her beliefs about that are wrong, she may refer to a thing to which she does not intend to refer. When we depart from paradigm cases, and consider ones in which the words chosen are inappropriate for the role the speaker intends to exploit, or when the speaker is misunderstood by careful hearers, things quickly get complicated. Basically, the speaker gets to choose which role she exploits, but then facts take over, and if the speaker's beliefs about those facts are wrong, she may not refer to the thing she intends to; but we won't look at these complications here.

5.3 The Target Intention

If S is at all adept at using language, she will not intend to get H to have a belief about some object, but will also have at least a vague intention of the type of cognitive fix on that object that H should have, in order to be in a position to have whatever further thoughts and actions S has in mind for him; that is, an apt cognitive fix. This is the *target intention*. In the case of passing the salt, the target intention is that the hearer think of the person referred to, the one who wants the salt, in some way that will afford passing the salt to that person. In the case of giving someone information about Cicero, say, to use on an exam, one will likely want the cognitive fix to be via the name that will be used to refer to Cicero.

5.4 The Path Intention

Moreover, if S is an adept speaker, she will have in mind some *path*, some reasoning, that will lead H from realizing what role the referent has in the speaker's life, that is, from grasping the direction intention, to the target intention, that is to the cognitive fix S wants H to have. When I say, "I'd like the salt," I expect you to realize that the person who wants the salt is the speaker of the utterance you hear, and so the person you see across from you; this is the target cognitive fix, the one that will enable you to pass the salt to the right person.

5.5 Examples

S and H are standing on the east side of Canal Street, just south of Adams, in Chicago. Union Station rises on either side of Canal Street, the main part of the station being underground, running under Canal Street, and connecting the parts above ground. S believes that H's train leaves from Union Station. She intends to impart that information to H, with the goal that H will walk into the nearest part of Union Station. She holds this belief via her notion of Union Station, usually detached, but now connected to perception. In this situation, there are (at least) three ways S could refer to Union Station, exploiting three different cognitive fixes she has on it. She could just say

(6) Your train leaves from Union Station.

But in order to meet *S*'s goal, *H* would have to recognize which building was Union Station, and *S* doesn't think he does. She could point to the part of Union Station that rises on the other side of Canal Street, and say,

(7) Your train leaves from that station.

But that would doubtless lead to *H*'s unnecessarily crossing busy Canal Street. Or *S* could point to the near part of Union Station, that rises on the east side of Canal Street, a short distance from where *S* and *H* are talking. This is clearly the way of referring that is most likely to lead to the effect on *H* that *S* wants; that is, to believe of Union Station, thought of as the building he sees on the same side of the street, that it is the place he needs to go to catch his train.

S's directing intention is to refer to the building she sees as she looks east, by using the demonstrative phrase "that station." This fixes the referent. This creates the possibility of a failing to refer to the object she intends to refer to, even though intentions fix reference. Suppose *S* is in error. Things have changed at Union Station. The above-ground part of structure that used to be the eastern wing of Union Station has been converted to a posh prison for Illinois politicians. Union Station is now just the structure west of Canal Street, plus the part under the street. *S* point to the structure on the east side, and says "Your train leaves from that station." In this case, even though *S*'s utterance was motivated by a belief about Union Station, and the primary referential intention was to refer to Union Station, she has not referred to Union Station, but to the Illinois Politicians' Prison.

In the original example, *S*, an adept speaker, chose the way of referring to Union Station that would most likely lead *H* to have an apt cognitive fix on the station. Here we have role-transfer; the kind of cognitive fix *S* intended for *H* to have was basically the same sort that was involved in *S*'s directing intention, that is, a perceptual fix. That path that *S* set up for *H* to follow was short and direct, basically from "the station *S* is looking at" to "the station I am looking at." *S*'s referential plan, then, is a complex intention to refer to an object, Union Station, in a way that will induce *H* to recognize *S*'s directing intention, and then following the *path* to a perceptual cognitive fix on the same building—the *target intention*.

But paths are not always simple and direct. *S* tells *H*,

(8) Mr. Muggs is wanted on the phone—would you tell him?

Perhaps *S* answered the phone, at a party, and someone asked for Muggs, whom *S* already knows. She has the sort of cognitive fix on Muggs that one has in such a situation; she isn't seeing or hearing Muggs, just thinking about him in the way one thinks about someone one knows, via a detached notion. But she wants H to have a perceptual fix on Muggs, for this is required to approach him and give him the message. S's plan puts a cognitive burden on H, to know, or be able to find out what Muggs looks like.

Or perhaps S is a professor in a large class and Muggs is a student, whose name S does not know. Muggs asks her if he can have an extension on his paper, and S agrees. She tells his teaching assistant H, "Make a note that he gets an extension." S is assuming the assistant will know the student's name, for this is required to make a useful note. S's plan, in some detail, is:

- H hears my utterance, and parses it;
- H has the fix: the person the speaker of the utterance refers to with "he";
- He realizes that I, the professor, am the speaker;
- He has the fix: the person the Professor is referring to with "he";
- H witnessed my conversation with the student, and realizes that he is who I have in mind;
- H has the fix: the student the Professor was just talking to;
- H is a responsible assistant and knows the names of his students;
- H has a fix on the student via the student's name;
- H will be in a position to make a useful note.

The pronoun "he" provides auxiliary information about the referent, that he is a male. It may be misinformation. In this case, the professor may not have realized that the student he was talking to was a female; it's not always easy to tell. Or the professor may be a fossil who thinks that girls should dress like girls and boys like boys; she was very aware that the student was a girl, but signaled her disapproval to the teaching assistant by using the wrong pronoun. Or maybe her native language is Basque, which doesn't have a gendered pronoun system, and she always says "he" rather than think about which English pronoun to use. In this case, it really doesn't matter. The teaching assistant will know to whom she is referring, and disregard the misinformation.

Sometimes it does matter. Perhaps two students have been making requests of the professor. She tells the teaching assistant, "Give *her* an extension, give *him* an incomplete." She is counting on the pronouns to distinguish between the two students, and if she gets it wrong, the wrong students may end up with the incomplete and the extension. This additional information, or misinformation as the case may be, does not affect who or what is being referred to, nor is it asserted of the referent. We say it is *projected*; but we won't have more to say about this here.[4]

6 Conclusion

If we are right, the pragmatic aspects of singular reference are largely a matter of role-management, and, in that sense, indexicals and demonstratives or more illuminating than the traditional paradigms, proper names and definite descriptions.

This doesn't mean that we're giving up the referentialist view on singular reference, according to which the contribution of the sub-utterance of the singular term to the proposition expressed (or what is said) by the whole utterance is a particular object. We are essentially referentialists to that extent. But we are critical referentialists, because we think that the *way* that a thing is referred to, and not just the identity of the referent, is required to deal with traditional problems of cognitive significance. Of course, if one cannot tell the difference between co-referential terms in one's theory, one will have little hope of explaining the difference that using one term over another might have, and little hope of explaining a speaker's reasons for choosing one rather than the other.

We refer to objects in the ways that we do in order to provide our hearers with an *apt* cognitive fix on the people or things or places we want to convey beliefs or other attitudes about, that is, one enables them to take whatever further actions we would like them to carry out with respect to this object. We hope that our GDTPA structure of speaker's plan makes clear the complexity of our referential intentions, and the relevance of roles and cognitive fixes in that respect.

Theories in the philosophy of action have long recognized the multi-level structure of action. An agent moves in certain circumstances, and the combination of the nature of the movement, and the nature of the circumstances, produces certain results, given the way the world works. I move my arm in a certain way unthinkingly, and because of the circumstances I'm in, I knock a cup to the floor. By knocking the cup to the floor, I cause it to break. By causing it to break, I make its owner angry. And so forth. The action is naturally viewed as having multiple informational contents, depending of the facts we take as given. In contrast, theories of the content of language and propositional attitudes are usually "mono-propositional." That is, there is a single proposition that is thought to capture the content of a belief, desire, or assertion. We contend that utterances, *qua* acts, also have a plurality of contents, that derive from facts about the speaker's plan, linguistic conventions

---

[4] But see our book *Critical Pragmatics* (2011), specially Chapter 8, on descriptions.

and the circumstances of utterance, and which of them are taken as given. Our analysis of referential acts is, hopefully, a step towards clarifying how that works.[5]

---

[5] The work of the first author has been partially supported by a grant of the Basque Government (IT323-10) and a grant by the Spanish Ministry of Science and Innovation (FFI2009-08574).

7

What is Said

KEPA KORTA AND JOHN PERRY

1 The Importance of What is Said

The nineteen sixties and seventies were exciting times for the philosophy of language. There was the "referential revolution": work by Saul Kripke, Keith Donnellan, David Kaplan, and others led to a shift in thinking about reference. Grice's theory of conversational implicatures provided a powerful new way of thinking about pragmatics, which has had deep influences not only in the philosophy of language but also in linguistics and artificial intelligence.

Both of these developments relied on the more or less common-sense notion of *what a person says,* or *what is said* by an utterance. For Grice, recognition of what is said is the "input" to reasoning about implicatures:

> He has said that *p*; there is no reason to suppose that he is not observing the maxims, ...; he could not be doing this unless he thought that *q*; he knows (and knows that I know that he knows) that I can see that the supposition that he thinks that *q* is *required*; he has done nothing to stop me thinking that *q*; he intends me to think, or is at least willing to allow me to think, that *q*; and so he has implicated that *q*. (Grice, 1967a [1989], 31. Our italics)

Kaplan explicitly grounds the key concept of the content of an utterance in the concept of what is said:

> Suppose I point at Paul and say,
>
> > He now lives in Princeton, New Jersey.
>
> Call *what I said*—i.e., the content of my utterance, the proposition expressed—"Pat." Is Pat true or false? True! Suppose that unbeknownst to me, Paul had moved to Santa Monica last week. Would Pat have then been true or false? False! Now, the tricky case: Suppose that Paul and Charles had each disguised themselves as the other and had switched places. If that had

happened, *and* I had uttered as I did, then the proposition I *would have* expressed would have been false. But in that possible context the proposition I would have expressed is not Pat. That is easy to see because the proposition I *would have* expressed, had I pointed to Charles instead of Paul—call this proposition "Mike"—not only *would have* been false but actually is false. Pat, I would claim, would still be true in the circumstances of the envisaged possible context provided that Paul—in whatever costume he appeared—were still residing in Princeton. (Kaplan, 1989a, 512–513).

Kaplan here grounds the more or less technical phrases "the content of an utterance" and "the proposition expressed by an utterance" in our ordinary concept of what is said. He assumes that we will have intuitive judgments about what is said that correspond with his. First of all, we will take it that in the original case he designates Paul, because Paul meets the condition of the person he is pointing to, and that what he says, Pat, will be true if Paul lives in Princeton, but false if he lives in Santa Monica. Second, we will take it that in the tricky case, he designates Charles, because he points to him, even though he thinks he is pointing at Paul; and that what he says, Mike, is false given that Charles does not live in Princeton.

All of these assumptions are consistent with Pat and Mike being the same proposition, viz.,

Erin: that the person to whom the speaker points lives in Princeton.[1]

But Kaplan thinks we will also find it plausible that Pat is not Mike, and neither of them is Erin. We should be convinced by the fact that they differ in their counterfactual properties. Pat is true in the original case, in which Kaplan points to Paul and Paul lives in New Jersey. But it is also true in the tricky case, in which both Mike and Erin are false. Mike is false in the original case, in which Pat and Erin are true, as well as in the tricky case. So Pat is not Mike, and neither of them is Erin. If we take Pat to be the singular proposition that Paul lives in Princeton, and Mike to be the singular proposition that Charles lives there, we get the right results.

Thus we have an argument that what is said is a singular proposition about the object designated, rather than a proposition that incorporates the identifying condition—here *being the person the speaker points to*. And it is our concept of what is said, so understood, that grounds the concepts of the proposition expressed by an utterance and the content of an utterance.

---

[1] For the sake of simplicity, we are leaving aside the meaning and contents of "now."

2   A Dilemma About What is Said

The situation in the sixties and seventies seems then to have been quite propitious. Gricean pragmatics rested on a concept of what is said, as the input to pragmatic reasoning. Referential semantics supplied a clear and well-argued account of what is said. Referential semantics seemed to supply what Gricean pragmatics needs.

But there is a problem. The concept of what is said as referential content does not seem to work for Gricean pragmatics; some "finer-grained" notion is needed. Suppose a group of strangers is having a meal at a soup kitchen, staffed by volunteers. Someone has spilled the salt and failed to clean it up. "Whoever spilled the salt, must clean it up," the volunteer waiter says. Elwood stands up and says, "I spilled the salt." He implicates that he will clean it up. But if he stood up and said, "Elwood spilled the salt," he would not have implicated this, but implicated instead that he had not done it, and had no intention of cleaning it up. The relevant difference seems to be the identifying conditions associated with the term Elwood used to refer to himself. The character of the word "I," that it refers to the speaker, seems to be just the element involved in the first case that generates the implicature; Elwood's implicature relies on the fact the hearers will realize that the speaker is the person who, according to the speaker, spilled the salt. In the second case, he relies on their lack of knowledge that the speaker is the referent of his use of "Elwood." The effect of these different ways of referring to Elwood, are just what singular propositions lose track of.

Or consider an elaboration on Kaplan's own case—the second, tricky case. Elwood wants to know where Charles lives. We all think that Kaplan is unusually knowledgeable about where his philosophical colleagues reside. Kaplan says, pointing to Charles, thinking he is Paul, "He lives in Princeton." If you say, pointing at Charles, "Kaplan said that man lives in Princeton," you may implicate that Kaplan did not realize that he was pointing to Charles. If you merely say, "Kaplan said that Charles lives in Princeton," you do not implicate this, and indeed most likely convey that there was no reason to doubt that Kaplan knew of whom he was speaking. The different manners in which you report what Kaplan said allow for different implicatures. But if in both cases what you said is simply that Kaplan said Mike, and what is said is the input to implicative reasoning, how can this be so?

So we seem to have a dilemma about what is said. It can be coarse-grained, and fit the arguments and serve the needs of referentialism. Or it can be fine-grained, and fit the examples and serve the needs of Gricean pragmatics.

We shall argue that the dilemma is only apparent. Or, more cautiously, we argue that there is a single account of saying and what is said, that both preserves the referentialist identification of what is said with referential content, and explains how what is said is, if not precisely the input to, a major constraint upon, Gricean reasoning.

3   Saying-Reports as Contextual Classifications of Content

We shall not take issue with the idea that the phrase "what is said" can be regarded as designating a proposition. But, unlike typical signature terms, the nominals "what is said," or "what she said" are closely related to interrogatives: "What was said?" or "what did she say?" Such questions are typically questions about particular utterances, or a circumscribed set of utterances, such as those that occur in a conversation. Further, such questions are typically focused on certain subject matter, as when one asks, "What did she say about *me?*" or "What did she say about *Obama?*" or "What did she say about *San Sebastian?*" The fact that specifying "what is said" is typically tied to answering questions with such foci is the key to understanding some of the complexities of our concept of what is said.

We'll consider an extended example concerning a conversation about San Sebastian. First, a brief geography lesson. San Sebastian is a city in the Basque Country, home of a campus of the University of the Basque Country, site of many conferences in the philosophy of language and related areas of linguistics, rhetoric and cognitive science. The name San Sebastian is an anglicized version of the Spanish name for the city, "San Sebastián"; Basques prefer to call the city "Donostia" whenever practical. Thus,

(1) Donostia and San Sebastian are the same city.

Now imagine the following. A group of philosophers and linguists are on their way to a conference. Most of them are veterans, and know that Donostia and San Sebastian are the same city. Further, they regularly refer to this city as "Donostia" when they are in the Basque Country. But one of them, the linguist Ivan, does not know this; this is his first trip to the Basque Country. All of the conference materials he looked at referred to the site of the conference as "San Sebastian." As the bus travels from the Hondarribia airport to the city, Ivan is struck by the fact that, according to the signs along the road, San Sebastian and Donostia, a city he'd never heard of, were exactly the same distance from the airport, first fifteen kilometers, then ten, then seven, then three, and so on.

During the trip Ivan muses out loud, saying "This bus is going to San Sebastian," and "This bus is not going to Donostia." The following are intuitively true reports about what Ivan said:

(2) Ivan said that the bus is going to San Sebastian.
(3) Ivan did not say that the bus is not going to San Sebastian.
(4) Ivan said that the bus is not going to Donostia.
(5) Ivan did not say that the bus is going to Donostia.

Suppose, for example, that Tom overhears Ivan's musings, and then provides the other veterans with reports (2)–(5). His hearers would grasp the situation; that Ivan has two notions of the same city that are unlinked in his mind. One of these notions is associated with the name "San Sebastian," the other with the name "Donostia." They would assume that Tom's reports (2) and (3) were based on utterances using the name "San Sebastian," while (4) and (5) were based on reports using "Donostia."

Now imagine a somewhat different situation. Because of his high energy level, Ivan is put in charge of finding the right bus for the group to take to the conference. The veterans are sure the information he needs will be available under the name "San Sebastián."[2] The tired, jaded veterans hop on the bus to which Ivan directs them. But after a while, for reasons that need not concern us, they begin to worry about whether they are on the right bus. They send Tom to check. At first Tom forgets that Ivan is not a veteran, and asks, "Is this bus going to Donostia." Ivan says, "This bus is not going to Donostia." Then Tom remembers that Ivan is likely ignorant of (1), and asks, "Is this bus going to San Sebastian?" Ivan replies, "This bus is going to San Sebastian."

Tom returns to the veterans and says:

(6) Ivan said that the bus is going to Donostia.

It seems to us that, in this context,[3] (6) is intuitively correct, and in fact true, and if Tom had uttered (4) it would have been incorrect, and arguably untrue.

To make sense of our intuitions, we introduce two contextual considerations. The first is the difference between using saying-reports as *explanations* and using them as *information* (about the subject-matter).

What a sincere person says reveals something about the state of their minds, states which may explain various things they do or don't do. Suppose for example that the bus passes a sign that says

Free Drinks for Linguists at Noam's Bar in Donostia

---

[2] Henceforth we ignore the difference between the Spanish and English names, although it wouldn't be hard to come up with examples where it was relevant.

[3] We use "context" in the sense of properties of an utterance that are relevant to understanding, rather than in Kaplan's technical sense of a quadruple of agent, location, time and world.

Tom sees the sign, and says to Ivan, "Hey, that's good news!" Ivan replies, "But this bus isn't going to Donostia." Tom reports to the other veterans, "Ivan says this bus isn't going to Donostia. That's why he wasn't cheered up by the sign about Noam's bar." Tom is providing a saying-report as an explanation of Ivan's behavior, or lack thereof.

But when a person is sincere and knowledgeable, what they say can also provide information about the world, about the object they are talking about. Ivan is knowledgeable about where the bus is going, since he is the one that checked the sign on the front before getting on board. When Tom is sent to check on where the bus is going, and reports back with (6), he is providing a saying-report as information.

Both uses of saying-reports get complicated when a person has two notions of the same thing without realizing it. When Ivan sees the sign about free drinks, it affects his beliefs about Donostia, but not all of his beliefs about Donostia; only those that involve his "Donostia" associated notion. This is a notion of the city he acquired when he first saw the mileage signs. The beliefs that involve this notion are about the city, in that it is facts about the city that determine whether they are true or false.

His other notion of the city, the one that is associated with the name "San Sebastian," was acquired years ago, when Ivan took geography in school. His recent reading of conference materials has resulted in a lot of new beliefs about the city involving this notion: that it is where the conference is being held; that it is an attractive city on a bay; and so forth.

The beliefs Ivan has that involve his "Donostia" notion and those that involve his "San Sebastian" notion are insulated from one another, both in terms of explanation and information. The belief Ivan has, that explains his lack of euphoria on learning of free drinks at Noam's bar, is the one he would express with "This bus is not going to Donostia." When Tom uses saying-report (4) to explain the lack of euphoria, the veterans infer a belief involving Ivan's "Donostia" notion, and it is this belief that does the explanatory work.

On the other hand, Ivan is a good guide to where the bus is going, only when he is drawing on the beliefs he has that involve his "San Sebastian" notion. It was a "San Sebastian" sign on the bus that led to the key beliefs; it is only his assertions involving the name "San Sebastian" that are a good guide to these beliefs.

This leads to our second contextually important factor, which we call a "conversational thread." A thread is part of a larger name-notion network.[4] Such a network begins with an origin, in this case the city of San Sebas-

---

[4] See Perry, 2001 [2012], 2nd edition, Chapter 10.

tian/Donostia, and extends through utterances, perceptions of utterances, notions formed on the basis of such perceptions, and then further utterances. At some point the city was named "Donostia"; people called it that for centuries; eventually a sign was put up along the road, "Donostia: 15 km."; Ivan saw the sign; he formed a notion of the city; his notion guided his utterances to Tom. Similarly with "San Sebastian"; this network intersected with Ivan in school, led to his "San Sebastian" notion, and all the beliefs associated with it lead to the utterances in which Ivan uses this name.

The "San Sebastian" and the "Donostia" networks have the same origin, the city, and intersect in many places, as in the minds of the English-speaking residents, and the minds of the veterans; when they hear or read something using the name "San Sebastian" or using the name "Donostia," the information gets associated with the same notion, one that is associated with both names. But in Ivan's head there are two *threads*; one through his "Donostia" notion, and one through his "San Sebastian" notion.

When Tom tells the veterans what Ivan said, he is implicitly talking about what Ivan said *along a conversational thread.* When he reports (4), using the report as an explanation, he is implicitly talking about the thread that goes through Ivan's Donostia notion, and through Ivan's utterances that use the name "Donostia." He is telling the veterans, more or less, "if you follow the thread back from my current utterance to Ivan's "Donostia" using utterances, you'll find one the content of which is that this bus isn't going to Donostia." This thread is relevant because the report is provided as an explanation of Ivan's lack of euphoria at seeing a sign with good news expressed using the term "Donostia."

On the other hand, when Tom reassures the veterans that the bus is going to Donostia, using (6), he is in effect telling them that if they follow the thread that leads back from his use of "Donostia" to Ivan's use of "San Sebastian," they will find an utterance whose content is that the bus is going to Donostia. This thread is relevant because Ivan's information about the bus was gained from a destination sign on the front that used the name "San Sebastian."

We can now provide an account of saying-reports that is modeled on the Crimmins-Perry analysis of belief reports.[5] In that theory, belief reports were taken to be about contextually determined *notions* or *types of notions*, in the mind of the believer. These were unarticulated constituents of the content of the belief report. Here we take threads running through notions and utterances of the sayer,[6] to the minds and utterances of the reporter to be contextually determined unarticulated constituents of the saying-report.

---

[5] See Crimmins and Perry, 1989; Crimmins, 1992.

[6] When discussing saying-reports, we use the somewhat unfamiliar "the sayer" rather than "the speaker," since both the sayer and reporter are speakers.

Where u is a saying-report of the form "X said that S," we use u_S for the subutterance of 'S'.

A report u of "X said that S," about thread T, is true iff:

a) there is an utterance u' that lies along T, and u is about u';
b) 'X' in u designates the agent of u';
c) the content of u' = the content of u_S.

When Tom is using his reports as explanation, (4) and (5) are true. Context determines that he is talking about the thread that runs through Ivan's "Donostia" notion. Along the "Donostia" thread, there are no utterances with the content that the bus is going to Donostia, and there is one with the content that the bus is not going to Donostia. When Tom uses them as evidence, he is talking about the "San Sebastian" thread. (4) and (5) are false and (6) is true; there is an utterance along the "San Sebastian" thread that has the content that the bus is going to Donostia.

Earlier, in introducing the example, we said that Tom's utterance of (4) seemed intuitively true. Consider the context of our remark. We had just introduced an example that called attention to Ivan's possessing two unlinked notions of the same city. Then we imagined Tom reporting what he had heard Ivan saying to himself. In this context, it was natural to take Tom's reports as explanations, or at least as a way of conveying to the veterans that Ivan hadn't grasped (1). That is, it was natural to take Tom's utterance as concerning the thread that ran through his Donostia-notion; along that thread there was not utterance to the effect that the bus was going to San Sebastian, so his report was true.

4   The Classificatory Role of Content

If this account, or something like it, is the right way to look at saying-reports, what does this imply about the claim that "what is said" is referential content? We think that it supports the claim, as long as we understand the role of the referential content, what is said, correctly.

It is misleading to think of a saying-report as simply a report of a relation that does or does not hold between the sayer and a certain object, one which happens to be a proposition. The job of the proposition is a bit more subtle. It plays a role in identifying a property the sayer does or does not have. A saying-report is a way of classifying an agent by the property of having produced an assertive utterance with certain truth-conditions. But not just any utterance will do. Context can constrain which conversation, or which part of a conversation, the utterance has to have been a part of, and along which track in that conversation the utterance must have lain.

That is, the job of the truth-conditions of the embedded sentence in the saying-report is to tell us something about the sayer's utterance *in addition to* the conditions it has to meet to be contextually relevant. In the case of Ivan and Noam's bar, the issue was whether Ivan believed, via some notion that was associated with being the place the bus was headed, that it was the site of Noam's bar. Assuming that Ivan saw and believed the sign, there will be associated with his "Donostia" notion, the property of being the site of a bar that serves linguists free drinks. Knowing that Ivan likes drinks, especially free ones, one assumes that if he believes he is heading to the site of Noam's bar he will be cheered up. The remaining question is whether he believes, via his "Donostia" notion, that the bus is headed there. If he is sincere, what he says about where the bus is heading, using the term "Donostia" will indicate the presence or absence of such a belief. Given that these are the issues in the air, Tom's report (4), tells the veterans what they need to know. The content of Ivan's *relevant* belief, the one involving his "Donostia" notion, is that the bus isn't going there. So he's not in the right mental state to be cheered up.

Suppose now that the context of Tom's remark isn't so clear to the veterans. That is, they are not sure at the outset what Tom is trying to communicate to them. A few minutes ago he reported (6), to reassure them the bus was headed to Donostia, on Ivan's authority. Now he says (4). Is his point that Ivan has changed his mind? Or is it rather that Tom's conversational goals are different? If the latter seems more plausible, one will fill in the missing contextual information in a way that makes sense. Before he was reporting what Ivan said relative to a thread relevant to his actions of getting us on this bus rather than another. Now he is reporting what Ivan said relative to a thread that is relevant to why seeing the sign about Noam's didn't cheer him up.

Now consider Kaplan's argument, in particular "the tricky case." Paul and Charles have disguised themselves as each other and changed places. Kaplan is looking at Charles. But he thinks he is looking at Paul. He says, "He now lives in Princeton, New Jersey." Kaplan argues that what he says in this case is false, and would have been false, even if the changing of places has not occurred, although in that case it would not have been what he said.

One can grant all of this, and still be dubious that in this circumstance the report, "Kaplan said that Charles lives in Princeton," would be true. Our account explains what is going on here. There are two threads in Kaplan's head, leading to Charles. One involves the notions that controls his use of "Charles," the other involves his perceptual notion, which is of Charles since Charles is the person he is looking at, and controls the use of "he." This latter thread is connected with his "Paul" notion, and the beliefs associated with that notion have become temporarily (until the ruse is disclosed) associated with his perceptual notion.

Suppose the issue is where Charles lives, and Kaplan is deemed to be an expert about where his philosophical friends reside. In this context, it would not be true to say "Kaplan said that Charles lives in Princeton." Of his two notions of Charles, the one that is authoritative about residence issues is the old one that controls his use of "Charles," not the new one that controls his use of "he." There is no utterance on a thread that goes through the authoritative "Charles" notion, and has the content that Charles lives in Princeton. This explanation of why it would be untrue in certain contexts to say "Kaplan said that Charles lives in Princeton" does not argue against the view that it is referential content that is at issue. The problem with the report is that in these contexts the speaker is talking about tracks on which authoritative utterances lie, and there is no authoritative utterance by Kaplan with the content that Charles lives in Princeton.

5 The General Theory of Content

The classificatory conception of content suggests the possibility of generalizing our ordinary concept of content in a way useful for theoretical purposes. Focusing on assertive utterances, one can think of contents as abstract objects that encode the truth-conditions of the utterances. But *the truth-conditions of an utterance* is a *relative* and *incremental* concept. That is, one is saying what *else* the world has to be like, for the utterance to be true, *given* certain facts about the utterance that are taken as fixed. The concept of the referential content of an utterance gets at what else the world has to be like for the utterance to be true, *given* the language of the utterance, the disambiguated meanings and syntax of the words and phrases, and the facts, including contextual facts, that determine the reference of the singular terms and other contextually sensitive items.

But one can naturally extend the concept of content, by considering the truth-conditions of an utterance with some of these items left *unfixed*. For example, the referential content of an utterance u of "I don't live in Princeton," spoken to Kaplan by Charles while disguised as Paul, is simply the proposition that Charles doesn't live in Princeton. An utterance of "Charles doesn't live in Princeton" would have had the same referential content. But if we abstract over the contextual fact that the speaker of the utterance is Charles, what else has to be the case for u to be true? The speaker of u has to not live in Princeton. This proposition, that the speaker of u doesn't live in Princeton, is a singular proposition about u and Princeton. It seems that this is the crucial bit of information that Charles is attempting to convey to Kaplan. Kaplan realizes that the person he is looking at, the one he has been taking to be Paul, is the speaker of u. So he learns that the person he is looking at, and has recently demonstrated with "he," does not live in Princeton. If he is confident that Paul has not moved, and he believes what he hears, we will have to conclude that the person he just demonstrated, the person he is talking to, is not Paul after all.

The proposition that the speaker of u does not live in Princeton what we call "utterance-bound" or "reflexive" truth-conditions of the utterance u; that is, truth-conditions that are conditions on the utterance u itself. These contents are not *alternatives* to the referential content, but supplement it and mesh with it. In the actual world, the proposition that the speaker of u doesn't live in Princeton, and the proposition that Charles doesn't live in Princeton, will have the same truth-value.

In his argument, Kaplan distinguishes between two different questions we might ask concerning the counterfactual circumstance, in which Charles disguised as Paul is the person he points to. One concerns the proposition Pat, the proposition that Kaplan actually expressed—that is, what he actually said, when he said "He lives in Princeton." Kaplan thinks Pat is the proposition that Paul lives in Princeton, and this proposition will still be true in the counterfactual circumstances.

The second question is whether Mike, what Kaplan would have said in the counterfactual circumstance, would have been true in that circumstance. What he would have said is that Charles lives in Princeton. That proposition is false, and would have been false, since we didn't build anything about Charles living anywhere else into the counterfactual circumstance.

Earlier we distinguished Pat and Mike from Erin, the proposition *that the person to whom the speaker points lives in Princeton.* Erin is neither what Kaplan actually said, nor what he would have said. Nevertheless, we think that Erin deserves a place in the account of what happened; that is the theorist can find a role for Erin, even though it is not what is said in either the actual or the counterfactual circumstance.

Although Erin is not what Kaplan said in the counterfactual situation, he committed himself to the truth of it, for it is a truth-condition of his utterance; it is what the world has to be like for the utterance to be true given the meaning of the words used in English and of the gesture of pointing. Since Kaplan realized that he was the speaker, he also committed himself to the content we get by fixing this fact:

Megan: that the person to whom Kaplan points lives in Princeton.

When Charles said "I don't live in Princeton," his plan is roughly as follows:

Kaplan knows English, so he will know that my utterance is true iff the speaker of it does not live in Princeton. He can see that I am the speaker, and he realizes that I am the very person he pointed to a few seconds ago. So he will realize that if my utterance is true, the proposition that the person to whom he pointed lives in Princeton (i.e. Megan) is false, and so realize that what he said was false.

It is Megan that Charles intends to convince Kaplan of the falsity of, when he says "I don't live in Princeton." It wouldn't have worked to say the same thing by saying "Charles doesn't live in Princeton," because the truth- conditions of that utterance don't conflict with Megan.

6   Plans and Implicatures

Understanding implicatures is a matter of intention discovery. Using language to generate implicatures is an intentional activity. But in both generation and understanding, the intentions are complex; they involve not a single intention, but a structure of intentions, to do one thing by doing another [see Chapter 6].

In the case of Charles in disguise, by saying "I don't live in Princeton," he intended to say that he didn't live in Princeton. By saying that, he intended for Kaplan to figure out that what he had just said was false, and that the person in front of him was not Paul. This was part of what Charles meant; that is, he intended for Kaplan to recognize his intention. That is to say, he implicated that Kaplan had said something false, and that it wasn't Paul that he demonstrated. In order for Charles to succeed in this, it didn't suffice to simply say that he didn't live in Princeton; he had to say it in a certain way. He had to say in such a way that the truth-conditions of his utterance were inconsistent with what Kaplan had said, given facts that he could count on Kaplan knowing, in particular that the speaker was the same person Kaplan had just referred to.

Charles plans for Kaplan's reasoning to begin with Kaplan hearing his utterance u, and grasping its utterance-bound content, that the speaker of u doesn't live in Princeton. Then he relies on Kaplan grasping its content given that the speaker is the person he sees in front of him, that that person doesn't live in Princeton. Then, since he will recognize the person he sees in front of him is the same person he just referred to, he will grasp that the person he sees in front of him does not live in Princeton, and that what he said was false. And given his firm belief that Paul lives in Princeton, he will grasp that he wasn't demonstrating Paul.

Charles plans on Kaplan's reasoning beginning with the utterance-bound content, not with what he says. Thus we distinguish between what Charles says, or what is said by his utterance *u*, and the *operative propositions*. These are the propositions that he counts on Kaplan grasping in order to grasp his implicatures.

This example is typical of implicatures; the operative propositions are typically *not* what is said, but propositions that correspond to various truth-conditions that abstract from some of the fact relevant to determining what is said.

Suppose that, having lunch around a table at Tresidder Union at Stanford, David, John and Dikran are talking about boring university towns. Dikran says, "Princeton is even more boring than Palo Alto. I can't imagine living in such a place." John whispers:

(7) He lives in Princeton,

moving his eyes toward a man sitting a couple of tables away from theirs. He implicates that they should lower their voices if they don't want to offend a Princetonian. Now, what's the operative content of John's utterance?

As a matter of fact, Dikran and David cannot see Paul, but John doesn't intend them to turn and look at Paul—causing an embarrassing situation, as Paul would think they were talking about him. In this case, the referential content of John's utterance, *that Paul lives in Princeton*—our old friend Pat—, is not what John intends to communicate to David and Dikran. For all we know, Pat can be a proposition that they both knew before John uttered anything. But John's point was not to remind them about that. In fact, as he didn't want them to turn around rudely to look at Paul, he couldn't reasonably intend them to grasp what he said, in any way that would allow them to recognize it as something they already knew. He is not trying to convince them that the actual world is one in which Paul lives in Princeton. He is trying to convince them that the actual world is one in which a Princetonian sits within earshot of them. It is by convincing them of this, that he hopes to instill in them the belief that it would be a good idea to lower their voices while saying negative things about Princeton.

John's plans more or less as follows.

> David and Dikran will hear my utterance (7). They understand English and realize that it is true iff the person I am referring to with "he" lives in Princeton. They will see me pointing, and although they cannot see to whom I am pointing, they will realize I am pointing to someone nearby, and he is the person to whom I'm referring. Thus they will realize that someone near them is from Princeton. Given a modicum of common sense and politeness, they will realize we should not continue our conversation about the dullness of Princeton, or at least not at such a level so that a person nearby can hear. They will also notice that I am whispering, and figure out that I am doing

that so the person I am referring to won't hear me, and will follow my example.

The operative proposition here, the key to Dikran and David grasping John's implicature, is the proposition that someone nearby them is from Princeton. This is the linchpin of the inferences he expects them to make, in figuring out what he is trying to convey to them and trying to get them to do. This is not what John said. Nor is it merely the utterance-bound content of his utterance. It is a proposition that encodes the truth-conditions of his utterance given a combination of semantical and contextual properties.

What about the proposition he expressed, what he says, that Paul is from Princeton? There is a sense in which David and Dikran will grasp this; they will have various utterance-bound and context-bound conceptions of this proposition:

> That the person referred to by the speaker of (7) is from Princeton;
> That the person John refers to is from Princeton
> That the person behind us and referred to by John is from Princeton.

But John does not plan on them being able to identify this proposition in any way that connects with their pre-existing notions of Paul; in that sense, his plan does not depend on them recognizing what he says.

So here again, the operative propositions are not the propositions that referentialism identifies with what is said. And yet, the referentialist account of what is said permits us to identify the propositions that are operative.

7 Conclusion

We agree with referentialism that what is said by simple utterances involving indexicals, demonstratives and names are singular propositions with the referents of those terms as constituents, in spite of the problems posed for this view by problems of cognitive significance. More is involved in reporting what a person says, and answering the question, "What did she say?" than simply identifying these singular propositions. The questions, to which saying reports provide answers, can be, and typically are, questions about what a person said, in the course of a certain conversation, with utterances that drew on certain notions and beliefs involving those notions, that are relevant to certain actions the sayer might or might not take, or certain sources of information, the sayer might or might not have. Given an appreciation of the complexity and subtlety of such questions and the reports that answer them, we can see how saying what a person said can provide information about utterances that goes beyond the bare identity of the singular propositions.

Grice is right that implicatures are generated by what a person says, if one interprets this to mean that the information needed to figure out the implicatures is the sort of information conveyed by answering questions about what is said. But, in line with what was said in the last paragraph, these answers will not simply identify the singular propositions expressed by the sayer. They will identify that proposition as the proposition expressed in the course of a conversation, with various contextual facts fixed in various ways. A person says something—expresses a singular proposition—by constructing an utterance that has certain truth-conditions. What is said will correspond to the referential content of the utterance, what the world has to be like for the utterance to be true, given facts about meaning and reference. But other truth-conditions of the utterance can be identified by abstracting from some reference-fixing facts, and fixing other contextual facts. The operative propositions, those the grasping of which will lead to grasping the implicatures, can be, and typically are, among these other truth-conditions of the utterance.

Thus, while the insights of Grice and those of the referentialists do not fit together in as simple a way as we conceived at the outset, with the "output" of semantics constituting the "input" to pragmatics, within a general theory of content the consistency of the insights can be appreciated. Referential semantics does provide what Gricean pragmatic needs.[7]

---

[7] The research of the first author was partially supported by a grant of the Spanish Ministry of Education (HUM2006-11663/FISO) and the University of the Basque Country (GIU 08/23). He is also thankful to the Institute for Logic, Cognition, Language and Information (ILCLI). The second author was supported by the University of California at Riverside and Stanford University.

8

Highlights of *Critical Pragmatics*: Reference and the Contents of the Utterance

KEPA KORTA AND JOHN PERRY

1 Introduction

The aim of this paper is to present in a somewhat abridged form the main ideas presented in our recent book *Critical pragmatics: An inquiry into reference and communication* (2011, Cambridge University Press). It should be an easy job, since the basic ideas or insights we attempted to develop there are just three:

1. *Language is a mode of action.* The source of this insight is obviously the English philosopher John L. Austin,[1] who famously claimed that language should be seen as a way of doing things with words. We follow his view, and see acts of using language, that is to say, *utterances*, as having a basic structure that is an instance of the general structure of actions: An agent by moving her body and its parts in various ways, in various circumstances, accomplishes various things. A speaker by making certain noises, performs a locutionary act (expresses a certain proposition), an illocutionary act (e.g., makes a claim, a prediction, a suggestion…), and typically a perlocutionary act (pleases or annoys someone, for instance). Giving an adequate account of utterance meaning and content that matches, and ultimately derives from a reasonable theory of action and mind can rightly be taken as the main goal of our project. [For more about language as a mode of action, see Chapter 16.]

---

[1] With distinguished precedents such as Wittgenstein and Malinowski (see Korta, 2008).

2. *Meaning and content ultimately derive from the speaker's intentions.* Our utterances typically have a communicative goal and are motivated by what Paul Grice called "M-intentions," now most commonly known as "communicative intentions." These are quite a special sort of intention. They have a feature that is characteristic, but not limited to, the use of language: Communicative intentions are overt, i.e., intended to be recognized. Understanding an utterance is basically a process of recognizing the speaker's communicative intentions, whether by guesswork or reasoned inference. This is in conflict with the well-known model of communication as a coding-decoding process, but it is just the natural consequence of the Gricean (and post- and neo-Gricean) approach to pragmatics. Offering a serious alternative to the "code" model of human communication is arguably one of the major contributions of current pragmatic theory, and we aim at contributing our bit.
3. *Utterances have different levels of contents or truth-conditions.* Utterances and other information-carrying events have a variety of truth-conditions or contents. This idea comes from John Perry's distinction between reflexive and referential truth-conditions (Perry 1993 [2000], 2001 [2012]).[2] Once we adopt the view of utterances as acts, the idea of a variety of contents for a single utterance sounds perfectly natural. The idea is that in assigning contents we consider what the rest of the world has to be like for the utterance to occur and be true. And what this amounts to, depends on what we take as fixed. Simply given the constraints on truth-conditions imposed by the meanings of words and phrases that are fixed by the conventions of language gives us one level on content. If we also take as fixed further facts about the utterance (such as the speaker, time, place, and addressee) or about the speaker's communicative intentions, we get further levels.

We see *Critical pragmatics* as a natural and consistent development of these insights. In our humble opinion, these basic points have not been sufficiently taken onboard by contemporary pragmatics. Speaking roughly and briefly, in current pragmatic theory, (1) the idea of language as action is vindicated in theory but forgotten in practice; (2) the role of speaker's intentions is sometimes overestimated (taking over any role that the circumstances of the utterance or conventions may play) and sometimes denounced as involving mysterious entities and processes; and (3) even if some authors provide more than one utterance content to account for certain phenomena,[3] most theories are tied to an assumption we call "mono-propositionalism," namely, the idea that

---

[2] With precedents in his joint work with Jon Barwise (Barwise and Perry, 1983 [1999]) and David Israel (Israel and Perry, 1990, 1991).

[3] Bach, 1999; Neale, 1999; Carston, 2002, are significant examples.

there is one and only one proposition that corresponds to the content of the utterance (once we exclude presuppositions, implicatures, and other non-literal contents).

In these respects, our view is critical of most current pragmatic theories. On the other hand, in our view, pragmatics is critical to linguistic inquiry. It is the branch that makes sense of every other branch of natural language studies; or, perhaps, it is rather the trunk (or the roots) than just a branch of linguistics. This central place we acknowledge to pragmatics and our general assessment of current pragmatic theory constitute the twofold motivation for calling our approach, "Critical Pragmatics."

With this framework for a general pragmatic theory, we take the study of singular reference as a starting point for a number of reasons. First, singular reference has been a central topic in the philosophy of language from its origins in the works of Frege and Russell. Pace Strawson (1950) or Donnellan (1966), it has usually been conceived to belong to the realm of semantics. This has not only distorted an adequate account of reference (that we take to be primarily a pragmatic phenomenon) but has also impeded the proper delimitation of pragmatics with respect to semantics. Second, the topic of reference is at the heart of the reflexive-referential theory of content (Perry, 2001 [2012]), which is in turn at the very heart of Critical Pragmatics. Our goal is to elaborate a fully pragmatic account of singular reference. Third, limiting our attention to singular reference in utterances of simple declarative sentences was a good initial test for our theory. If it doesn't work well enough in this relatively simple case, it won't work with more complicated ones.

Here we are not going to spend much effort to assess other theories. We will start by introducing some basic notions on our theory of action and mind that are required for the presentation of Critical Pragmatics. Then we will discuss, one by one, the main linguistic tools for singular reference. And, finally, we will draw some comparisons at the end of the paper.

2 Acts, Roles, and Files

Acts involve agents at times and places, doing mental operations, and moving their bodies and their parts (including vocal cords). The term "token" is sometimes used for what we call the utterance, which is also sometimes called the "tokening." The term is also used for the product or result of such acts, the burst of sound or the marks on paper. We distinguish between utterances, acts, and tokens, products, to avoid this "process/product" ambiguity. We call such basic actions "executions." Depending on the circumstances in which they occur, executions have various results. The acts of an agent have a direct effect on objects that play various roles in the agent's life. Given the role-structure of those objects, acts have more and more remote effects. Following

Israel, Perry and Tutiya (1993), we call all these results "accomplishments," whether or not the agent had them in mind or not, intended to achieve them or not.

Typically, when an agent acts, she perceives the object or objects to which she stands in a "direct pragmatic relation," that is to say, she can directly act upon them, or perform acts the results of which directly depend on these objects. These objects are perceived as standing in relation to other objects, which are the ones that the agent wants to have an (indirect) effect on. Agents take objects they want to act upon as playing certain roles in their lives, roles in which the roles of the objects with which we have a direct pragmatic relation are nested. This information about the objects with which the agent is in a direct relation are stored in a special kind of file or *notion*, which we call the *agent's buffer*. Let us clarify a bit what we mean by "roles," "notions," and "buffers."

2.1 Roles

Roles are functional relations between objects that humans use to organize information about them. To provide important facts about an object we often provide a list of key roles, and the objects that play those roles with respect to that object. Suppose we want to know more about Jennifer. We can ask: Who's your mother? Your father? Birthplace? Year of birth? Those roles and the objects that play them give us information about her. Sometimes a single object plays various roles with respect to the agent: The thing she sees, the thing in front of her that she takes and is now in her hands, the thing in her mouth, the thing with a certain taste, etc. When a single object plays various different roles with respect to some other object, we'll say that the roles are *linked*. Role-linking is crucial in our account. Often roles like "the person in front of me," "the speaker of the utterance," and "the referent of that use of 'I'" will be linked for the person who perceives an utterance. *Nested* roles will also be important. That's the basic structure of relations we exploit to achieve results of distant objects, that is, objects with which we have an indirect pragmatic relation. I pick up the phone and talk to its mouthpiece, because it is (somehow) connected to another phone, and thus I will create some sounds on this that the person at the other end will hear: "the phone I'm talking to," "the phone (somehow) connected to the phone I'm talking to," "the person holding the phone (somehow) connected to the phone I'm talking to" are just simple examples of increasingly nested roles.[4]

Of course, among all the roles we will consider, *utterance-relative* roles are going to occupy a prominent role. Roles such as "the speaker of the

---

[4] This paper, as the book, is co-authored, but here again we find the use of the first-person singular pronoun too useful to give it up.

utterance," "the place of the utterance," and "the time of the utterance," not only have a distinguished function in determining the contents of the utterance, but, as we shall see, also are essential to our account of the pragmatics of reference, for indexicals, which are designed to exploit utterance-relative roles, are our paradigms of reference.

It seems clear then that information about the roles that objects play in our lives, directly and as parts of the remote environment, is useful information about them. The agent's information about singular objects is stored in "mental files" that we call *notions*.[5]

2.2 Notions, Buffers, and Cognitive Fixes

Notions store the information (or misinformation) we have about an object. Notions are created in different ways, when we meet people, or see buildings, or read about them, or hear about them, for instance. A notion is *of* the object it was introduced to keep track of.

We further distinguish between *detached notions* and *buffers*. Notions are born as buffers. Typically, buffers are more or less ephemeral notions that store the contemporary roles than an object in our immediate surrounding plays. Think about the cup of coffee you're holding, the coffee it contains, its aroma, its temperature. Your notions about the cup and the coffee are buffers. They originated when you took the cup and prepared your espresso. Once you drink the coffee and place the cup in the dishwasher, they will no longer be buffers but possibly *detached* notions.

Detached notions are relatively stable, and usually include information (and misinformation) obtained in multifarious ways. Identifying or recognizing a particular basically consists in linking a buffer of an object with a detached notion of the same object.

Buffers and detached notions are a useful way to talk about the ways agents "have objects in mind" to borrow Keith Donnellan's phrase. There are different ways of having objects in mind, depending on what kind of notion one has—detached or buffer—and how it was formed. If it is a buffer, it may be visual, auditory, tactual, olfactory, or one in which these roles are linked and nested in various ways. Most importantly for our account, it may involve roles such as being the person one is reading about, or the person the speaker of the utterance is referring to. If it is a detached notion it may involve information such as its name, an image, or its past role in one's life. Borrowing a phrase from another referentialist, Howard Wettstein, we call these ways of having objects in mind "cognitive fixes," and with many referentialists, we think they have a critical role in an account of how and why we manage to refer to objects by our utterances.

---

[5] See Recanati, 2012, for a recent monograph.

In a nutshell, our basic view on reference is the following one: In trying to refer to an object O by the sub-utterance of a particular singular term T, in a typical communicative setting, the speaker exploits a particular cognitive fix she has on O, intending the hearer H to get his particular cognitive fix on O, such that it facilitates the comprehension of the whole utterance contents and implicatures. That is to say that reference is a process of management of cognitive fixes by the speaker. The speaker wants the hearer to have a cognitive fix on a certain object. To do this she creates another object, the utterance. She plans on the hearer first thinking of the object as the referent of the utterance, and then, using knowledge of language and context, to that cognitive fix. We see this as constituting a basic but subtle structure of referential plans that we dub GDTPA structure, for Grammar, Directing, Target, Path, and Auxiliary intentions and roles. We will focus here on the three most important.

3   Directing, Path, and Target Intentions

Suppose I see an object across the street that I identify as a man. I want to refer to him. I have various cognitive fixes on him. Some come from my buffer on him: "short guy walking across the street," "man across the street moving in a strange way." Some come from recognition; a previously detached notion of him is combined with the buffer: "the person named 'George W. Bush,'" "one of the most regrettable characters in recent US history," "the president who had an accident while watching TV," "the man Jon Stewart was referring to in his show once again last night…" It is up to me to decide which of these cognitive fixes I choose to exploit when I try to refer to him. If I choose "man over there," my perceptual cognitive fix on the object, a typical way to refer to him will be to use the third-person pronoun "he." My intention to refer to an object exploiting a particular cognitive fix is what we call the "directing intention."[6] It is up to the speaker as to which cognitive fix she chooses, but it is a matter of facts, to begin with, whether there is anything out there upon which she has a cognitive fix or there is nothing. If the latter, when I utter "he" my attempt ends in a failure. If the former, I'll refer to whatever object is there. It might not be a person but a statue; or it might be a person, but not a man; it might be a man, but not George W. Bush, if it wasn't the person I took him to be. It doesn't matter. I'll refer to whatever is there as the origin of my cognitive fix. So, again, I'm authoritative about

---

[6] Inspired on, and hopefully not deviating too much from, Kaplan's (1989a) notion of directing intention. [See Chapter 6, "Intentions to refer," for more on the GDTPA structure of referential plans; and Chapter 15, "Language and luck", for a further discussion on cognitive fixes and referential convergence of demonstratives.]

which cognitive fix I exploit when intending to refer, but what I achieve in referring to with my utterance is a matter of facts. Intentions and facts cooperate when we succeed in referring to whom or what we intend to refer.

Suppose that, by referring to the man over there, I intended to refer to George W. Bush, and, contrary to my beliefs, the man I see over there is not George W. Bush. Uttering "he" and exploiting my perceptual cognitive fix on the man over there, I will refer to the man over there, not to George W. Bush.

A more secure way to refer to George W. Bush in that situation would be to exploit my detached notion on George W. Bush while uttering the name "George W. Bush." Given my belief that the man over there is George W. Bush, I might well intend to refer to the man over there using that name. But if the world doesn't cooperate and my belief is false, in using the name I will refer to its bearer, to George W. Bush, and not to the man over there. My directing intention, plus the facts, determine to whom I refer.

A third option is to use "he," with the directing intention of referring to the person you are thinking about via your detached notion. "He" is flexible in this way; its reference can be governed by the perceptual buffer, or by the detached notion. That latter use is common when you remember almost everything about a person except their name. In this case I'd refer to the origin of the detached notion—that is, George W. Bush, and not to the man over there, given that, in the imagined circumstances, he is not George W. Bush.

So the directing intention that concerns the cognitive fix being exploited, and facts about the actual object occupying that role jointly determine the object referred to. The choice of a demonstrative over a name, or the other way around, gives evidence of my intentions. Demonstratives seem most naturally useful when exploiting a perceptual cognitive fix or buffer; names seem the natural option when detached notions are at stake. We'll study below the cases of indexicals and descriptions, but notice that typically in communicative situations that will not be enough. The third option was a simple way for me to refer to George W. Bush without having to pronounce his name. On the other hand, it provides almost no information to the hearer. This is the case with most demonstratives (Russell's logically proper names among them): easy devices for referring; not very useful for getting understood. If, thinking about George W. Bush, I utter, "He is a moron," I would be referring to George W. Bush, but I wouldn't be giving you much information about the person I'm referring to. And usually I would be interested in giving you a bit more than, say, "the person I'm referring to by my use of 'he.'" It might be crucial to my communicative plan that my hearer recognizes him as the man over there that happens to be George W. Bush: Given the impulsive nature of my hearer, he will likely react with a smart, not very nasty, but fair insult that George W. Bush will no doubt hear as well as the members of the secret service, who will react against my hearer and not me. Suppose that's my plan: to get George W. Bush publicly insulted without the risks of delivering the insult.

In a typical communicative situation, the speaker intends the hearer to have a certain cognitive fix on the object that she's referring to. We call this the "target intention." And this also affects the speaker's choice of referential term. Her referential plan does not aim simply to succeed in reference, but also to succeed in the hearer getting the appropriate cognitive fix on the object she's referring to. So, the speaker's plan includes an intention about the cognitive fix she exploits to refer to the object she's trying to refer, the directing intention, and an intention about the hearer's cognitive fix on the very same object. It is natural to add a third type of intention about the linking of the various roles that the object referred to plays in the lives of the speaker and the hearer. The speaker has to anticipate, however loosely, a path from the cognitive fix she has on the object—for instance, "the man I see over there"—through the role she creates—"the object I'm referring to"—via the object she produces—the utterance—to the cognitive fix the hearers get on the intended referent—say, "the short man I see over there"—via the linking of other roles that the object plays—"the object the speaker is referring to by his use of 'he'"—via the perception of the utterance. This is what we call the "path intention."

These three intentions (plus the grammatical and auxiliary intention) explain the different aspects of our referential intentions in our communicative acts. These intentions are Gricean; that is, they are overt, intended to be recognized by the hearer. And the goal is not simply to refer to a certain individual but to do it in a certain way: exploiting a particular cognitive fix, which opens a certain path of links between roles of that object to get a certain cognitive fix on the part of the hearer.

We can sum up the paradigmatic relation between the types of referential terms and the types of cognitive fix exploited in the following table:

Table 1

Type of expression	Type of cognitive fix
Demonstrative	Perceptual (broadly)
Indexical	Utterance-bound
Name	Network-bound
Description	Descriptive

This gives a correct overall picture of that relation. We will now present the details for each type of referential term in turn.

4 Demonstratives

Despite the title of his monograph "Demonstratives" (1989a), Kaplan didn't offer a formal treatment of demonstratives, but both the monograph and its sequel "Afterthoughts" (1989b) contain a lot of thinking that has been largely responsible for the debate about how these devices of direct reference get their referents. Do they have a meaning that, without entering into the proposition expressed, determines the referent? Is it the speaker's intention, the "directing intention" as Kaplan dubs it, determinative? Or is it the act of demonstrating, e.g., the pointing, which does the job? We advanced our view in the previous section. We will now illustrate it slightly adapting one of Kaplan's (1975) best-known examples.

A philosophy professor is giving a lecture in a familiar lecture hall at UCLA. For years, a portrait of Rudolf Carnap has hung behind the podium on the stage of the hall. At one point the professor points behind himself, without looking, and says,

(1) That's a painting of the greatest philosopher of the 20th Century.

But some graduate students have replaced the portrait of Carnap with one of Dick Cheney. Did the professor say something false about a portrait of Cheney? That seems to be the unequivocal verdict of the theory that holds that demonstrations are determinative. Did he say something true about the portrait of Carnap, the one he intended to point to, in a rather misleading way? If intention simply determined reference, that would be the verdict.

Our concepts of directing intentions and target intentions permit a more subtle view. The cognitive fix on the portrait the professor intended to establish for his hearers was perceptual; that's why he pointed; he wanted the audience to see the portrait behind him, and impart the belief that it portrayed the greatest philosopher of the 20th Century. This intention was successful; the audience did come to have a perceptual fix on the portrait. But he intended that, by having a cognitive fix on the portrait to which he drew their intention, they would have a cognitive fix on the portrait he remembered, which his motivating belief was about, and that he would impart a belief about that portrait; these further intentions did not succeed.

This is how it works on our theory in more detail. The professor has a detached notion of the portrait, associated with the idea of being a portrait of Carnap, and hence the greatest philosopher of the 20th Century. This notion is a component of his primary referential intention, to refer to that very portrait. He has a false belief, that the portrait is hanging behind him and is thus playing an epistemic-pragmatic role in his life. It is the portrait he would see if he turned around, and that he can point to by pointing behind himself. Thus, he believes it is the portrait he can refer to using the demonstrative "that," which is suited by its meaning for referring to things the speaker can draw a hearer's attention to by pointing. His directing intention is to exploit this role the portrait is playing in his life, and refer to it with "that." The portrait that plays that role is the one he refers to, for the directing intention is determinative. So, although his plan is to refer to the Carnap portrait, he in fact refers to the Cheney portrait.

The path intention is pretty straightforward. He intends that the audience will hear his utterance, see that he is the speaker, notice his gesture, and come to have a perceptual fix on the portrait. He probably has the further intention of getting them to believe that Carnap is the greatest philosopher of the 20th Century (or at least to realize that that is his opinion); some of them will recognize that the portrait is of Carnap, and they will soon tell the others. But things don't go according to plan. Since he doesn't refer to the object he planned to refer to, he doesn't say what he planned to say. In fact he says something quite false, and he is responsible for doing so. This seems to account for the intuitions about the case.

Thus, on our theory, what one refers to is determined by a mix of internal and external factors. The speaker's directing intention determines that the referent will be the object that plays the intended epistemic-pragmatic role. But which object plays that role isn't up to the speaker, but to the rest of the world, which may include pranksters. The concept of the directing intention draws the line between the internal contribution and the external contribution.

This view of demonstratives combined with the concept of *relativized* truth-conditions, that we will clarify below, allow us to deal with the various problems raised about the cognitive significance of utterances containing co-referential demonstrative uses and cases of no-reference, that is, uses of demonstratives that demonstrate nothing. Space limitations don't allow us to present that here; see Chapter 5 of *Critical pragmatics*.

5 The Essential Indexical and Varieties of Truth-Conditions

Chapter 6 of *Critical pragmatics* is devoted to our view on what are known as "pure indexicals," with special attention to the first-person singular pronoun "I," and the adverbs "here" and "now." Here we will briefly introduce a few basic ideas about "I" to present another key concept of our theory about the variety of the contents of truth-conditions of an utterance.

The paradigmatic structure of intentions for the use of "I" is straightforward. The first person is standardly used to convey to others the content of beliefs about oneself with one's self-notion as a component. The directing intention is to use the first person to convey a belief about oneself; the target intention will be to make the hearer have a belief with the same content, but a different cognitive fix—except in the case where a person leaves a reminder to himself. The intended path will begin with the fix the hearer has on the speaker as the speaker of the perceived utterance, and then, if it is a face-to-face conversation, as the person the hearer is perceiving and interacting with, and from there to whatever the target role is.

Suppose that Larraitz meets John at a conference and introduces herself saying,

(2) I am Larraitz.

If we assume a referential semantics for indexicals and names, Larraitz could have expressed the same thing by saying,

(3) I am I

or

(4) Larraitz is Larraitz.

But neither of these utterances would have achieved what she achieved with (2). John's first fix on the subject will be as "speaker of the utterance I am hearing"; then he will link this role with "person I am seeing before me." Then he will realize that if the statement is true, the person he sees before him is Larraitz, and this is Larraitz's goal.

Larraitz here exploits the fact that she has two cognitive fixes on herself. She has her self-notion. But she also, like her friends, neighbors, and associates, has her name. She wants to impart to John two cognitive fixes, one as the person talking to him, one as Larraitz.

The semantics of "I" is exhausted by our adaptation of Kaplan's character rule: An utterance of "I" refers to the speaker of the utterance. That is, "I" is a device a speaker can use, no matter who he is, or how self-deluded he is, to refer to himself or herself; that is, to refer to the person with whom he or she is identical. As referentialists about indexicals, we think that an utterance containing the pronoun "I" expresses a proposition about the person who utters it; i.e., the proposition expressed includes the speaker, and not any condition on her, not even the condition of being the speaker. Thus, (2), (3) and (4) express the same proposition, namely, that Larraitz is identical with herself. That's why an utterance by Kepa, produced in Donostia on August 15, 2012, at 17:00 UTC, of

(5) I am here now

expresses the proposition that Kepa is in Donostia on August 15, 2012, at 17:00 UTC, a proposition that would have been true even if Kepa hadn't uttered it, or Donostia had another name, or the Radio Consultative Committee didn't establish the Coordinated Universal Time as the standard. We follow Kaplan in taking these truth-conditions as the proposition expressed by the speaker who produces (5). This is a contingent proposition. Kepa was in fact there at that particular time, but he might have been somewhere else.

However, as Kaplan notes, there is a sense in which (5) is analytically true, because any utterance u of "I am here now" by anyone, anywhere, at any time will be true if and only if the speaker of u is at the place of u at the time of u. This is not the proposition expressed by the speaker. Kepa didn't say that by producing (5): He said something contingent about himself, Donostia and that particular holiday at 17:00 UTC (7:00 pm local time); and he said nothing necessary about the speaker, the place and the time of (5). We conceive these set of truth-conditions not as two different propositions Kepa expressed, or two different things he said, but as two different kinds of truth-conditions that all utterances systematically have: "utterance-bound" and "utterance-independent" truth-conditions. The utterance-bound truth-conditions of an utterance are determined by the conventional meaning of the sentence uttered and the fact that the utterance has occurred. In the case of (5), the utterance-bound truth-conditions would yield

(6) That (5) is true if and only if the speaker of (5) is at the place of (5) at the time of (5)

The utterance-independent or referential truth-conditions of (5), on the other hand, are

(7) That (5) is true if and only if Kepa is in Donostia on August 15, 2012, at 17:00 UTC.

and they are obtained once we set the referents for the indexicals "I," "here," and "now."

In general, the referential truth-conditions of utterances containing indexicals, demonstratives, and names are determined once the referents for the referential devices are fixed by facts about the speaker's intentions, context, and, as we shall see below, by naming conventions, and they correspond to what referentialists take to be the only truth-conditions of utterances of this sort: their only content; the only proposition they expressed. We are referentialist and we agree that this kind of utterances express what philosophers call *singular* propositions and that they (usually) encode what the speaker says in uttering them.[7] But we contend that, besides referential or utterance-independent truth-conditions, there are also utterance-bound truth-conditions that derive naturally from our view of utterances as acts and fit perfectly with the picture of referential expressions as role-management devices. In fact, there is a variety of truth-conditions from the most utterance-bound to the most utterance-independent, depending on the facts that are taken as given. We will introduce them in the following section while we present our account of proper names.[8]

6 Proper Names

For an individual to be referentially accessible to a speaker via a name "N," the speaker needs to be able to utter "N" as a part of what we call a "name-notion network" or "network" for short (see also Perry, 2012a). The idea is similar to Kripke's "chains of communication," Donnellan's "referential chains," or Chastain's "anaphoric chains" (Kripke, 1980; Donnellan, 1970; Chastain, 1975). Except in the few cases in which the speaker performs an act of "baptism," in using a proper name the speaker intends to co-refer with a previous use of that name by another speaker, or at least intends to co-refer with a previous utterance of the name, if the previous utterance referred to anything. The practices of co-referring and conditional co-referring (or "coco-referring," see Chapter 7 of *Critical pragmatics*) form a network that supports a convention to refer to an individual with a name. A use of a name that exploits a convention refers to the origin of the network that supports the convention, if it has one; otherwise, the conventions and the use are empty.

If referring to an object using a name can just consist in an act of coco-referring, it seems to follow that there are very few conditions on referring via names, and this seems right. In particular, you don't need an utterance-independent description that identifies the referent.

But names can also point to information that one has about an individual. Names also involve cognitive fixes we have on objects. A nominal cognitive fix involves a name, a (detached) notion associated with the name that

---

[7] We qualify the sentence with a bracketed "usually" because we think that in cases like (2) above other truth-conditions are "promoted" to the category of what is said. This might even be the general case when we consider Grice's category of what is said versus the implicatures of an utterance. See Chapter 11 of *Critical pragmatics*.

[8] With a different terminology the distinction responds to Perry's (2001) distinction between "reflexive" and "referential" truth-conditions at the two extremes of a family or more or less incremental truth-conditions.

involves all sorts of information (and possibly misinformation) about the object, and a network of which that notion is a part. The object plays a role in the life of a person, in virtue of having such a cognitive fix.

Names are not as clearly related to perceptual and utterance-relative roles as demonstratives and indexicals are. But they also work as role-management devices. Suppose the famous actress Meg Ryan sits to John's right at dinner, and tells him she wants the salt. The salt shaker is by his left but out of his reach so he tells Kepa,

(8) Meg Ryan would like the salt.

Kepa has a nominal cognitive fix with the name "Meg Ryan," a detached notion of her, and an accessible network. In this case, John expects Kepa to link that notion with a buffer or a perceptual cognitive fix of her as "the person sitting to John's right," so that he hands him the salt-shaker and he satisfies Meg's desire for salt. Here John exploits his nominal cognitive fix on Meg Ryan and aims at Kepa's role-linking between his own nominal cognitive fix on her (path) and his perceptual cognitive fix on her as the person to John's right (target).

Suppose now that after a conference reception, John is tired and asks Kepa if someone could drive him to the hotel. Kepa says,

(9) Joana is very nice.

Let's suppose John recognizes Joana as a proper name for a person but knows nothing about its bearer. On the basis only of his knowledge of English, he would only understand the "utterance-bound" truth-conditions of Kepa's utterance:

Utterance-bound truth-conditions
Given that (9) is in English, has the syntax it does,
and "is very nice" means what it does in English,
(9) is true if and only if
$\exists x, \exists N, \exists y$ such that x is the speaker of (9),
N is the network x exploits with "Joana,"
y is the origin of N
and y is very nice.

Of course, he heard Kepa saying it, and recognized him as the speaker of (9), so he understood something like:

Speaker-bound truth-conditions
   Given that (9) is in English, has the syntax it does,
   "is very nice" means what it does in English,
   and Kepa is the speaker of (9),
   (9) is true if and only if
   ∃N, ∃y such that N is the network Kepa exploits with "Joana,"
   y is the origin of N
   and y is very nice.

Now, suppose that John remembers nothing about N_{Joana}, except that it's the network Kepa is exploiting by his use of "Joana." In that case, we could describe the content he gets from (9) as:

Network-bound truth-conditions
   Given that (9) is in English, has the syntax it does,
   "is very nice" means what it does in English,
   Kepa is the speaker of (2),
   and N_{Joana} is the network Kepa exploits with "Joana,"
   (9) is true if and only if
   ∃y such that y is the origin of N_{Joana} and y is very nice.

Knowing the network-bound truth-conditions doesn't count as understanding what Kepa said by (9), but John will still be in position to refer to Joana, that is, to coco-refer with Kepa's utterance, for instance, by asking, "Who is Joana?" The network-bound truth-conditions are probably what we most often understand when understanding an utterance containing a proper name. And that is probably all we rely on to produce an utterance containing a proper name. Contrary to what Russell claimed, we need not be acquainted with the bearer of the name to use and understand the use of proper names. Now, for various reasons, we keep the concept of what is said (the proposition expressed, the content) to apply to the content that includes the referent itself; to the referential truth-conditions of the utterance.

If John remembers something about Joana, namely, the origin of the network N_{Joana}, he will get what Kepa said, the "official content" of (9) or its

Referential truth-conditions
   Given that (9) is in English, has the syntax it does,
   "is very nice" means what it does in English,
   Kepa is the speaker of (9),
   N_{Joana} is the network Kepa exploits with "Joana"
   and y is the origin of N_{Joana},

(9) is true if and only if
y is very nice.

To sum up, even though names do not involve any description uniquely selecting the individual referred to, naming involves a network of utterances and (possibly thin) notions that supports coco-referring. If the network has an origin, we manage to refer to an individual. If it doesn't, we don't refer (and, then, we don't co-refer) to anything. But the plurality of contents and the use of names as role-management devices allow us to relate our use of names in both cases to the plans the speaker has in mind; this provides us with the tools we need to understand the cognitive significance of co-referring names, and the content of empty names. But we cannot go into more details here now. [See Chapter 12, for fictional names, in particular.]

7 Definite Descriptions

Our view on definite descriptions and their referential and attributive uses is quite close to Donnellan's (1966). It locates the critical difference between the two kinds of use at the level of the speaker's intentions, but it is finer-grained when spelling out the difference. Put it shortly, the speaker's directing, path, and target intentions in the attributive use involve a mere descriptive fix on the individual. On the referential use, even if the path intention involves the descriptive fix, the directing and target intentions involve a perceptual or notional fix the speaker exploits and expects the hearer to be able to grasp.

The distinction can be made clearer using the various kinds of utterance contents. So far we had utterance-bound, speaker-bound, network-bound, and referential truth-conditions of an utterance. Referential truth-conditions is the level that usually corresponds to the proposition expressed or the content of the utterance. At this level, we adopt a Russellian (though not exactly Russell's) theory of descriptions, in that they include an identifying condition of the individual, not the individual itself. The referential truth-conditions of an utterance u of "Smith's murderer is insane" would be the following ones:

Given that u is in English,
its syntax, the meaning of the words,
and the fact that Smith is the origin of the exploited Smith-network,
u is true if and only if
there is a unique person who murdered Smith, and that person is insane.

This would be the content of the utterance when the speaker is looking at Smith's mutilated body, and with nobody in mind, she utters u. The content of the belief she wants to impart is that whoever murdered Smith is insane. Her target cognitive fix is merely descriptive.

In Donnellan's example of the referential use, speaker and hearer are at the trial of Jones, who, we assume, did actually murder Smith. Watching Jones's strange behavior, the speaker intends to impart the belief that Jones is insane by her utterance u' of "Smith's murderer is insane." In this case, the speaker aims at the "designational" or "referential*" truth-conditions of her utterance:

> Given that u' is in English, its syntax,
> the meaning of the words,
> the fact that Smith is the origin of the exploited Smith-network, and the fact that Jones murdered Smith,
> u' is true if and only if
> Jones is insane.

This amounts to a singular proposition with Jones as a constituent. Now, the difference between a referential and an attributive use of "Smith's murderer" is in the speaker's intention, as Donnellan suggested. Is the speaker intending to impart the referential* truth-conditions of her utterance? Or is she just intending the hearer's understanding to stop at the referential truth-conditions? Or both?

The last is a real option. Whenever there is an individual uniquely satisfying a description, an utterance containing it will have both referential and referential* truth-conditions. The latter has to be true for the former to be true. And that can be the speaker's intention: using a description essentially to designate the individual that uniquely fits the description. So, our account allows a double attributive-referential use of a description. When there is no intention to use the description essentially, but just as a means—as good as a name, a demonstrative, or a complex demonstrative—to designate Jones, we would have a referential use, in which the speaker intentionally imparts the referential* truth-conditions of her utterance. When the speaker just wants to impart a descriptive cognitive fix with no further target intention, her use is merely attributive.

The description "Smith's murderer" is a complete description, since it provides an identifying condition that applies to one and only one individual. But most often we use incomplete definite descriptions like "the table," "my neighbor," "the book," "the computer," which are insufficient to pick out a unique individual. Our account of incomplete descriptions goes along with Perry's (1986) concept of unarticulated constituents. Again, we cannot go into that here, but Chapter 8 and Chapter 9 of *Critical pragmatics* will give you all the specifics of our view on descriptions and unarticulated constituents.

8 Utterance Contents and Implicatures

For many people, one of the most innovative and controversial contributions of *Critical pragmatics* is our assumption that utterances have a variety of truth-conditions. Of course, this insight comes from Perry (2001 [2012]) and is present in earlier works by him. What we do in critical pragmatics is to use it in the account of a variety of phenomena in pragmatic theory. The idea seems pretty natural to us; a natural consequence of the serious consideration of utterances as acts. However, it has distinguished our approach from practically all contemporary pragmatic theories, which are, as we like to put it, by and large mono-propositionalist. That is to say, leaving implicatures and presuppositions aside, they take utterances to have one single content, or one single set of truth-conditions. They can be referentialist or descriptivist about the proposition expressed; they can be contextualist, minimalist or indexicalist, moderate or radical about the amount of pragmatic "intrusion" into what is said; but they will all consider that the proposition expressed or what is said coincides with the unique content of the utterance, its single set of truth-conditions. We disagree.[9]

We claim that utterances systematically have a variety of contents or truth-conditions, from the minimal utterance-bound (reflexive) to the utterance-independent (referential and referential*). We are happy to agree that only one of these contents should be taken as "what is said" or "the proposition expressed" by the speaker. But this is no reason to ignore the other kinds of content that explain, for instance, the workings of reference, with referential expressions as devices of role management.

We hope we have shown convincingly the advantages of adopting our content-pluralistic view. The problems with mono-propositionalism seem quite clear to us. Basically, they come to the following: one is inevitably led to impose too many, possibly incompatible requirements on a single proposition. Take, for example, Searle's speech act theory and his notion of propositional content (Searle, 1969). On the one hand, being, together with the illocutionary force, the main component of an elementary speech act, we are told that, in the right circumstances, the following utterances may share a common propositional content:[10]

---

[9] On how we see our position on the debate between minimalism and contextualism, see Korta and Perry, 2007b [Chapter 2 of this volume], 2007c.

[10] For keeping things easy, we are just considering three kinds of illocutionary force: assertive, directive, and commissive.

(10) John shut the door.
(11) John, please, shut the door!
(12) I will shut door [uttered by John].

Their propositional content includes John, a particular door, and the action of shutting it. Their illocutionary force is different—e.g., (10) is an assertion, (11) a request, and (12) a promise—but their propositional content is the same. If this is so, the proposition needs to include John himself, and not any description, name, demonstrative or indexical referring to him, and the time parameter needs to be "detensed." Otherwise, we would have different propositional contents for (10), (11), and (12).

On the other hand, when the theory considers "propositional content conditions" of a speech act, the requirements on the proposition change. A promise like (12), for instance, establishes that the propositional content must represent a future act of the speaker and a request, in contrast, determines that the propositional content must represent a future act by the addressee. This means that speaker and addressee, and the future tense need to be represented in the propositional content, but this goes against our initial characterization of propositional content. As we argue in Chapter 10 of *Critical pragmatics* (see also Chapter 3 of this volume), speech act theory demands a pluralistic theory of contents, with utterance-bound and utterance-independent propositions to do the various jobs.

With regard to Sperber and Wilson's Relevance Theory (Sperber and Wilson, 1986; Wilson and Sperber, 2012), we think that their account of utterance understanding also demands the variety of contents of the utterance that we distinguish. Take their utterance comprehension strategy or heuristics:

(a) Follow a path of least effort in constructing an interpretation of the utterance (and in particular **in resolving ambiguities and referential indeterminacies, in going beyond linguistic meaning,** in supplying contextual assumptions, computing implicatures, etc.).
(b) Stop when your expectations of relevance are satisfied.
(Quoted in Wilson and Sperber, 2012: 7, emphasis added)

There is a clear sense in which this relevance-theoretic comprehension strategy predicts the existence of a variety of contents. Interpreted according to our view, the hearer might well stop at the utterance-bound content, without "going beyond linguistic meaning" and without "resolving referential indeterminacies," because the utterance-bound content is relevant enough. Or she might go a bit further and stop at the speaker-bound content, or the network-bound content, without going through the reasoning required to fix the referents of referential expressions. In other words, the relevance-theoretic "explicature" does not amount to a fully enriched referential content but to any of a variety of contents, from utterance-bound to utterance-independent, depending on considerations of relevance. In that sense, relevance theory is not a mono-propositionalist view on utterance content, but it requires a pluralistic view like ours. The differences between critical pragmatics and relevance theory, then, if any, lie elsewhere.

9 Conclusions

Unfortunately, we cannot extend our space and time limits further. There are many issues that we barely mentioned and some that we didn't mention at all. Unarticulated constituents and the solutions to various classic reference puzzles are some of the former. The delimitation between semantics and pragmatics and the solution to Grice's circle are some of the latter. They are all discussed in *Critical pragmatics* (see also Chapter 4 and Chapter 9 in this volume).

During the last few years, a number of people have been working on various applications of the insights of critical pragmatics. Joana Garmendia (2010, 2011) has elaborated a theory of irony; Larraitz Zubeldia (2010) applied it to the pragmatic study of reportative particles; María de Ponte (Ponte and Vázquez, 2012; Korta and de Ponte, 2014) used it for the analysis of tense and time; Eros Corazza (Corazza and Korta, 2010; Corazza, 2011) showed its value for the explanation of subsentential utterances, among other things; and Richard Vallée (2012) developed it for the analysis of relational adjectives. The journey of critical pragmatics has just started, but it promises to bring some bits of truth and lots of fun.[11]

---

[11] The work of the first author has been partially supported by a grant of the Basque Government (IT32310) and the Spanish Ministry of Economy and Competitive ness (FFI200908574 and FFI201237726). He would like to thank the members of the group on Language, Action and Thought at the Institute for Logic, Cognition, Language and Information (ILCLI) of the University of the Basque Country (UPVEHU). The second author thanks for support to the Philosophy Department at the University of California Riverside and to CSLI at Stanford University. Both authors want to thank Istvan Kecskes for his enormous patience and invaluable help.

9

Squaring the Circle

KEPA KORTA AND JOHN PERRY

1 Introduction

Grice (1967a [1989]) famously distinguished between what a speaker said by an utterance, on the one hand, and what she implicated by saying what she said, on the other. This was widely taken, at the time, as providing a clear-cut distinction between semantics and pragmatics. Semantics would deal with "what is said," also known as "the proposition expressed" by the utterance (or sentence in context), its "propositional content."[1] (See Kaplan, 1989a, for a classic statement). Pragmatics would be concerned with implicatures and any other aspect of meaning not pertaining to the truth-conditional content of the utterance. As Gazdar (1979) famously put it

PRAGMATICS = MEANING − TRUTH-CONDITIONS.

But things were soon shown to be not so simple. Figuring out the reference of many natural language expressions seems to require reasoning the same sorts of pragmatic reasoning involved in the generation and understanding of Gricean implicatures. We have pragmatics intruding on the realm of semantics.[2]

Grice's initial impact on pragmatic theory was due to the wide range of applications for his theory, but as with all philosophical theories, considerable critical attention was paid to fundamental ideas and distinctions. Interest first focused on his distinctions between conventional and conversational

---

[1] The category of conventional implicatures doesn't fit this picture, however, since being the result of the semantics (of certain words) of the sentence uttered, they do not contribute, according to Grice, to what is said.

[2] For a recent defense of Gazdar's view on the semantics/pragmatics divide that attempts to avoid Grice's circle, see Capone, 2006.

143

implicatures, and particularized and generalized ones. With time, attention turned to the concept of "what is said" and the extent to which this is affected by "pragmatic intrusion," that is, the extent to which understanding what is said by the speaker requires the intervention of pragmatic processes.

The issue of the amount of pragmatic intrusion into the semantic content of the utterance is at the heart of the debate held by literalists (or minimalists) and contextualists and a number of positions in between (indexicalists, situationalists, and radical and moderate of all sorts). Despite their differences, they seem subject to what Levinson (2000) dubbed "Grice's circle":

> Grice's account makes implicature dependent on a prior determination of "the said." The said in turn depends on disambiguation, indexical resolution, reference fixing, not to mention ellipsis unpacking and generality narrowing. But each of these processes, which are prerequisites to determining the proposition expressed, may themselves depend crucially on processes that look indistinguishable from implicatures. Thus what is said seems both to determine and to be determined by implicature (Levinson, 2000, 186).

Thus, within the Gricean picture, the processes of intention-recognition that invoke the Cooperative Principle and the conversational maxims seem to be needed to determine the proposition expressed by the utterance; but, at the same time, the proposition expressed seems to be required for these processes to get started. Many working practitioners accept that semantics and pragmatics are irremediably entangled in the determination of utterance content. There is no clear-cut delimitation between semantics and pragmatics. They ignore the Gordian knot, rather than trying to untie it.[3]

We have a bit of terminology we find useful in thinking about this. What is said, or the proposition expressed, plays a central role in the classic picture. We call pragmatics in the service of figuring what is said, "near-side pragmatics" (see Korta and Perry, 2006b). This is the pragmatic reasoning that seems to be intruding into something that is none of its business on the classical conception. Pragmatic reasoning that starts with what is said, and seeks

---

[3] According to Bach (2011), Levinson makes a mistake to the extent that he sees Grice himself as having the views that lead to the circle. According to Bach, Levinson conflates two senses of "determine": one related to what the grammar delivers in combination with context, the other with the psychological process of ascertaining the content by a hearer:

> He [Grice] never claimed that the hearer's inference proceeds from first identifying what the speaker says to *then* considering whether there is any ostensible breach of the maxims and, if so and assuming the speaker is being cooperative and is aiming to communicate something, to seek a plausible candidate for what that could be.

This is doubtless a correct point about Grice, and shows that the circle need not to be temporal. But it does not explain how Gricean considerations are brought to bear prior to identifying what is said; this is what we try to do.

to discover what one is doing in saying or by saying it—what illocutionary and perlocutionary speech acts were performed—we call "far-side pragmatics." So the question is, how does near-side pragmatics make sense?

Some tried a somewhat different approach: to assume that, all in all, semantics does *not* yield fully truth-conditional content. The "output" of semantics is the "input" to pragmatics, but this output is not a fully determined proposition, and not *what is said.* Instead of talking about "pragmatic intrusion," we should accept that *what is said* is systematically a pragmatically determined content and not the input to pragmatics; the input to pragmatics is just what semantics gives us. This approach has been seen as undermining truth-conditional semantics, as cutting through the knot rather than untying it, to pursue one of our metaphors. But of course some are happy to cry "Truth conditional semantics is dead! Long live truth-conditional pragmatics!"[4]

In this paper, we'll argue that there are two false assumptions that generate the circle. One is that we need to identify what is said, in a canonical way, before Gricean considerations can be applied. The other is that simply because semantics underdetermines what is said, it does not provide a propositional content that can be the basis of reasoning. We'll show that these assumptions are wrong and that abandoning them gives way to a natural account of the semantic content of an utterance, what is said, and the semantics/pragmatics distinction. So we claim, in terms of our metaphors, to square Grice's circle, or untie the knot without slicing it, that is, without undermining truth-conditional semantics. We'll start by considering Grice's concept of what is said.

2 Grice on What is Said

Grice (1967a [1989]) famously distinguished between *what a speaker says* and *what she implicates* by uttering a sentence. Think about Anne and Bob talking about their common friend Carol, who both know that she recently started working in a bank. Anne asks: "How is Carol getting on in her job?" Bob replies: "Oh quite well… She hasn't been to prison yet." Bob is clearly suggesting something here; something related to Carol's tendency to yield to the temptation provided by her occupation, as Grice would put it. However, that's not something he said, but something he implicated in saying what he said.[5] But what did he say?

Grice's remarks suggest that his concept of "what is said" can be taken as equivalent to "the proposition expressed" or "the content" of the

---

[4] See Recanati, 2010.

[5] Grice included in his overall picture of meaning and communication non-linguistic "utterances" like gestures and movements, but we will limit the discussion to linguistic utterances.

utterance.[6] He claims that to know what someone said by uttering a sentence one has to know

(1) the conventional meaning of the sentence uttered;
(2) the disambiguated meaning of the sentence in that particular occasion of use; and
(3) the referents of referential expressions (Grice, 1967a [1989], 25).

This view of what is said fits well with Kaplan's (1989a) distinction between the character of a sentence, and the content of an utterance (or sentence-in-context). This also results in a seemingly perfect match between semantics and pragmatics: semantics deals with what is said; pragmatics deals with implicatures. The input to pragmatics is the output of semantics, in the form of disambiguated meaning plus context and fixing the reference of names.

But Grice's concept of what is said turned out to be less simple and clear as initially thought. Perry (1986) argued that someone who utters "It is raining" normally expresses a proposition that includes the place of the raining event, even if the sentence does not include any expression *articulating* that element of the proposition expressed. A variety of phenomena arguably showed a similar point: quantifier domain restrictions, comparative adjectives, assertions about taste, and a long list of other phenomena seem to involve constituents of the proposition expressed that are not articulated by any element in the sentence uttered. A significant part of the debate between minimalism and contextualism, and all the *isms* around them, concerns the analysis of these elements: whether they are actually part of what is said or should be relegated to some other category, like the category of *implicitures* (Bach, 1994a) or generalized conversational implicatures; whether they are actually unarticulated or they are values for some "hidden" indexicals in the logical form of the sentence uttered.

One might think that this kind of pragmatic intrusion into determining what is said is all there is to the circle; and that just a minimalist approach as found in, for instance, (Cappelen and Lepore, 2005), is enough to square it. The product of sentence meaning plus disambiguation and reference-fixing of names and indexicals might not yield what intuitively is said by the

---

[6] These more technical terms used by philosophers are not without problems, since they can suggest that implicatures are not contents of the utterance, or they are not propositional. Gricean implicatures (at least conversational particularized ones) are also full-blown truth-conditional (though more or less indeterminate) contents of the utterance, but we ignore this issue here, and follow common practice using "content" only to talk about the contents that are on the "what-is-said" part of the Gricean divide.

speaker, but it would have the merit of giving us a clear-cut notion of *semantically expressed proposition*. If you say, "It is raining," the semantically expressed proposition is simply *that it is raining*; something true if it raining anywhere (roughly). That proposition is trivial, so pragmatics takes the hearer to a more promising one as what the speaker conveys: *It is raining in X*, where the identity of X is determined pragmatically.

Another view is that semantics alone doesn't (always) get us to a proposition at all, even if we assume disambiguation and add context and reference fixing. We can only rely on obtaining a "proposition template" (Carston) or a "propositional radical" (Bach). Moreover, whatever exactly the result is, it does not seem to constitute the right "input" for implicatures; their derivation requires an "enriched" proposition to serve as "what is said": the content of the utterance with its *implicitures*.

On this issue, we side with Cappelen and Lepore, although with important differences. Like them, our view is that semantics provides us with propositions, and these propositions are not what is said. But our account is even more minimalist a conception than the one Cappelen and Lepore provide, and, we think, much more intuitive in a wide variety of cases.

To see the merits of our position, it is helpful to note that a Cappelen and Lepore style minimalism does not actually get us out of the Gricean circle. This is because the factors they fold into semantics: disambiguation and reference-fixing in particular, are often only resolved using pragmatic methods. As Levinson notes, reference fixing and indexical resolution and disambiguation, "which are prerequisites to determining the proposition expressed, may themselves depend crucially on processes that look indistinguishable from implicatures." (Levinson 2000, 186)

Here is an example involving reference-fixing. Suppose that the Stanford Philosophy Department is meeting in the 1980s, with John Perry, John Etchemendy, John Dupre and Jon Barwise all in attendance. John Perry has been talking at length, while Jon Barwise has been waiting impatiently to say something. The chair, Nancy Cartwright says, "/djon/ needs some time to develop his views." Is she referring to John Perry, using the name "John," or one of the other Johns, or Jon Barwise, using his name? It seems that the listener will most likely try to figure out whether she is speaking literally, referring to John Perry and implicating that Barwise should calm down (unlikely), being non-literal, referring to John Perry, and implicating that he should shut up, (more likely, postulating a sarcasm within Cartwright's repertoire), or speaking literally, referring to Jon Barwise (using the name "Jon"), and implicating that time is running out so he needs to be given a turn (most straightforward), or referring to Etchemendy or Dupre, and implicating that they should quit dozing and get involved (a distinct possibility).

What seems beyond question is the principle of underdetermination,

> The linguistic meaning of a sentence underdetermines what is said by a speaker uttering that sentence.

If all there is to semantics is to give the linguistic meaning of sentences (types), then there is an obvious sense in which that claim is true. Sentences say nothing; utterances do or, better, speakers do by uttering sentences. The semantic meaning of a sentence type uttered on a particular occasion is not (often, according to "moderate" contextualists; always, according to "radical" ones) enough to determine what the speaker said by the utterance. She might not have *said* anything, but have been asking a question, giving an example, or rehearsing a line for a play. More relevantly for our purposes, the linguistic meaning of the uttered sentence does not seem to yield a fully truth-conditional or propositional content.

3 Minimal but Complete Semantic Contents

It's helpful to start with indexicals. Suppose, out of the blue, in a crowded room, you hear the utterance

(1) I am French.

You don't even see who is doing the talking. Having no clue about who is talking, you would not really be able to say what the speaker said. Your semantic competence gets you only so far; it seems you wouldn't grasp a proposition, but just a propositional template or propositional "radical"; a predicate like

(2) x is French.

Since you don't know who is speaking, you don't know who this predicate has to be true of, for the utterance to be true.

On the other hand, semantics does provide you with enough to get started. You know that (1) is true iff,

(3) $\exists x$ (x is the utterer of (1) & x is French)

(3) Gives you a proposition, which may serve to get some reasoning started. Perhaps you reason that most likely (1) is true, and whoever said it is French; you can't think offhand of any reason why someone would be claiming to be French if they weren't; it didn't sound sarcastic, but had more of an

informative tone. This may be rather weak pragmatic reasoning, but it is pragmatic. You might look around for some reliable signs of a French person—someone who is smoking Gauloises cigarettes, for example. If you spot such a person, and are right, you will have used pragmatic reasoning and semantics (what is required for the utterance to be true, plus what seems to be the intention behind the utterance) to help you figure out who said it, which allows you to figure out *what is said.*

This illustrates our basic strategy. Semantics provides slots, which provides truth-conditions for utterances; by existentially quantifying we get a proposition; this proposition usually won't be *what is said,* but it provides us with what is needed to start what we call "near-side reasoning"; that is reasoning that gets us *from* perception of an utterance of a sentence and a grasp of the semantics, *to* what is said.

This picture is pretty much in tune with Borg's (2004) minimalist view of semantic content, and with Grice's comments on what one understands from an utterance in virtue of knowing the language. About an utterance of "He was in the grip of a vice," he makes the following remark:

> Given a knowledge of the English language, but no knowledge of the circumstances of the utterance, one would know something about what the speaker had said, on the assumption that he was speaking standard English, and speaking literally. One would know that he had said, about some particular male person or animal x, that at the time of utterance (whatever that was), either (1) x was unable to rid himself of a certain kind of bad character trait or (2) some part of x's person was caught in a certain kind of tool or instrument (approximate account, of course) (Grice, 1967a [1989], 25).[7]

As Grice's remark suggests, we don't even need disambiguation to get these sorts of truth-conditions. Given the meanings in (British) English of "He was in the grip of a vice," there is a fully propositional if utterance-bound content of **u**, namely,

(4) $\exists x \exists t$ (x is the person or animal the speaker of **u** is talking about and t is the time of **u** & at t either x was unable to rid himself of a certain kind of bad character trait or some part of x's person was caught in a certain kind of tool or instrument)

Suppose you receive an unsigned postcard that reads

---

[7] In American English this is an example of two words, "vice" and "vise," both pronounced /vais/. Parallel considerations would apply. But we follow British English, and Grice, in taking it to be an ambiguity.

(5) I am having a good time here.

Without identifying the writer, the time and the place of the writing, you would not know what she or he was saying to you. But this does not mean that you would fail to grasp a complete proposition from the postcard on the basis of your semantic competence. You would understand that the utterance would be true if and only if its author was having a good time at the time of the utterance at the place of the utterance. This is a perfectly truth-conditionally complete content.

These propositions are not what is said, and they aren't even *about* the same things the speaker is talking about. (4) is about the utterance **u**, not about the person the speaker refers to with "he," or even about the speaker himself or herself. We call such propositions *utterance-bound* contents. We want to emphasize three things about such contents before going further:

(a) Utterance-bound contents are utterance-bound with respect to the utterance they are about. (4) is the utterance-bound content of **u**, but it is not the utterance-bound content of (4).
(b) We do not claim, to repeat ourselves, that the utterance-bound content of an utterance is what the utterance expresses, or what the utterance says, or what the speaker of the utterance says.
(c) We do claim that the utterance-bound content gives the truth-conditions of the utterance. That is, it gives the conditions that the utterance must meet, in order to be true; there must be various things, speakers, things the speaker refers to and the like, that stand in various relations to the utterance and fulfill further conditions. But saying this can be misleading. In philosophy, at least, one typically uses the term "truth-conditions" for the *counterfactual* truth-conditions, the conditions that a situation or world must satisfy, to be one in which the proposition expressed, or what is said, is true. The counterfactual truth-conditions usually line up with what we call the *referential* truth-conditions, which is what you get when you identify the witnesses of the various existential quantifiers and plug them in for the variables. For example, with respect to our last example, this might be the proposition

That Hiram is/was having a good time on March 4, in Hawaii.

This proposition isn't about an utterance, and could be true in worlds in which the utterance **u** did not occur.

Although potentially misleading, we think our use is a correct and literal use of the term "truth-conditions." You get different truth-conditions for an utterance, depending on what you hold fixed and what you allow to vary. The truth-conditions are *what else* has to be the case, *given* what is held fixed, for the utterance to be true. Both utterance-bound and referential truth-conditions are truth-conditions; we aren't replacing the ordinary philosophical concept, but noticing that it is part of a system of truth-conditions, or contents, that an utterance can have.

4 Utterance Contents and Implicatures

Even admitting that an utterance has a truth-conditionally complete content before disambiguation, reference fixing and any other near-side pragmatic considerations, it can be argued that, since this content does not amount to what the speaker said by her utterance, we need to perform disambiguation and reference assignment and even further pragmatic processes (like so-called "free enrichment" processes) to get the content that can appropriately be called what is said (or the "explicature"). This would be required by Grice's picture of the inference of implicatures. Minimalists like Cappelen and Lepore share this view with contextualists like Carston (2002):

> We agree with her that you need a contextually shaped content to generate implicatures in all of the cases she discusses. (...) What's needed in order to derive the implicature in these cases is a contextually shaped content, i.e., a contextually shaped what-is-said. (...)
>
> More generally: We are happy to agree with Carston that an appropriate notion of what the speaker said must allow for contextual influences that go far beyond what the speaker said (Cappelen and Lepore, 2005: 180–181).

So, if this morning someone invited you to a coffee and you uttered

(6) I've had breakfast,

trying to implicate a negative answer, the implicature wouldn't have gone through, had he only got its utterance-bound content (7), or what Cappelen and Lepore take to be the proposition semantically expressed (8) (the result of semantic meaning plus disambiguation and reference assignment to referential expressions). Something like (9) which, arguably, includes elements that are not articulated in the uttered sentence, needs to be determined to infer the implicature:

(7) There is a time previous to the utterance of (6), when the speaker of (6) has had breakfast.
(8) X has had breakfast at some point or other.
(9) X has had breakfast this morning.

In this and other examples, the concept of what is said required by Grice's theory of implicatures seems to go beyond our fully truth-conditional but minimal level of content. Hence, we seem condemned to Grice's circle, after all.

But we are not. First, and most importantly, we have a truth-conditionally complete content whose determination is independent of pragmatic reasoning, and thus keep us out of the circle. And, second, because, contrary to what Cappelen and Lepore suggest, it is not generally the case that the hearer needs arriving at a "contextually shaped" what is said to understand the implicatures of an utterance. It is not even necessary that he gets what is said or what they call the proposition semantically expressed. It is sometimes enough to get the utterance-bound content of the utterance, or a content that with some undetermined (but existentially bound) element.[8] Suppose Kepa asked John for suggestions about whom to invite for an upcoming pragmatics conference. The conversation runs like this:

J: He is rather unreliable, doesn't have much to say, and always takes a long time to say it.
K: Next.

In this case, Kepa need not resolve the referent for John's use of the demonstrative "he," and maybe John doesn't intend him to resolve it. He trusts that grasping the utterance-bound truth-conditions of his utterance,[9] Kepa will infer that that guy would not be an appropriate candidate for lecturing at the conference. Or take our postcard example. You can guess, say, who the author is, but not the place he is talking about. You can, however, understand that he is implying he is postponing his trip back home. The moral is that even without determining what is said in the sense of disambiguating the expressions used and fixing the referents involved, Gricean inference of implicatures is often possible.

---

[8] See Chapter 1 and Chapter 4 of this volume, and Korta and Perry 2011. In the latter we distinguish utterance-bound, speaker-bound, network-bound, referential and designational contents. We contend that any of those can be and is the right "input" for the inference of implicatures.

[9] Or, more precisely, the speaker-bound truth-conditions. See Korta and Perry, 2011, and Chapter 8 of this volume.

To sum up, Grice's circle is avoided once a fully truth-conditional minimal semantic content is provided. This is our utterance-bound content, which does not require any pragmatic process of disambiguation, anaphora resolution or any other process that looks practically indistinguishable from implicature inference. The utterance-bound content itself can constitute a sufficient input for figuring out an implicature in some cases, while in other cases more facts about the utterance may need to be fixed. In some cases, the referential content of the utterance may suffice, in others one may need "the contextually-shaped what is said." But even in these cases the pragmatic reasoning can begin with the utterance-bound content, and can be used to arrive at the more specific contents that are required. Suppose you take your watch to be repaired and the watchmaker tells you:

(10) It will take some time to fix this watch.

The referential content of (10) is trivially true; any human act takes some time to perform. The enriched content of (10) (with the *implicature* within brackets) would be something like

(11) It will take some time [more than you might expect] to fix this watch,

which would allow you to infer the intended implicature, say, that you should take it easy. Now, some other shopper who overhears the conversation without being in position to fix the reference of the speaker's use of "this watch" would easily understand the implicate and implicature at issue. The inference of pragmatic contents starts from the utterance-bound content with or without reference fixing, disambiguation and other near-side pragmatic processes.

5 Truth-Conditional Semantics and Pragmatics

In our view semantics has to do with the conventional meanings of words and modes of combination, and its most central part is truth-conditional semantics. Truth-conditional semantics gives us the truth-conditions of utterances in terms of the constraints imposed by these meanings. They give us the utterance-bound or reflexive truth-conditions in terms of the utterance itself. They do not give us what is said or the proposition expressed by the speaker—speakers most often attempt to talk about things in the world, not about their own utterances. So our view of semantics is minimalist.

But being minimalist without allowing pragmatic "intrusion" into semantic content does not necessarily involve sacrificing truth-conditional semantics, and being pushed into Grice's circle. Our approach allows a clear-cut distinction between semantics and pragmatics that avoids it and offers the ideal toolkit to account for the relation between our knowledge of language and its use in communication.[10]

---

[10] The first author is grateful to his colleagues of the group "Language, Action and Thought" at the Institute for Logic, Cognition, Language and Information (ILCLI) for their comments and criticisms, especially to Eros Corazza, Joana Garmendia, María de Ponte and Larraitz Zubeldia. This work was partially supported by grants of the Basque Government (IT323-10 and IT780-13) and the Spanish Ministry of Science and Innovation (FFI2009-08574 and FFI2012-37726).

The second author appreciates the support of the philosophy department at the University of California, Riverside, the Center for the Study of Language and Information at Stanford University, and conversations with many colleagues and students.

Both authors want to thank Alessandro Capone for his infinite enthusiasm and patience.

10

Full but Not Saturated: The Myth of Mandatory Primary Pragmatic Processes

KEPA KORTA AND JOHN PERRY

1 Introduction

There are few assumptions in contemporary pragmatic theory as universal as what we will call "incompletism." With this ugly word, we refer to the claim that, in utterance comprehension, in the absence of the operation of certain pragmatic processes, an utterance often fails to determine a complete, fully truth-evaluable proposition. It delivers only an *incomplete* proposition, something that in and by itself cannot have a truth-value. This may be identified as a subpropositional "logical form," a "partial" or "gappy" proposition, a propositional "fragment," "schema," "radical," "skeleton," "template," "matrix," or "scaffolding."[1] All serve as propositional *function,* to use a more traditional term. Unless values are given for this entity's variables—or gaps or slots—it will not have a truth-value, i.e., it will not be a (full) proposition.[2]

The ubiquity of *incompletism* is a matter of dispute. It depends on (i) the number of context-sensitive expressions admitted and (ii) the nature of context-sensitivity envisaged as well as (iii) what is taken to be a complete, fully truth-evaluable proposition. Cappelen & Lepore (2005) are a good example

---

[1] We lack the scholarly instincts to track each term to its original author, but we think it is fair enough to say they collectively belong to Kent Bach (1994a, 1994b), Robyn Carston (2002), François Recanati (2004), Dan Sperber & Deirdre Wilson (1986), Ken Taylor (2001) and others.

[2] Bach claims that there is not much sense in talking about *incomplete* propositions: "An incomplete proposition is no more a proposition than a sentence fragment is a sentence or a rubber duck is a duck" (Bach 2006, 441–2). That's why he opts for the term "propositional radical." Nevertheless, Bach himself talked about incomplete propositions in "Conversational impliciture" (1994a) and many other places.

of a minimalist position on the first two issues: the number of context-sensitive expressions is limited to what they call "the Basic Set," namely, the pronouns "I," "you," "he," "she," "it," "this," and "that" in all their cases and numbers, the adverbs "here," "there," "now," "today," "yesterday," "tomorrow" "ago," "henceforth," the adjectives "actual" and "present," tense words and morphemes, nouns like "enemy," "outsider," "foreigner," "alien," "immigrant," "friend," and "native," and adjectives like "foreign," "local," "domestic," "national," "imported," and "exported." Hence, the only kind of context-sensitivity admitted is indexicality (which alludes to the context-sensitivity proper of indexicals, demonstratives and contextuals). About the third issue, they are almost alone in holding that, for example, an utterance of "It's raining" expresses a complete proposition even without the pragmatic provision of a location for the raining-event; and so does an utterance of "Tipper is ready" even without knowing what she is supposed to be ready for. When pressed, they are happy to answer in the following terms:

- An utterance of "It is raining" expresses the proposition that it is raining, which is true if and only if it is raining.
- An utterance of "Tipper is ready" expresses the proposition that Tipper is ready, which is true if and only if Tipper is ready.

Most people disagree with Cappelen & Lepore, and think that locations must be provided for weather reports, and some other parameters are required by gradable adjectives, relational adjectives and a variety of expressions that show, at the same time, that there are more kinds of context-sensitivity besides indexicality. Among those who disagree are contextualists such as Charles Travis (1997), François Recanati (2004), Dan Sperber & Deirdre Wilson (1986) and Robyn Carston (2002).[3] But there is a point on which all, minimalists and contextualists alike, come to terms: the case of indexicals and demonstratives.[4]

Suppose that suddenly, without any given context, somewhat out of the blue, you hear the utterance

(1) I am French.

As long as you have a basic knowledge of English, and you assume that the speaker is talking literally, with the ordinary meaning of those words and

---

[3] Indexicalists such as Jason Stanley and Zoltan Szabo (2000) take the set of indexicals to be much larger than the Basic Set but they add a new kind of context-sensitivity: hidden indexicality.

[4] There is no consensus about contextuals, and we won't deal with them in this paper.

their composition, and that she is making an assertion and not, for instance, just reading aloud a poem she just wrote, there is a sense in which you can rightly say that you understood the utterance. You understood the words uttered but you didn't understand what the speaker said, in the philosophers' and linguists' usual favored sense of the verb "to say." The fact that you have no clue about the context of the utterance that permits you to identify the speaker of (1) makes your understanding of (1) incomplete. You cannot assign a referent to the speaker's use of "I," so you don't understand what the speaker said in uttering (1). Your understanding falls short of determining a complete proposition. Instead, you just get an *incomplete* proposition. Something like

(2) x is French.

Given this, pragmatic processes of provision of referents would be mandatory to obtain a fully truth-conditional proposition, or, what amounts to the same thing, to get a candidate for the proposition that counts as what is said by the utterance.

Recanati (2004) calls the pragmatic processes that "intrude" in the determination of *what is said* "primary" pragmatic processes and claims that, among them, there is one kind, which he calls "saturation," which is mandatory, unlike all the other pragmatic processes, which are optional. Not everybody agrees that there is a fundamental distinction to be made between primary and secondary pragmatic processes; Sperber & Wilson (1986, 2002), Carston (2007) and Curcó (2013) argue against Recanati on this point. But they all agree, minimalists and contextualists alike, that saturation, whatever you call it and however you characterize it, is a mandatory pragmatic process. And it is mandatory for the sole reason that, otherwise, the utterance would provide only an incomplete proposition.

In this paper, we argue against this consensus opinion. We argue that 1) there are no mandatory primary pragmatic processes; because 2) even without the provision of referents for referential expressions (or locations for weather reports) an utterance does determine a complete proposition. This proposition will typically not be "the proposition expressed" or "what is said" by the speaker. But it is a complete proposition that captures truth-conditions for the utterance. Thus, primary pragmatic processes are not needed to have such a proposition. If primary pragmatic processes are mandatory, it is not due to *incompletism*.

We'll start by summing up the differences between primary and secondary pragmatic processes according to Recanati (2004) and the allegedly mandatory nature of some of the former. Then we'll focus on the assumptions behind the main argument for that mandatory nature: together with incompletism, it depends on semantic underdeterminacy and propositionalism. We will show, in section 4, what's wrong with these assumptions or, rather, what's wrong with the use of these assumptions in arguing for incompletism. Their force ends when we recall that we are dealing, not with mere sentences, but with utterances of them. With that in mind, it is natural to consider a variety of truth-conditions or contents beginning with a level that is clearly complete but not saturated: the utterance-bound or reflexive content. In section 5, we'll consider various objections: (i) that the utterance-bound content is saturated after all (ii) that it's not sufficient for understanding and (iii) that it should be ignored, since it plays no role in a theory of utterance comprehension. Needless to say, we'll rebut all these charges. In section 6, we'll show how our view fits perfectly with Grice's view on what is said and, perhaps despite appearances, with the relevance-theoretic notion of explicature. We'll end by drawing some general conclusions.

We need to emphasize that we are adopting the hearer's perspective on utterance contents and truth-conditions. That is, we are talking about the understanding rather than the production of utterances. When we take the speaker's point of view and think about utterance planning and production, the debate does not make much sense. In all the relevant cases under discussion here the speaker does have a complete thought, i.e., a belief or another doxastic attitude with a complete truth-conditional content she intends to express via her utterance: there is no primary or secondary pragmatic process to be undertaken by the speaker. Typically she will know the (intended) referents for her referential expressions before they are uttered. The present debate, like many others in pragmatics, concerns utterance comprehension, but that shouldn't hide the fact that pragmatics is also concerned with what the speaker means and does in uttering what she does.

2 Recanati on Pragmatic Processes

Recanati (2004) has insisted on the distinction between primary and secondary pragmatic processes and its importance. Against this, some other authors, like Sperber & Wilson (1986, 2002), Carston (2007) and Curcó (2013), have argued that there is no significant psychological difference between them, even if some theoretical distinction may be justified.

According to Recanati (2004), primary pragmatic processes (henceforth PPPs) are those involved, together with the semantic meaning of the sentence uttered, in determining the proposition expressed or *what is said*. These include disambiguation, reference fixing and, depending on your minimalist or contextualist allegiances, other processes of "enrichment." In other words, PPPs belong to what Korta & Perry (2006b) called "near-side pragmatics," as they are prior to the determination of *what is said*. Secondary pragmatic processes (henceforth SPPs), belong to "far-side pragmatics," given that, of course, they go further than what is said:

> In contrast, *secondary* pragmatic processes are ordinary inferential taking us from what is said, or rather from the speaker's saying of what is said, to something that (under standard assumptions of rationality and cooperativeness) follows from the fact that the speaker has said what she has said. (Recanati, 2004, 17)

Recanati makes a related distinction that concerns the level of operation of the pragmatic processes. Given that PPPs intervene on sentence meaning to jointly determine the proposition expressed, they can be said to work at the *pre*-propositional level. SPPs, on the other hand, typically take the proposition expressed, *what is said*, as input; so, in that sense, they operate at the *post*-propositional level.

A third difference has to do with the kind of cognitive system responsible for the process. Thus, PPPs typically are not available to consciousness, but rather belong to sub-personal cognitive processes. In contrast, the determination of implicatures, typically with *what is said* as input, occurs at the personal level, and so it is available to consciousness.

This is related to the fact that SPPs are inferential processes, while PPPs would be blind, mechanical, i.e., non- inferential and mostly associative. This is always the case according to Recanati (2004). Sperber & Wilson (1986), among others, argue that pragmatic processes are all inferential and guided by considerations of relevance. Given this, the distinction between PPPs and SPPs does not make much sense; it would concern only the level of utterance content to which these processes contribute: the level of what is said (or the *explicature*, in their terms) or the level of implicatures. However, practically all authors, including Sperber & Wilson, agree that there are some pragmatic processes that are mandatory, and that those are processes that contribute to *what is said*, that is, they are PPPs, if the distinction is to be kept.[5]

---

[5] The optionality of SPPs and PPPs other than saturation seems related to the cancelability of pragmatically determined aspects of content. Grice (1967a [1989], 1967b [1989]) indicated that conversational implicatures are cancelable, and Sperber & Wilson (1986), Carston (2002), Recanati (2004) and many others extended it to all pragmatically determined elements. Now, if saturation is mandatory, it is inconsistent to claim that an element determined by saturation is cancelable, if we interpret being cancelable roughly as being eliminable, and not as being merely revisable (see Korta, 1997, for discussion).

Table 1. Differences between PPPs and SPPs according to Recanati

PPPs	SPPs
Involved in determining what is said	Take what is said as input
Work at the pre-propositional level	Work at the post-propositional level
Operate at the sub-personal level (they are not consciously available)	Operate at the personal level (they are consciously available)
Blind, mechanical	Inferential
Mandatory (saturation) or optional (enrichment)	Optional

Recanati, being a contextualist about *what is said,* admits that some PPPs such as enrichment are optional as all SPPs are. But he insists that some PPPs are mandatory, since they are required for the utterance to express a complete proposition. Recanati's label for these PPPs is "saturation." Under this label he includes not only reference assignment and disambiguation but also the provision of unarticulated constituents, when they are needed to get a full proposition:

> Saturation is the process whereby the meaning of the sentence *is completed and made propositional* through the assignment of semantic values to the constituents of the sentence whose interpretation is context-dependent (and possibly through the contextual provision of unarticulated constituents, if one assumes, as some philosophers do, that such constituents are sometimes needed to make the sentence fully propositional).
> (Recanati, 2004, 7. Our emphasis).

The critical function of the process of saturation is, then, to complete what otherwise would be incomplete and pre-propositional. The key is then to provide the elements to get a complete proposition. And that's the reason why saturation is a *mandatory* process:

> Whenever saturation is in order, appeal to the context is necessary for the utterance to express a complete proposition: from a semantic point of view, saturation is a *mandatory* contextual process.
> (Recanati, 2004, 7. His emphasis)

Recanati's "saturation" is very similar to Kent Bach's "completion":

> When a sentence is in this way *semantically under-determinate,* understanding its utterance requires a process of *completion* to produce a full proposition. (Bach, 1994a, 125)

Without completion (or saturation), no full proposition, *ergo* no understanding. That's the claim.

3 Underdeterminacy, Propositionalism and Incompletism

The main argument for the obligatory nature of saturation or completion is incompletism. But the route from incompletism to mandatory PPPs goes through two other widely held assumptions: semantic underdeterminacy and propositionalism. Semantic underdeterminacy has been much discussed in relation to the contextualist/minimalism debate, and it has been interpreted in related but significantly different ways. In particular, the following three somewhat different failures have been labeled "semantic underdeterminacy":

1. The linguistic meaning of the sentence uttered fails to determine a complete proposition; or
2. The linguistic meaning of the sentence uttered fails to determine the literal truth-conditions of the utterance; or
3. The linguistic meaning of the sentence uttered fails to determine the intuitive truth-conditions of the utterance.

There are various positions regarding underdeterminacy. If you are a contextualist, for instance, you probably think that all three varieties are pervasive in natural language; that the role of context in identifying propositions is not limited to indexicals, and that there is no coherent notion of literal meaning separable from the intuitive truth-conditions of the utterance, which linguistic meaning systematically underdetermines. But you don't need to be a contextualist to embrace semantic underdeterminacy. And we are not going to take sides in the debate. We will deal with the non-controversial part of semantic underdeterminacy, namely, 1). This is always true when we consider sentences containing indexicals and demonstratives—the meaning of the sentence does not provide a complete proposition. Nobody denies that, nor do we. In fact, it sounds very much like a truism; the contextualist truism: Sentences do not express propositions, utterances of sentences (that is, speakers uttering sentences) do. What we call "incompletism," and deny, is version 1) of indeterminacy applied to utterances.

The second leg of the argument for the mandatory nature of saturation is propositionalism, the idea that the performance (and understanding) of a full speech act like an assertion, a command or a promise involve the expression (and understanding) of a complete proposition. Of course, we are leaving aside *wh*-interrogatives and other cases that may induce more or less controversy. We do not argue against it. So, we deny neither underdeterminacy nor propositionalism, but the assumption that they jointly lead to incompletism.

162 / Three Demonstrations and A Funeral and Other Essays

The key to our objection requires attention to the distinction between sentence meaning and utterance content(s).[6]

4   Sentence versus Utterance

Consider again the sentence uttered in (1), namely, "I am French." The sentence itself does not determine a complete proposition. If we adopt a token-reflexive account of indexicals and assume that the meaning of "I" is something like "the speaker of *this* utterance" then, at most we will have a "gappy" proposition with a slot to be filled in by a particular utterance of that sentence, something like:

(3) The speaker of x is French.

This is indeed a propositional function, that is, an incomplete proposition. That's the most an indexical sentence can aspire to provide in propositional terms: a semi-gappy-incomplete propositional function-radical-template.

Now, as soon as we consider not just sentences but utterances of sentences, that is, acts performed by a certain agent, the speaker, at a certain time, in a certain place, things are crucially different. To begin with, if we take again utterance (1), we don't have just a propositional function like (2) or (3), but a full proposition like

(4) The speaker of **(1)** is French.[7]

Even if you heard (1) out of the blue, without any chance to identify the speaker, not even to guess her or his gender or age, this is available to you given your knowledge of the English language, the identification of the sentence uttered, and your perception of the utterance or, in some cases, your inference that there was an utterance.

In face-to-face communication you are usually able to directly identify the speaker, the time and the place of the utterance you're hearing. You may not know the speaker's name, or what time it is, or where exactly it is, but you have direct knowledge of those parameters, and they permit you to close the propositional function provided and have access to further contents. If

---

[6] The reason for the parenthetical plural is that as a natural consequence of our discussion, we will argue that the utterance, not the sentence, has a variety of contents or truth-conditions.

[7] We'll follow the notational convention of Perry (2001 [2012]) and use boldface to indicate that the propositional constituent is the referent itself and not any identifying condition on it. On the other hand, we will use small capitals for propositions, contents or truth-conditions.

you had the speaker of (1) in front of you, you would be able to grasp the following proposition:

(5) THE PERSON IN FRONT OF **ME** IS FRENCH,

and even, given your perceptual identification of the speaker, the following one:

(6) **THIS GUY** IS FRENCH,

with the speaker himself, not any identifying conditions on him, as a constituent. This is usually considered as the proposition expressed by the utterance, what the speaker said in uttering (1). We also consider it so—usually (see Chapter 3 and Chapter 8 of this volume, and Korta and Perry 2011).

When not communicating orally or face-to-face, often we do not perceive the utterance itself; we do not perceive the act of uttering a sentence, but only its product, what Perry (2001 [2012]) calls a "token." In that case, we might be unable to identify the speaker of the utterance, or the time, or the place, independently of the utterance—which may itself only be identifiable as "the production of *this* token." Hence we talk of "utterance-bound" identification of the speaker, the time, the place, and in fact of the truth-conditions of the utterance.

Suppose you find an anonymous hand-written note, apparently slid under your office-door, that reads

(n) You are Spanish.

You don't have any hint about its author,[8] its addressee or addressees, the time it was written or placed there, or its purpose. The utterance-bound truth-conditions, or utterance-bound content, of (n), however, is available to you:

(7) THE ADDRESSEE(S) OF **N** MEET THE CONDITIONS THE AUTHOR OF **N** MEANS BY "SPANISH" AT THE TIME OF BEING SAID.

Whether the referent of "you" is a sole person, all the occupants of the office or just some of them and who exactly he, she or they is/are is a matter of the speaker's intention that goes further than the facts determining the minimal

---

[8] We should rather say its user, since being a token, can be used and re-used by other people other than its author; that's why the relevant time is the time of sliding the note (or perhaps even the time the user expects the addressee to read the note; see Perry, 2003).

utterance-bound content. About the meaning of "Spanish" opinions can differ about whether it denotes a perfectly identifiable current European citizenship quite permanent in time, or it involves a few things other than a passport which makes the denotation more intention-dependent and temporary. (7) stands for the latter option. Anyway, we know that the note has an author and has an issuing time, and that's all we need to existentially close our propositional function and have a complete proposition.

Coming back to (6), we call it the referential content or referential truth-conditions of the utterance, as we take utterances to have a variety of truth-conditions or contents; a variety of truth-conditions or contents that are set relative to various kinds of facts:

- The utterance-bound truth-conditions; set by the meaning of the sentence uttered plus the fact that an utterance has been produced.
- The speaker-bound truth-conditions; set by the above facts plus the identity of the speaker.
- The network-bound truth-conditions; set by the above facts plus the notion-network supporting the use of a certain proper name.
- The referential truth-conditions; set by the above facts plus facts about the speaker's intentions and contextual facts that set the values for context-sensitive expressions as well as unarticulated constituents.
- and some other truth-conditions that can be distinguished as the product of all the various facts about conventions, intentions and circumstances involved.

To our present purposes, however, it is the first level of truth-conditions which is critical: the level of utterance-bound or reflexive truth-conditions, for they provide the proof that incompletism is false. It is false that without saturation we do not have a complete proposition. And thus it is false that saturation is mandatory to get a complete proposition.

5 Against Utterance-Bound or Reflexive Content

Suppose you are quite convinced by our arguments, but still you wish to defend that saturation is mandatory. You might try to object as follows. The closure of the incomplete parameters through the utterance parameters of the speaker, time and place is just another way of saturating the incomplete proposition delivered by sentence meaning. If right, this would be a fatal objection to our argument, we would be just begging the question by an excessive narrow interpretation of "saturation," and we wouldn't have refuted incompletism.

Remember that we deliberately choose to discuss only the non-controversial cases, indexicals and demonstratives. These are supposed to leave, in virtue of their context-sensitive meaning, a "gap," "slot," or a free variable that is to be saturated to have a complete proposition. Saturation in this case amounts to providing the referents for the indexicals and demonstratives, their "semantic" values as they are often called (misleadingly, since their determination is not semantic, but pragmatic, as it involves intention recognition). Utterances containing indexical or demonstrative pronouns express singular propositions, with their referents as constituents, and saturation, as far as indexicals and demonstratives are concerned, is the process of fixing them. That is at least what Recanati (2004) clearly has in mind. Saturation provides the referents for indexicals and demonstratives. Without saturation we are left with gaps, slots of free variables.

In other words, our utterance-bound content, by definition, involves no saturation. Recanati (2004) himself acknowledges this when he takes the utterance-bound or reflexive proposition as the only coherent notion of minimal proposition:

> *[T]he reflexive proposition is determined before the process of saturation takes place*. The reflexive proposition can't be determined unless the sentence is tokened, but no substantial knowledge of the context of utterance is required to determine it. Thus an utterance *u* of the sentence "I am French" expresses the reflexive proposition that the utterer of *u* is French. That it does not presuppose saturation is precisely what makes the reflexive proposition useful, since in most cases saturation proceeds by appeal to speaker's meaning. (Recanati, 2004, 65. Our emphasis.)

Saturation and existential quantification are two different ways of getting from sentence meaning to a complete proposition. It is contrary to Recanati's understanding of his own term, and unhelpful, to use the term "saturation" with this portmanteau sense.

Another possible objection could go along the following lines:

> Ok, let's accept that your utterance-bound or reflexive content is a complete proposition that is determined before saturation. Incompletism is false. *But the utterance-bound content does not amount to what is said,* so understanding the utterance-bound content does not count as understanding the utterance. So, even if saturation is not mandatory for reasons of incompletism, it is mandatory for reasons of full understanding of the utterance.

This is not an objection but a concession of our main claim: incompletism is false, so saturation is not mandatory for that reason. But it can be used as a preliminary move to a further point: that the utterance-bound content has no role in a psychologically plausible account of utterance understanding.[9]

Concerning the first point. The notion of utterance-bound content is not intended to capture "what is said" or "the proposition expressed." Quite the opposite, we claimed that typically what is said corresponds to what we call the "referential content" of the utterance. Typically, but not always. For example with identity statements the referential content seldom captures what the speaker means to convey.

Recanati himself does not take the reflexive proposition to be what is said:

> The reflexive proposition is admittedly distinct from that which the speaker asserts... but why is this an objection? [The reflexive proposition] comes as close as one can get to capturing, in propositional format, the information provided by the utterance in virtue solely of the linguistic meaning of the sentence "I am French." (Recanati 2004, 66)

However, we think that equating full understanding of an utterance with understanding of what is said is incorrect. Leaving aside that *full* understanding is most likely a chimera, we'd like to show, first, that understanding what is said is not necessary to adequately understand an utterance. Consider the following example:[10]

> In New Orleans, after hurricane Katrina, Davis McAlary checks regularly his ex-girlfriend's mailbox since she moved to New York City. This time he sees the front door is open, it has been forced; he enters; there is a mess; he hesitates; he hears a noise upstairs; he utters "Who's that? Who's that? Anybody there? Hey! This is the Police! Anybody up there?"; he takes his cell phone from his pocket and holding it like a gun he shouts "I'm a cop with a gun, seriously!"; more noises upstairs; he runs out like crazy.

Consider McAlary's last utterance:

(8) I'm a cop with a gun, seriously.

---

[9] These two objections are the transposition of Recanati's objections to the minimalist notion of what is said à la Cappelen & Lepore or Bach. Obviously, for a contextualist that notion does not correspond with an adequate notion of what is said; and, according to Recanati (and others like Sperber & Wilson or Carston) it plays no role, anyway, in a psychologically plausible explanation of utterance understanding. For some experimental work on the psychological role of (not so) minimal propositions, see Bezuidenhout & Cooper Cutting, 2002.

[10] From the TV series *Treme*, second season, third episode (2011), entitled "On your way down."

Forget about "seriously." Now, what is the relevant content? Perhaps, it's a gappy proposition like

(9) X IS A COP WITH A GUN.

We can discard that already. What he said by (8) is surely

(10) **DAVIS MCALARY** IS A COP WITH A GUN.

But was saying this Davis's goal? Whatever counts as identifying an individual in a singular proposition, it involves identifying the individual in other ways than as the referent of the uttered referential expression; that is, not simply in an utterance-bound way. Either directly, seeing him, for instance, or by a description like "the sweet but hopeless music lover who is an heterodox radio DJ and a frustrated musician." Any of these would be fatal for McAlary's purpose. He wants the hearer to think that there is an armed policeman downstairs, where the utterance clearly takes place. Anyone who sees him or has heard about him would definitely not be scared and would not fly from the scene. It seems clear that in this case the content that McAlary intends to convey to the hearer is rather

(11) THE SPEAKER OF **(8)** IS A COP WITH A GUN,

i.e., the utterance-bound content. That's what they are to grasp, and from which they are to infer that there is an armed policeman in the house, and it's best to leave the house.[11]

The example shows that the objections are misguided if directed to utterance-bound content. It doesn't amount to what is said—we never said that—but it explains what understanding consists in in many cases and, hence, it plays an important role in explaining utterance understanding.

Thus, understanding what a speaker says in uttering a sentence is not necessary to understand the communicative act. And it is not sufficient either. This morning the first words Kepa told his friends were:

(12) I am Basque.

---

[11] One can build alternative explanations like: "they just heard an utterance; they didn't even understand the sentence; hearing a voice downstairs did all the work; Davis could have just uttered *"Kennst du das Land, wo die Zitronen blühen?"* and the robbers would have run all the same." These are all possible stories, but not the story we are using as an example. Our story is possible, and that's all that matters.

They looked at him with puzzled faces. His communicative plan was to exploit the widely recognized fact that Basques are punctual, and so to complain that they were late and accuse them thereby for not being good Basques. It was probably too complicated early in the morning. Kepa failed. But no doubt they understood what he said. The problem is that they didn't understand what he meant, that is, they didn't understand why Kepa said what he said or, what amounts to the same thing, which the implicatures of his utterance were.

This reveals a curious tendency in contemporary pragmatics: After 50 plus years of Gricean (and Austinian) pragmatics, the attention is centered on *what is said* (and its neighbor contents) rather than on *implicatures*. As we like to put it, the focus in pragmatics started on the far-side and then slowly moved to the near-side. That is, it started by calling attention to phenomena and concepts that went far beyond what is said (illocutions, implicatures, presuppositions...) and came to scrutinize the notion of what is said and facts in its vicinity. This is not good or bad in itself, research on both-sides pragmatics is surely important. But it could be the sign of a regress to the old code model of communication, a model that, as it is shown by Grice's work, is essentially insufficient to account for human communication and demands to be supplemented (or substituted, depending how you interpret it) by a model that takes language as action. This emphasis on what is said as the measure of utterance understanding, forgetting about the importance of implicatures is, in our humble opinion, a remnant of the code model that we should discard.

6 True Neo-Griceans (or Neo-Relevantists)

Perhaps contrary to appearances, our view on utterance contents is well-rooted in Grice's seminal work. It is also in substantial agreement with relevance theory, an important contemporary theory of utterance understanding that is rooted in Grice's ideas.

Our utterance-bound content sounds as an echo of the following passage of "Logic and Conversation," in which Grice is discussing what is said by an utterance of "He was in the grip of a vice":

> *Given a knowledge of the English language, but no knowledge of the circumstances of the utterance, one would know something about what the speaker had said*, on the assumption that he was speaking standard English, and speaking literally. One would know that he had said, about some particular male person or animal x, that at the time of utterance (whatever that was), either (1) x was unable to rid himself of a certain kind of bad character trait or (2) some part of x's person was caught in a certain kind of tool or instrument (approximate account, of course). (Grice, 1967a [1989], 25. Our emphasis.)

This is precisely how we characterize utterance-bound content: the content determined by the knowledge of the language and the fact that an utterance has been made, nothing else. Referents for referential expressions are not assigned, the time of the utterance is not determined and ambiguities are not resolved. It is not what is said, but it is looks like a complete content. So, leaving implicatures aside, Grice seems to explicitly admit at least two contents for the utterance: what we call the utterance-bound and referential contents. The others are admitted implicitly since they derive naturally as the remaining information is "loaded."[12]

As for relevance theory, the relevant comparison seems the one between our variety of contents and their "explicature." The explicature has often been taken to be a proposition that results from processes of ambiguity and vagueness resolution, reference assignment and other pragmatics processes (roughly called enrichment processes) performed on the "logical form" of the sentence uttered. Or, following Recanati's distinction, it is the result of applying the mandatory PPPs and, eventually, the optional PPPs to the initial—and incomplete—proposition that is the product of decoding. The "fully developed" proposition would constitute the input for the inference of implicatures. Cappelen and Lepore, to cite just one case, assume just that:

> We agree with her [Carston] that you need a contextually shaped content to generate implicatures in all of the cases she discusses... What's needed in order to derive the implicature in these cases is a contextually shaped content, i.e., a contextually shaped what-is-said. (Cappelen and Lepore, 2005, 180)[13]

But we don't think this is the right interpretation of the input of implicatures within relevance theory. Instead, as we understand the theory, it is assumed that both explicatures and implicatures are derived fast, on-line and parallel, and the inferences are carried out following what they call the Relevance-theoretic comprehension strategy:

(a) Follow a path of least effort in constructing an interpretation of the utterance (and in particular in resolving ambiguities and referential

---

[12] For a discussion of Grice's notion of what is said see Korta, 2013.

[13] To be honest, in this passage they agree with Carston in "these cases," the cases presented by contextualists in favor of an enriched notion of what is said. It's not clear what Cappelen and Lepore think about other cases, but we think it is fair to say that many authors identify the concept of relevance-theoretic explicature with the fully enriched proposition. For instance, Yan Huang tells this in his entry on explicature: "An explicature corresponds roughly to the American philosopher Kent Bach's notion of impliciture and the French philosopher François Recanati's notion of pragmatically enriched said." (Huang, 2012, 110-111).

indeterminacies, in going beyond linguistic meaning, in supplying contextual assumptions, computing implicatures, etc.).
(b) Stop when your expectations of relevance are satisfied.
(Wilson and Sperber, 2012, 7)

Interpreted according to our view, the hearer might well stop at the utterance-bound content, without "going beyond linguistic meaning" and without "resolving referential indeterminacies," because the utterance-bound content is relevant enough—as in the McAlary example. Or she might go a bit further and stop at the speaker-bound content, or the network-bound content, without going through the process required to fix the referents of referential expressions. This is all that is needed for the inference of implicatures (which can be on-line, and in parallel), and other perlocutionary effects the speaker intends to generate. There is nothing that demands the PPPs to operate at all, because the utterance-bound content might be relevant enough, and being complete, there is no necessity of any saturation process to work.

7 Conclusions

We think it is now sufficiently clear that incompletism is false, and that, consequently, it does not justify the claim that saturation is mandatory. Reasons of "full" utterance understanding are also wanting. Understanding "what is said" is neither necessary nor sufficient to understand an utterance, and we believe that insisting on the contrary is the product of the old code model of human linguistic communication, according to which successful communication consists in transmitting a proposition from the speaker's mind to the hearer's mind.

In our picture, what the speaker says, or, rather, the referential content of an utterance, is one content among others, and may or may not be the appropriate content to grasp in order to understand further contents of the utterance like implicatures and other perlocutionary contents. This seems to be much more in line with Gricean and Austinian views of language as action.

Our pluralistic view on contents seems the only way to naturally explain actual communicative phenomena and overcome sterile debates caused by "mono-propositionalism" and other remnants of the code model.

It is true that abandoning incompletism even for the case of utterances containing indexicals and demonstratives would deprive both minimalism and contextualism of one of their few points of agreement. However, they would each gain on significant issues. The level of utterance-bound or reflexive content offers the minimalist a truly minimal, pragmatics-free kind of semantic content. Its determination does not require any appeal to context or to the speaker's intention. Semantic content is immune to pragmatic intrusion.

The price to pay is to admit that the minimal content does not amount to what the speaker says, but that's a bullet most minimalist are ready to bite for their pragmatically-blended semantic content, anyway.

As for contextualism, the case for the pragmatic determinants of what is said remains strong. Anything beyond the utterance-bound content requires pragmatic processes (be they primary non-inferential or secondary inferential), so what is said by a speaker in uttering a sentence, our referential truth-conditions, would be highly context-dependent.[14]

What both minimalism and contextualism would lose together with incompletism is the mandatory nature of any pragmatic process. There is no mandatory PPP or SPP. At least not for reasons of incompletism. And if we consider reasons of good utterance understanding, PPPs are neither sufficient nor necessary.[15]

---

[14] For our position regarding the minimalism/contextualism debate, see Chapter 2 of this volume.

[15] Earlier primitive versions of this paper were presented at "AMPRA. Pragmatics of the Americas Conference" (Charlotte, NC, USA), "IV Congreso Iberoamericano de Filosofía" (Santiago, Chile) and the "2nd ILCLI- IFFs Workshop on Language, Cognition, and Logic" (Mexico City). We thank the audiences at these places and, in particular, Axel Barceló, Robyn Carston, Eros Corazza, Carmen Curcó, Wayne Davis, Justina Díaz Legaspe, Maite Ezcurdia, Eduardo García-Ramírez, Larry Horn, Yan Huang, Nicolás Lo Guercio, Alfonso Losada, Eleonora Orlando, María de Ponte and Deirdre Wilson for their comments, suggestions and criticisms. We benefited from grants by the Spanish Ministry of Economy and Competitivity (FFI2015-63719-P (MINECO/FEDER)), Basque Government (IT1032-16). The first author also benefited from a grant of the University of the Basque Country (UTR/PIU/UFI 11/18). The second author thanks the University of California, Riverside and Stanford University for their support. Sarah-Jane Conrad deserves special credit for her immense patience.

11

New Thoughts about Old Facts: On Prior's Root Canal

María de Ponte and Kepa Korta

1 Introduction

In his 1908 paper "The Unreality of Time," McTaggart introduced some terminology that has perdured until now. He distinguished between different ways in which positions in time could be ordered. On the A-series, positions are ordered according to their having the property of being past, present, or future. These properties have come to be known as "A-properties." On the B-series, positions are ordered by two-place relations: earlier than, simultaneous with, and later than. These have come to be known as "B-relations."

This terminology has permeated the debate on the philosophy of time over the last century. The disagreement between A- and B-theorists is at the heart of the ontological debate on the nature of time: Is there an objective difference between past, present, and future or not? Are past, present, and future key pieces of reality's furniture, or are they rather part of humans' cognitive and linguistic apparatus? Both, perhaps?[1]

A-theorists defend that A-properties are fundamental and B-relations derivative. They believe there is an objective distinction among past, present, and future events and that the flow of time is real. It is in this sense that they are said to defend a "tensed" view of time.

B-theorists take B-relations as fundamental and deny the objective character of past, present, and future. There is no past, only events that happen earlier than other events. Consequently, when we talk about an event's being past, we are not describing a fact about the world or about time; rather what we are doing is describing the way we perceive, think, and talk about time.

---

[1] For a discussion of the A and B dichotomy with respect to time, see Le Poidevin, 1998; Markosian, 2014; and Mellor, 1998.

The flow of time is thus a mere appearance, the result of the way our cognitive and linguistic apparatuses are shaped. All there is to time, they claim, is an event's temporal position in relation with another event's temporal position. They are said to defend a "tenseless" view of time.

In discussions of the role of time in language and thought, it is often unclear how the various aspects of what is being said are related to each other. Ontological (and physical) considerations about the nature of time are raised, together with epistemological (and phenomenological) aspects of how we experience the flow and the direction of time, and even semantic (and pragmatic) insights into our talk about time, without clear connections and distinctions between the arguments at each level. We think that some of the most pervasive arguments in favor of the A-theories are epistemic ones, although they are disguised as either ontological or linguistic.

Prior's famous paper "Thank goodness that's over" (1959) is a clear case at hand: Ontological, epistemic, and linguistic considerations are entangled in a way that creates the illusion of an ontological argument about the nature of time. In this essay we defend the thesis that Prior's argument and those akin to it are best interpreted as "knowledge arguments," similar to the one raised by Frank Jackson (1986) against physicalism. We start by summing up Prior's challenge (section 2) and Jackson's knowledge argument (section 3). Our discussion comes then in three main steps. In section 4, which is about our various tools for referring to time, we challenge the assumption that utterances containing temporal indexicals and utterances containing dates, when made in the same circumstances, express different propositions. In section 5, which deals with the way we represent time in thought, we go back to the analogy with Jackson's argument and claim that in both cases there are different motivating thoughts involved. Realizing and explaining this fact is key to rejecting the ontological conclusions that both Prior and Jackson get to. We offer an explanation in section 6, making use of identity statements and thoughts. We reject the alleged ontological implications of Prior's paper in the concluding section.

2 Thank Goodness That's Over

According to the A-theory, the passage of time is a real feature of the world, and not merely some mind-dependent phenomenon. Many arguments in its favor, however, rely on issues about temporal knowledge and the cognitive significance of time to conclude to the inexorability of A-properties. The basic idea underlying these arguments is that a view that denies the existence of A-properties (e.g. being past) and reduces it to B-relations (happening earlier than) offers no grounds for tensed thoughts and tensed emotions. That is, B-theories lack the tools to warrant thoughts about past events and the emotions they elicit—regret, relief, and the like—and the essential differences with thoughts about future events and the emotions they elicit—anxiety, hope, and so on.

One such argument was presented by Prior (1959). Consider this repeatedly quoted fragment:

> [H]alf the time I personally have forgotten what the date is and have to look it up or ask somebody when I need it for writing cheques, etc.; yet even in this perpetual dateless haze one somehow communicates, one makes oneself understood, and with time references too. One says, e.g. "Thank goodness that's over!"… says something which it is impossible that any use of a tenseless copula with a date should convey. It certainly doesn't mean the same as, e.g. "Thank goodness the date of the conclusion of that thing is Friday, June 15, 1954," even if it be said then. (Nor, for that matter, does it mean "Thank goodness the conclusion of that thing is contemporaneous with this utterance." Why would anyone thank goodness for that?).
> (Prior, 1959, 17)

This short paragraph encapsulates remarks with an impact at different levels: linguistic, epistemological, and ontological. The clearest point, however, is the linguistic claim to the effect that, in the imagined circumstances, the following utterances wouldn't say (or mean) the same thing:

(1) Thank goodness the root canal is over (now).[2]
(2) Thank goodness the date of the conclusion of the root canal is Friday, June 15, 1954.
(3) Thank goodness the conclusion of the root canal is contemporaneous with this utterance.

Utterance (1) is an A-utterance that through an (implicit) indexical expression refers to the (then) present day. Utterance (2) is a B-utterance that includes a particular date. Utterance (3) is a B-utterance that some authors (not Prior, of course) take to be the appropriate utterance-reflexive rendering of the meaning of (1).

Pace Prior, it is not obvious that in the right circumstances (1)–(3) express different propositions or say different things, but there is certainly little room for discussion that, as he claims, (2), and in particular (3), are very odd utterances to make in those circumstances. A semantic and pragmatic account

---

[2] We write "now" within brackets to make clear that, in this case, the present tense designates the present time (the time of the utterance), and not a "zero-tense" as in "2 plus 2 equals 4." On many occasions an explicit "now," though arguably redundant, might be useful to avoid this ambiguity (see de Ponte, 2017).

should clarify the content and the cognitive significance of our tensed and tenseless ways of referring to time. As Prior claims in his closing rhetorical question, it is very difficult to imagine why anyone should utter (2) or (3) in those circumstances or, moving from the linguistic level to the psychological, why anyone should feel thankful that the conclusion of the root canal is contemporaneous with that feeling.

Interestingly, most readings of Prior's argument take it to be basically about ontology (Maclaurin and Dyke, 2002; Zimmerman, 2008). If these readings are right, Prior is arguing against B-theories, or against the tenseless view of time. From the implausibility of B-utterances like (2) and (3) and the perfect plausibility of an A-utterance like (1), the implausibility of the B-series and the plausibility of A-series would naturally follow. Or so it is claimed.

The key question would then be: What is it that makes people exclaim (1), and not (2) or (3), upon leaving the dentist's office? The answer, according to the ontological reading, requires including A-properties into the basic furniture of the world. One feels thankful, when the root canal finishes, because one takes the event to have a certain property: the property of being over, that is, the property of being past. An utterance referring to that A-property makes sense. When the reference to the A-property is substituted by a reference to a B-relation or a date (like in (2) and (3)), the utterance sounds awkward. The difference in the meanings (and contents) of (1), (2), and (3) amounts, according to this interpretation, to a difference in the properties of the events that are talked about. In a nutshell, A-utterances like (1) (and their corresponding A-thoughts) require the existence of A-properties.

We agree, to a certain extent, with Prior. Indeed, we take it to be an almost trivial fact about human cognition: (1) must involve A-thoughts that include tensed reference to the past for humans to be able to feel anything like happiness about the conclusion of some unpleasant event; and similarly for the presentness of pain and the anxiety about a future event. B-thoughts about the temporal relations of precedence, simultaneity, or succession of a pair of events are not enough. We need something else.

What this something else might be, though, is far from clear. Embedded within Prior's challenge is a claim about the object of emotional reactions, utterances, and thoughts. The idea is that A-properties—past, present, and future—must get into the picture first as fundamental elements of reality and, second, as ingredients of the content of our utterances and thoughts. We agree, with qualifications, with the second requirement.[3] We argue that the

---

[3] The qualifications are important, though. We use "A-thoughts" and "A-utterances" for the kind of utterances or thoughts that, according to Prior, involve A-properties but that, in our approach, need not do so; they just contain "tensed" expressions and thought components (i.e.

first one is unjustified and superfluous. On the one hand, the inference from the tensed nature of some of our utterances and thoughts to the fundamentally tensed nature of time is unjustified. On the other hand, even if we were to accept this inference, that wouldn't give us an explanation of our different cognitive and emotional reactions to time. After all, why would the fact that a certain event—say, a root canal—has a certain property—say, of "being past"—account for the agent's emotions?

Applying our views on the semantics and pragmatics of temporal reference (see Korta and Ponte, 2015, for a detailed account), which combine a direct reference theory of singular terms with a token-reflexive theory of indexicals, we contend, *contra* Prior, that, in the imagined circumstances, (1)–(3) express the same proposition, that is, say the same thing. Nevertheless, as Prior insists, they are utterances of different sentences with different meanings. They have therefore different cognitive significance. With this at hand, we show that Prior's linguistic remarks do not have any ontological impact.

As hinted above, Prior's challenge to B-theories seems to involve not only the difference between A- and B-utterances but also basic considerations about the corresponding distinction between A- and B-thoughts.[4] In this essay we take Prior's challenge as a kind of "knowledge argument," analogous to the one presented by Jackson (1986) against physicalism, and we claim that, likewise, Prior's epistemic claim fails to have any ontological impact either.

3   The Knowledge Argument and Prior's Challenge

Let us consider first Prior's example in some detail. Imagine that Arthur had a particularly painful root canal performed on him on Friday, June 15, 1954. By noon the root canal is over, the procedure is finished and the aftereffects are gone, something he is truly thankful for, so he utters (1), repeated here:

(1) Thank goodness the root canal is over (now).

Leaving aside exactly what the emotion of relief expressed in "thank goodness" amounts to, it is clear that, in order to be thankful, Arthur needs to have certain thoughts. He needs to think that the root canal has finished, that it is

---

indexicals and their thought equivalents). So we agree with Prior that A-utterances and A-thoughts must get into the picture; we disagree that A-properties must also do so. See section 4 below.

[4] We use the term "thought" (and the verb "to think") to talk about mental states or propositional attitudes, including not only beliefs (either conscious or implicit), but also more basic forms of "attunement" with reality that guide our cognition and action.

over, that it is no longer happening at the time of (1). This, Prior suggests, entails thinking that the root canal is a past event.

As we said above, Prior's dilemma can be seen as a type of knowledge argument, similar to Frank Jackson's (1986) argument against physicalism, which, roughly, reads like this.[5]

A bright scientist called Mary has been confined in a black-and-white room all her life. Unlucky as she is, her education is thorough and she has access to all the information there is to have about colors. She lives in a very advanced society and this information is complete, so, through her noncolored books and black-and-white TV, she gets to know all there is to know about the physical properties of colors. Now, if physicalism is correct, we have to accept that Mary has all the information about colors simpliciter. Nevertheless, she has never seen a color. One day Mary is released and the first thing she sees is a red tomato. Does she learn anything? Does she acquire a new piece of information about the color red? Jackson argues that she learns "what it is like to see something red" (Jackson, 1986, 291) and that this proves that physicalism is wrong. Mary did not have all the knowledge about colors before her release, and this means that there are certain nonphysical facts she didn't know.

There are various takes on Jackson's argument. It can be interpreted merely as an epistemological argument, with no consequences for the metaphysics of qualia. But that's not Jackson's own purport. He clearly takes it to be an argument against physicalism that shows that not all facts (and properties) are physical.[6]

Let us consider the argument in greater detail:

(A) If physicalism is true, then all facts are physical.
(B) If all facts are physical, then all knowledge is about physical facts.
(C) Mary knows all physical facts about color, so she knows everything about colors.
(D) When Mary sees the red tomato after her release, she gains new knowledge.
(E) What Mary learns must be nonphysical.

---

[5] Kiernan-Lewis (1991) also defends the view that Prior's challenge should be taken as a type of knowledge argument. His conclusions, however, differ substantially from ours. For one, he endorses the challenge, while we take it as a nonstarter. See Oaklander, 1992, for a criticism of Kiernan-Lewis' proposal.

[6] Jackson changed his views on the matter after the publication of the argument, adopting a form of physicalism and thus rejecting the strong reading of it. See Nida-Rümelin, 2015, for a detailed account of the different interpretations of the argument.

(F) Hence physicalism is false.

Jackson's argument starts with an ontological premise, followed by various epistemological premises about Mary's knowledge that lead to an ontological conclusion to the effect that qualia, that is, the qualitative features of our conscious experience, are nonphysical, and hence physicalism is false.

Most physicalists have adopted what Nida-Rümelin (2015) calls the "new knowledge/old fact view," which basically consists in accepting premises (A)–(D) while rejecting (E) and (F). Or, better said, rejecting the ontological reading of (E); because, as it stands, (E) is ambiguous between an epistemic and an ontological reading. If (E) just claims that the kind of new knowledge that Mary acquires after being released is nonphysical, physicalists can accept it, since it wouldn't yield (F) as a conclusion. They would still have to clarify what kind of knowledge such new nonphysical knowledge was; but physicalism would be untouched by the knowledge argument. If, on the other hand, what (E) claims is that what Mary learns is a new nonphysical fact, physicalists should reject it.

Whatever the reactions to Jackson's knowledge argument, we want to compare it with Prior's point in the root canal example. In our reconstruction, we are presented with Arthur, about whom we know very little. We know that he had a root canal performed on him on Friday, June 15, 1954 and that, upon finishing, he's feeling thankful because it's over, and thus utters (1). Now, according to B-theories, all there is to time is the B-relations and there is no ontological difference between past, present, and future. If we accept this view, all Arthur thinks is that the conclusion of his root canal happened at a time that is earlier than the time of (1). But this, Prior suggests, is insufficient to generate emotions of thankfulness. It would certainly be odd if Arthur were to exclaim, referring to the end of the root canal,

(4) Thank goodness that's earlier than the time of this utterance!

or any of the other tenseless alternatives, such as (2) and (3). Arthur needs a different type of thought, an A-thought, to feel thankful. If B-thoughts were all the knowledge Arthur had, there would be certain non-B facts about time he wouldn't know. Hence B-theories are wrong and A-properties are fundamental elements of reality. We can reformulate Prior's challenge as follows:

(a) If B-theory is true, then reality is tenseless (all events are ordered by B-relations and there are no A-properties).
(b) If reality is tenseless, then all knowledge is about tenseless reality (events ordered by B-relations).

(c) Arthur knows that the date of the conclusion of the root canal is Friday, June 15, 1954 (a B-thought), so he knows all there is to know about the time of conclusion of the root canal.
(d) On Friday, June 15, 1954, it should be reasonable for him to utter (3) ("Thank goodness the conclusion of the root canal is contemporaneous with this utterance"), but this is not the case; uttering (1) is reasonable.
(e) What Arthur thinks when uttering (1) must be tensed (an A-thought).
(f) Hence B-theory is false.

The structure of Prior's argument resembles the structure of the knowledge argument. Facing it, B-theorists are in a position similar to that of physicalists facing Jackson's argument. They can accept premises (a)–(d) with no qualms. What they need to reject is conclusion (f) and the ontological reading of (e). If all (e) says is that the kind of thought that Arthur has to have in order to motivate him to utter (1) is an A-thought, then the B-theorists can accept it.[7] If what (e) claims is that the A-thought is about an A-fact, then the B-theorists should reject it.

Going further in the parallelism, the position of the B-theorist who accepts (a)–(d) plus the epistemological reading of (e) and rejects the ontological reading of (e) plus (f) can be tagged as a "new A-thought/old B-fact" sort of view. We show now how such a view would account for Prior's insights.

4 New A-Thought/Old B-Fact

Prior's argument, as we reconstruct it, makes the following assumptions about language, thought, and reality:

i. Utterances (1)–(3) express different propositions.
ii. Utterances (1)–(3) are associated with different thoughts.
iii. The proposition related to utterance (1) and its associated thought require the existence of an A-property of events.[8]

---

[7] This would essentially be the position of so-called "new B-theorists" like Mellor (1998) and Oaklander (1994).

[8] It could be argued that Prior's challenge suggests the stronger assumption that *all* utterances (1)–(3) and their associated thoughts require the existence of A-properties. We stick to the weaker claim, first, because it seems to be all he is clearly committing to in his 1959 paper and, second, because, if our criticism of the weaker assumption is right, then it will also be valid against the stronger one.

Our approach makes different assumptions. To begin with, we deny assumption (i). The sentences used in (1)–(3) have different meanings but, in the imagined circumstances, Arthur says the same thing; he expresses the same proposition. This is implied by a direct reference theory of indexicals like "I," "here," and "now," demonstratives like "she," "he," "this," and "that," names like "Jones," "Arthur," and "Mary," and (referential uses of) definite descriptions like "Smith's murderer," "the queen of England," and "the time of this utterance." In the right circumstances (described in brackets), the speaker says the same thing in uttering (5)–(8).

(5) I am insane (uttered by Jones).
(6) He is insane (uttered by Williams pointing to Jones).
(7) Jones is insane.
(8) Smith's murderer is insane (uttered intending the audience to pick out Jones).

The proposition expressed here is a singular proposition involving the individual Jones and the property of being insane. This is true if and only if the individual Jones is insane, regardless of what his name is, of whether or not he uttered (5), and of whether or not he murdered Smith.[9] Barcan Marcus (1961), Donnellan (1966), Kaplan (1989a, 1989b), Kripke (1980), Perry (1977, 1979) and others have provided convincing arguments that all these noun phrases contribute an individual to the proposition expressed by the utterance containing them. Using them in the appropriate circumstances, the speakers would express the same proposition; they would say the same thing.[10]

Along the same lines, we contend that (1)–(3) express the same proposition, a proposition that has the same time—Friday, June 15, 1954—referred to by the utterance of the (implicit) indexical "now" in (1), by the name "Friday, June 15, 1954" in (2), and by the predicate "being contemporaneous with this utterance" in (3).[11] There is no difference in what the speaker says by uttering (1)–(3) in the imagined circumstances. We agree with Prior, however, that utterances (1)–(3)—like (5)–(8)—are associated with different thoughts. What we mean by this is that their cognitive significance is

---

[9] For the sake of simplicity, in these examples we ignore issues concerning tense and time.

[10] Concerning (8), Donnellan (1966, 1978) and Kripke (1977) disagree on whether the referential use of the definite description is semantic or pragmatic, but that should not bother us here.

[11] Dates are better considered as descriptions, we believe, since they provide systematic information about the position of their referents with respect to other days. Also, an account is due of how the predicate "being contemporaneous with this utterance" refers to a particular time or day; but we ignore these complications, assuming that they bear no relevance for our present purposes.

different; or, more precisely, that in each utterance the thought that likely motivates the speaker (and the thought that the hearer likely acquires) are different. Take (5)–(8) again. If Jones wants to express the proposition that he is insane in a communicatively apt way, (5) would be typically his most likely choice. To begin with, the normal way of thinking about oneself is essentially indexical: This is a kind of thought that each of us would express using the first-person singular pronoun. Besides, this is the most direct way for his audience to identify the guy whom Jones is talking about: himself or, better, the guy talking in front of it. He could have expressed the same proposition with (6)–(8), but in normal circumstances the use of "he," "Jones," or "Smith's murderer" would impose an extra cognitive burden on the audience. Something similar happens in Prior's example.

Ex hypothesi, Arthur is in "a perceptual dateless haze" (Prior, 1959, 17) when he utters (1), and this is why it is clearly his most natural and practically only choice: (2) is unavailable to him, and (3) is an unnecessarily verbose (token-reflexive) rendering of "now." His motivating thought is essentially indexical: It contains (the mental equivalent of) "now" and the present tense. That is to say, it is essentially tensed: an A-thought. It is also the most direct way to communicate his thought to the audience: Its members identify the moment (day) of the utterance they're hearing. Utterance (2) imposes extra cognitive burden not only on the audience but on Arthur himself. It requires from him a knowledge about dates that he doesn't have, in his dazed condition, and from audience members an identification of the calendar date with the day of the utterance they are hearing. So, in those circumstances, (1) is the only natural utterance, as Prior says.

Suppose, however, that the New Zealand Dental Association announced that, starting on Monday, June 18, 1954 new prices for dental practices will be in force and that the new price for a root canal will be twice the previous one. In this context, once the root canal is concluded, Arthur's uttering (2) would sound perfectly natural when he is presented with the bill. He could also have uttered (1), but that wouldn't be communicatively very helpful to people who don't remember that the following Monday is June 18, 1954, the day the price of a root canal is going to double.

Or suppose that Arthur, still in his "perceptual dateless haze," reads in a newspaper "Root canals to double in price starting Monday, June 18" and in his diary "Root canal" as an entry under Friday, June 15. As far as he knows, those dates can be situated in his past, his extended present, or his future. He just has the B-thought that his root canal be (tenseless) Friday, June 15, which is a couple of days earlier than the day of the rise in price: Monday, June 18. Thus he sincerely utters (2).

To sum up, (1)–(3) express the same proposition as (5)–(8) do, even if they are communicatively apt in different circumstances, because they are associated with different cognitive routes for their respective audiences. Now, does this have any consequence for the existence of A-properties of events? If we are right, the answer is no.

The only fact that makes (5)–(8) true is that a certain individual—regardless of his name—referred to by himself with the indexical "I" or by someone else with a name, a demonstrative, or a description, is insane. Analogously, since (1)–(3) are taken to occur exactly at the same time, they are all made true by the same fact: a fact involving Arthur and his thankfulness regarding a root canal performed and concluded at a particular time on a particular date. It does not matter whether the event that Arthur is thankful about is in Arthur's past, present, or future (and then it would not yet exist). The only thing that matters for the truth of (1)–(3) is that at the time of the utterance Arthur is thankful about an event that occurs (tenselessly) on Friday, June 15, 1954—a B-event; and, if real, an old B-fact.

5 Back to Mary

In section 3 we showed how Prior's argument is similar to Jackson's knowledge argument. Both go from predominantly epistemological premises to ontological conclusions. We claim now that Jackson's knowledge argument can also be viewed as involving various assumptions about the content of certain utterances that contain color terms, their cognitive significance, and the kind of things that make them true. Suppose that Mary—who knows everything there is to know about the physical properties of colors but has never seen anything red—upon seeing a red tomato for the first time expresses her happiness at having her first color experience. Sentence (9) sounds like a natural utterance.[12] Utterance (10) sounds bizarre. Why would anyone thank goodness about that?

   (9) Thank goodness I finally see red!
   (10) Thank goodness I finally see the color evoked by light with a predominant wavelength of roughly 620–740 nm.!

"Priorized" Jackson makes the following three assumptions:

---

[12] Utterance (9) might sound misleading. Arguably, Mary has seen red things in the past (say, on her black-and-white TV). What is new is knowing what it is like to see red. Mary's new knowledge is about the color red: "Red has the property of being like *this* to see (for a normal person)." That is what she is expressing by uttering (9). (Thanks to John Perry for raising this point.)

(I) Utterances (9) and (10) express different propositions.
(II) Utterances (9) and (10) are associated with different thoughts.
(III) The proposition related to utterance (9) and its associated thought require the existence of nonphysical properties of visual experiences of color.

If (I) is rejected and (II) accepted, there is a pretty straightforward way to account for the intuitions raised by the example, without needing to accept anything like (III).

Direct reference theories of natural kind colors, like Kripke's (1980), for instance, tell us that, if an identity statement like "red is the color evoked by light with a predominant wavelength of roughly 620–740 nm." is true, then it is necessarily true.[13] Hence there is nothing more to the meaning of a natural kind term like "red" than its theoretical (and physicalist) definition, and the contributions each term makes to the proposition expressed by (9) and (10) is exactly the same—their common referent.

Utterances (9) and (10) have different cognitive significance, however. They are associated with different thoughts. One can believe that (11) is true and disbelieve, or at least suspend belief about, (12).

(11) This tomato is red.
(12) This tomato is the color evoked by light with a predominant wavelength of roughly 620–740 nm.

Of course, the difference lies in the different thoughts associated to each utterance. Utterances (9) and (11) use the ordinary concept "red"; (10) and (12) use the theoretical description "the color evoked by light with a predominant wavelength of roughly 620–740 nm." They constitute different motivating thoughts and, typically, they produce a different impact on their audience.

In the imagined circumstances, (9) sounds natural whereas its cumbersome counterpart (10) sounds anything but natural. But there might be circumstances in which (10) could be more natural. Suppose that Mary forgets for a second the color name associated with the description "the color evoked by light with a predominant wavelength of roughly 620–740 nm.," but remembers perfectly that the predominant wavelength of approximately 620–740 nm. is the one corresponding to tomatoes, fire hydrants and the typical neck scarfs, belts, and berets of bull runners in Iruñea (Pamplona). Sentence (12) is, then, if not the most natural, the only available means to express the

---

[13] Necessarily true but known a posteriori.

proposition Mary wants to express. Or imagine that Mary is with her grandpa Frank, a philosopher and a physicist, the person responsible for her perfect knowledge of the physics of colors as well as for her confinement in the black-and-white room. Utterance (9) can be quite an imprecise way of talking about colors, so the most communicatively apt way for her to talk with him would be (10), not (9).

The point is that (9) and (10) express the same proposition involving the perception of a certain color, even if they are associated with different motivating thoughts that account for their differing cognitive significance. The examples, so accounted, bear no impact on the metaphysics of colors or on our conscious experience of them. The colors and our experience of them remain the same. It is in our linguistic practices and in the thoughts that motivate them that the relevant difference lies, not in the ontology of colors or in our experiences.

6 Linking A- and B-Thoughts

Going further into the interpretation of Prior's challenge to B-theories as a knowledge argument, it is worth noticing that this challenge involves an epistemic issue regarding the connection between different kinds of thoughts *via* pertinent identity relations. Let us turn now to explain this.

In the initial circumstances envisioned by Prior, with Arthur in a "perceptual dateless haze," the only available option to express himself is an A-utterance, (1), associated with an A-thought regarding the conclusion of the root canal. Utterance (2), which includes the date of the root canal, is clearly not an option, given that he lacks the relevant B-thought.

Or, better said, he lacks knowledge of a particular identity (13) that would allow him to link the two relevant A- and B-thoughts:

(13) Today is Friday, June 15, 1954.

This crucial role of identity thoughts like (13) is not restricted to knowledge about time, as has been duly noticed. Take a well-known example discussed by Perry (2002):

> Ernest Mach tells of getting on the end of a bus and seeing a scruffy, unkempt bookish looking sort of person at the other end. He thought to himself:
>
> (14) That man is a shabby pedagogue.
>
> In fact, Mach was seeing himself in a large mirror at the far end of the bus, of the sort conductors use to help keep track of things. He eventually realized this and thought to himself:

> (15) I am that man.
> (16) I am a shabby pedagogue.
>
> Now consider Mach at the earlier time. Did Mach have self-knowledge?... it seems that he did. After all, he knew that a certain person was a shabby pedagogue. Furthermore, that person was, in fact, him. The knower and the person known about were the same. But this case isn't really what we have in mind when we talk of self-knowledge. Self-knowledge is something Mach really only had when he got to step (16), when he would have used the word "I" to express what he knew. (Perry, 2002, 192; examples are renumbered)

Coming to know the identity expressed as (15)—that is, recognizing the man in the mirror as himself—allows Mach to link a demonstrative thought like (14) to an indexically expressible thought like (16), which will prompt him to take some action, say, put his shirt into his trousers or tidy up his bow tie.

A similar case can be built around our temporal reasoning. Imagine that Anna is planning to go on a trip to Iceland on September 18, 2015. That trip is important for her, she is really looking forward to it, and she needs to make different arrangements to make it happen. Knowing that she is a very absent-minded person and fearing she might forget the date of the trip, she fills her house with post-its that read: "Trip to Iceland, September 18."

On the morning of September 18, however, Anna wakes up not knowing what day it is. She goes to the kitchen and sees one of her Iceland post-its but, not knowing the truth about the identity statement saying that "September 18 is today," she goes on with her daily routines. Despite her best efforts, she fails to go to the airport in time and she sadly misses her trip.

Anna's case is similar to Mach's. In like manner, we could ask: Did Anna know that her trip was to take place on the same day she was living in? Well, in a sense, she did. She knew that the trip was to take place on September 18, 2015, and September 18 was in fact the day she was living in. But, as in Mach's case, this isn't what we have in mind when we say that someone knows what day she is living in—and what happens on that day. Anna only gets to know (18) when she realizes that this is the case (17):

> (17) Today is September 18, 2015
> (18) Hence the trip to Iceland is today.

Paraphrasing Perry, this is when she would have used the word "today" to express what she knew. What she needs, in other words, is to realize that she is looking at one object, the day she is living in, from two different angles. She needs to realize that her B-thought is about the same day as the day she is living in—today.

Taking it one step further, establishing the analogy between Anna's case and Arthur's is also quite straightforward. Anna has a B-thought about the trip—she knows the date—but, given her ignorance of the relevant identity, she has no A-thought about it, in other words she doesn't know that the trip is today, or present. And, just as B-thoughts alone would have been insufficient to bring about Arthur's thankfulness, B-thoughts alone are insufficient to bring about the appropriate actions from Anna. In Prior's terms, the knowledge she needs in order to act is "something which it is impossible that any use of a tenseless copula with a date should convey" (Prior, 1959, 17).

7   Conclusion

So far, we have defended that utterances (1)–(3) express the same proposition, but that they are associated with different thoughts. That is, we reject Prior's first assumption—utterances (1)–(3) express different propositions—and accept, with qualifications, the second one—utterances (1)–(3) are associated with different thoughts. We have also asserted that this should not have any ontological bearing, that is, that Prior's third assumption—the proposition related to utterance (1) and with its associated thought requires the existence of an A-property of events—should be rejected. We now elaborate a bit on this.

One can look at time from what we might call an absolutist or external perspective or a participant's or internal perspective. The first is the perspective adopted by physicists and metaphysicians. It brings about "objective" thoughts or B-thoughts, and it is usually expressed by indexicals such as "now," "today," or "present."

The internal perspective on time and the resulting A-thoughts, which are closely tied to the agent's cognitive capacities and limitations and to what happens or not in the agent's surroundings, set some requirements and limitations to events in time, or rather to the way these events are presented to us. A-thoughts about the present are intimately related to events the agent can perceive, to what is happening in the agent's surroundings.[14] A-thoughts about the present include, then, whatever could be perceived by the agent, if she were in the appropriate spatial location. The movement of my fingers as I write is present in relation to me,[15] and that generates some A-thoughts about it, which could be expressed as

---

[14] Note that all animals have a special way of knowing what goes on "now, here, to me," even though they don't have a language. The indexicals are connected to those primitive sorts of thoughts. See Perry, 2017, section 8.2.

[15] The use of the first-person singular pronoun is too expedient to abandon just because we happen to be two authors.

(19) My fingers are moving (now).

Notice, however, that I could also have A-thoughts about somebody moving her fingers in Buckingham Palace now, just because, if I were in Buckingham Palace right now, I would be able to perceive it. Being perceivable is thus a requisite for having an A-thought about the present.

A requisite for having A-thoughts about the past is being memorable. A-thoughts about the past involve all that could be remembered by the agent or, more broadly, all the events the agent thinks have happened but can no longer be perceived by her. Thus I can think of the concert I attended in Albert Hall last summer as past, that is, I can have an A-thought about it, because I can no longer perceive it. It is only a memory. The natural language expression of that thought would then be something like,

(20) The concert at Albert Hall is over.

Also, I can have A-thoughts about a concert played in Albert Hall in, say, 1959, even though I wasn't born in 1959 and so that cannot be one of my memories. It is past because, had I been there, I would be able to remember it now. It is past also because it is an event that has already happened, one that I think has happened, and one that I cannot perceive, no matter where I am.[16]

Notice that this is completely independent of what time is, ontologically speaking. Ours is not an ontological proposal, but an epistemic and a linguistic one. Indeed, the agent's time and physical time, or time simpliciter, don't have to coincide.[17] It seems clear that being a memory is linked with being past, being predictable with being future, and being perceivable with being present, but this is restricted to the internal perspective. From this perspective, then, past, present, and future are indeed real and fundamental elements without which no explanation of our thoughts, emotions, and actions would be possible. But that carries no fundamental ontological weight. It is an epistemic thesis. It talks about how we, as agents, perceive and think about time, and about how events have a different impact on us depending on their

---

[16] For simplicity's sake, we ignore the possibility of watching or listening to a recording of the concert. Also, we leave aside A-thoughts about the future.

[17] And indeed it seems that they don't. Take the case of the present. According to special relativity, there is no such thing as absolute simultaneity, and thus the circumstance that something is present can hardly be an objective fact. How to interpret special relativity is a complex issue, though, as is its relevance to philosophical debate. Prior, for instance, rejected this interpretation of special relativity. See Prior (1970) and Godfrey-Smith (1979)

temporal relation to us. It is neutral on how or what time really is. What characterizes both A-thoughts and self-knowledge, we are claiming, is not *what* is thought but *how* it is thought. Prior's mistake, we think, was to confuse these two aspects.

Needless to say, this would have to be further developed in order to be a compelling account of temporal knowledge and temporal ontology. We believe, though, that even at this primitive level of elaboration, it presents a much more commonsense view on Arthur's thoughts, emotions, and utterances, and in particular, on differences in our ways of referring to time in language and representing it in thought. One clear advantage of our proposal over Prior's is that it keeps ontology simple. Or as simple as it can be. The same could be said of "new knowledge/old fact" types for answers to Jackson's knowledge argument. We haven't presented any definite ontological argument in defense of B-theories but hopefully we have outlined a way to resist one type of argument in favor of adding new entities to the world, namely A-properties. Prior's challenge, taken as an ontological argument, is a red herring.[18]

---

[18] Thanks to Eros Corazza, John Perry, and an anonymous referee for their comments and suggestions. The final version was prepared during a stay at the Center for the Study of Language and Information (CSLI), Stanford University, and we are thankful to John Perry, Chris Potts, Dikran Karagueuzian, Emma Pease, and Michelle Lodwick for hosting us. This work was partially supported by the Basque Government (IT1032-16), as well as by the Spanish Ministries of Economy and Competitivity (FFI2012-37726; FFI2015- 63719-P MINECO/FEDER, UE) and Education, Culture, and Sports (PRX15/00481).

12

Truth without Reference: The Use of Fictional Names

María de Ponte, Kepa Korta, and John Perry

1 Introduction

Singular terms without referents are called *empty* or *vacuous* terms. But not all of them are equally empty. In particular, not all proper names that fail to name an existing object fail in the same way: Although they are all empty, they are not all equally vacuous. "Vulcan," "Jacob Horn," "Odysseus," and "Sherlock Holmes," for instance, are all empty. They have no referents. But they are not entirely vacuous or useless. They convey information. They are empty in different ways, and thus some of them at least are not-so-vacuous. Consider the following statements:

(1) Vulcan causes the perturbations of Mercury's orbit.
(2) Odysseus was set ashore at Ithaca while sound asleep.
(3) Zeus was chief of the gods.
(4) Jacob Horn was an important person in Colonial America.
(5) Sherlock Holmes lived in 221B Baker Street, London, England.

Any of these might appear on a true/false exam, in the appropriate class. In an Astronomy Class, the right answer for (1) would be "F." In an American History Class, the right answer for (4) would be "F." But in Literature or Classics courses, the right answer to (2), (3) and (5) would be "T." This doesn't settle the issue of whether statements with empty names have truth-values. But it shows that there are correct and incorrect answers, and that the mere fact that the names contained in them are empty is not enough to decide on this issue.

Let us analyze each statement in a bit more detail. (1) is a scientific hypothesis about a planet called "Vulcan," which, as it turned out, doesn't really exist. (1) is nowadays taken to be false, and the discovery of its falsity is a piece of astronomic knowledge. Though empty, "Vulcan" is not so vacuous. One might agree that empty names have no place in science, if by "science" one means "finished science." But they play key roles in scientific practice and they have played important roles in the history of science.

(2) belongs to Homer's poem and is one of Frege's famous examples. He says that "it is a matter of no concern to us whether the name 'Odysseus' … has a *Bedeutung,* so long as we accept the poem as a work of art." But, if the name is empty, then (2) lacks a truth-value: "…since it is doubtful whether the name 'Odysseus' … has a *Bedeutung,* it is also doubtful whether the whole sentence does" (Frege, 1892 [1997], 157). Frege takes (2), and any simple statement containing empty names, to be neither true nor false. Russell takes them to be false.

Things are a bit more complicated. Our intuitions about the truth-value of statements containing empty names diverge. Sometimes, we tend to agree with Frege that they lack a truth-value, but often we tend to take them as true or false, depending on whether the names purport to refer to actual, mythological, or fictional "objects." The scare quotes are due, of course, to our resistance to calling the referents of fictional or mythological names "objects." In our view, all these names are empty, i.e., there is no object to which they refer, but from that it does not follow that all statements containing them are false, or that they lack truth-value.

Take (3). We are now fairly confident that "Zeus" does not refer to an existent object, but presumably many ancient Greeks thought it did, and believed that (3) was true. Once we identify Zeus as a myth and "Zeus" as empty, however, we generally keep the intuition that (3) is nonetheless true, because it is an accepted part of the myth. So, in contrast,

(6) Aphrodite was chief of the gods,

is false. In other words, in a Classics class "T" would be the right answer for (3) and "F" for (6). Actually, things can get even more complicated. While in a Classics class "T" might be the right answer for (3), in a Basic Dogma class in a Catholic High School, the right answer would be "F."

That is not what happens with (4). With the publication of *The Horn Papers* by William Horn in 1945 as the diary of Jacob Horn,[1] people came to believe (4) to be true. But, when it was discovered that the diary was a hoax, that Jacob Horn didn't actually exist, everyone took it not only to be untrue—

---

[1] Example of Perry, 2001 [2012], 2012a, after Donnellan, 1974.

for lack of a truth-value, as Fregeans would conclude—but false. They realized they had been fooled, and that what they believed to be true was not.

Again, with (5), things are quite different. We all know that Sherlock Holmes is a fictional character created by Arthur Conan Doyle, and that there was no actual person to whom the name "Sherlock Holmes" refers. Our intuition, however, is that (5) is true, while (7), for instance, is false:

(7) Sherlock Holmes lived in 221B Boulanger Street, Paris, France.

Fictional names—like "Sherlock Holmes"—seem to have more in common with mythological names—like "Zeus" or "Aphrodite"—than with hoax names—like "Jacob Horn." At least in the sense indicated here. Finally, all seven statements above differ from

(8) Ignatius P. Thunderbold had five arms.

We just made this name up. It isn't part of a myth or a story or a legend or a fraud. It is not even part of a story we are telling. You might suppose that the sentence must be correct, since we made up the name, and we said it. But we didn't assert it. It's just an example of a completely and utterly vacuous name. As such it differs from the ones in the list. There is no standard for correctness, there is no class where an answer to (8) might be correct or incorrect.

We are basically referentialists about proper names. The ordinary semantic function of a proper name is to refer to an object, and to do it directly, that is, without semantically providing any identifying condition that the object should meet to be the referent. To put it differently, we agree that statements containing proper names express *singular* propositions, i.e., that their truth-conditions involve the referent of the proper name, if it exists, and not any identifying condition of it. Now, since empty names lack a referent, and therefore would not express such a singular proposition, how do we explain that some, if not all, the statements (1)–(7) have a truth-value? Answering this question is the aim of this paper.

We begin with a preliminary discussion of fictional and non-fictional names in Sect. 2. Then, in Sect. 3, we present our account of ordinary uses of ordinary (non-fictional, non-mythological, non-empty) names, which is based on *Critical Referentialism* (Perry, 2001 [2012], 2012a), and *Critical Pragmatics* (Korta and Perry, 2011). In Sect. 4, we elaborate the explanation to cover the cases of ordinary uses of empty names. In Sect. 5, we present our account of fictional names, and, in Sect. 6, we conclude.

2 Fictional and Non-Fictional Names

To repeat, not all empty names are equally empty. For present purposes, we will take fictional names to be those proper names that are initially used in works of fiction to *fictionally refer* to particular people, places, objects and so on, and later to talk, outside fiction, about those fictional people, places, objects and so forth.[2] Our particular focus will be on the uses of fictional names in statements like (2), (5) and (7) above, which purportedly express *fictional truths* (or *falsities),* addressing mythology, frauds and empty names in ordinary discourse only as important preliminaries.

A fictional truth concerns a fictional story and the facts according to the story. These facts can be explicit or implicit in the story. We call statements about fictional facts made, so to speak, outside fiction *parafictional* statements. They are actual statements made by actual speakers (or writers) about fictional states of affairs, i.e. about states of affairs explicitly or implicitly depicted in a work of fiction; states of affairs that are part of the story told. Parafictional statements are not fictional statements. Neither (5) nor (7) are lines from any of Sherlock Holmes's stories. Watson never uttered (5) or (7), neither as narrator nor as a character. No other character or narrator ever fictionally uttered (5) or (7).

We call the statements (or pseudo-statements, or pretense- statements, if you prefer) made by the author, the narrator or the characters of a work of fiction *fictional* statements. Fictional statements are part of the work of fiction; parafictional statements are not; they designate fictional states of affairs that belong (or not) to the fictional story.

Any ordinary (*full* or *empty*) proper name, say, "Gaius Julius Caesar" or "Vulcan" can become fictional, if it's used in a work of fiction to identify a fictional character or a planet, for instance. That is, if they are used in fictional statements. And then, exploiting what we call a name-notion-network of co-reference, we use those names in statements about the events in the work of fiction, that is to say, in producing parafictional statements.

Consider how the proper names in a very well-known fiction were first introduced. The first mention of "Sherlock Holmes" is in the title of Chapter I ("Mr. Sherlock Holmes") of *A Study in Scarlet*, whose Part I is presented as a non-fictional diary of John H. Watson, M.D., setting the latter as the narrator.

---

[2] Given that we are talking about empty names, it might be more appropriate to avoid "refer" and use "identify" "as a way of picking out the phenomenon of aboutness, or object-directedness, without ontological commitment" (Friend, 2014, 307) to the existence of a reference, but we think it will be enough to keep in mind that, in our account, whatever the speaker's or hearer's intentions and beliefs, if a name is empty then it cannot be successfully used to refer to any object, be it actual, fictional, or mythological.

The first mention of Baker Street is part of a *fictional* utterance by Sherlock Holmes in his first conversation with Watson, in their first appearance in a fictional story:

> "I have my eye on a suite in Baker Street," he [Holmes] said, "which would suit us down to the ground." (Conan Doyle, 1887 [2010], 4)

The narrator—Watson—says a little later

> We met next day as he had arranged, and inspected the rooms at No. 221B, Baker Street, of which he had spoken at our meeting. (Conan Doyle, 1887 [2010], 4)

London appears in the first sentence of Chapter I: "In the year 1878 I took my degree of Doctor of Medicine of the University of London," (Conan Doyle, 1887 [2010], 1).

This is how the fictional names "Sherlock Holmes" and "[Doctor] John H. Watson" are introduced. As names for fictional characters made up by Arthur Conan Doyle,[3] whose adventures will be narrated in a number of novels and short stories from 1887 to 1927.[4] In our view, this is the beginning of a wide network of what we call "coco-reference" that reaches to the present day.[5]

There are a huge number of novels, movies, and TV series based on these two characters, with the very same names and—roughly—similar features. One might wonder whether the uses of "Sherlock Holmes" related to, for instance, the recent BBC series do co-refer with the uses of the name in statements about Conan Doyle's stories; that is to say, whether we are talking about the same fictional character or not. We are not going to discuss this question in detail, but our intuitions lead us to suspect that, despite their many similarities, in these particular examples the two Sherlock Holmeses are two different fictional characters. For instance, the parafictional statement

(9) Doctor Watson and Mary Morstan got married in 1889,

---

[3] Reportedly, "Arthur Ignatius Conan" was the author's given name and "Doyle" his surname. Sometime after high school he started using "Conan Doyle" as a sort of compound surname. So technically his family name was just "Doyle," but we would rather respect his wishes and follow common practice by referring to him as "Conan Doyle."

[4] We think that "London" and "Baker Street" are also fictional names. We discuss these cases below.

[5] More about networks and coco-reference below. See Chaps. 8 and 9 of Perry, 2001 [2012] and Chap. 7 of Korta and Perry, 2011.

is true if the names correspond to the characters in Conan Doyle's stories, but false if they correspond to the characters in the BBC series, which situates the action in the twenty-first century. To be sure, this is not a definite argument for the "two-character" view, but it certainly triggers intuitions in its favor.

Coming back to Conan Doyle's stories, are "221B Baker street" and "London" fictional names? Are they empty, or do they actually refer to actual London, and actual 221B Baker Street? In this respect, we side with Frege (1897 [1997]) and against Kripke (2013): We think they do not refer to actual cities and streets.[6] And, consequently, "London" and "221B Baker Street," both in parafictional statements like (5) and in fictional statements uttered by fictional characters, are as fictional as "Sherlock Holmes." The fact that there was and still is a *real* city called "London," in a *real* country, and in the *real* world, doesn't mean that this city is the one referred to by all uses of "London," and it certainly doesn't mean that *real* London is the city referred to with the use of "London" in Conan Doyle's stories or in parafictional statements like (5). Similarly, the existence of a *real* person called "Sherlock Holmes," if there is one, would not make all uses of "Sherlock Holmes" refer to this *real* person and it wouldn't mean that all uses of the name in Conan Doyle's stories refer to this *real* person.

To be sure, at the time when Conan Doyle published the stories, addresses in Baker Street did not go as high as 221, so the name "221B Baker Street, London" in (5), if taken as an ordinary non-fictional name, is empty at the relevant time, so (5) should be deemed false. In any case, even if there was such an address in the *real* world, the idea of a fictional character living in an actual flat in London is nonsense.[7] In fictional stories and parafictional

---

[6] Frege says:

> If Schiller's *Don Carlos* were to be regarded as a piece of history, then to a large extent the drama would be false. But a work of fiction is not meant to be taken seriously in this way at all: it is all play. Even the proper names in the drama, though they correspond to names of historical persons, are mock proper names; they are not meant to be taken seriously in the work. (Frege, 1897 [1997], 230)

Kripke says:

> Just because something occurs in the story, it does not mean that the entity so named is fictional. There are fictional stories, for example, about Napoleon—a real person—and in commenting on those stories one says that Napoleon really existed, but his faithful dog Fido in the story did not—he is from the fictional part. (Kripke, 2013, 20)

We disagree with Kripke.

[7] Consider the case of a parent who tells their child "Sherlock Holmes lives in this street" or "Sherlock Holmes lives here." Of course, these statements make perfect sense, but we think that the demonstratives are used metonymically, that is, that by referring to the real street the speaker is making a parafictional statement involving a fictional place. They would need to make this explicit if, for instance, the child asks "Where exactly?", and acknowledge that there is no real

statements, then, we assume that proper names *are about* fictional people, places, pets, et cetera.[8] Of course, it remains to explain how this works, what fictional characters are, and what we mean by "aboutness" if the names are empty.

We should distinguish the following kinds of statements:

(i) *ordinary "literal" statements* containing proper names that are purported to refer to actual objects,[9] and whose truth concerns actual facts;
(ii) fictional *statements* by authors, narrators and characters in works of fiction;
(iii) parafictional *statements* that concern the fictional facts; and
(iv) metafictional *statements*. These are ordinary statements about actual facts about the fiction. For instance,

(10) Sherlock Holmes is a fictional character created by Arthur Conan Doyle.

This is a true statement because it corresponds to actual facts. We have to be careful to make these distinctions appropriately, because sometimes our intuitions about the truth-value of these kinds of statements depends on whether we interpret them as ordinary, fictional, parafictional or metafictional. Take

(11) Sherlock Holmes does not exist.[10]

"here" or "this street," no 221B Baker Street, where Sherlock Holmes lives. Thanks to an anonymous referee for raising the issue.

[8] We think this is compatible with the Reality Assumption. The Reality Assumption as formulated by Friend (2017) says that "everything that is true or obtains in the real world is storified ... unless it is excluded by the work." (Friend, 2017, 31). We are justified to assume that what is really true (false) about the real London of the 1880s is fictionally true (false) about Doyle's fictional London *unless excluded by the work*. Thus, there is no 221B Baker Street in actual London, but we cannot assume that for fictional London, because it is excluded by the Holmes stories. Anyhow, it may be worth reminding that the reality assumption "is not a mechanism for generating implied story-truths" but just "a starting point for specifying the input into any such mechanism" (Friend, 2017, 34).

[9] We don't like to apply "literal" to ordinary non-fictional discourse, because, as Searle (1975) says, it wrongly suggests that fiction is somehow figurative or non-literal speech.

[10] As is usual in philosophy, negative existential statements like (11) should be taken as tenseless, equivalent to "X didn't, doesn't and will not exist." Thus, people like Socrates and Aristotle exist, even if defunct.

If taken as an ordinary statement, it seems perfectly true, but if considered as a parafictional statement, it is false—Sherlock exists and lives in 221B Baker Street, in the fiction. And perhaps it is also false as a metafictional statement—Sherlock, the fictional character, exists since it was created by Conan Doyle. Actually, things are more complicated, since we can have ordinary/parafictional/metafictional *mixed statements*. Take

(12) Sherlock Holmes does not exist—he's a fictional character.

In the most charitable interpretation, the first statement should be taken as an ordinary statement while the second should be interpreted as metafictional. But, if taken as parafictional, for instance, they would both be false. Eventually, a full account of fictional names would have to cover all these cases,[11] but we'll concentrate on their use in parafictional statements.

Also, notice that all these distinctions should also apply to mythology, that is, to ordinary vs. mythological vs. *paramythological* vs. *metamythological* statements. The main difference is that mythological names, at least in many cases, were once thought to name existing objects. But this should not be too relevant for our present purposes. In any case, to introduce our take on fictional names, we have to start discussing the case of ordinary non-empty names.

3 Ordinary Non-Empty Names

As referentialists, we assume that an utterance of

(13) Cicero was a Roman Senator,

is true if and only if a certain person, the referent of the use of "Cicero" in (13), had the property of being a member of the Roman Senate. These truth-conditions involve an existing object (a certain person) and a property (we can ignore tense and time issues for present purposes), and, using common philosophical parlance, we can represent it as a singular proposition; a proposition that, if true, would remain true whatever the name of the object, and whether or not (13) was ever produced as an utterance. Philosophers often represent this proposition as

---

[11] The previous list of uses is not meant to be exhaustive. We ignore, for instance, *interfictional* statements such as "Sherlock Holmes is taller than Hercules Poirot" which, by the way, we think is true—Holmes "was rather over 6 feet" while Poirot was 5'4". Anyhow, as one of the referees observes, in our account, one and the same sentence can be used in more than one way, so the speaker's intentions are needed to determine which sort of statement she makes.

(14) <*Roman-Senator,* **c**>,

and say that (13) expresses it.

Notice, however, that this way of putting things might obscure the fact that different kinds of truth-conditions are in place. For (13) to be true the following conditions must obtain:[12]

E (existential condition). That **c** exists.
R (reference condition). That the use of "Cicero" in (13) refers to **c**.
S (satisfaction condition). That **c** is a Roman senator.

The satisfaction condition S, which is basically equivalent to the proposition (14), requires that "Cicero" refers to **c** (R), which, in turn, requires that **c** exists (E). Distinguishing among these sorts of truth-conditions is critical, for instance, when we want to distinguish between the truth-conditions of (13) and (15):

(15) Tully was a Roman senator.

As referentialists, we acknowledge that (15) also expresses the proposition (14), with object **c** and property *Roman-senator* as constituents. In other words, the same satisfaction condition S applies. The existential condition E is also the same—**c** must exist. But the reference condition is different. R puts conditions on the use of the name "Cicero" but the truth of (15) doesn't require anything from the name "Cicero." Rather, what we find in (15) is a condition on the use of the name "Tully," i.e. that it must refer to **c**.

Acknowledging this is not tantamount to the abandonment of referentialism about proper names; we are not assuming that an identifying condition is associated with names as part of their meaning. We are just assuming that proper names are not semantically associated with a single actual object. Following Strawson, we claim that proper names do not refer, people do, by using names and other expressions (indexicals, demonstratives, descriptions), or even with no expressions (with referents as unarticulated constituents).[13]

---

[12] For the sake of simplicity, we ignore the conditions for the predicate "is a Roman Senator" to denote the property it does.

[13] It's become customary to credit Strawson with this view about reference and truth as opposed to Frege's. Frege's own words do not exclude speakers as the agents of the acts of designating a referent and expressing a sense; quite the opposite. He says, "A proper name (word, sign, combination of signs, expression) *expresses* its sense, and *stands for [bedeutet]* or *designates [bezeichnet]* its *Bedeutung.*" But he immediately adds, "By employing a sign we express its sense and designate its *Bedeutung.*" (Frege, 1892 [1997], 156, emphasis in the original).

But of course, people err, and sometimes, even when we intend to refer, we do not do so. So, in our view, the reference condition is not *straightforwardly given* for any use of a name. But then, what are the conditions for reference?

Our complete picture of reference by proper names is Perry's conception of notion-name-network, which is inspired in turn by Chastain's (1975), Donnellan's (1970), Evan's (1973) and Kripke's (1980) view of chains of reference. In this paper, however, we skip many details of the proposal, to focus on the most relevant ones for present purposes: the concepts of a *network* and a *notion*.[14]

3.1 Networks

Proper names are easy to use. We don't have to have much information about the referent to be able to refer to it using a name. Except for the few occasions in which we choose a name for a child, a pet or a nickname for a friend, we rely on previous uses of the names we heard. And learning the name is precisely a way to know about it by asking questions or googling.

Imagine María tells you,

(16) Juana is coming,

you have no idea who she is referring to, apart from the fact that she's probably referring to a female person.[15] Regardless of this, if you want to get more information and you ask "Who is Juana?" you are referring to the same person that María is referring to, assuming she exists. If María answers "My mum," then you acquire some information about her, for instance, that she is alive. According to Critical Referentialism, your utterances of "Juana" refer, co-refer, and *coco*-refer (that is, *conditionally co-refer;* see Korta and Perry, 2011), because with your use of "Juana" you intend to refer to the same person that María's use of "Juana" refers to, assuming again that there is such a referent.[16]

---

[14] For other proposals about fictional names—and other singular terms used in fiction—inspired by Perry's critical referentialism (2001 [2012]), see Corazza and Whitsey, 2003, and Vallée, 2018.

[15] The use of names in natural languages often provides information about the kind of object we are referring to (city, person, pet, river, mountain, valley...) and in the case of names for people, their gender, culture, and the like. See Corazza, 2017, for an extensive discussion.

[16] In Perry's words:

> A later utterance *co-refers* with an earlier one, if both utterances refer, and refer to the same thing. A later utterance *conditionally* co-refers, or *coco-refers*, with an earlier one, if conditions are such that the later utterance will refer if the earlier one does, and refer to the same thing. So there are cases of coco-reference that are not cases of reference, and so not cases of co-reference. (Perry, 2001 [2012], 172)]

These relations of coco-reference form a *network* of coco-reference for the name, a convention that by coco-reference allows one to refer to the *origin* of that network.[17] When her parents decided to name María's mum "Juana," they established a convention that allowed speakers to refer to her with that name, creating a network of coco-reference (and co-reference, in this case) with her as origin. But what happens with empty names? That is, how do we account for networks that do not have an object at their origin?

Consider the following scenario. John tells you (4) "Jacob Horn was an important person in Colonial America." You don't want to show your ignorance about US history—while you show, without noticing, your ignorance about Donnellan's 1974 paper—so you just smile and go to Wikipedia. You are redirected to "Jakob Horn," (https://en.wikipedia.org/wiki/Jakob_Horn, accessed August 9, 2017), who is said to be a German mathematician, famous for his *Horn* functions. It rings a bell from your Logic courses. But that's not the guy John is referring to by his use of the name. You somehow arrive at the entry for *The Horn papers,* where you read that

> The Horn Papers were a genealogical hoax consisting of forged historical records pertaining to the northeastern United States for the period from 1765 to 1795. They were published by William F. Horn of Topeka, Kansas between 1933 and 1936, and presented as a transcription of documents of his great-great-great grandfather, Jacob Horn (died 1778), and other members of the Horn family. (https://en.wikipedia.org/wiki/Horn_Papers, accessed August 9, 2017)

This is the Jacob Horn John is talking about or, rather, the one he is not talking about, given that this Jacob Horn never existed. So perhaps John is teasing you, or wants to discuss Donnellan's paper, or both.

This case illustrates two things. First, that we have many networks associated to the same name. There are many Juanas in the world. We can use "Juana" exploiting the particular network of coco-reference that has María's mother as origin, or a different one, picking a different referent for our utterance. In other words, proper names are *nambiguous*, and it is a matter of a speaker's intentions which network she is trying to exploit. Consequently, we can use "Jacob/Jakob Horn" exploiting a network of coco-reference with the German mathematician as origin and, thus, refer to him; or we can exploit another network, coco-referring with John's use in (4), and fail to refer to

---

[17] In Perry's (2001 [2012]) terminology, "origin" refers to the object that is at the beginning of the name-notion-network in virtue of which an utterance of the name refers to that object. If there is no object, there is no origin, the name-notion-networks ends in a block. It is important not to confuse it with other uses of the term "origin" meant to talk about the creation by baptism, for instance, of a certain name convention.

anyone. And this is the second point. The second network, exploited by John, has no origin or, as Donnellan (1974) puts it, ends in a block. In other words, it is an empty name. In this case we have a network of coco-reference, with utterances that do not co-refer, because they don't refer. And this leads us to the main theme of the paper. Before elaborating our account of empty names, though, let us briefly present our account for the name "Cicero," as used in (13) above.

Simplifying a bit, we can assume that there is a wide network of coco-reference of the name "Cicero," with the Roman citizen Marcus Tullius Cicero (106 BCE–43 BCE) as its origin. Call it N_C. There is a smaller network for the name "Tullius" (sometimes anglicized as "Tully"), with the same individual as its origin. Call it N_T. They are not the only networks associated to these names, however. Both "Cicero" and "Tullius" are nambiguous. The speaker may intend to refer to his brother Quintus Tullius Cicero, for instance, via smaller networks with Quintus as its origin. Leaving this complication aside, we can elaborate the reference condition R of (13), making explicit the conditions on reference via networks, as follows:

RN (reference-network condition). (i) That there is a network N_C such that the use of "Cicero" in (13) exploits N_C; and (ii) has **c** as its origin.

The E and S conditions are the same as before. In the case of (11), we have a different name, "Tully" and a different network, N_T, which explains why, even if (13) and (15) are true if and only if *Roman-senator,* **c** is a fact, a competent speaker/hearer of English might believe that one is true and not the other. They share the same E and S conditions but they have different R conditions that, though true, might be unknown to such a speaker/hearer. To complete our picture of reference and cognitive significance, we need to invoke another important concept of Perry's (2001 [2012]) critical referentialism: *notions.*

3.2 Notions

Notions are mental files that store information (and misinformation) about the individuals we think and talk about. The three of us have our own separate notions of Cicero, which were born when each of us was separately—at different times on different continents—reading Ancient Roman history. Notions include ideas, and our notions of Cicero probably include similar ones, that is, ideas of being a powerful senator and brilliant orator. Those of us who took Latin courses would have richer notions, and might have later included in the notion the famous lines *"Quo usque tamdem abutere, Catilina, patientia nostra...*" that reportedly open his speech against Catiline.[18] But not all of us had included them in our Cicero notion, not until now, at least. Anyway, for one of us to utter (11), s/he doesn't need to have a rich notion of Cicero; proper names are especially apt tools to refer to individuals with whom we do not have any opportunity to interact directly, because they are dead, like Cicero, or because they are remote in space, like Venus.

Other singular terms are particularly apt for referring to individuals, when we have a specific kind of notion that involves particular *cognitive fixes* of them: demonstratives, for instance, are suited to exploit perceptual information; indexicals to exploit utterance-bound fixes. Proper names are paradigmatically associated to standing notions that participate in intersubjective notion-networks.[19] Notion-networks provide a natural account of the cognitive significance of statements containing proper names. They explain a speaker's particular choice of a singular term (a demonstrative over a proper name, e.g. "she" instead of "Livia"; a proper name over another, "Tully" instead of "Cicero"), and they explain also why a hearer can get different information from utterances of different co-referential terms. Notion-networks also offer an account of how the reference, if any, of a proper name is determined: It is the origin of the notion-network. Typically, however, it is just the origin of the notion-network, if there is any, which counts for the truth of what the speaker says.

As we said above, what a speaker says when she utters (13) is the same as what she says when she utters (15), and what she says involves the origin of the name-notion-network, **c**, and the property predicated of it—the S condition—but not the names and the notion-networks associated to them. This is the typical case. But things are different with empty names.

An empty name is a name whose notion-network ends in a block. Perry (2001 [2012], 205–208) distinguishes three kinds of blocks:[20]

(E-1) blocks that are created by perceptual experiences wrongly taken as being caused by an object;
(E-3) blocks that are created by utterance comprehension processes that interpret a referring act when there is none; and
(E-5) blocks that are freely created.

The notion-networks associated to fictional names are of the last kind. So are hoaxes like Jacob Horn. There is no wrong perception or any other kind of

---

[18] There is no way to know whether these particular lines of the written version correspond word-to-word to the opening of the spoken version. See Beard, 2015, 41–44.

[19] See Korta and Perry, 2011.

[20] His numbering.

mistake, rather, there was an act of (free) creation of notions without origins. The case of myths is a bit more problematic. They can be taken to be cases of E-5 too, but most likely they should be taken as E-1 blocks; as cases in which perceptual experiences of events were wrongly interpreted to have "supernatural" individuals as their causes. Finally, it seems there are also cases of (E-3) blocks with myths too.[21] The important point, however, is that when using fictional (and mythical) proper names in parafictional (and paramythical) statements, notions become exceptionally (and, perhaps, exclusively) important for their truth. Unlike ordinary proper names, fictional names are not purported to refer to their origin. They are not purported to refer to a notion either; they are not purported to refer at all.[22] But a particular notion is involved in the truth-conditions of the parafictional statement such that the statement can be true or false, even if the notion has no origin, and, hence, the name is empty.

We call *fictional* notions those notions that are freely created by authors without an origin in a work of fiction. In this sense, what Conan Doyle did by writing the Holmes stories was to create a fictional notion associated to the proper name "Sherlock Holmes," filling it with many explicit and implicit ideas. Once created, and because it is a fictional notion, it gets more ideas from the application of the Reality Principle, which assumes that everything that is true in reality is also fictionally true unless it is excluded (explicitly or implicitly) by the work. That is why it is fictionally true that Sherlock Holmes has a great-grandfather, even if he is never mentioned in the Holmes stories (as far as we can remember).

Fictional names are importantly different from other empty names like "Jacob Horn" and "Vulcan," which once were taken to have a referent, but didn't. We will start by discussing the latter before turning to fictional names.

---

[21] According to Kripke (2013, 70–71) there are various theories that take "Moloch"—the name of a pagan god—to be created out of linguistic misinterpretations of various kinds. The word "Moloch" might have been interpreted as a proper name when it was really the noun "melech," Hebrew for "king"; or it was a name but for a kind of sacrifice, not a god.

[22] Let us emphasize that we *do not* claim that fictional names in parafictional statements refer to notions. Take the parafictional statement "Batman is Bruce Wayne." We do not claim that the statement is true because it expresses a singular proposition containing a single Batman/Wayne notion and the identity relation. In our view, there is no singular proposition expressed here. The statement is true because there are two name-networks that end in a single notion, which contains the idea of being a superhero called Batman and the idea of being a businessman called Bruce Wayne. See below. Thanks to an anonymous referee for raising the issue.

4 Ordinary Empty Names

Le Verrier explained the perturbations of Uranus's orbit by the presence of a planet that was unknown at the time, Neptune. The success of his hypothesis gave much credit to the hypothesis expressed by (1) "Vulcan causes the perturbations of Mercury's orbit." According to our previous account,[23] this hypothesis has the following truth-conditions:

E. That **v** exists.
RN. (i) That there is a network **N**v such that the use of "Vulcan" in
   (1) exploits **N**v; and (ii) has **v** as its origin.
S. That **v** causes the perturbations of Mercury's orbit.

Now, the hypothesis turned out to be false. There is no such planet. There is no **v**, so all conditions turn out to fail.[24] This also means that there is no proposition <*Cause-the-perturbations-of-Mercury's-orbit,* **v**>, but at most an incomplete or gappy proposition like <*Cause-the-perturbations-of-Mercury's-orbit, [empty slot]*>. Referentialists that assume a unique proposition—the proposition expressed—to encode the truth-conditions of statements containing proper names, have a problem with this, for various reasons. But we won't press the issue here. Let us just note here that that's no problem for our account. The truth-conditions of (1) are complete, but, because E is not met, R and S are not met either. In our account then (1) is clearly not true, but: Is it false, as Russell would conclude? Or does it lack a truth-value, as claimed by Frege?

Both options are available to our account. If we side with Frege and Strawson, we could take condition E to be a presupposition of (1), so that when the utterance fails to meet this condition, the proposition would be neither true nor false. This would accord with the idea that actually there is no proposition expressed. We would have to explain away, however, the strong intuition that (1) is false, and its negation is true. We would also need to explain away the intuition that (17) is true, and its negation false:

   (17) Vulcan does not exist.

So we rather align with Russell, without needing to treat proper names as definite descriptions in disguise. (1) is false because if we take the negation

---

[23] For the sake of simplicity, we leave notions aside for the moment. They don't play a decisive role for the truth of ordinary statements, as they do for the truth of parafictional statements, as we'll see below.
[24] Actually, the condition RN(i) about the existence of the network **N**v is met. See below.

of (1) as taking wide scope, it would amount to denying that the conditions E, RN and S are met; which is obviously true. With narrow scope, it would amount to asserting that E and R are met but not S, which is obviously false.

The truth conditions of negative existentials like (17) are a bit special, of course. They don't include anything like the E condition or the S condition but just the RN. The affirmative counterpart of (17) has the following ones:

RN. (i) That there is a network N_V such that the use of "Vulcan" in (17) exploits N_V; and (ii) has **v** as its origin.

Now (17) denies RN, which is false, so (17) is true, its positive counterpart false. But arguably RN(i) is left intact, since the speaker of (17) is exploiting the name network of coco-reference N_V created with Le Verrier's hypothesis, and not any other network associated to that name (like the one that is associated to a planet in the BBC series *Doctor Who* or in the American series *Star Trek*). In uttering (1) ("Vulcan causes the perturbations of Mercury's orbit.") or its negation, (17) or its negation, the speaker does not suspend her commitment to RN(i), the existence of a network N_V associated with the name "Vulcan" that she is exploiting.[25]

We suggest that this commitment to the existence of a particular network of coco-reference associated to the name is generalized to all uses of proper names in statements, except perhaps in the quite extraordinary cases of initial baptism, which constitute the very creation of the network for a name.

The application of this account to the case of Jacob Horn and statement (4) above is left as an exercise for the reader. We turn now to fictional names.

5 Fictional Names

We turn back to Sherlock Holmes now. How can we take (5) to be true and (7) to be false, if Sherlock Holmes is a fictional character, i.e., if *he* doesn't exist?

(5) Sherlock Holmes lived in 221B Baker Street, London, England.
(7) Sherlock Holmes lived in 221B Boulanger Street, Paris, France.

If we apply our account taking them as ordinary statements, we would render the truth conditions of (5) as follows:

---

[25] Our knowledgeable readers can recognize here Perry's (2001 [2012], 2012a) view about existential statements, according to which they lack referential truth-conditions and their network truth-conditions are promoted to the category of what is said.

E. that **sh** exists.
RN. (i) that there is a network **N**$_{SH}$ such that the use of "Sherlock Holmes" in (5) exploits **N**$_{SH}$; and (ii) has **sh** as its origin.
S. that **sh** lived in 221B Baker Street, London, England.

There is no **sh**, so (5) is false, just as (1) is. This seems favored by the fact that (11) seems as true as (17) ("Vulcan does not exist"), for the same reasons:

(11) Sherlock Holmes does not exist.

(11) lacks S conditions, and it asserts that the RN(ii) condition is not met—which is true.

If we interpret (5) as an ordinary statement as above, this would be an appropriate account. (5) would be false, as false as (7)—if this is also interpreted as an ordinary statement—as long as condition E is not met, and, consequently, conditions RN(ii) and S are not met.

It is only if (5) and (7) are taken as parafictional statements that we take them to be true and false, respectively. The question now is, how does the fact that a statement is parafictional affect its truth-conditions?

A first immediate answer comes from the notions of mimesis, pretense or make-believe. According to such a view, in making a parafictional statement we wouldn't be making an actual statement, but only pretending or acting *as if* we were making it. We would know that conditions E, RN(ii) and S do not obtain, but we would pretend they do. Perhaps this makes sense for fictional statements (except for the fact that we are not the authors, narrators, or characters in a work of fiction). As Searle (1975) puts it, "the author of a work of fiction pretends to perform a series of illocutionary acts" (p. 325) such as statements, assertions, descriptions, and so on. But it's not clear that it is the right approach for parafictional statements, which, to repeat, are real statements by real speakers. Do speakers of parafictional statements pretend that they refer to a person, even if they are not doing so?

It seems clear that the sincere speaker of the parafictional statement (5) is not committed to conditions E, RN(ii) and S: she does not believe that **sh** exists, so she doesn't believe that it is the origin of any network, or that **sh** lives anywhere. She is committed to RN(i)—the existence of the network **N**$_{SH}$ associated to her use of "Sherlock Holmes"—, that's quite clear. But what do we do with the other conditions? That is where fictional notions enter forcefully into the picture.

In our view, fictional names are not purported to refer to any individual. Any speaker or hearer who believes that the uses of "Sherlock Holmes" in (5), (7), (9), (10) and (11) are purported to refer to a real person—in other words, who takes them to be ordinary statements—is not getting at the right truth-conditions of those utterances.

Take (5). The informed speaker does not intend to refer to a nonexistent individual **sh**; but she is assuming the existence of a network N_{SH} and a notion n_{sh} at the end of the network (just before the block), associated to the name "Sherlock Holmes," such that the notion includes the idea expressed by the predicate "lived in 221B Baker Street, London, England." Or, to put it differently, the truth-conditions for (5) are the following ones:

> E. That a notion n_{sh} exists
> RN. (i) That there is a network N_{SH} such that the use of "Sherlock Holmes" in (5) exploits N_{SH}; and (ii) has no origin, but ends in the notion n_{sh}.[26]
> S. That the notion n_{sh} includes the idea "lived in 221B Baker Street, London, England."

As we saw, the fictional notion n_{sh} includes the idea "lived in 221B Baker Street, London, England." The information is given by Doctor Watson himself playing the role of the (fictional) narrator.[27] That's why we take the parafictional statement (5) to be true. And this is why we take (7) to be a false statement: the S condition for (7) is not met, n_{sh} does not include "lived in 221B Boulanger Street, Paris, France." It does not include it, not because Conan Doyle or anyone in the works tells us otherwise, but because it contradicts what is explicitly true in the stories, that is to say, (5).

Take now the case of (10), "Sherlock Holmes does not exist." If we interpret it as an ordinary statement, its truth-conditions are just the RN-conditions.

> RN. (i) That there is a network N_{sh} such that the use of "Sherlock Holmes" in (10) exploits N_{sh}; and (ii) N_{sh} has no origin.

which is obviously true, since the name is empty. If we interpret it as a parafictional statement, however, the name is still empty, but the fictional notion

---

[26] The abbreviation "RN" (for "reference-network condition") can be misleading here, since, as we argue, this is not a case of reference and, besides, we have a notion along with a network. So, something like FNN ("fiction-network-notion condition") might be more correct, but we suspect this would be even more misleading.

[27] Of course, this idea includes the proper name "Baker Street, London, England," which, if we are right, is also fictional and, thus, empty, with no origin. It would involve the same kind of analysis as "Sherlock Holmes." The fact that it is clearly connected to an ordinary proper name makes it possible to transport information from the notion corresponding to the real city to the fictional notion. But we leave these issues for another occasion.

n_{sh} comes to the fore, and so for (10) to be true, the following truth-conditions must obtain:

> RN. (i) That there is a network N_{SH} such that the use of "Sherlock Holmes" in (5) exploits N_{SH}; and (ii) has no origin, and doesn't end in the notion n_{sh}.

The network N_{SH} does end in the notion n_{sh}, so (10) is false in this interpretation.

6 Conclusions

To recapitulate, our account of fictional proper names in parafictional statements takes them to be really *empty*: that is, names whose uses don't refer to anything, and, in particular, they don't refer to *ficta* or any other individual entity of dubious metaphysical status.

We want to emphasize that, in our view, they don't refer to (fictional) notions either. Notions are a critical element of the truth-conditions of parafictional statements, but that doesn't make them the referents of fictional proper names. Are we saying that what we call fictional characters are notions? Yes, we are. Writing a novel, after all, seems to basically consist in creating a bunch of characters with their properties and relations among them, in imagined places and times with imagined events happening to them. All of these are freely created notions with no origins. The work of fiction consists in those notions, but it is not about them.

Speakers using a proper name are not talking about notions or networks, but make (implicit) use of them. Knowing how to use ordinary proper names shows (implicit) knowledge of networks, notions and origins in a play of coco-referring (conditional co-referring). Using fictional proper names in parafictional statements properly is similar except that the existential condition, along with reference, is dropped and notions come to play a role in its truth.

To be sure, there is an important difference between truth in fiction (or the truth of parafictional statements) and truth *tout court*. Perry says that in fiction

> ...we drop realism and completeness—the principle of excluded middle. No one supposes there is a truth to the matter of how many hairs Sherlock Holmes had on the back of his neck on his forty-fifth birthday, or whether Holmes's great-grandfather had more grandchildren than Professor Moriarty's great-grandfather did. (Perry, 2001 [2012], 231.)

That's why he proposes to distinguish between *truth*, which is a matter of correspondence with (actual) facts, and *accuracy* or *fit*, which would be a matter of "agreement with the contents of canonical representations" (Perry, 2001 [2012], 231). In the terminology we use here, we would say that the truth of parafictional statements is a matter of correspondence with *fictional* facts, that is, facts as established by the author of the (canonical) work explicitly or implicitly via the creation of notions without origins, which are also fed by the reality assumption. Realism is dropped, that's quite clear. That completeness is also dropped is not so clear. Arguably, Sherlock Holmes either had 10,000 hairs on the back of his neck on his 45th birthday or he hadn't; and either Holmes's great-grandfather had more grandchildren than Moriarty's or he hadn't. As parafictional statements, it is pretty obvious that the disjunctions are true; but it seems to us that the truth (or falsity) of any of the disjuncts is not only epistemically undetermined but also metaphysically so. What the consequences of these facts are is a matter we are not going to pursue in this paper.[28]

---

[28] The authors are particularly grateful to Tadeusz Ciecierski and Pawel Grabarczyk for their encouragement and patience. They also want to thank the Spanish Government (FFI2015-63719-P (MINECO/FEDER)) and the Basque Government (IT1032-16) for their grants, and the Institute for Logic, Cognition, Language and Information (ILCLI) of the University of the Basque Country (UPV-EHU), the Department of Philosophy and the Center for the Study of Language and Information (CSLI) at Stanford, and the Diamond XX Philosophy Institute in Copperopolis, CA, for the many direct and indirect benefits the three of them have had through their involvement with the activities of these institutions. We also thank *Topoi*'s two anonymous referees for their helpful comments and suggestions.

13

Utterance and Context

María de Ponte, Kepa Korta, and John Perry

1 Introduction

If JP[1] says, "I live in California," he says something true about JP. If MDP says, "I live in California," she says something false about MDP. Utterances of sentences with indexicals such as "I" express different propositions, depending on *context,* in this case the speaker. Similarly with tense. An utterance by KK of "I am tired," early Sunday morning as he gets out of bed, may be false. But ninety minutes later, returning from running his daily 5K to get ready for mass, his utterance of the same words will be true.

In this essay we consider what seems to be an issue of detail. On Kaplan's approach, contexts are sets, quadruples of a speaker, time, location and world. Utterances do not appear in the theory, but are modeled by pairs of expressions and contexts. An expression has a *character* (meaning); an expression-in-context has a *content* (proposition or component thereof.)

On the account we favor, the "reflexive-referential" theory, utterances appear in the theory; they are what the theory is about. Speaker-of, time-of, and location-of are *roles*, that is, functions from an utterance to the object that stands in the appropriate relation. The term "context" is used with its usual meanings for the truth-conditionally relevant circumstances of an utterance, but contexts as such are not entities within the theory.

We argue that this difference is more significant than it might seem, and that our approach has advantages for understanding the relation between the content of utterances (and other contentful episodes), their causal roles and their cognitive significance. On the other hand, we do not deny Kaplan's point, that modelling utterances as pairs of expressions and context has advantages in developing a logic of indexicals and demonstratives.

---

[1] We refer to ourselves in this paper as MDP, KK, and JP.

2 Prior's Root Canal

Here is a famous quote from Arthur Prior:

> [H]alf the time I personally have forgotten what the date is and have to look it up or ask somebody when I need it for writing cheques, etc.; yet even in this perpetual dateless haze one somehow communicates, one makes oneself understood, and with time references too. One says, e.g. "Thank goodness that's over!" . . . says something which it is impossible that any use of a tenseless copula with a date should convey. It certainly doesn't mean the same as, e.g. "Thank goodness the date of the conclusion of that thing is Friday, June 15, 1954," even if it be said then. (Nor, for that matter, does it mean "Thank goodness the conclusion of that thing is contemporaneous with this utterance." Why would anyone thank goodness for that?). (Prior, 1959, 17)

Consider two sentences Prior might have used to give thanks on June 15, 1954 at 7 p.m.

> Thank goodness that…
> (1) the root canal is over (now).
> (2) the root canal is over as of Friday evening, June 15, 1954.[2]

(1) seems a normal thing for a person who has just undergone a root canal to say. (2) does not, although with a bit of effort one can construct an example where it makes a bit of sense—perhaps one's dental insurance lapses on June 16. The cognitive and emotional significance of (1) and (2)—the doxastic and emotional states that would typically cause such utterances and of which such utterances would be signs—are different.

MDP and KK argue that if one supposes, as Prior does, that the difference in cognitive significance must be due to difference in the propositions expressed by (1) and (2), then metaphysical consequences loom. And Prior draws such conclusions. If we confine ourselves to objective facts about the temporal events—the "B-series" in McTaggart's (1908) terminology—then we can give the truth-conditions of (2). But to get at the different truth-conditions of (1) we need "A-properties," such properties as being past, present and future. Objective facts about insurance coverage dates might make one happy that one's root canal did/is/will take place before June 15, 1954. But it is the diminution of fear and apprehension of *future* pain that makes one happy that one's root canal has *already* taken place.

---

[2] Actually, June 15, 1954 was Tuesday, and not Friday, as Prior indicates. We will, however, keep Prior's example as it is.

MDP and KK point out that the metaphysical conclusion depends on taking the difference in cognitive significance to be a difference in proposition expressed.[3] On either Kaplan's approach or on our approach, there is a more plausible alternative; one can believe the same proposition in more than one way, and the different ways of believing account for differences in cognitive significance.

2.1 Kaplan's Approach

In Kaplan's theory, a context is a set, a quadruple of a speaker, a time, a location, and a world. A proper context is one in which the speaker is in the location at the time in the world. The meaning, or *character* of an expression is a function from contexts to *contents*. The content of a sentence is a proposition, that of other expressions is their contribution to the proposition expressed by sentences in which they occur, basically an object, property, or relation. Thus (1) and (2) have the same content in the circumstances we are imagining, that Prior's root canal occurs prior to Friday evening, June 15, 1954.

In a series of essays, JP defended Kaplan's theory, and argued that Kaplan's concept of character was not only a contribution to understanding how indexicals and demonstratives work, but also to understanding intentionality in general.[4] Basically, JP claimed that the causal roles of perceptual states, states of belief and desire, and intentions and volitions can only be understood in terms of character. JP's term for this generalized concept of character was "role." The causal role of a visual state, for example, is to carry information about the objects in view of the perceiver at the time and place of perception. The same state can carry information about different objects at different locations at different times, for different perceivers or the same perceiver at different times and places. We cannot understand this simply in terms of propositions that encapsulate the information captured, but must also bring in roles, functions from the circumstances the perceiver is in to *what* is perceived.

---

[3] See Chapter 11 of the present volume.

[4] See the early essays collected in JP's *The Problem of the Essential Indexical and Other Essays* (1993 [2000]). The move to the reflexive-referential begins in the essay "Cognitive Significance and New Theories of Reference" (1988), with the concept of "the proposition created." This essay was a reply to Howard Wettstein's important essay "Has Semantics Rested on a Mistake?" (1986). In his essay, Wettstein introduced examples in which the expression, character, and context are basically the same, but the cognitive significance is nevertheless different. The reflexive- referential theory is developed in *Reference and Reflexivity* (2001 [2012]) and in Korta and Perry's *Critical Pragmatics* (2011). The notion of episode was first introduced in Crimmins and Perry's "The Prince and the Phone Booth: Reporting Puzzling Beliefs" (1989), in their account of beliefs as concrete cognitive particulars.

2.2 The Reflexive-Referential Approach

Our position differs somewhat from Kaplan's view, and the view that JP defended. Kaplan discusses utterances to motivate his theory, but he does not bring them into his theory as such; they are replaced by, or perhaps modeled as, pairs of expressions and contexts: "expressions-in-context." Kaplan's main interest was developing a logic of demonstratives and indexicals. For this purpose, he regarded utterances as an unnecessary complication. For one thing, a pair of context and expression can have a content, even if the speaker of the context does not utter the expression at the time and place of the context in the world under consideration. More importantly, utterances take time; the validity of an argument with one hundred steps might depend on the context being the same for all of them, but we can't talk or write that fast. So, for logical purposes, utterances can get in the way.

From the point of view of understanding the relations between the contents of states and their causal roles, however, it is very helpful to have *episodes*—paradigmatically, utterances, but also perceptions, thoughts, and actions—in our theory, as well as more extended "episodes" such as beliefs, desires and intentions. It is such episodes that *have* contents, have causes, and have effects. So, in the theory of intentionality, episodes and, in particular, utterances are too important to ignore, in spite of the complications they pose for logic.

For this purpose, we consider the elements of Kaplan's contexts to simply be properties of utterances, which objects fill the roles of speaker-of, time-of, and location-of. The fact that utterances have speakers and occur in locations at times clearly inspired Kaplan's concepts of context and character. We promote these inspiring episodes to first-class status.

The chief advantage of our view is simply that it accounts for—and makes use of—the fact that utterances have many other properties in addition to having speakers, locations, and times, that can be relevant to understanding their cognitive significance.[5]

One way to handle these, while sticking with Kaplan's approach, is to add more members to the context set, or to introduce additional sets. The latter is more or less the approach of Jon Barwise and JP in *Situations and Attitudes* (1983 [1999]). On the "relational theory of meaning" advocated there, the meaning of a sentence is taken to be a relation among various situations connected to an utterance, although the utterance itself is, as in Kaplan's theory, only modelled and not introduced directly into the theory. The basic relation is between the utterance situation, which determines the speaker, location and time, and, in lieu of propositions, described situations.

---

[5] We consider the issue of possibilities and worlds in the last section.

But various other situations are added to the range of the relation, for dealing with names, descriptions, ambiguity and other phenomena.

On the reflexive-referential account, however, the treatment of such factors is simpler and more straightforward. They are all properties of the utterance, which can be recognized as necessary to handle various phenomena.

On the reflexive-referential theory, truth and falsity are regarded as properties of episodes. An utterance has truth-conditions, and is true if it satisfies them. Take a simple example, JP's utterance **u** of "I am sitting." For **u** to be true, there must be a speaker of **u** and a time of **u**, and the speaker must be sitting at the time. These are the *reflexive* truth-conditions. Then, *given* that JP is the speaker and noon August 28 is the time of **u**, JP must be sitting at that time for it to be true. That is, by identifying the occupants of the roles in the reflexive truth-conditions, we obtain the *referential* truth-conditions. The latter are not, in themselves, conditions on the utterance. JP could be sitting at that time without uttering anything. But if we conceive of the referential truth-conditions as giving *what else* has to be the case for the utterance to be true, *given* the referential facts, the referential truth-conditions are conditions on the utterance.

In the referential-reflexive theory, we distinguish being true and being factual. Truth is a property of utterances and other episodes. Being a fact is a property of a state of affairs, or circumstances, or whatever else one takes to serve as *possibilities*.

That JP is sitting at noon is a fact, because he is. No utterance or episode is required. It would be a fact that Venus is the second planet from the sun, even if no one ever said so, even if there were no language, or even no life on earth, and no utterances. But for an utterance of "Venus is the second planet from the sun" to be true, life, language, and speakers are all required.

Thus, the truth-conditions of each utterance are determined by the expressions used and the occupants of relevant roles. Utterances with different expressions, and different occupants of the relevant roles, will have different truth-conditions. Truth, the property that all true utterances have in common, is the property of meeting the truth-conditions that an utterance provides for itself.

Usually the phrase "truth-conditions" is used in contemporary philosophy for what we call "referential truth-conditions," what *else* has to be the case for the utterance to be true, *given* the facts of reference. In this sense, quite different utterances can have the same truth-conditions, for example JP's utterance of "I like philosophy now" and KK's simultaneous utterance to JP of "You like philosophy now." But the reflexive truth-conditions will not be the same; the former requires the speaker of that very utterance to like philosophy to be true, the latter requires that the person the speaker of that utterance is addressing likes philosophy.

Let **u** be an utterance of "I love sailing now." Taking just the meaning into account, we can say:

> **u** is true iff the speaker of **u** loves sailing at the time of **u**.

As noted, these are conditions on the utterance **u**, properties *it* must have to be true; that is, conditions on the utterance *itself,* and hence *reflexive truth-conditions.*

Suppose MDP is the speaker of **u**, and July 2017 is the time. Given that, we can give the *referential* truth-conditions of **u**, that is, what else has to be the case for **u**, given the reference of "I" and "now." Note that they put *no* conditions on **u**, but on MDP and July 2017. They are also the referential truth-conditions of KK's utterance at the same time to MDP, "You love sailing now!"

We argue that the reflexive-referential theory inherits a key insight of Kaplan's theory, and JP's earlier view, but the inclusion of utterances gives it two advantages. The inherited key insight is the distinction between different ways in which information can be discovered, believed and asserted.

The first advantage is that the cognitive significance of an utterance for different hearers can depend on the perceptual and causal relations the hearer has to the utterance, and which reference-determining referential facts they know, and how they think of them. To account for this, we need to bring in additional properties of the utterance, and in particular causal properties. These are not modelled by Kaplan's expressions-in-context.

The second advantage concern certain possibilities that are hard to find unless, again, we have utterances—or more generally cognitive and linguistic episodes—in our account. We elaborate on these two advantages below. We start with the first one, on sections 3 and 4, and we discuss the second one on sections 5 and 6.

One final point, before we leave Prior's examples for a bit. On his list of things it would be strange to thank goodness for, he includes

> (3) the conclusion of the root canal is contemporaneous with this utterance.

The referential truth-conditions of (3) are that the conclusion of the root canal is contemporaneous with the utterance (3). This is about the same as the reflexive truth-conditions of (1).

(1) the root canal is over (now).

The reflexive truth-conditions of (1) are that the root canal is over at the time of utterance (1).

In general, an utterance that elevates the relevant reflexive truth-conditions of an original utterance to referential truth-conditions will not have the same cognitive significance as the original. Compare, "I need some salt," "KK needs some salt" and "the speaker of this utterance needs some salt," all said at dinner by KK. The relevant reflexive truth-conditions of the first are that the speaker of the utterance needs some salt. This is what KK intends to convey; that is, he wants others at the dinner table, who can reach the salt, to be able to identify the one who needs salt in a way that will lead them to pass the salt in the right direction. They hear the utterance; they can easily identify the speaker, they know where the speaker is in comparison to them, so they will know how to get the salt to the person that needs it. The second utterance does not have these virtues; it will help KK's fellow diners to help the person who needs the salt only if they know who KK is; even if this can be assumed it sounds pretentious.[6] The third utterance is better than the second. As long as his fellow diners know that KK is referring to his own utterance with "this," they can figure out where to pass the salt. Otherwise they might wonder what utterance he is referring to—perhaps something he reads on the menu. By referring to his own utterance, rather than simply making it, KK makes the utterance part of the referential content, that is, part of what he is talking about. Even if they realize which utterance he demonstratively refers to, and manage to pass the salt in the right direction, this will strike his fellow diners as odd—perhaps a way of emphasizing KK's obsession with utterances.

Similarly, in (3), Arthur Prior refers to his own utterance, instead of simply producing it, making the utterance itself part of the referential content, that is, part of what he is talking about. To understand him, the audience would need to know what utterance he is referring to; and even if they do, it will strike them as odd. Thus, the cognitive significance of (3)—which talks about (1) or, in other words, includes (1) in its referential truth-conditions—is different from the cognitive significance of (1).

3 Varieties of Cognitive Significance

The first advantage mentioned above is that in the reflexive-referential theory there is a simple account of how utterances have different cognitive significance for different people, depending on their relation to the utterance. To

---
[6] See Korta and Perry, 2011, Chapter 7.

account for this, we need to bring in additional truth-conditions of the utterance; and additional properties. Utterances have reflexive and referential truth-conditions, as we noted. But many other levels of truth-conditions can be considered for different purposes. The reflexive content of MDP's utterance **u** is simply that the speaker of **u** loves sailing at the time of **u**. Suppose MDP steps off the boat at a pier in San Francisco Bay after an afternoon of sailing. After accidentally falling in the cold water of San Francisco Bay during the sail, she had said to KK, "Sometimes I hate sailing." But as she steps off the boat she utters **u**, "I love sailing now." A stranger who, like Prior, is in a dateless haze, and is looking in the opposite direction, hears her. Initially, he has only an utterance-bound "cognitive fix" on the speaker of **u**: whoever is the speaker of the utterance he hears.[7] Then he turns, and recognizes that the speaker of the utterance is the young lady he sees. Now he knows that she is the person who must now love sailing for the utterance he heard to be true. Also, the stranger originally has only an utterance-bound fix on the time of **u**: the time of the utterance he hears. Once he turns, and realizes that he is hearing the utterance at the same time it occurs—rather than hearing it over the radio—he realizes that the time of the utterance is also the time of his hearing of it; it is the time that, even in his dateless haze, he thinks of as "now." So, as he gains more knowledge about the properties of the utterance, he moves from only grasping the reflexive truth-conditions to grasping the referential truth-conditions, which he can express with "She likes sailing now."

Suppose you see a video of MDP, whom you recognize, uttering **u**, but have no idea when the video was taken. If you believe her, you would come to believe that at the time of the utterance she enjoyed sailing. Your understanding is utterance-bound, for you can identify the time at which she loved sailing only as the time at which **u** occurred. But since you recognize MDP, you have more than a reflexive understanding. The relevant truth-conditions are conditions both on the time of the utterance and on MDP. In *Critical Pragmatics,* KK and JP call such truth-conditions "utterance-bound," and considered a large number of examples and issues in which utterance-bound truth-conditions (and other "hybrid" truth-conditions) are crucial to understanding semantic and, in particular, pragmatic issues.

4 Back to Prior

On both Kaplan's approach and the reflexive-referential approach, Prior's utterances (1) and (2) are importantly different in cognitive significance. On both approaches, the explanation for the difference need not rely on the

---

[7] We own the phrase "cognitive fix" to Howard Wettstein.

proposition expressed, but in the way of apprehending or asserting that proposition. So either approach can avoid Prior's metaphysical conclusions.

To see the advantages, we claim for the reflexive-referential approach, let's assume that Prior's philosophical thoughts were inspired by a real root canal that he had on June 15, 1954, in the early afternoon. Towards evening he went to a bar with friends, all of whom, like Prior, went around in dateless hazes. It hurt him to talk, but he wrote a note and showed it to his friends:

(4) I had a root canal earlier today.

The note is preserved in the Museum of Tense Logic in Auckland, together with a little explanation of how it came to be written. We examine it, more than half a century later. The cognitive significance of the note was much different for his friends at the bar than it will be for us.

Such a note is a token, the physical product of an act of writing, which we take to be a species of uttering. When one takes a note to be meaningful, one thinks of it as the results of an intentional act of writing. The context for the expression-in-context, or the occupants of the relevant roles for an utterance based theory, is provided by the intentional act that produced the token.[8]

Thus the context, character, and content of writing the note don't change between 1954 and 2017. And it is the same utterance of the same expression and the same objects filling the utterance-relative roles and the same reflexive and referential contents, in 1954 and 2017.

Let's imagine that Prior's friends and the museum-goers both were in dateless but not totally clueless hazes. That is, they couldn't provide the date and time they became aware of the note, but they knew the year—1954 and 2017 respectively.

Thus, when they inspected the note, both groups would understand its truth-conditions at an incremental but still utterance-bound level:

> The display of this note was true, iff it occurred on a day when Prior had a root canal, later in the day than the root canal.

The difference is that the two groups, although both in dateless hazes, know different things about the utterance. Prior's friends, who witnessed the display, know that it occurred on the same day that they are sitting with Prior in the pub and can offer him a drink. The museum-goers, aware that Prior died in 1969, know that whatever the exact date of the utterance, or the exact date of their inspection, the first occurred many years before the second. And this

---

[8] See Predelli 1998, 2011 and Perry 2003 for complications.

difference explains why the first group offers Prior a drink, but the second group makes no such effort.

Kaplan's theory also has the resources to explain the difference. Kaplan's contexts contain not only speakers, locations, and times, but also possible worlds. So the context of Prior's utterance contains all the facts that could be possibly relevant, including all facts about his utterance, its effects in the bar, and much later in the museum. Even if we do not have utterances in our basic semantics, we can bring them in through the "back-door," by finding them in the possible world in the context.

To us, this seems a bit roundabout. The utterances, and other episodes the truth-conditions and cognitive significance of which we want to understand, are what our semantic and pragmatic theories are ultimately theories about. It seems natural to give them a central place in our theories. In addition, the inclusion of utterances in our theory brings a second advantage for the reflexive-referential theory over the Kaplan-Perry one.

5 Wettstein's Challenge

In his important essay, "Has semantics rested on a mistake?" Howard Wettstein pointed out that whatever the virtues of what he called the "Kaplan-Perry" account has in explaining cognitive significance of cases involving indexicals, it does not handle Frege's *Begriffsschrift* (1879 [1967]) problem, the origin of worries about cognitive significance, which involves proper names. "Hesperus is Hesperus" and "Hesperus is Phosphorus" clearly have different cognitive significance; one learns from the second that the names co-refer, but not from the first. On a directly referential account of proper names, which is more or less what Frege had in the *Begriffsschrift,* this is hard to account for. On Kaplan's account, the character of a proper name is a constant function, from any context to the bearer of the name. The two sentences have the same content, a singular proposition to the effect that Venus is Venus. So, whatever the virtues of the Kaplan-Perry thesis for cases involving indexicals, it does not help with proper names.

In response to Wettstein's essay, JP introduced the concept of the proposition created by an utterance, in contrast with the proposition expressed by an utterance, which was basically the distinction between reflexive and referential content.

On the reflexive-referential account, the two utterances have different reflexive truth-conditions. The first is true if and only if there is an object named by "Hesperus" which is self-identical. The second is true if and only if there is such an object, and there is also an object named by "Phosphorus," and the objects are identical. So, even though the contents of referential truth-conditions of the two utterances are the same, they differ in cognitive significance, in virtue of their different reflexive truth-conditions.

6 More Hazes

As noted, certain possibilities are hard to find unless we have utterances—and other episodes—in our account. We turn now to the discussion of this second advantage.

One can be in a dateless haze without knowing it; that is, one can be quite certain about the date, but be wrong. In such a case, it is natural to think, in retrospect, that one *might have* been correct; even that one's false belief was justified. This seems to provide another advantage for the reflexive-referential theory.

Suppose JP and Dan are planning to go to the Giants game on August 22, 2017. The day before, JP types out a reminder: "The Giants game is tomorrow. Don't forget." But he forgets to hit the "send" button. He notices that the message has not been sent just before retiring, and hits the button. But he doesn't notice that it is already after midnight.

Dan, a dateless-hazer, sees the reminder, "The Giants game is tomorrow," when he wakes up on August 22, and sees that date on the email heading. He knows that the game is on August 22, and reasons, given JP's notorious reliability, "Today must be August 21." He then immerses himself in linguistic esoterica until late in the evening, when JP calls and says, "You missed the game!"

Dan thought, on August 22, that it was August 21. He had good reason for this belief. The game was scheduled for August 22. JP said, in an email this morning, that the game was tomorrow. JP is pretty reliable. Therefore, today must be August 21.

Could Dan have been right? It seems not, because for his belief to be true, August 22 would have to be August 21, which is not possible. Surely had Dan said,

(5) August 22 is August 21

we could diagnose some kind of irrationality (or that he was making some subtle linguistic point). But if he just says, as he did:

(6) Today is August 21

on August 22, this doesn't seem like the right diagnosis.

But there is a way Dan's utterance could have been true: If it had occurred on August 21 rather than August 22. That is, specifically, if the role of time-of for the utterance of "today" had been filled by some moment occurring on August 21, the utterance would have been true.

On the expression-in-context approach, this doesn't seem like an option. Since the pair of expression and context is individuated by its members, we wouldn't have the same pair if the time of the context was August 21. So we have another advantage for the reflexive-referential theory and granting utterances first-class status in the semantics of tense and indexicals.

As Richard Vallée has pointed out,[9] there is an objection to our strategy. One theory of events is that they are *individuated* by the time at which they occur, *where* they occur, and *which* object and properties are involved. If we accept this account of event individuation, the reflexive-referential account is no better off than the expressions-in-context account.

We reject this account of the individuation of events; it is a plausible account of the individuation of facts, but not of events. Being a fact is, as noted, a property of whatever one takes to serve as possibilities, be it circumstances, states of affairs or whatever. We will not here develop an account of events, which we regard as very basic elements of reality. But we think an adequate account must allow for counterfactuals of the form, "if the election had occurred two weeks earlier, Clinton would have won," or, to follow with our example, "if Dan's utterance had occurred on August 21, he wouldn't have missed the Giant's game." It is a fact that he missed it and that he made his utterance on August 22. Nothing can change that. But the episodes involved, Dan's belief and Dan's utterance "Today is August 21" could have been true, had they occurred on August 21.

In his paper "Frege on Demonstratives" (1977), JP introduced the example of Heimson, who thought he was David Hume. Let's suppose instead that Heimson thought he was Bob Dylan, which will make it easier to make a case for his rationality. Here is the background story. Heimson falls, hits his head, and has amnesia as a result. He doesn't know who he is. He carries no identification. He awakes in a hospital where no one has any idea who he is. Heimson decides to figure out who he is. Heimson's amnesia is of a rather peculiar sort; he retains "third-person" memories about lots of people, he simply doesn't remember which of them he is. He assumes he is one of the people about whom he knows a great deal. He notices that he knows all of Bob Dylan's songs by heart, the date of every concert where he performed, and loads of other things. He also knows a lot about a fellow named "Heimson," but not nearly as much as he knows about Dylan. He decides he is Dylan, and thinks, with some confidence, "I am Bob Dylan."

---

[9] Personal communication.

His thought cannot be true. Indeed, it seems necessarily false. But it might be rational. And we think it does get at a possibility, even if a rather remote one. The possibility is found at the reflexive level. Call his thought—the event of thinking, the episode, not its content—*T*. If Bob Dylan had the thought *T*, rather than Heimson, *T* would be true. This is the possibility that Heimson's sifting of the evidence available to him led him to think was the case.

David Lewis (1979), considering JP's original example, comes to the opposite conclusion. In "Frege on demonstratives," JP advocated a version of the Kaplan-Perry view, that he called the two-tiered view. In a nutshell, to deal with the attitudes we need to recognize two levels of content for beliefs. *What* is believed is a proposition, often a singular proposition. *How* it is believed corresponds to character or role.

Lewis had nice things to say about this account, but thought that the level corresponding to character or role could serve as what is believed, and the upper tier could be jettisoned. Lewis noted that a character, a function from contexts to propositions, could be regarded as a property: the property an agent has at a time iff the character, applied to that agent and time, yields a true proposition. So, when JP says, "I am sitting," he "self-ascribes" the property $P_{sitting}$:

$P_{sitting}=$
the property x has iff the character of "I am sitting," with arguments x and t, yields a true proposition, that is,
the property someone x has at time t, iff x is sitting at t.

On Lewis's view, properties, rather than propositions, are the true "objects" of beliefs. A belief consists of an agent at a time self-ascribing a property.

Lewis's view, like the Kaplan-Perry approach, does not involve episodes. We have agents, times, the relation of self-ascription, and properties. Lewis (1979, footnote 16) regards singular propositions and "de re" beliefs as unnecessary intrusions into the theory of the attitudes based on preoccupation with the analysis of our customs for reporting beliefs.

Lewis's view incorporates much of the traditional picture that belief is a relation between an agent at a time and a proposition. His innovation is to replace propositions with properties. But we think the idea of objects of beliefs in this sense is a mistake. A belief consists in an agent at a time being in a mental state, an episode. This episode has truth-conditions, which can be characterized by propositions, many different propositions, depending on what is taken as given. But neither propositions, nor characters, nor characters construed as properties, are objects of belief in the sense that belief consists of a relation to them. Propositions, in our sense, are tools we used to characterize and keep track of the truth-conditions of the episode.

Lewis's account, like the Kaplan-Perry account, does not have episodes, utterances or beliefs, as elements. So, on Lewis's view, Heimson's belief, whether he thinks he is Hume or thinks he is Dylan, cannot be true in the strong sense that there is no possible way it could be true. On his view, the belief consists of Heimson, the relevant time, and the attitude of self-ascription to the property of being Hume/being Bob Dylan. Since there is no possibility that Heimson at the time has that property, there is no way the belief can be true. Heimson is irrational in all possible circumstances.

So, we count it as a defect of the Kaplan-Perry account, and of Lewis's account, that it is unfair to Heimson. To paraphrase Billy Joel, Heimson may be crazy, but often in philosophy we are looking for a lunatic, to uncover hidden corners in the realm of possibilities.[10]

7 Conclusion

The topic of this volume is contexts in general. We do not hold that theories that treat contexts as abstract entities, sets that encode relevant contextual information, are necessarily wrong-headed. For the purposes of formal theories that lend themselves to axiomatization and computation, such theories have many virtues. But we think that in order to fully understand what is going on for many philosophical purposes, it must be kept in mind that possession and transfer of information are always a matter of complex relations between the contents of episodes—thoughts, utterances, signals—and their other properties. In the reflexive-referential theory we advocate, episodes and their properties are not only kept in mind, but in the theory.[11]

---

[10] Billy Joel "You might be right," in *Glass Houses* (1980).

[11] The authors want to thank the Spanish Government (FFI2015-63719-P (MINECO/FEDER)) and the Basque Government (IT1032-16) for their grants, and the Institute for Logic, Cognition, Language and Information (ILCLI) of the University of the Basque Country (UPV-EHU), the Department of Philosophy and the Center for the Study of Language and Information (CSLI) at Stanford, and the Diamond XX Philosophy Institute in Copperopolis, CA, for the many direct and indirect benefits the three of them have had through their involvement with the activities of these institutions.

14

Four Puzzling Paragraphs. Frege on "≡" and "="

María de Ponte, Kepa Korta, and John Perry

1 Introduction

In §8 of his *Begriffsschrift* (1879 [1967]), Gottlob Frege discusses issues related to identity. Frege begins his most famous essay, "On Sense and Reference" (1892 [1997]), published thirteen years later, by criticizing the view advocated in §8. He returns once more to these issues in the concluding paragraph. Controversies continue over these historically important passages. We offer an interpretation and discuss some alternatives. Starting with the negative points, we argue that

> (i) In the *Begriffsschrift,* Frege does not hold that identity is a relation between signs; that is, he doesn't hold what is sometimes known as the *Name view* on identity, not even in §8.
> (ii) What Frege introduces in §8 of the *Begriffsschrift,* and represents by "≡," is not identity but a different relation called "identity of content," which presupposes but is different from identity, represented by "=."
> (iii) Neither in the *Begriffsschrift* nor in "On Sense and Reference," does Frege explain what we call the *Name Problem:* the issue of how we get the information that two signs "*a*" and "*b*" designate the same thing from a sentence like "*a = b*."

On a more positive vein, we claim that

> (iv) §8 of the *Begriffsschrift* is motivated by the conflict between two different criteria for sameness of conceptual content of sentences: the *inferential criterion* and the *sameness of circumstance criterion*.

225

(v) To resolve that conflict, Frege introduces "≡" in §8 and, thus, circumstances with names as constituents.

(vi) To the same end, in "On Sense and Reference," Frege introduces senses and Thoughts and abandons both "≡" and circumstances. He solves what we call the *Co-instantiation problem,* and disregards, but does not solve, the *Name problem.*

We proceed by discussing the four critical paragraphs in Sections 2 to 4: the two paragraphs of §8 of the *Begriffsschrift,* and the opening and closing paragraphs of "On Sense and Reference." In Section 5, we focus on the *Name problem,* a problem Frege identified but did not quite solve in the *Begriffsschrift,* and that he discarded as a pseudo-problem without argument in "On Sense and Reference." Finally, in Section 6 we briefly compare our interpretation with some alternatives.

2 The Two Paragraphs of §8 of the *Begriffsschrift*

We"ll begin by noting a mistaken view about §8:

> [In his *Begriffsschrift,* Frege] adds a special treatment of identity statements to the theory of conceptual content: "$a = a$" has the content that the sign "a" stands for the same thing as the sign "a" itself, while "$a = b$" has the content that the sign "a" stands for the same thing as the sign "b". (Perry, 2001 [2012], 141)

This view is suggested by the first paragraph of "On Sense and Reference," and is widely accepted by those who write about Frege.[1] But it is wrong.

Frege says *nothing* about the sentences "$a = a$" and "$a = b$" in §8, or anywhere else in the *Begriffsschrift.* The symbol "=" occurs only twice, in an example at the beginning of §8 and in another example, in §5. He also does not, contrary to what he says in "On Sense and Reference," maintain in the *Begriffsschrift* that identity is a relation between signs or names, and indeed seems extremely careful not to say that.

2.1 Text
Here is the passage from the *Begriffsschrift*:

---

[1] A classic formulation can be found in Dummett, "In *Begriffsschrift* Frege held that identity was a relation between names and not between things" (1981a, 544). See also Salmon, 1986: 51–4 and Sluga, 1980, 151. A more recent formulation can also be found in Corazza and Korta, 2015.

Identity of Content

§8. Identity of content differs from conditionality and negation in that it applies to names and not to contents. Whereas in other contexts signs are merely representatives of their content, so that every combination into which they enter expresses only a relation between their respective contents, they suddenly display their own selves when they are combined by means of the sign for identity of content, for it expresses the circumstance that two names have the same content. Hence the introduction of a sign for identity of content necessarily produces a bifurcation in the meaning of all signs: they stand at times for their content, at times for themselves. At first we have the impression that what we are dealing with pertains merely to the *expression* and *not to the thought*, that we do not need different signs at all for the same content and hence no sign whatsoever for identity of content. To show that this is an empty illusion I take the following example from geometry. Assume that on the circumference of a circle there is a fixed point A about which a ray revolves. When this ray passes through the center of the circle, we call the other point at which it intersects the circle the point B associated with this position of the ray. The point of intersection, other than A, of the ray and the circumference will then be called the point B associated with the position of the ray at any time; this point is such that continuous variations in its position must always correspond to continuous variations in the point of the ray. Hence the name B refers to something indeterminate so long as the corresponding position of the ray has not been specified. We can now ask: what point is associated with the position of the ray when it is perpendicular to the diameter? The answer will be: the point A. In this case, therefore, the name B has the same content as has the name A; and yet we could not have used only one name from the beginning, since the justification for that is given only by the answer. One point is determined in two ways: (1) immediately through intuition and (2) as a point B associated with the ray perpendicular to the diameter.

(*Begriffsschrift,* 20–21)

Geach provides this diagram to illustrate Frege's example:[2]

---

[2] Peter Geach and Max Black (eds.) (1952). *Translations From the Philosophical Writings of Gottlob Frege.*

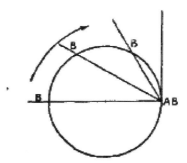

As the line turns in the direction of the arrow, B moves towards A, till they coincide.

At the end of §8, Frege introduces a new sign, "≡," which he calls *identity of content* and gives a definition:

> Now let
>
> ⊢ A≡B
>
> mean that *the sign A and the sign B have the same conceptual content, so that we can everywhere put B for A and conversely.* (*Begriffsschrift*, 21)

Before going on with the interpretation, a note on translation. The verb *bedeuten* is in some contexts naturally translated as "stands for" and other times as "means" or "refers." We use "stands for," "means" and "refers" as a translation for "*bedeuten*" as it occurs in the *Begriffsschrift,* and "denotes" as it occurs in "On Sense and Reference." This is simply for our convenience; Frege has a somewhat different view of *Bedeutung* in the two works, the result of splitting the concept of *Bedeutung* in the former into *Sinn* and *Bedeutung* in the latter.

2.2 Interpretation

In the *Begriffsschrift,* Frege does not discuss sentences with "=," he does not use the identity sign, and he only mentions it twice in two examples, in §1 and §5. He introduces "≡," which stands for a relation between expressions:

identity of content. It is the contents that stand in the relation of identity, not the expressions. In the *Begriffsschrift*, the *conceptual contents* of names, predicates and sentences are their referents, that is, objects, concepts, and circumstances. So Frege is using "identity" in the phrase "identity of content" in the normal sense, for the relation each object has to itself, and no other. If he didn't mean identity by "identity," his explanation of his new symbol would make no sense.

Later in the *Begriffsschrift*, in §20, Frege uses his new symbol to formulate his version of Leibniz's Law:

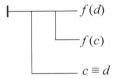

In more familiar notation:

$((c \equiv d) \rightarrow (f(c) \rightarrow f(d)))$

He provides this gloss:

> The case in which the content of c is identical with the content of d and in which $f(c)$ is affirmed and $f(d)$ is denied does not take place. This proposition means that, if $c \equiv d$, we could everywhere put d for c.
> (*Begriffsschrift*, 50)

In this passage, Frege is using the new sign "≡" where logicians would normally use "=," and he would use "=" after the *Begriffsschrift*. But "≡" is *not* a new sign for identity, but a sign for a different relationship, between expressions, identity of content.

This all seems a bit puzzling. Frege does not hold that identity is a relation between names, but that identity of content is, which seems like a reasonable view. He introduces the new symbol "≡" for this relation, and basically retires "=." But he doesn't explain why he retires "=."[3]

---

[3] He doesn't define "=" either, but this is not too surprising, considering that he only uses it in cases of arithmetical equality. Much later, in the introduction to *Grundgesetze* (1893, 1903 [1952]), Frege details the changes he has made to his formal language since *Begriffsschrift*:

> The fundamental signs employed in my *Begriffsschrift* have, with one exception, been used again here. Instead of the three parallel lines I have chosen the ordinary symbol of equality because I convinced myself that it is used in arithmetic to stand for the very thing that I wish to symbolize. In fact, I use the expression "equal" to stand for the same as "coinciding

2.3 Conceptual Content and Circumstances

A key notion in the *Begriffsschrift* is *conceptual content.* Consider:

⊢── The Greeks defeated the Persians at Plataea

The vertical bar indicates that we have a judgement; we are asserting that the Greeks defeated the Persians at Plataea. It does not occur, for example, in the antecedent or consequent of a conditional. The horizontal bar is the content stroke; what follows must provide the judgeable content, that is, it must be a sentence. He often calls such contents "circumstances" ("*Umstand*"), a choice of terminology on which we put some weight. Sentences *bedeuten* circumstances. At this point Frege was not making the distinction between sense (*Sinn*) and denotation (*Bedeutung*), but dealing with a single concept of content.

Conceptual contents and circumstances are important for our interpretation, and we need to emphasize that Frege doesn't treat "circumstance" (*Umstand*) as a technical term, or even one that needs explanation in the *Begriffsschrift*. But he regularly says that sentences stand for or mean (*bedeuten*) circumstances. A couple of examples:

From §5:

[L]et ⊢──*A* stand for (*bedeuten*) $3 \times 7 = 21$ and *B* for the circumstance that the sun is shining...
(*Begriffsschrift*, 14)

From §15:

Let *d* mean (*bedeuten*) the circumstance that the piston *K* of an air pump is moved..., *c* the circumstance that the valve *H* is in position *I*, *b* the circumstance that... (*Begriffsschrift*, 36)

So, where we write "It is a fact that S," Frege writes

⊢── S

---

or identical with," and this is just how the sign of equality is actually used in arithmetic to stand for the very thing that I wish to symbolize. (*Grundgesetze*, 140–141)

This is consistent with what he says in the *Begriffsschrift*. His notion of identity is the usual relation of an object with itself, and the notion of identity of content is not needed, he assumes, when talking about arithmetic. See May, 2001, and Heck, 2003, for an extensive discussion of Frege's view of arithmetical equality.

The vertical line is for assertion, and corresponds to "it is a fact." The horizontal line corresponds to "that." So

─── S

identifies the conceptual content, *that S*. The formula,

corresponds to "It is a fact that not-S."

Following Frege, we use "conceptual content" for a "content that can become a judgement," (§3), which is the only kind of content that can follow the content stroke, i.e. circumstances. The conceptual content of the whole sentence is determined by the contents of its parts. The content of a name is the object it stands for. The content of a predicate is a property or relation, the condition that the object or objects named must meet for the sentence to be true.[4]

If a bird flies, the bird *falls under* the concept *( ) is flying*. Flying is an activity; that is, the concept *( ) flies* falls under the concept *( ) is an activity*. So *falling under* is a relation objects have to the properties they instantiate, and properties have to the higher-level properties they instantiate. By "properties" we mean "properties and relations." Circumstances involve objects falling under concepts, i.e. having properties, and concepts falling under higher-level properties, as well as various combinations.

In the terminology we employ, *first-level* circumstances consist of objects having properties and standing in relations. If the objects have the properties and stand in the relations, the circumstance is a fact. Higher-level circumstances consist of concepts falling under concepts. It is a second-level fact, for example, that there are philosophers; that is, that *being a philosopher* falls under *being instantiated*. We call any circumstances a first-level circumstance if it involves objects, even if it also involves properties having properties and standing in relations.

2.4 Content Problems

Frege tells us that if two sentences have the same conceptual content, they have the same logical consequences (§3). We call this his *inference criterion* for identity of content. As Warren Goldfarb cogently explains in his fine

---

[4] Dummett questions the importance of Frege's notion of conceptual content in the *Begriffsschrift*, claiming that it is "plainly a matter which Frege had not at that stage thought through" (Dummett, 1981b, 299). We disagree. See Beaney, 1996, and Kremer, 2010, for a discussion of Frege's notion of content.

essay "Frege's Conception of Logic" (2010), Frege had a very straightforward view of logic, but one quite different than the view or views of logic that have developed since the works of Tarski and Gödel. Frege thought that logic, like any science, consists of truths, at least in its finished state. It differs from other sciences in being the most general. He thought that the truths of logic were *analytic,* in (more or less) Kant's sense. If we understand them— which may require a lot of work—we will see that they are true, without having to consult what is going on in the world. To see that two sentences have the same content—have the same consequences—one may have to put in a lot of work developing a proof of this fact. But one should not have to go outside one's study to establish some empirical facts.

First-level circumstances, especially those involving concrete things like rocks, humans, planets, and words, don't provide contents that meet these criteria. It is a sufficient condition for two sentences to stand for the same circumstance, that they name the same object and predicate the same properties. And, as we will see, there is a conflict between these two criteria for sameness of conceptual content: the inference criterion and the sameness of circumstance criterion.

Consider:

(1) Hesperus = Hesperus
(2) Hesperus = Phosphorus
(3) Hesperus has no moons
(4) Phosphorus has no moons

(1) and (2) stand for the same circumstance, and so have the same conceptual content, according to the sameness of circumstance criterion. Given that they have the same conceptual concept, they should have the same logical consequences by the inference criterion. But (4) follows from (2) and (3), and not from (1) and (3).

Our hypothesis is that it is this problem with conceptual content that led to §8. Frege does *not* tell us that in the *Begriffsschrift,* but, as we shall see, he suggests this motivation in "On Sense and Reference." To appreciate the problem we think was bothering Frege, consider a standard formulation of Leibniz's Law using Frege's notation:

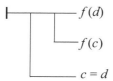

Stare at this, keeping in mind that sentences stand for circumstances, and that involving the same objects and properties is a sufficient condition for the identity of circumstances, and hence for identity of conceptual content. Keep the inference criterion for identity of conceptual content firmly in mind; set aside whatever you know about model theory. If you do this, it should seem very puzzling.

The Law *seems* to guarantee that the substitution of "*d*" for "*c*" in "*f(c)*" will preserve truth, given that "*c = d*" is true. But "*c = d*" doesn't seem to tell us anything that justifies the substitution. For "*c = d*," if true, stands for the same circumstance as "*c = c.*" The two sentences have the same conceptual content. The circumstance they both stand for has a certain object and the relation of identity as constituents. It has no names as constituents. How can this circumstance justify the substitution of names?

There are various ways Frege might have resolved the conflict in criteria. He might have abandoned the inference criterion, but it was very central to his conception of what logic is all about. He might have jettisoned first-level circumstances from his theory, and this is what he eventually does in his theory of sense and denotation. But in the *Begriffsschrift*, he *would* make the inference legitimate. His answer is the circumstance that $c \equiv d$. This circumstance *does* have names as constituents. Its truth requires that the two names stand for the same thing, so its truth requires that *c* and *d* are the same thing. But the circumstance that object *c* is identical with object *d* is not the conceptual content of "$c \equiv d$." And this sentence does not stand for the same circumstance as "$c \equiv c$." The difference in inferential power coincides with, and is explained by, the difference in circumstance.

Given this understanding, Frege is dealing with two connected problems in §8. The first we'll call the *Name Problem*. How do we learn from "*a = b*" that "*a*" and "*b*" stand for the same object? And, why can we infer from "*a = b*" that "*a*" and "*b*" stand for the same object, but not from "*a = a*," if they both stand for the same circumstance? Frege doesn't formulate the problem, and he doesn't solve it. He simply makes sure that it doesn't arise in Begriffsschrift, i.e. Concept-Writing. In Concept-Writing, in the *Begriffsschrift*, we use "$a \equiv b$" which states in a straightforward way what we *seem* to use "*a = b*" to communicate, in spite of its meaning, namely, that "*a*" and "*b*" have the relation of identity of content, that is, stand for, refer to the same thing.

The second problem we'll call the *Co-instantiation Problem*. This is the problem he uses the diagram to explain. We'll use a simpler example. Why would the Babylonians have two names, "Hesperus" and "Phosphorus" for the same heavenly body? Because there were two "ways of determination" associated with them. "Hesperus" was associated with the property of being the first heavenly body, other than the Sun or the Moon, to appear in the night sky. "Phosphorus" was associated with the property of being the last heavenly body to disappear from the morning sky, leaving only the Sun and (perhaps) the Moon.

Given this, it seems that one can learn from "Hesperus = Phosphorus" that the properties of being the first heavenly body to appear at night and the last to disappear in the morning are co-instantiated. But again, this is puzzling; one couldn't learn this from "Hesperus = Hesperus," which stands for the same circumstance. But with "≡" things become clear. "Hesperus ≡ Phosphorus" tells us that the names stand for the same thing; hence that thing must co-instantiate both ways of determination. "Hesperus ≡ Hesperus" doesn't tell us this.

Summing up, we think Frege's motivation for §8 comes from a conflict between criteria for sameness of conceptual content:

The Inference Criterion: two sentences have the same conceptual content if and only if they have the same logical consequences,

and

The Sameness of Circumstance Criterion: two sentences have the same conceptual content if and only if they stand for the same circumstance.

The conflict stems from the fact that two sentences can stand for the same circumstance and yet have different logical consequences. In particular, different consequences regarding the names and the properties involved. In other words, assuming that "$a = b$" and "$a = a$" both stand for the same circumstance, we get two problems:

The Name Problem: From "$a = b$" we can infer that "a" and "b" stand for the same thing, but not from "$a = a$;"

and

The Co-instantiation Problem: From "$a = b$" we can infer that a and b co-instantiate the same properties, but not from "$a = a$."

3 Sense and Reference: First Paragraph

Thirteen years after the *Begriffsschrift*, Frege criticized it in the opening paragraph of "On Sense and Reference." But something a bit odd seems to have been going on. He attributed to himself a view he didn't seem to hold, and then criticized this view, instead of the one he did hold.[5]

3.1 The Text and its Interpretation

Here is the first part of the first paragraph of "On Sense and Reference," broken into passages by us, followed by our interpretations:

> (A)
> Equality gives rise to challenging questions which are not altogether easy to answer. Is it a relation? A relation between objects, or between names or signs of objects? In my *Begriffsschrift* I assumed the latter.
> ("On Sense and Reference," 151)

This passage is very puzzling, given what he actually said in the *Begriffsschrift*. He never said that identity was a relation between names or signs. He never held what some people call the *Name view, Metalinguistic View* or the *Co-Reference Theory* of identity.[6] Our hypothesis is that he is telling us, in a rather opaque way, about the problem that was bothering him when he wrote the *Begriffsschrift* rather than the actual treatment of it that he was led to.[7] A clearer account might have been:

> Identity sentences such as "$a = b$" are puzzling. The "=" signifies a relation that holds between an object and itself. But what we seem to learn from such a sentence is that a certain relation holds between the names "a" and "b."

Instead, the paragraph goes on like this:

> (B)
> The reasons which seem to favor [the *Name view*] are the following: $a = a$ and $a = b$ are obviously statements of differing cognitive value; $a = a$ holds *a priori* and, according to Kant, is to be labelled analytic, while statements of the form $a = b$ often contain very valuable extensions of our knowledge and cannot always be established *a priori*. The discovery that the rising sun is not new every morning, but always the same, was one of the most fertile

---

[5] See Perry, 2019a, for an in-depth discussion of "On Sense and Reference," and for a presentation of Perry's "integrated account," a proposal that integrates Frege's theory in *Begriffsschrift*, with his theory of sense and denotation.

[6] See, for example, Thau and Caplan, 2001; Heck, 2003; Bar-Elli, 2006; Dickie, 2008; and May, 2012.

[7] That Frege's presentation of his view in the *Begriffsschrift* is misleading has also been suggested by Mendelsohn, 1982, and Angelelli, 1967. On the other hand, whether or not Frege was aware of the so-called "Frege problem" at the time he wrote *Begriffsschrifft* is a matter of controversy. Sluga (1980) believes he did, Dummett (1981b) disagrees.

astronomical discoveries. Even today the reidentification of a small planet or a comet is not always a matter of course.
("On Sense and Reference," 151)

Here Frege seems to bring up both the Name Problem and the Co-instantiation Problem, without distinguishing them very clearly. In terms of our example, "Hesperus = Hesperus" is analytic, while "Hesperus = Phosphorus" is not. That observation seems true, independently of the names being associated with ways of determination—what he will call "senses." But the fact that "Hesperus" and "Phosphorus" stand for the same thing doesn't seem to qualify as a valuable extension of our knowledge. He seems to be moving seamlessly from the Name Problem to the Co-instantiation Problem.

(C)
Now if we were to regard equality as a relation between that which the names "a" and "b" designate, it would seem that $a = b$ could not differ from $a = a$, i.e. provided $a = b$ is true). A relation would thereby be expressed of a thing to itself, and indeed one in which each thing stands to itself but to no other thing. What we apparently want to state by $a = b$ is that the signs or names "a" and "b" designate the same thing, so that those signs themselves would be under discussion; a relation between them would be asserted.
("On Sense and Reference," 151)

In (C), as we interpret it, Frege is telling us more about his motivation for what he said in the *Begriffsschrift* rather than telling us what he actually said there. The last sentence in (C) provide the missing motivations for §8: "What is intended to be said by $a = b$ seems to be that the signs or names "a" and "b" designate the same thing..." In the *Begriffsschrift*, however, this motivated Frege to retire "=" as a symbol, and replace it with "≡," rather than draw the conclusion that with "$a = b$" the signs themselves are under discussion, and "=" asserts a relation between signs.

(D)
But this relation would hold between the names or signs only in so far as they named or designated something. It would be mediated by the connection of each of the two signs with the same designated thing. But this is arbitrary. Nobody can be forbidden to use any arbitrarily producible event or object as a sign for something. In that case the sentence $a = b$ would no longer be concerned with the subject matter,[8] but only with its mode of designation; we would express no proper knowledge by its means. But in many cases this is just what we want to do. If the sign "a" is distinguished from

---

[8] Following Beaney, 1997, we translate "*betreffen*" as "be concerned with," instead of "refer," as it appears in the translation by Black in Geach and Black (1952).

the sign "b" only as object (here, by means of its shape), not as sign (i.e., not by the manner in which it designates something), the cognitive value of $a = a$ becomes essentially equal to that of $a = b$, provided $a = b$ is true. A difference can arise only if the difference between the signs corresponds to a difference in the mode of presentation of the thing designated. ("On Sense and Reference," 151–152.)

With the "But" at the beginning of this passage, Frege moves from exposition and apparent justification of his *Begriffsschrift* view, or what he is presenting as his *Begriffsschrift* view, to a critique of the view. After passage (D) Frege moves, still in the same paragraph, to the explanation of his new theory, the theory of sense and denotation.

Frege seems quite right that the relation of identity of content, or co-designation, would hold between names in virtue of their designating something. And, at least as long as we are talking about ordinary proper names, this does seem arbitrary. Just about anything can be used as a name. And it seems that "$a \equiv b$," or "$a = b$" if we interpret "=" to mean $\equiv$, doesn't say anything about the subject matter, and expresses no "proper knowledge," in the sense of no knowledge of any but linguistic interest. This is basically the same point he made in §8, with his geometrical example. And it is surely correct that we often do want to say something of interest with a sentence like "Hesperus = Phosphorus."[9]

But what comes next is puzzling. Suppose we don't know the ways of determination associated with "Hesperus" and "Phosphorus." Suppose we are told "Hesperus = Phosphorus" *before* we are told what ways of determination are associated with them. And suppose that, in fact, "Hesperus = Phosphorus" is true. Why does that mean that the cognitive value of "Hesperus = Phosphorus" becomes "essentially equal" to that of "Hesperus = Hesperus"?

This claim seems wrong. For one thing "Hesperus = Hesperus" is analytic, on the assumption that "Hesperus" names something, while "Hesperus = Phosphorus" is not, even on the assumption that both names name something.

For another, the sentences differ in content according to the inference criterion. As we showed above, (4) follows from (2) and (3) but it doesn't follow from (1) and (3). Suppose now that someone is told (2) "Hesperus = Phosphorus" and then, that evening and the next morning, has the ways of determination explained to her. She won't learn anything of much interest until she learns the ways of determination, but it seems she will learn something that, once the ways of determination are presented, allows her to make a somewhat astonishing inference, namely, that the first heavenly object to

---

[9] See also Perry, 2001 [2012], and Corazza and Korta, 2015.

appear in the night sky is the same as the last to disappear from the morning sky. Had she been told (1) "Hesperus = Hesperus" she would not have been able to make this inference.

3.2 The Missing Solution

It seems that in "On Sense and Reference," Frege sees his actual *Begriffsschrift* analysis as involving an extra and unnecessary step. He sees the sentence "Hesperus = Phosphorus" *itself,* not some other sentence involving ≡, as carrying, for semantically competent speakers, the information that the property of being the first planet to appear in the evening and the property of being the last planet to disappear in the morning are co-instantiated.

The "ways of determination" of the *Begriffsschrift* have become senses in "On Sense and Reference." So they are part of the content, the Thought expressed. The sentence "Hesperus = Phosphorus" doesn't express the circumstance that Venus is Venus, but rather expresses the Thought that one thing is both the first planet to appear in the evening and the last planet to disappear in the morning. If we understand the identity sentence (2), we grasp this Thought. There is no need to go through the "≡" step. We get from "Hesperus = Phosphorus" to a Thought involving significant astronomical information without going through the intermediate step that "Hesperus ≡ Phosphorus."

But, on this account, what is the solution to the Name Problem? That is, how can one learn that "Hesperus" and "Phosphorus" co-refer from "Hesperus = Phosphorus"?

When Frege says in (D),

> If the sign "a" is distinguished from the sign "b" only as object (here, by means of its shape), not as a sign (i.e., not by the manner in which it designates), *the cognitive value of $a = a$ becomes essentially equal to that of $a = b$, provided $a = b$ is true.* [emphasis added],
>
> ("On Sense and Reference," 152.)

one might think he is thinking about the case in which "a" and "b" are just marks, not yet assigned as names to anything. But then it would make no sense to say, "provided $a = b$ is true."

In "On Sense and Reference," Frege denies that the Name Problem, the difference in what we can learn about *names* from (1) and (2), is a problem after all. He seems to have come to see this as a *pseudo-problem*. But Frege doesn't tell us *why* this is so.

In fact, Frege's theory of sense and denotation does not seem to provide a solution to the Name Problem. On the theory of sense and denotation, sentences express Thoughts. Although (1) and (2) denote the same truth-value, they do not express the same Thought. The Thoughts incorporate the senses corresponding to the different names. (1) and (2) differ in content; we learn something of astronomical importance from (2) that we do not learn from (1).

This is a solution to the Co-instantiation problem, but not to the Name Problem. Consider (5):

> (5) The first planet to appear in the evening sky is the last planet to disappear from the morning sky.

(5) seems to capture the Thought expressed by (2), since it is the senses of "Hesperus" and "Phosphorus," not the names, that are contributed to the Thought. But there is nothing about "Hesperus" and "Phosphorus" in (5). Frege's theory provides no route back from sense to name, and so no solution to the Name Problem.

To treat the problem within his theory of sense and denotation, Frege needs to provide us with a Thought that is about names, just as he provided a circumstance involving names in the *Begriffsschrift*. This would require senses of the names themselves, in addition to the senses with which the names are associated. Then he needs to explain how we grasp *that* Thought.

4 Sense and Reference: Last Paragraph

In the last paragraph of "Sense and Reference" Frege returns to identity sentences.

4.1 Text

Let us return to our starting-point.
If we found "$a = a$" and "$a = b$" to have different cognitive values, the explanation is that for the purpose of knowledge, the sense of the sentence, viz., the thought expressed by it, is no less relevant than its denotation, i.e. its truth-value. If now $a = b$, then indeed the referent of "b" is the same as that of "a," and hence the truth-value of "$a = b$" is the same as that of "$a = a$." In spite of this, the sense of "b" may differ from that of "a," and thereby the sense expressed by "$a = b$" will differ from that expressed by "$a = a$." In that case the two sentences do not have the same cognitive value. If we understand by "judgement" the advance from the thought to its truth-value, as in the present paper, we can also say that the judgments are different.
("On Sense and Reference," 171)

4.2 Interpretation

Here he treats the Name Problem rather succinctly, with the word "indeed":

> If now $a = b$, then *indeed* the referent of "b" is the same as that of "a," and hence the truth-value of "$a = b$" is the same as that of "$a = a$."
> ("On Sense and Reference," 171, emphasis added.)

He then notes that the two sentences have different senses, without explaining the "indeed"; that is, without explaining how we get information about names from a sentence that denotes a truth-value, and expresses a thought that is not about the names, but their denotations—without explaining the Name Problem.

In between the opening and closing paragraphs, Frege has given us an account of quotation:

> If words are used in the ordinary way, what one intends to speak of is their referents. It can also happen, however, that one wishes to talk about the words themselves or their sense. This happens, for instance, when the words of another are quoted. One's own words then first designate words of the other speaker, and only the latter have their usual referents. We then have signs of signs. In writing, the words are in this case enclosed in quotation marks. Accordingly, a word standing between quotation marks must not be taken as having its ordinary referent.
> ("On Sense and Reference," 153–154)

> Exceptions [to preservation of truth-value upon substitution] are to be expected when the whole sentence or its part is direct or indirect quotation; for in such cases, as we have seen, the words do not have their customary referents. In direct quotation, a sentence designates another sentence, and in indirect speech a thought. ("On Sense and Reference," 159)

Does this provide an explanation to the Name Problem? It doesn't seem so. The issue is how we learn from

(2) Hesperus = Phosphorus

that "Hesperus" and "Phosphorus" stand for the same object, not how we learn from

(2') "Hesperus = Phosphorus"

or

(2") "Hesperus = Phosphorus" is true

that they do. The last two sentences express what we seem to learn when we read (2), but it doesn't explain how we learn it.

It seems most plausible that Frege still thinks that the Name Problem is a pseudo-problem, rather than thinking it is a real problem he has solved by the end of "On Sense and Reference."

5   Is the Name Problem a Pseudo-Problem?

Suppose a bright, but philosophically gifted, student stares at a formulation of Leibniz's Law such as,

$$(a = b) \rightarrow (f(a) \rightarrow f(b))$$

and finds it mysterious, in the way we imagined Frege to have found it mysterious, and encouraged the reader to find it mysterious. "If the antecedent is true," she says to her instructor, "it puts the same requirements, on the same object(s), as '$a = a$.' But we couldn't draw the inference in that case. The antecedent seems to tell us that "a" and "b" co-refer—but isn't that a "use-mention" confusion? How does the identity of object(s) tell us anything that permits substituting the names?" The instructor might reply, "Look at it from the model-theoretic point of view. Any model in which '$a = b$' and '$f(a)$' is true will be one in which '$f(b)$' is true. You don't get that result with '$a = a$'."

The instructor might be impressed with the student's bafflement. But she regards it as a pseudo-problem. It evaporates as soon as one looks at the truth-conditions of the sentence from another angle, not in terms of what it *says*, but what the semantics of the language requires for a sentence like it to be true.

From what "Hesperus = Phosphorus" says, one can learn that Hesperus and Phosphorus are the same planet, but not that the names used refer to the same thing. On Frege's view, the sentence expresses a Thought; something like, *There is a planet that is both the first planet to appear in the night sky and the last to disappear from the morning sky*. On a direct reference view, it expresses the singular proposition that Venus is Venus. On neither view does the truth of what it expresses put any conditions on the names "Hesperus" and "Phosphorus."

If we don't worry about what the sentence says, but simply the conditions of truth imposed by its semantics, we see that the sentence is true in all models in which "=" is assigned a relation that holds between the referents of the two names. If we assume that "=" is a logical term, so is in effect assigned to identity in all models, we learn that in all models in which the sentence is true, "Hesperus" and "Phosphorus" are assigned to the same object. If the sentence is true, the names co-designate.

We agree with the later Frege that this was a pseudo-problem for the earlier Frege, that he could ignore, and the earlier Frege should have ignored.

But the later Frege doesn't say *why* it is a pseudo-problem. Since he had no opportunity to study Tarski and Gödel one can hardly blame him.

Still, we think the earlier Frege has the equipment for such a treatment almost in his grasp with his concept of bifurcation, and his clear if not explicit semantics in terms of conceptual content. Suppose Frege wrote the *Begriffsschrift* without §8 and without replacing "=" with "≡." He found one of his students staring at the version of Leibniz's Law in this hypothetical version:

$$\vdash \begin{array}{l} f(d) \\ f(c) \\ c = d \end{array}$$

When asked what's bothering her, the students says, "if '$c = d$' is true, it stands for the same circumstance as '$c = c$.' So if we replace the first by the second, since they have the same conceptual content, the same things should follow. But surely, given the replacement it wouldn't follow that $f(d)$."

At that point, it seems to us, Frege could have said something like this:

> You have to keep in mind how my theory of the truth-conditions of sentences works. On that theory, a sentence of the form "cRd" is true iff "c" stands for an object, "d" stands for an object, and the two objects stand in the relation meant by "R". Since "R" means identity, the sentence "$c = d$" is true iff "c" and "d" stand for the same object. This assures us that replacing "c" with "d" won't affect the truth-value. But it doesn't work with "$c = c$."
>
> You must keep in mind that there is always a bifurcation in our use of language. Sometimes we are happy to grasp what the sentence says, the circumstance it stands for, the conditions its truth imposes on the properties and objects the expressions stand for. At other times, we need to reflect on *how* it says what it says; that is, what conditions its truth imposes on the expressions used, simply in virtue of the structure of the sentence and the way the language works.

If the student then says, "Does that mean you are changing your conception of logic?," we aren't sure what Frege should say.

6 Conclusion

The first paragraph of "On Sense and Reference" is probably the single most-read paragraph in analytic philosophy. It is remarkable how misleading it is. The author attributes himself a view on identity that never held, the Name

View, and proceeds to criticize it. The standard interpretation takes the paragraph at face value and attributes Frege the Name View, first, and the Object View later on. Further, the standard interpretation does not distinguish between two different relations that are present in the *Begriffsschrift*, identity (=) and identity of content (≡).

On a recent set of papers, Thau and Caplan (2001), Heck (2003) and Bar-Elli (2006)[10] have had an interesting discussion about the standard interpretation, its vices and virtues. Without getting into much detail, we think our proposal sheds light on some critical points of the discussion.

First, it is surprising that not many commentators pay attention to the difference between = and ≡, and very few take them to be *two different relations*.[11] Thau and Caplan, and Heck, for instance, accept the common view in this regard, and take "=" and "≡" to be notational variants of the same relation—identity. But this is quite surprising, why would Frege introduce a new symbol for identity? Why have two symbols for the same relation in the *Begriffsschrift*? He used two symbols, so it seems reasonable to conclude that he thought they had two different meanings. To repeat, "=" and "≡" stand for different relations. Frege never held the Name View about identity in the *Begriffsschrift*, or anywhere else for that matter. He held that *identity of content* is a relation between names, but not that *identity* is.

Second, the Name View of identity, which is misattributed to the *Begriffsschrift* by many—including, perhaps, Frege himself in "On Sense and Reference"—, is also often called the *Metalinguistic View*. These terms are used quite differently by Thau and Caplan (2001). For these authors,

> On the first, metalinguistic view—which we'll call the *name view*—"α = β" expresses the thought that the *names* α and β have the same referent; whereas, on the second view, non-metalinguistic view—which we'll call the *object view*—"α = β" expresses the thought that a and b are the same object, where a and b are the objects named by α and β. (Thau and Caplan 2001, 161)

Notice that the distinction here is not between two views about identity but between two views about the meaning of identity statements or, rather, as they put it, about the kind of thoughts expressed by identity statements. They argue that Frege holds the metalinguistic view on the meaning of identity statements in *Begriffsschrift* and that he *never abandons* it.

---

[10] See also Dickie, 2008.
[11] This might have been caused by Frege's own confusing remarks in "On Sense and Reference," as we have discussed. Also, most of the key literature on Frege, and in particular Dummett, 1981a, 1981b, accord with this. For exceptions, see Mendelsohn, 1982; May 2001, 2012; and Bar-Elli, 2006.

We think that framing the discussion like that is misleading. First, because there is no metalinguistic view about *identity* statements in *Begriffsschrift,* there is a *Name View* of *identity-of-content* statements. But, second, and even focusing on the latter, what an identity-of-content statement says is: "$\alpha \equiv \beta$" stand for the circumstance where the *names* α and β have the same content. "Have the same content" and "have the same referent/denotation" might be practically synonyms, but substituting "expressing a thought" for "stand for a circumstance," as Thau and Caplan seem to do, is far from innocuous, especially when talking about the similarities and differences between *Begriffsschrift* and "On Sense and Reference." In the former, first-level circumstances contain objects and relations, so the circumstances that identity-of-content statements stand for contain two names and a relation. In the latter, the thoughts expressed by identity statements contain senses, and not names or relations.

Contrary to what Thau and Caplan claim, what Frege holds in *Begriffsschrift,* and never rejects in "On Sense and Reference," is the view that if "$a \equiv b$" is true and, therefore, "$a = b$" is also true, then the referent of "b" is the same as the referent of "a." He says as much in the last paragraph of "On Sense and Reference." But this view is neither the Name View of identity, as we understand it, nor the metalinguistic view of identity statements, as Thau and Caplan (2001) understand it.

According to our interpretation, Frege found it natural at this point in his thinking to take sentences as standing for or meaning circumstances, in pretty much the sense the phrase "states of affairs" is now commonly used. We are taking the word seriously, perhaps more seriously than Frege himself did, but it is helpful in understanding the problems Frege had in the *Begriffsschrift* with identity, problems which he thought he solved later with his theory of sense and reference.[12]

---

[12] This paper was inspired by our dissatisfaction with the discussion of these problems in an early draft of Perry's *Frege's Detour* (2019), and inspired the discussion in later drafts. We are grateful to the members of the Zoom group, and the audience of the World Philosophy Congress at Beijing (August 2018), where we presented an early version of it. The first two authors benefitted from grants by the Spanish Government (FFI2015- 63719-P (MINECO/FEDER, UE); PID2019-106078GB-I00 (MCI/AEI/FEDER, UE)) and the Basque Government (IT1032-16). We are very thankful for the comments of an anonymous reviewer. We are particularly very grateful to Tadeusz Ciecierski for his invitation and his help and patience during the process.

15

Language and Luck

María de Ponte, Kepa Korta and John Perry

1 Introduction

In this essay we consider three cases of luck, only one of which deserves the title "linguistic luck." In all three cases a phrase of the form "It was lucky for A at t that S" is a natural description. This phrase suggests that being lucky is a relation an agent has to a proposition at a time, just as "propositional attitude" reports suggest that believing, hoping, or saying are relations an agent has to a proposition at a time. We have argued that this picture is too simple in the case of propositional attitude reports, and put forward what we call the "reflexive-referential" account, or "critical referentialism" as an improvement. Here we argue this account is very helpful in dealing with luck and the natural way of describing it.

The first case is historically important but not philosophically problematic in any obvious way. We use it to motivate our working definition of "luck." Consider:

> When he crossed the Delaware early in the morning December 26, 1776 in order to mount a surprise attack on the British garrison of Hessian soldiers near Trenton, George Washington was lucky that most of them were not awake.

This tells us quite a bit about a lucky incident (A). We elaborate a little.

(A)
1. What was lucky: That most of the Hessians were not awake;
2. Who was lucky: George Washington;
3. What he was trying to do: To mount a surprise attack on the Hessian garrison;
4. When he was lucky: The morning of December 26, 1776;

5. Why he was lucky: Because most of the British were not awake, Washington was able to destroy a garrison of over 1,000 Hessian soldiers, weakening the British and having a positive effect on the morale of his own troops.

The *Oxford English Dictionary* (*OED*) offers many definitions of "luck," including

> The chance occurrence of situations or events either favourable or unfavourable to a person's interests. (*OED*)

The term "chance" suggests "random." We think this narrows things too much and prefer:

> The occurrence of situations or events, either favorable or unfavorable to a person's interests, which are contingent, and not completely under that person's control.

Washington had good reasons to think it likely that the Hessians, or most of them, would be asleep fairly late the morning after Christmas, for he had good reasons to believe that like good Hessians they would have done a lot of celebrating the day before, probably ingesting significant amounts of alcohol. He wasn't just relying on chance. But, of course, he couldn't be certain, and had no control over how late they would sleep. Indeed, the British were warned of his attack, but the Hessian in command thought the Americans were pretty feeble, and that it wouldn't be necessary to wake all of his troops to defeat the Americans.

Here is our working definition of luck:

> An agent A is lucky at t that S, if S is a contingent fact, uncertain and favorable to A's interests, and the contingencies are not under A's control.

> An agent A is *un*lucky at t that S, if S is contingent fact, uncertain and *un*favorable to A's interests, and the contingencies are not under A's control.

This is a broad definition, which accords more or less with plausible accounts of luck available in the literature. In what follows, we first discuss a case of a lucky necessity, which allegedly contradicts our working definition (and other common accounts of luck). We argue, using the "reflexive-referential" account, that it does not. We then apply this account to a well-known case of linguistic luck presented by Brian Loar (1976).

2 Lucky Necessities

In "Why Every Theory of Luck is Wrong," Stephen Hales (2016) offers a short and clear presentation of the most common accounts of luck: in terms of probability, in terms of modality, and in terms of the agent's control over the events leading to the bit of luck. It seems that if it is lucky for A that S, then S must be a truth that is improbable, or at least not certain; contingent, rather than necessary; and the sort of thing an agent might control, but in this case does not.

But then Hales gives several examples where the bit of luck in question seems to be a necessary truth. According to him, such cases are a threat to all three accounts of luck. If this is so, they would also challenge our working definition. We will focus on this example:

> Jack the Ripper is terrorizing the neighborhood. There's a knock on your door, which you promptly and thoughtlessly open. It is your friend Bob (who is not Jack the Ripper). Bob rolls his eyes at your carelessness and says, "You're lucky I'm not Jack the Ripper." It is metaphysically necessary that things (and people) are self-identical. Given that Bob is not Jack the Ripper, it is metaphysically impossible for him to be Jack the Ripper. Bob cannot be other than what he is. (Hales, 2016, 495)

On our working definition, a bit of luck must be a contingent fact, and this requirement is explicitly or implicitly shared by the three accounts. So it seems such accounts are defective.

Let us modify some details of the example. We'll let Enid answer the door instead of you. We'll move the example back a bit more than a century, to June 12, 1888, and locate it in London's East End, where Jack the Ripper, Enid, and Bob were all living. Bob says to Enid, "You are lucky that I am not Jack the Ripper." The embedded sentence, "I am not Jack the Ripper" identifies the bit of luck: *That Bob is not Jack the Ripper*. If he had been Jack the Ripper, he would have likely killed her. This is what this example (B) seems to tell us about this lucky incident:

(B)
1. What was lucky: That Bob is not Jack the Ripper;
2. Who was lucky: Enid;
3. What she was trying to do: To answer the door (without getting killed);
4. When she was lucky: June 12, 1888 (when Jack the Ripper was alive and terrorizing London neighborhoods);
5. Why she was lucky: Because had Bob been Jack the Ripper, she would have been painfully killed.

In (B), like in (A), the bit of luck is identified with a sentence embedded in a "that"-clause. This suggests that bits of luck can be propositions. But the proposition that Bob is not Jack the Ripper is necessarily true. How can something that is necessarily true be lucky?

If luck is a matter of something with relatively low probability happening, metaphysical necessities are not matters of luck. The modality explanation doesn't fare better. Luck, according to this view, involves modal fragility, that is, a lucky event is one that happens but could easily have not happened. It doesn't happen in many "close possible worlds." But Bob being Jack the Ripper, given that he is not, simply could not have happened. It's not a contingent fact; we won't find it in any world in which either of them exists, however distant.

Finally, the control explanation claims that lucky events are those over which we have little control. Enid certainly has no control over whether Bob is or is not Jack the Ripper. But, clearly, this case isn't what the defenders of the control explanation have in mind. An extra element is needed: A lucky event is a contingent event we cannot control. That is, an event that might or might not happen, and about which we can do little or nothing. But we cannot control whether or not something impossible happens.[1]

It seems to us that the problem comes from a wrong understanding of Bob's utterance of "I'm not Jack the Ripper." This, in turn, results in a wrong understanding of what is *the piece of luck*—what Enid is lucky for and why. We suggest that this case can be handled by using the reflexive-referential account of the contents of utterances and thoughts, which we now explain.

3   The Reflexive-Referential Account

The account focuses on contentful *episodes*: utterances, thoughts, perceptions, actions, beliefs, desires, intentions, etc. These things occur in space and time and have causes and effects. They involve cognition; we'll call them "cognitive episodes." In so doing we stretch the phrase. As we use the term, an episode can be very brief, as one's perception of a bolt of lightning, or very long, as one's subsequent fear of lightning might be. Beliefs and desires are states one may be in for a long time, but we'll include them as episodes.

---

[1] In "Luck and Risk and the Lack of Control" (2015), Fernando Broncano-Berrocal develops a plausible account of luck that incorporates ideas from the probability, modality, and especially the lack of control accounts, and emphasizes the element of risk. But risk doesn't seem to provide an answer to Hales challenge either. Enid was not at any risk that Bob would be Jack the Ripper, since it was metaphysically impossible.

Cognitive episodes have *contents*. The truth-conditions of a statement or a belief are the paradigm case, but orders have fulfilment-conditions, desires have satisfaction-conditions, and so forth. We use "contents" for all such conditions. We think of contents as propositions that encode the conditions of truth for statements, conditions of satisfaction for expressions of hopes and desires, conditions of compliance for orders, and so forth. We take propositions to be abstract objects that are useful for classifying episodes in terms of their conditions of truth, etc. We agree with Frege that propositions (his "Thoughts") are not mental or physical episodes or states and so have no causes or effects. We don't, however, accept everything Frege says about propositions.

We do not regard episodes of belief, desire, etc., as consisting of relations to propositions. These episodes have causes and effects. We think propositions are abstract objects that have been designed to be useful in classifying events in the causal realm, but not themselves as causes and effects. To be useful, such propositions need to be well-behaved and well-understood abstract objects, usually sets. The language that is used for propositions needs to be correlated with the elements of utterances and thoughts that determine their truth-conditions. Sentences play a major role in identifying these elements in the case of utterances and thoughts that can be expressed with sentences.

We repeat, with emphasis: Propositions, in our account, are tools to keep track of the contents of cognitive episodes. Saying, believing, hoping, and other "propositional attitudes" do not consist in relations of a speaker or thinker to propositions, although they induce such relations. One of the authors is 79 years old. This fact puts him into a relation to the number 79 and the numeral "79" because they are the number and numeral used to classify and refer to his age. But being 79 years old doesn't consist in having these relations to numbers and numerals. It involves living for a long time, however we measure or refer to lengths of time. Similarly, having the belief that the Canary Islands are beautiful induces a relation to the proposition *that the Canary Islands are beautiful.* The belief induces the relation to a proposition, just as a person's height induces a relation to the number assigned to that height by some system of measurement. But the belief does not consist in the relation to this abstract object. It consists in having memories and images of the Canary Islands and a concept of beauty that these memories and images fit.

On the reflexive-referential account such cognitive episodes have multiple consistent layers of content that can be classified with propositions.[2] As

---

[2] For more about the reflexive-referential account, see Perry, 2001 [2012], Korta & Perry, 2011, and Chapter 8 of this volume.

we said, the time is June 12, 1888, and the place is East End of London, where Bob, Enid, and Jack all reside. Bob knocks on Enid's door. Bob and Enid are old friends, but today he has just moved into a flat near hers in Whitechapel. Before uttering the remark about luck already quoted, Bob says to her, "Today you and I are neighbors." We'll call this utterance **u**. Then, on many accounts, Bob said the proposition:

P: *That Bob is Enid's neighbor on June 12, 1888*

On a simple account this proposition is a set consisting of the relation of x being a neighbor of y at t, and the sequence of Bob, Enid, and June 12, 1888. One might take it to be the set of possible worlds in which Bob is a neighbor of Enid's on that day. Or perhaps the set of worlds w in which Bob's counterpart in w be a neighbor of Enid's counterpart in w on that day, or perhaps on that day's counterpart. Indeed, there are many kinds of abstract objects philosophers have taken to be propositions. We'll stick with the simple account, and assume that the reader gets the general idea.

We agree that the proposition P is *a* truth-condition of Bob's utterance. But we don't agree that it is *the* truth-condition. On our account, the truth-conditions of an utterance are *relative* to a set of facts that are taken as *given*. The truth-condition of an utterance, relative to a set of facts g, is *what else* has to be the case for the utterance to be true, *given g*.

Suppose we start with the fact that **u** is "Today you and I are neighbors," and that the sentence is in English. Given that, do we have truth-conditions for **u**? Of course we do:

P_{ub}: *There is a day* d *on which* **u** *occurs, a day* d' *to which "today" in* **u** *refers, persons* x, y *to whom the utterances of "you" and "I" in* **u** *refer, a relation* R *to which the utterance of "are neighbors" in* **u** *refers, and on day* d', x, *and* y *stand in relation* R.

We call P_{ub} an *utterance-bound* truth-condition of **u**.[3] The references of the expressions are identified only in terms the utterance **u**. P_{ub} is certainly not what Bob said, as we ordinarily use "said." To get at what Bob would ordinarily be taken to have said, we need information about **u** that allows us to instantiate on the variables, so that we can free the identification of the referents from their dependence on **u**. In this case:

---

[3] We do not call P_{ub} "*the* utterance-bound truth-conditions." We started by giving the language and expressions of **u**. At an even more utterance-bound level these might only be identified relative to the utterance. For example, the language might be identified as "the language of **u**" rather than as "English."

d = June 12, 1888, and, given the conventions of English for the utterances of "today," "you," "I," and "are neighbors": $d' = d$, x = Enid, y = Bob, and R = the relation of living close to.

To get to what Bob said, ordinarily construed, we need to identify referents independently of **u**. So, given, in addition to P_{ub}, the information that **u** occurs on June 12, 1888, that "today" refers to the day of utterance, that "I" refers to the speaker and Bob is the speaker, that "you" refers to the person spoken to and Enid is the person spoken to, so x and y are Bob and Enid, and that "are neighbors" refers to the relation of being neighbors, *what else* has to be the case for **u** to be true? Just our old friend P:

P: *That Bob is Enid's neighbor on June 12, 1888*

P_{ub} gave us an utterance-bound truth-condition for **u**. To get from there to what we would normally regard as "the proposition expressed" or "what was said," we need the instantiating information. But P does not encode or entail all of the information we need to get to it. For example, P does not entail that Bob is the speaker of **u**, or that Enid was the audience of **u**, or even that **u** occurred.

P doesn't put any conditions on **u**. The conditions can be met even if **u** doesn't happen. It puts conditions on Bob, Enid, the relation of being a neighbor of, and June 12, 1888. That is, it gives us conditions on the referents of the expressions in the utterance, but not on the utterance itself. So it is the *reference-bound* content, or simply the *referential* content.

Suppose for instance we didn't bother to tell you *when* this all happened, that is, what day "today" referred to. Would you know conditions of truth for Bob's utterance? Of course you would. Bob's utterance is true iff

P_h: *There is some day* d *during which the utterance* **u** *occurred, and Bob and Enid were neighbors on* d

P_h, like P_{ub} is utterance-bound. But not every referring term in P_h is utterance-bound, only "today." We'll call such a content *hybrid*. There are many hybrid contents on the way from P_{ub} to P, which might be relevant in variations on the case.

P_{ub}, P_h, and P are different propositions. The first two are independent of the third. But they are consistent with it. P_h follows from P_{ub} when we add the meanings of "I," "you," the reference of "are neighbors" and the facts that the speaker was Bob and the audience was Enid. P follows from P_h when we give the date of **u**.

Our claim is that utterance-bound contents can be used by theories of luck to handle Hales' lucky necessities. We'll now recycle **u** for Bob's utterance of "You're lucky I'm not Jack the Ripper," in the original example. We'll use **u'** for the sub-utterance of "I'm not Jack the Ripper." Given the details we supplied, the referential content of **u'** is the necessary truth:

Q: *That Bob is not Jack the Ripper on June 12, 1888*

The date is irrelevant and we'll usually ignore it. We agree that it is hard to see the necessary truth *Q* as a matter of luck. But consider the hybrid content of **u'** given everything except the identity of the speaker:

Q_h: *Someone* x *is the speaker of **u'**, and* x *is not Jack the Ripper*

Enid knows, before opening the door, that the person knocking on her door is on her porch. She knows that when she opens the door, she will be face to face with this person, with at most a screen door between them. She realizes, or would if she thought about it, that it would be dangerous to be in that situation with Jack the Ripper. She opens the door, sees Bob, hears his utterance **u'** and believes it. The speaker doesn't look like a deranged killer, and isn't doing anything threatening towards her. So when she opens the door and hears Bob utterance **u'** she learns that Jack the Ripper is not the person on her front porch, she is not face to face with him, and is in no danger. So Q_h conjoined with something obvious to Enid, that the speaker of **u'** is the person on her front porch, gives us the contingency that Enid was lucky about: That the person on her front porch is not Jack the Ripper.

Looking at things this way, what the example tells us about the lucky incident is:

(B')
1. What was lucky: That the speaker of **u'** (the person on the porch) is not Jack the Ripper;
2. Who was lucky: Enid;
3. What she was trying to do: To answer the door without being killed;
4. When she was lucky: June 12, 1888 (when Jack the Ripper was alive and terrorizing neighborhoods);
5. Why she was lucky: Because had Jack the Ripper been the speaker of **u'** (the person on the porch), she would likely have been killed.

There is nothing particularly problematic here, nothing that differentiates this case from any other lucky episode, such as (A) above. What is more, looking at things this way, the three approaches to luck seem to at least contribute something to understanding Enid's luck:

- Most of us, not living in London's East End in the late nineteenth century, don't have to be lucky to open our front door and not be face to face with Jack the Ripper. That scenario would be extremely improbable, occurring only in possible worlds very remote from our own. For Enid, living in London's East End in 1888, the probability that the person knocking on one's door was Jack the Ripper was still low, but not negligible; and the consequences would likely be terrible for Enid. So Enid is lucky that the person on her front porch is not Jack the Ripper, and probability seems at least part of the story.
- It is metaphysically impossible that Bob is Jack the Ripper. But it was not metaphysically impossible that the person on Enid's front porch that afternoon was Jack the Ripper. Suppose Knute says to Mary, as she goes to answer the front door, in Donostia in the twenty-first century, "If that's Jack the Ripper, you are in trouble." She might reasonably reply, "Well, perhaps the antecedent of your weird remark isn't metaphysically impossible; maybe Jack has been in Hell all these years and has somehow escaped. But that's a very remote possibility at best. So I'm not going to worry about it." But Jack the Ripper being on the front porch knocking on her door would not have been a remote possibility for Enid in London's East End in 1888. Given the likely consequence, Enid was lucky it wasn't him, and modality has a role in the explanation.
- It wasn't under Enid's control whether Bob was or was not Jack the Ripper. Since he is not, Enid is lucky. But the issue of control seems irrelevant. No one can do anything to control whether Bob is Jack the Ripper. Metaphysics settled that. But it was under her control whether she opened the door without further investigation of who was there. That was stupid on her part. Given the likely consequences, she was lucky that Jack the Ripper wasn't on her front porch and control seems relevant.

So, in our view, a proper account of cases of "lucky necessities" does not require giving up otherwise plausible accounts of luck. What is needed is a proper understanding of the truth-conditions of luck-utterances (of the type "X is lucky that S").

Of course, one might object: What Bob *said* was *that he was not Jack the Ripper*. He did not say anything about the front porch or who was standing there. We agree, pretty much. The default choice for "what is said" by an utterance is the referential content of the utterance. But a proper understanding of how this works makes it clear that what is said does not exhaust the information that an utterance can convey, and be intended to convey, to a semantically competent hearer. Any of the information of the utterance-bound or the hybrid contents can be conveyed, and often, the intent of the speaker is to do so.

In this case it seems clear that the utterance-bound content that Bob wants to convey to Enid is a hybrid one with all the references unbound except "I." Regardless of what Bob *actually* said, a topic on which philosophers of language might engage in long discussions, it seems clear that what he meant to convey was not that Enid was lucky that he was not Jack the Ripper, but rather that the speaker on the porch could have been Jack the Ripper, and Enid was lucky because he was not. This is actually a quite common sort of case, not in any way restricted to lucky necessities or to luck-utterances. Let us look at a couple more examples:

> Fred puts a big platter of kale before his young children and says "You will love this kale."

He knows his children have never seen this ugly vegetable before. But he thinks they will learn the name for it from his utterance. They will realize that his utterance is true iff there is some stuff Fred is referring to with "this kale" and they will love it. They realize that "kale," in the singular "this kale," is most likely a name of the kind of stuff he is pointing at. That is, they know how English works. They don't know this in the way people who have taken a linguistics or even a philosophy of language class know it. They may not know what an utterance is, or what referring is, or what a singular term is. But they are *attuned* to these facts about English, and are capable of making inferences from them, without being able to articulate the premises of their reasoning. What explains their inference is an utterance-bound content of Fred's utterance, given the meaning of the sentence and the fact, conveyed by glance and gesture, that he was referring to the green stuff on the platter. Given all of that, *what else* had to be the case, for Fred's utterance to be true? That "kale" is a name for the ugly green stuff. Note that in this case Fred succeeds in teaching his children something, that "kale" names kale, even though what he says is almost certainly false.

> John tells Frenchie that he is going to San Sebastian in the Basque Country for a week. She looks at the map of the Basque Country in John's office for "San Sebastian" but can't find it. He says, "San Sebastian is Donostia." Frenchie finds "Donostia" on the map, points to it and says, "That's where you are going?" and John says "yes."

John has conveyed to Frenchie that "Donostia" and "San Sebastian" are names for the same city. But what he said was simply that San Sebastian was Donostia, a necessary truth, which is the same thing he would have said with "San Sebastian is San Sebastian" and "Donostia is Donostia," if what is said is always to be identified with referential content. But those utterances would not have been helpful. A philosophical rule of thumb should be that the information conveyed by utterances of identity sentences can almost never be understood simply in terms of their referential content. If you insist on doing that, you will be lucky to get much of anything right.

4 Linguistic Luck

So far, this hasn't been a philosophy essay on linguistic luck, but rather a linguistic philosophy essay on luck. Now, we will use the reflexive-referential account to address a well-known issue concerning a possible case of linguistic luck, according to our working definition. Consider Brian Loar's example:

> Suppose that Smith and Jones are unaware that the man being interviewed on television is someone they see on the train every morning and about whom, in that latter role, they have just been talking. Smith says "He is a stockbroker," intending to refer to the man on television; Jones takes Smith to be referring to the man on the train. Now Jones, as it happens, has correctly identified Smith's referent, since the man on the television is the man on the train; but he has somehow failed to understand Smith's utterance. It would seem that, as Frege held, some "manner of presentation" of the referent is, even on referential uses, essential to what is being communicated. (Loar, 1976, 357)

Suppose the man on the train and on television is Peters. In the standard interpretation of Loar cases, Smith intends to communicate the singular proposition P, that Peters is a stockbroker, by uttering "He is a stockbroker." Jones grasps P, but "it turns out to be merely a matter of luck that both interlocutors entertained the same proposition" (Peet, 2017, 381). Either that or direct reference theories of demonstratives are wrong and they must be replaced by a Fregean theory, or at least supplemented with Fregean "manners of presentation."

Briefly, what Loar's example shows, in our view and terminology, is that the referential content is not enough to correctly explain linguistic understanding and communication, and failures of such endeavors. In particular, when singular terms are involved, communication is not merely a matter of correct referent assignment by whatever means. We agree with Loar that there is some communicative mismatch between Smith and Jones, but we wouldn't just say that Jones "has failed to understand Smith's utterance." It is a bit more complicated than that.

To understand the misunderstanding, we need something in addition to the expressions Smith and Jones both use and the entities that they both refer to. For that purpose, we bring in *notions*. Here is the explanation of this concept from *Critical Pragmatics*.

> We think the ideas we have of particular objects—we call them "notions"—are in many ways like files. They are relatively stable, more or less concrete structures in our minds. We establish them, when we meet people, or see buildings, or read about them, or hear about them. We use them to store information, some accurate, some inaccurate, about those things. This information is in the form of ideas of properties, relations, and notions of other things that we associate with the notions. Each association is a cognition—a belief, a desire, a hope, an expectation, a memory perhaps. The notion is a *component* of the cognition. We use that information when we interact with the objects, or engage in conversations about them. A notion is *of* the object it was introduced to keep track of, however poorly or well the associated ideas may fit [the object].
> (Korta & Perry, 2011, 38–9)

The reference of an utterance of a personal pronoun is typically determined, in part, by the intentions of the speaker and the notions that are part of that intention. We are standing at a corner, looking at a pair of women across the street. I nod in their direction and say "She looks like Kamala Harris." You ask, "Who?" or perhaps "To whom are you referring?" "The one on the right," I answer. In this case, I acquired two notions when I observed the scene across the street. When I added the information picked up visually to my stock of memories and beliefs, and after thinking a little I concluded that one of the women, whom we'll call X, looks a bit like Kamala Harris. I formed the intention to call this to your attention, and fulfilled that intention by uttering a sentence, by referring to X with "She" and predicating the resemblance with "looks like Kamala Harris." My notion of this woman plays a causal role in my action. X is a cause of my perception, which is a cause of my notion, which is a part of the intention that caused of my utterance of "She." Given those facts, our identification of the referent of "She" no longer needs to be utterance-bound. It can be *notion-bound*. The referent of my utterance of "She" is the person the notion that motivates that utterance is of.

Now that notion will have content. It may be part belief (There is a woman across the street who looks like such and such ...), part memory (I think Kamala Harris looked such and such when I met her at a campaign event ...), or part conjecture (I don't think even being vice-president she would have changed that much ...). The content may add up to something that doesn't fit X at all. But it is *of* X, because X was its origin, regardless of the fact that the machinations of an aged mind may have made it one that doesn't fit her all that well.

In natural language, the intentions of the speaker are often crucial in determining reference. Suppose I say, "George Bush was from Texas." You might reasonably ask, "Which George Bush, the father or the son?" Both are equally salient, so it seems that it is up to me to decide to whom I refer with my use of "George Bush." Or course I may be confused, absent-minded, or plainly wrong, but paradigmatically, it is the job of the speaker to resolve such "nambiguities."[4] Further, the notion involved can outweigh the meaning: "That wolf is going to eat your golf-ball." "That's not a wolf, it's a fox." "Well whatever it is, it's chasing on your golf ball."

Notions might be compared with Frege's "modes of presentation." Fregean modes of presentations have two roles. First, they help in explaining recognition and reasoning about things. This is also a role that notions have. But for Frege modes of presentation also have the job of *determining* reference, and this is where modes and notions differ. Names and other forms of reference are associated with modes of presentation, their "senses," and are *of* the object that the mode of presentation identifies, the one that has the properties and stands in the relations. This is not how we regard notions. They don't do the second job. The reference of names (or other forms of reference) is determined by their causal source, by the thing they were introduced to organize information about, and not by their satisfying the conditions that the images and descriptions in the notion identify.

We regard notions as crucial parts of the sorts of historical/causal chains that many philosophers plausibly take to establish reference. These may be short, as the one that goes from your sighting of X to your use of "That person." They may be longer, thousands of years longer, as the one that stretches from Aristotle's parents giving him a name to Chris Bobonich's use of "Aristotle" in a lecture to refer to him. The chains will involve many persons with many quite different notions of Aristotle, a great many of which may be mistaken in the properties attributed to him. Information can be passed along such chains, but also misinformation.[5]

The term "direct reference" employs a rather odd use of "direct." It basically means the connection does not involve Fregean senses. The paradigms of direct reference are not very direct in the ordinary sense of the word. The path from Aristotle's parents' use of some Greek precursor of "Aristotle" to a contemporary use of "Aristotle" in a Stanford classroom is not very direct.

---

[4] See Korta & Perry, 2011, Chapter 7, for more on names and ambiguities.
[5] See Perry, 2001 [2012], and Korta & Perry, 2011.

And it involves many notions in the many heads that have passed on information and misinformation about Aristotle. It involves many "manners of presentation," but they don't serve as Fregean senses, fixing the reference of use of the name. They are the information and misinformation passed along the historical chain, from one person thinking and talking about Aristotle to another.

Indexicals and demonstratives are paradigms of "direct reference." But again, there is nothing very direct about them in the ordinary sense of "direct." An utterance of "you" by B is determined by the character of "you"; it is the person B is addressing. But B may have an audience of dozens. Does her use of "you" refer to all of them, to some of them, to one of them? This is determined by all sorts of facts, but they pretty much boil down to the intentions of the speaker. Perhaps she is lecturing in classroom at UCLA, but "you" is directed at an Asian spy she takes to be listening in via a chain of events that goes from the classroom to a satellite and then to another and then to a listening base in Beijing or Vladivostok. Again, pretty non-Fregean, but not direct in any other sense.

Returning to Loar's example and to Smith's utterance **u**: "He is a stockbroker." A personal pronoun like "he" can be used deictically or anaphorically. If deictic, the referent is something that the speaker is thinking of—"has a notion of," in our lingo—and to which he is (typically) trying to draw audience's attention. Anaphorically, the pronoun picks up the reference of an earlier use of a singular term, possibly by a different speaker, even if the speaker of the anaphor has no idea what or who that is. But there is still a weak and fleeting notion involved: The speaker intends to refer to whatever the earlier utterance referred to. For this essay, however, we'll simply assume that Smith's use of "he" is deictic.

On the reflexive-referential account, Smith's utterance **u** has at least three different relevant contents or truth-conditions. The referential content, which is a singular proposition involving the individual—Peters—and the property of being a stockbroker.[6] An utterance-bound content, or the content that is determined by the rules of English and the fact that utterance **u** has been made. And the notion-bound content, which includes the notion or mental file—call it N_{TV}—that is motivating the speaker's use of "he," and that in the example is perceptually created by the image on the TV screen.

What we call "pure referentialism" will take the only content of Smith utterance to be the referential content, identified as "what is said." But what we call "critical referentialism," while recognizing singular propositions and referential content, and the fact that this content is usually the default

---

[6] We will leave time issues aside, since they are not relevant for our argument.

candidate for "what is said," will insist that other contents, with less taken as given, must be recognized for referentialism to be viable. With regard to the case under discussion, these other contents must be recognized for referentialism to be a plausible explanation. In this case, three contents of Smith's utterance **u** are crucial to understand what is going on:

- P_u: *That the person referred to by the utterance of "he" in* **u** *is a stockbroker*
- P_h: *That the origin of* N_{TV} *is a stockbroker*
- P: *That* **Peters** *is a stockbroker*

With these contents at hand, we can see where the communicative (mis)match in Smith's and Jones exchange lies. Assuming that Jones is a competent English speaker, alert and with no hearing problems, he can certainly identify the utterance-bound content of **u**. He correctly identifies the sentence uttered and its meaning. For **u** to be true, "he" has to refer to a male person and that person has to be a stockbroker. That is not what the speaker said, but assuming that Jones' understanding process has not completely failed him, P_u is a content he can easily identify. Also, by hypothesis, Jones also identifies **u**'s referential content P correctly. He correctly identifies Peters as the referent of "he" and understand that the property of being a stockbroker is being attributed to him. So, the mismatch must take place at the notion-bound content P_h.

Jones does not identify N_{TV}, the type of perceptual notion that both minds instantiate as they watch TV, and the one that motivates Smith's use of "he." Rather, he takes the notion that motivates Smith's use of "he" to be N_{Train}, the detached notion that both have of the person they see every day in the train but don't attach to any present perception.[7] Now, both notions do in fact correspond to the same person, and that's the source of the alleged luck in Smith's and Jones's convergence onto the same referential content.

When he introduced the example of Smith and Jones, Loar suggested that it seems to show that "[as] Frege held, some 'manner of presentation' of the referent is, even on referential uses, essential to what is being communicated." We agree. But, as we have argued, that doesn't mean we agree with Frege's theory of sense and reference. We agree with Frege that senses, or at least manners of presentation, and references are a crucial part of semantics. But their relation is more complicated than his theory envisages.

---

[7] We could also track the difference to a kind of *refined* utterance-bound content that distinguishes between anaphoric and deictic uses of demonstrative pronouns. Smith uses the pronoun deictically, and Jones takes him to be using it anaphorically, and that's what lead Jones to a different notion-bound content.

We claim to be referentialists, but critical referentialists, not direct referentialists. Does that mean we think the semantical views about names and indexicals and demonstratives and such espoused by "direct referentialist" are incorrect? No, mainly we think it is misleading—extraordinarily so—to call this "direct reference." There are many steps between utterance and reference, and these are systematically exploited to convey all sort of information other than referential content—what we sometimes have called "official" content.

So, given all this, where is the luck in Loar's example? It is not lucky or unlucky that the man they see every morning in the train is the same as the man on TV—that Peters is Peters. That Peters is Peters is as necessary as that Bob was not Jack the Ripper. But it is a matter of luck that they both identify the same content as **u**'s referential content, given that they are making use of different notions. Again, the identity that Smith and Jones ignore is not the trivial fact that Peters is Peters, but the non-trivial identity that can be rendered as

(*) *The origin of* N_{TV} = *The origin of* N_{Train}

In other words, there is a true identity relevant to the coherence of the conversation, the referents of the two uses of "he" are the same. They both believe this. But they each believe it on the basis of a mistake. Jones thinks Smith is thinking of the referent of his use as the man on the train, but he is not. Smith thinks Jones is thinking of the referent of his use as the man on TV, but he is not. An interesting case, but is this a matter of luck? Good luck? Or bad luck?

It seems there is linguistic luck involved in this case and that it is due to the fact that Smith and Jones did not know that the identity (*) above is true. Taking this into account, what the example tells us about luck and lucky referential convergence is something like:

(C)
1. What was lucky: That Jones identified the referential content of Smith's utterance correctly;
2. Who was lucky: Smith;[8]
3. What he was trying to do: To refer to the origin of N_{TV}—Peters—and to state that he is a stockbroker;

---

[8] Perhaps a better answer would be "both," since Jones was also lucky in having understood what Smith said, that is, he correctly identified the referential content of Smith's utterance. We will focus on Smith, just to keep things simpler. Adding Jones to this schema would not modify it significantly.

4. When he was lucky: At the time of the utterance;
5. Why he was lucky: Because Jones identified the reference of Smith's use of "he," even if he, unknowingly, employed a different notion, and neither knew that and, hence, that the origins of both notions were the same.

There is nothing exceptional here. Nothing to differentiate this episode from any other lucky one, like (A) and (B') above. Also, like in (B'), the three main approaches of luck can contribute to understanding it. The probability of Smith and Jones' referential convergence onto Peters, taking that they were both associating different notions to their uses of "he" and that they didn't know this, is quite low. Also, the outcome, although not dramatically important for their lives (as it was for Enid in the previous example), is still relevant. It is not clear, however, whether it is a positive or a negative outcome, and this is why it is not clear if this is a case of good or bad linguistic luck. The fact that they converge onto the same referential content of Smith's utterance is a good outcome. The fact that they did this on the basis of a mistake might cause further complications along the line.

Referring is an action. People perform the same action in different ways, and different actions in the same way. Smith performs the action of referring to Peters with "he"; Jones perform the action of identifying Peters as the referent of Smith's action. But they do what they do in different ways, relying on different circumstances. Smith refers to Peters in virtue of Peters having being on TV, and so the historical/causal source of the notion that motivates his utterance. Jones identifies Peters in virtue of Peters having been the man seen on the train, and so being the causal/historical source of the notion he employs. Given this, referential convergence is a matter of pure luck, being good or bad and for whom depending on how we continue the story.

Suppose that the man they see on the train wears bib overalls while on the train, because he fears spilling coffee on his shirt and tie while on a moving train. He changes into a suit when he gets to work at the brokerage or the television studio. So he doesn't look much like a stockbroker while on the train. The conversation continues, after Smith's utterance **u**, "He is a stockbroker."

> JONES: I doubt very much that what you just said is true.
> SMITH: I can't imagine why. It's obvious. I'm sure of it.
> JONES: I can't imagine why you think so. I'll bet you $10 that he isn't a stockbroker.
> SMITH: I accept.

Eventually they figure things out and Smith wins the bet. It is good luck for Smith that neither realized they were using different notions of the same man; if Jones, in particular, had realized that (*) was true he would have realized that what Smith said was likely true, and wouldn't have offered the bet. Smith didn't control this; he didn't even realize that (*) was relevant until after the bet was made. It was a bit of bad luck for Jones that their notions were of the same person. Otherwise, he could have declared the bet moot, since he would think they were talking about different people. Or at least he could put off paying until they had done a thorough study of the notion Smith was employing in such a case, and its relation to his own notion of Peters. Smith clearly intended to refer to the man he saw on TV. But didn't he also intend to refer to the man they were both thinking of? Well, they were thinking of the same man, but they didn't know they were thinking of him in different manners, and, Jones at least, didn't know that these manners had the same origin, so, was there really a proposition to serve as the basis of the wager? Perhaps in another year or so they could agree on this. Our point is simply that our critical referentialism would be the best framework in which to debate the question. Also, that probability can contribute to understanding the luck element.

On the other hand, although it is not metaphysically possible for Peters not to be Peters, the identity (*) is non-trivial. It is a contingent fact that the origin of N_{TV} is the same as the origin of N_{Train}. So this is a modally fragile situation. There are many possible situations where the mismatch could have not ended in referential convergence.

Finally, it is not under Smith's control that Jones identifies the intended notion-bound content. It is quite normal for him to assume that Jones would identify it, and would also make use of N_{TV}; after all, they are both watching TV together. But, since he doesn't realize that the man on TV is the man they see on the train, it is not under his control to anticipate Jones identifying N_{Train} instead. Had he been aware of the fact that the man on TV is the same as the man they see on the train, then, maybe, he should have made this connection explicit, to avoid possible complications and to make sure Jones understand he is talking about Peters by his use of "he."

In any case, what is most relevant for us is not what "luck" is, but rather how to account for this lucky incident from a linguistic perspective. Critical referentialism can easily account for this and similar cases, where two (or more) people refer to or think of the same object in different ways or, conversely, where they refer to or think of different objects in the same way. In most, if not all of them, luck will surely play an important role. Just as it does here. But these are not unusual or particularly complicated situations. Quite the contrary. These are cases where the speaker and the hearer identify different notions as motivating different uses of the same demonstrative. But that is not an extraordinary feature in communicative exchanges, by itself a matter of good or bad luck. It certainly does not justify the claim that Jones does not understand Smith. Jones actually understands quite well Smith's utterance. He identifies the utterance-bound content and, most importantly, the referential one. So he understands quite a lot of what Smith is saying.

Loar's claim was that his example posed a problem for direct referentialist theories: "It would seem that, as Frege held, some 'manner of presentation' of the referent is, even on referential uses, essential to what is being communicated" (Loar, 1976, 357). We agree. Fregean modes of presentations, or something along their lines, is needed. Direct or "pure" referentialists are in trouble. Critical referentialism introduces the idea of notions, similar to modes of presentation, but not quite the same thing as Fregean senses. With it, we can explain how the misunderstanding occurs and why; the amount of things Jones actually understands; referential convergence; and the role luck plays in it.

We don't claim to have provided a theory of luck in language, or an account of what we assume when we believe we have good reason to suppose we are talking or thinking about the same person. But we hope to have shown that critical referentialism provides a promising framework for further development. It allows us, as referentialists, to discard Frege's theory of sense and reference, without discarding the insights that made it plausible enough to be the accepted theory of names for most of a century.[9]

---

[9] We are grateful to the members of the Zoom group. The first two authors benefitted from grants by the Spanish Government (PID2019-106078GB-I00; MCI/AEI/FEDER, UE) and the Basque Government (IT1612-22). We are particularly grateful to the editors of this volume, Abrol Fairweather and Carlos Montemayor, for their invitation and their help and patience during the process.

16

Philosophy of Language and Action Theory

María de Ponte, Kepa Korta and John Perry

1 Introduction

Language is paradigmatically a human activity, largely consisting of speakers saying things in order to inform, warn, misinform, threat, sell, and so on. Usually, the plans that motivate such utterances include being understood by others and having an effect on their behavior as a result. The use of language belongs squarely in what Frege called the causal realms, the physical and the mental. Language is important because it is a system for doing things. This suggests that the philosophy of action should be a part—a very important part—of the philosophy of language.

To a certain extent it is. Charles Morris, in *Signs, Language, and Behavior* (1946), divided "semiotics," the study of signs, into three parts: syntax, semantics, and pragmatics.[1] Taking language as a system of signs, pragmatics is the study of how language is used, "how to do things with words," as Austin says. Austin developed his theory of speech acts in the 1950s, and Searle and others have further criticized and developed it (Searle 1969). Speech act theory categorizes and describes actions in terms of what we do to perform them, and what we do in and by performing them. Perhaps by uttering a sentence I say something about a politician (a locutionary act); in saying that, I *insult* the politician (an illocutionary act); by insulting the politician I *annoy* his powerful friends (a perlocutionary act), and so on. All of this depends on syntax and semantics to get started, but it is basically pragmatics.

A bit later, H. P. Grice (1967a [1989]) introduced the concept of implicature, which is something conveyed by an utterance beyond the proposition

---

[1] The term "semiotics" is due to Ferdinand de Saussure (1916 [1977]) and was adopted by Charles Peirce (1931–1958); neither used it in exactly the same way Morris did.

it expresses, beyond what the speaker says in uttering a sentence in a certain occasion. You ask me if I am going to a talk by X; I say "X is a complete idiot." I have not said that I am not going but have *implicated* that I won't. This, however, is not a matter of logic; I can consistently "cancel" the implicature by saying, "but I promised Y I would introduce X, so I'll be there."

Grice intended his influential theory to be a contribution to semantics. He thought that by taking what is implicated to be what is said, we make mistakes about what words and sentences mean. His original targets were claims, "common-place of philosophical logic" (Grice 1967a [1989], 22),[2] that the truth-conditional analyses logic provides for words like "or," "and," "if" do not give their meaning in natural language. But the theory of implicatures, regardless of what Grice intended, is a pragmatic theory, a theory of conversation taken as a "collaborative effort" (26), "a special case or variety of purposive, indeed rational, behavior" (28) where participants observe, or can be expected to observe, rational principles and maxims for (cooperative) action.

By and large, semantics itself was "utterance-free" until about the middle of the last century. Not that philosophers and logicians were unaware of utterances until then. But the working assumption was that semantics, the study of meaning and reference, should focus on what all utterances of an expression or sentence have in common, due to meaning, and not on how they differ, due to the particular facts of the utterance.

In this essay we "first consider how this assumption was challenged when the philosophy of language began to think about natural languages, as opposed to what Frege called "perfect languages." We discuss how, in the face of these challenges, attempts were made to "finesse utterances, in the analyses of names, and indexicals, by creating what one might call "expression-hybrids," particularly by David Kaplan. While appreciating the brilliance behind these attempts, we express reservations. Then we turn to our own theory, the reflexive-referential theory, which takes utterances as basic to the semantics and pragmatics of natural language.

2   Utterances Lost

Discussion of utterances is not common in the philosophy of language developed in the "first half of the twentieth century, at least in the analytic tradition inaugurated by Gottlob Frege and Bertrand Russell. The focus was the truth-conditions of sentences, and how they were based on the meanings and references of its parts. It was not the utterances of sentences and their parts that

---

[2] In earlier papers, the targets were claims by Ryle, Malcolm, Wittgenstein, Austin, Strawson, and others, about the meanings of expressions like "X looks φ to A" or "A tried to do x" (see Grice's "Prolegomena," in Grice 1989).

were studied, but the expressions themselves, the meanings they have in virtue of the conventions of the language to which they belong, the references they have in virtue of the world, and the truth-values the sentence of which they are parts have in virtue of all of these things.

In their early works, neither Frege nor Russell were particularly interested in natural languages except as the inspiration for better, more perfect, languages, like Frege's *Begriffsschrift*, or the language of Whitehead and Russell's *Principia Mathematica* were intended to be. They hoped to use these languages to show that arithmetic could be reduced to logic, a doctrine Russell labeled "logicism."[3] While their efforts did not fulfill their logicist ambitions, they produced a revolution in logic that had a profound effect on the next generation of logicians and philosophers of language.

Logic was the main interest of Frege and Russell, at least in his early years. Logic is centrally the study of valid inference. This suggests the activity of saying things that are true or are not and of drawing conclusions. But it was not these activities that were the focus, but rather the properties of sentences, considered as abstract objects, independently of their being spoken or written. How can the truth of one sentence, the conclusion, be guaranteed by the truth of others, the premises? Whether the premises are asserted, and if so by whom, when, and where, and whether the asserter is a reliable person with honorable intentions, is not of any interest. The question is whether what the truth of the premises requires of the world guarantees that the requirements for the truth of the conclusion will be met. So, although actual inferences are actions, with all sorts of causes and effects, it is validity as a property determined by structures of an ordered set of sentences that mainly fascinates logicians. And it was topics connected to this issue that dominated the philosophy of language for the first half of the twentieth century, following Frege's writings on these topics and Russell and Whitehead's watershed work, *Principia Mathematica*.

Frege and Russell's ideas about meaning, reference, truth, and the nature of the propositions gave philosophers of language a lot to think about. It was these ideas, often labeled the "Frege–Russell" theory, that dominated the philosophy of language for the first half of the twentieth century. They are still very much present in contemporary discussions, although their effects are somehow mitigated, or at least combined, with the effects of another "trend" that originated a few decades later, which placed the focus on the study of natural language. This trend, championed by philosophers like Strawson, Austin, and Grice, among others, was not concerned with logic (or not

---

[3] The origins of the term "logicism" are not clear. Logicism has its origins in Dedekind's work and, most importantly, on Frege's. But neither Dedekind nor Frege, as far as we know, used the term. Russell started using it around 1919, and so did Carnap and others.

merely) or with the development of any formal language, but rather with understanding the ways in which ordinary languages work and the ways speakers use expressions and sentences to do different things. When the attention of many analytic philosophers turned to natural language, the philosophy of action began to intrude into the citadel of the philosophy of language.

3   Reference: Natural Language Intrudes

From the end of World War II on, philosophers of language paid increasing attention to natural language, and to the extent to which the language of logic can mislead us as to how the corresponding expressions are used in natural language. The later Wittgenstein at Cambridge; Urmson, Austin, Grice, Anscombe, and others at Oxford; Peter Geach at Leeds; Max Black, Norman Malcolm, and Keith Donnellan at Cornell; and many others around the world pursued this theme in various ways, seldom in complete agreement with one another. In common to all was the increased attention to action, "how to do things with words," in Austin's phrase.

We start by describing the effects of this change of focus to the analysis of singular reference and, specifically, to the classic debates about definite descriptions (which are thought by some to refer, but not by all) and about names and indexicals (which are widely thought to refer to things). We pay special attention to indexicals, which might seem the natural candidates for the philosophy of action to intrude into the philosophy of language.

3.1   Definite Descriptions

Definite descriptions were an early target of philosophers concerned with natural language. Peter Geach in "Russell's Theory of Descriptions" (1950) and Peter Strawson in "On Referring" (1950) raised a number of objections to Russell's theory. Geach focused on Russell's example, "The King of France is bald," Strawson on a slight variation, "The king of France is wise." They raised a number of problems, but both focused on presupposition, a key factor in understanding descriptions in natural language.

They both were quite clear that they were doing the philosophy of natural language, a somewhat different project from Russell's. Geach said: "The incorrectness of Russell's theory as an account of ordinary language in no way goes against it as a proposed convention of symbolism" (1950, 86). And Strawson also makes it clear that his target is natural language: "I think it is true to say that Russell's Theory of Descriptions…is still widely accepted among logicians as giving a correct account of the use of such expressions in ordinary language. I want to show, in the first place, that this theory, so regarded, embodies some fundamental mistakes" (1950, 321).

Geach says that Russell's theory commits "the fallacy of many questions":

> the question "Is the present King of France bald" involves two other questions ...
> (4) Is anybody at the moment a King of France?
> (5) Are there at the moment different people each of whom is a King of France?
> The question does not arise unless the answer to (4) is positive and the answer to (5) is negative. (1950, 84–85)

Geach uses the term "presuppose" for what is going on. And this seems an apt term for the phenomenon Strawson describes:

> to use such an expression as "The king of France" at the beginning of a sentence was, in some sense of "imply," to imply that there was a king of France. When a man uses such an expression, he does not assert, nor does what he says entail, a uniquely existential proposition. But one of the conventional functions of the definite article is to act as a *signal* that a unique reference is being made—a *signal*, not a disguised assertion. When we begin a sentence with "the such- and-such" the use of "the" shows, but does not state, that we are, or intend to be, referring to one particular individual of the species "such-and-such." (1950, 331)

Strawson forcefully argued for a distinction between the properties that belong to sentences and expressions—meaning—and properties belonging to utterances or uses of sentences or expressions. It's clear that it is the speaker who does the presupposing, *by* uttering a sentence at a certain time in a certain situation.[4] If, in Oslo, I tell you "The King of Norway is wise," I am presupposing that there is such a king. I also presuppose, or at least assume, that you know that Norway is a monarchy. Both presuppositions are acts; I perform these acts *by* uttering a sentence.

3.2 Names

> Proper names are a nightmare for semantics. If it weren't for their use in calling the kids for dinner, I'd just as soon junk the whole category. (David Kaplan)[5]

---

[4] To be sure, Strawson's concept of presupposition, characterized in terms of the conditions for the truth of a statement, is semantic. A pragmatic definition of presupposition, in terms of what the speaker does, is due to Stalnaker (1970).

[5] John Perry remembers Kaplan saying this, or words to this effect, on several occasions. We have not been able to find a textual reference.

A natural approach to ordinary proper names is to suppose that they are just words assigned to people and things, and it is those things that they contribute to the truth-conditions of the sentences in which they occur. "Francisco Franco was a dictator" is true because the person "Francisco Franco" stands for a dictator. Sometimes nobles have names that contain more information, but we can just call those "titles" and ignore them for the purpose of logic, a democratic enterprise.

That seems to have been Frege's attitude in the *Begriffsschrift*. The semantics of a sentence of the form "F(a)" is that it stands for the circumstance that the individual "a" refers to falls under the concept referred to by "F." But then he saw a problem. Suppose "a" and "b" are two different names for the same object. Then "a = b" and "a = a" will refer to the same circumstance. This didn't seem right. In the *Begriffsschrift*, he thought this was a problem with the identity sign "=," which he jettisoned in favor of "≡," which stood for a relation between names that had the same referent. But before long he realized that the problem was not with the identity sign, but with identity itself and with what he called "cognitive content" (Chapter 14 of this volume). Consider "Mark Twain wrote *Huckleberry Finn*" and "Samuel Clemens wrote *Huckleberry Finn*." Both sentences are true, for "Mark Twain" and "Samuel Clemens" are two names for the same person. But a rational and semantically competent speaker might accept "Mark Twain wrote *Huckleberry Finn*" while rejecting, or at least having doubts about "Samuel Clemens wrote *Huckleberry Finn*."

At this point Frege made his distinction between sense and reference (1892 [1997]). Expressions have a sense assigned to them by the conventions of the language of which they are a part. The sense is a set of conditions that an object must fulfill to be the reference of the expression. Expressions with different senses can have the same reference. So "the first planet to appear in the evening sky" and "the last planet to disappear from the morning sky" both refer to Venus, which satisfies both conditions. Names are assigned senses which, at least in all the examples Frege ever gave us, can be captured with definite descriptions. So, in ancient Babylonia, the name "Phosphorus" might be assigned to the condition of being the last planet to disappear in the morning sky, while "Hesperus" is assigned to being the first planet to appear in the evening sky.[6] The two names have different senses, but the same reference. As a result, sentences containing them have different *cognitive content*, or, as modern philosophers of language want to put it, different *cognitive significance*.

---

[6] We are cheating a little to make our life simpler, since the Babylonians did not know that Hesperus and Phosphorus were planets

So Frege's distinction between sense and reference seems capable of dealing with differences in cognitive significance. Russell's theory, which takes names to be abbreviated descriptions, would not have problems with it either. Until the 1950s and 1960s, there was a general consensus on how singular terms, like names and definite descriptions, refer. Definite descriptions refer by describing objects, and names refer by having descriptions associated to them, or by abbreviating those descriptions. But that consensus was broken by ideas championed by "referentialists," as we will call them; philosophers like Ruth Barcan Marcus (1961), Dagfinn Føllesdal (1966 [2004]), Keith Donnellan (1966, 1970), Kaplan (1989), and, perhaps most importantly, Saul Kripke (1980), who argued that proper names were "rigid designators": expressions that pick up an object independently of any description, and which pick up the same object in every possible world.[7]

The label "referentialism" encodes ideas about two different issues (Martí 1995): the mechanism of reference and the contribution of reference. According to referentialists, a name refers to an object by picking it out through an assignment of the expression to the individual: a tagging of sorts. There is no associated sense, description, or identifying condition. The mechanism of reference is a bit more complex and usually involves a causal- historical process that links the name with the object.

Referentialism, at least with regard to the contribution of reference, is quite similar to the view defended by Frege in the *Begriffsschrift*. And, as Frege's early view, it faces the problem of accounting for cognitive significance. For the referentialist view, "Mark Twain wrote *Huckleberry Finn*" and "Samuel Clemens wrote *Huckleberry Finn*" express the same singular proposition, one involving a person who happened to have two names, and that person having written *Huckleberry Finn*. But then, if they both express the same singular proposition, how is it that a person who knows that "Mark Twain wrote *Huckleberry Finn*" learns something when she is told that "Mark Twain" is "Samuel Clemens"? And what is it that she learns?

Discussions of names, or singular reference in general, are usually regarded as discussions in semantics. But the problem of cognitive significance is very closely connected with pragmatics. The things we do with words, the speech acts we perform, and the effects these acts have on others, depend greatly on the singular terms we use to refer. Even if "Mark Twain" and "Samuel Clemens" refer to the same man (as does "the author of *Huckleberry Finn*"), the use of one or other name (or definite description) will have a significant impact on the situation in which they are used. Whether the speaker

---

[7] See Wettstein, 1986 who famously called these ideas "the new theory of reference." As early as 1961, Føllesdal used the phrase "genuine singular terms" for rigid designators (1966 [2004]).

uses one name or the other depends on her communicative intention, and which name she uses will have a quite different effect on the hearer.

3.3 Indexicals

In "On Denoting" Russell does not start with the example, "The King of France is bald" but rather "The *present* King of France is bald" (our italics.) There were many Kings of France, some no doubt bald. But there was no King of France in 1905. In the parts of the essay where Russell explains how the meaning of the expressions contribute to the meanings of the sentence in which the description is contained, he leaves out the word "present."

If we say "The present President of the US was born in Pennsylvania," we identify Joe Biden by the job he has as we write, and predicate something true of him. "Present" seems to be an indexical, referring to the period of time we write, late in 2021. Similarly, if we say "In 2011 the present president was vice-president," our description refers to Joe Biden and says something true about him.

In a later paper, "Mr. Strawson on Referring" (1957), Russell, answering Strawson, claims that he did not discuss "present" because he was concerned with definite descriptions and not with the "problem of egocentricity," a problem, he claims, he had already discussed in previous works. To use his own self-citation, in *Human Knowledge*, he claims:

> When a word is not egocentric, there is no need to distinguish between different occasions when it is used, but we must make this distinction with egocentric words, since what they indicate is something having a different relation to the particular use of the word. (1948, 107)

Russell clearly acknowledged the role of indexicals, and their importance. And so did Frege, who admitted that indexical expressions pose a special problem for his theory of the sense and reference of sentences; that sentences containing indexicals require "the knowledge of certain accompanying conditions of utterance"; without those conditions, "the mere wording…is not the complete expression of the thought" (1918 [1967], 24). Neither Russell nor Frege, however, developed their insights, and they are mainly of interest with respect to Frege or Russell interpretation. The fact remains that they did not develop the required semantic tools to deal with them.

There seems to be no way that indexicals such as "I," "now," and "present" can be handled with the sparse semantical apparatus Russell provides. We have an expression, "present." It means something, as Russell uses the terms "means," in the sense that there is a period of time, the period in which we are writing this essay, that contributes to the truth-conditions of the sentence in which it occurs. But referring to this period of time is not a property of the word "present." It is a property our utterance of the word "present," the time at which that event occurred.

Strawson points out that his distinctions among sentences/expressions, utterances of sentences/expressions, and uses of sentences/expressions are undeniable when we consider sentences containing indexicals. The sentence "I am hungry now" has a meaning that any competent speaker of English is attuned to. But the sentence, qua sentence, is neither true nor false, since the words "I" and "now," qua words, do not have a reference. We need to consider utterances of the sentence—that is, particular acts[8] of uttering the sentence—a speaker and its time of occurrence, to assign references and, eventually, a truth-value to the utterance. Indexicals—or, "egocentric particulars," as Russell called them—were promptly admitted to be clear cases of content-sensitivity.

In the 1970s Kaplan (1989) formulated an elegant formal theory of indexicals, based on intuitions about the meaning and truth of sentences containing them that are pretty undeniable. Basically, the meaning of indexicals—their "characters"—are functions from "contexts" to references of the sort their grammatical type requires. For Kaplan, the context of an expression is a quadruple of a (potential) speaker, location, time, and possible world. Suppose that Ethel says to Fred, in the afternoon of November 1, 2021: "You must fix dinner today. I have a paper to finish. And I fixed dinner yesterday. So it's your turn. You'll find the groceries here, in this bag." And then suppose that the next day Fred uses the very same sentence to tell Ethel that it is her turn to fix dinner.

In the first case the uses of "I" refer to Ethel. The uses of "you" refer to Fred. Uses of "today" refer to November 1, those of "yesterday" refer to October 31. "Here" refers to the kitchen, where Ethel is standing, and "this bag" refers to the bag she is indicating at that moment. If, on the other hand, Fred had said the exact same thing to Ethel, while he was standing in the living room holding a different bag, the truth-conditions of his utterance would be quite different, even though the meanings of the words were the same.

Indexicals might seem a natural place for the philosophy of action to stick its nose under the tent occupied by the philosophy of language. When we consider indexicals, it becomes clear that in many cases meaningful sentences

---

[8] As we use the terms, acts are particular events, actions are properties or types of such events. Agents *perform* actions at times, thereby producing acts. The act produced is often designated with a gerund phrase that specifies the agent, time, and action: "Fred's swimming across the lake earlier this morning." We basically adopt Goldman's *A Theory of Human Action* (1970) account of action, with some changes in terminology. For more about the theory of action, see Anscombe, 1957 [2000]; Bratman, 1987; Davidson, 1980 [2001]; and Grice, 1971.

with their meaning will not get us all the way to reference and truth-conditions. It seems that, as Strawson suggested, we need to consider *utterances* of sentences and expressions.

But Kaplan did not present his account as a move toward integrating the philosophy of language and the philosophy of action. His aim was to develop a logic of indexicals and demonstratives. He wanted to show the flexibility of logic, rather than its limits. The present authors think he succeeded in this endeavor. But in doing so, he raised issues that help us to understand the referential role, not only of indexicals and demonstratives in natural language, but also of names and definite descriptions, in the context of action.

Any utterance has countless properties. But for the basic indexicals "I," "here," and "now," three parameters suffice to determine reference: the speaker, the time, and the location. Call these the "bare context" of an utterance. An utterance of "I" refers to the speaker; and utterance of "now" to the time, and an utterance of "here" to the location. For "you" we need to bring in the audience, and perhaps those in the audience that speaker takes himself to be addressing. That is, the speaker intention is relevant. We need to add more and more facts to our utterance. But they all derive, it seems, from properties of the utterance.

Indexicals and demonstratives determine reference and truth-condition relative to such contexts. These don't have to be the speaker, time, and location and circumstances of any actual utterance. But if the speaker is in the location at the time, the context is *proper*.

Consider the following sentence:

(1) You are right about everything we have ever disagreed about.

Let the speaker be John Searle, and the time be November 1, 2021. The location isn't that relevant, but for the record, let us say it is a pub in Berkeley. The circumstances include John Perry being the person to whom the remark is directed. The sentence is true if, as of November 1, John Perry is right about everything he and Searle have ever disagreed about up to that point.

As we write, it is late in the evening November 1, and John Perry is not in a pub in Berkeley talking to John Searle, pleasant as that would be. No utterance of (1), with Searle as speaker and Perry as audience has ever occurred, or is likely to ever occur. Still, we can assess the proposition that would be expressed with the sentence given these parameters. (It would no doubt be false.)

So, if we take our subject matter to be sentences in such contexts, as Kaplan did, we can have a sensible concept of the logic of demonstratives and indexicals. A sentence is a logical truth, in the logic of demonstratives, if it is true in any proper context. Kaplan's example of a theorem in the logic of demonstratives: "I am here now." An argument will be valid if relative to the same context; truth of the premises guarantees truth of the conclusion. So "You live in Palo Alto, Palo Alto is in California, so you live in California" is valid. And validity may be achieved by additional premises, relating parameters of the contexts.

Kaplan took sentences-in-context as the subject matter, which sounds like the formal equivalent of possible utterances. But he did not put utterances at the center. Perry used Kaplan's work to argue that there were profound difficulties in treating indexicals and demonstratives within a Fregean framework. Eventually he concluded that in order to understand the role of sentences with demonstratives and indexical in action, in particular the role of "I" in expressing self-knowledge, we needed to take a step further than Kaplan had and take utterances to be the primary subject matter.

The result of this was the reflexive-referential theory.[9] The main departure from Kaplan's proposal is that, rather than modeling utterances in terms of expressions and contexts, the reflexive-referential theory brings utterances to the fore: it is, actually, a theory about utterances or, more generally, about *cognitive episodes*. Cognitive episodes are particular types of acts that happen during an interval of time that can be pretty short—in the case of utterances or perceptions—or relatively long—in the case of beliefs, desires, or intentions. We call them "cognitive" because they are intentional and all have contents, which encode the conditions that make them true, satisfied or fulfilled.

We will be mostly concerned here with utterances, which are acts of using language, with different contents and properties, all of them causally relevant. By focusing on utterances, rather than modeling them away, we somehow divert from the tradition started by Frege and Russell and continued by Kaplan, and follow instead a tradition originated in the philosophy of language that took language as action, championed by John Austin and Paul Grice. This tradition, however, focused on the study of speech acts and implicatures, and left pretty much aside the study of issues regarding reference and cognitive significance. In other words, pragmatics started as *far-side pragmatics*—the study of issues that goes beyond saying, such as illocutionary acts and implicatures—leaving *near-side pragmatics*—the study of the facts that determine what the speaker says, such as reference—to

---

[9] The reflexive-referential was developed in Perry's *Reference and Reflexivity* (2001 [2012]), in Korta and Perry's *Critical Pragmatics* (2011), and in Chapter 8 of this volume. This essay heavily relies on the ideas presented in *Critical Pragmatics*, where the idea of language as action and pragmatic aspects of the theory are extensively explored and discussed. See also Chapter 13 of this volume.

semanticists.[10] Austin–Grice is where philosophy of language meets the philosophy of action, producing pragmatics, and Perry is where pragmatically oriented philosophy of language comes to look back at issues of reference and cognitive significance or, if you prefer, where Austin–Grice turned to look back to Frege–Russell.

4 The Reflexive-Referential Account

The reflexive-referential account focuses on *episodes*: utterances, thoughts, perceptions, acts, beliefs, desires, intentions, etc. These things occur in space and time and have causes and effects. We take the relevant utterances to be intentional acts and so call all such episodes "cognitive." Cognitive episodes have *contents*. The truth-conditions of a statement or a belief are the paradigm case, but promises and intentions have fulfillment conditions, orders and desires have satisfaction conditions, and so forth. We use "contents" for all such conditions. Contents can be thought of as propositions that encode the conditions of truth for statements, conditions of satisfaction for expressions of hopes and desires, conditions of compliance for orders, and so forth. We take propositions to be abstract objects that are useful for classifying episodes in terms of their conditions of truth, satisfaction, and compliance. We agree with Frege that propositions ("Thoughts") are not mental or physical episodes or states and so have no causes or effects. We do not, however, accept everything Frege says about propositions.

We cannot, for instance, regard mental states, such as belief, desire, and the like, merely as relations to abstract objects, for beliefs and desires have causes and effects. We think that propositions are abstract objects that have been designed to be useful in classifying events in the causal realm. To be useful, such propositions need to be well-behaved and well-understood abstract objects, usually sets. The language that is used for propositions needs to be correlated with the elements of utterances and thoughts that determine their truth-conditions. Sentences play a major role in identifying these elements in the case of utterances and thoughts that can be expressed with sentences.

On the reflexive-referential account cognitive episodes have multiple consistent layers of content that can be classified with propositions.[11] Consider the follow example. Robyn and Fred are old friends, but up to now

---

[10] On the distinction between near-side and far-side pragmatics, see Korta and Perry, 2006b.

[11] Somehow confusingly, the reflexive-referential explanation has been labeled as "multi-" or "pluri-propositionalism." But, since in our account propositions are not the (main) constituents of cognitive episodes, but rather abstract tools to classify the variety of contents, we prefer avoiding this label. See Chapter 17 of this volume.

they've always lived in different cities. Today, however, Robyn has just moved into Fred's neighborhood in San Francisco. Suppose this is all happening on June 12, 2021, in a particular neighborhood in San Francisco, say, in the Mission. Robyn knocks on Fred's door and says to Fred, "Today you and I are neighbors." Call that utterance **u**. Then on many accounts, Robyn said the proposition *P: That Robyn is Fred's neighbor on June 12, 2021*. On a simple account this proposition is a set consisting of the relation of x being a neighbor of y at t; and the sequence of Robyn, Fred, and June 12, 2021. One might take it to be the set of possible worlds in which Robyn be Fred's neighbor on that day. Or perhaps the set of worlds w in which Robyn's counterpart in w be a neighbor of Fred's counterpart in w on that day, or perhaps its counterpart. Indeed, there are many kinds of abstract objects philosophers have taken to be propositions. We'll stick with the simple account and assume that the reader gets the general idea.

We agree that the proposition *P* is a truth-condition of Robyn's utterance. But we don't agree that it is *the* truth-condition. On our account, attributions of truth-conditions are ascribed to an utterance *relative* to what is taken as *given*. The truth-condition of an utterance, relative to a set of facts g, is *what else* has to be the case for the utterance to be true, *given g*. With regard to Robyn's utterance, we gave you the facts that determined the references of the parts of his utterance. "I" referred to Robyn, "you" referred to Fred, "today" referred to June 12, 2021, the language was English, so "are neighbors" refers to the relation, between two or more people, of *living near* to. Given all these facts, what else has to be the case for Robyn's utterance to be true is

P: That Robyn is Fred's neighbor on June 12, 2021.

Now suppose we didn't bother to tell you *when* this all happened. Do you know conditions of truth of Robyn's utterance? Of course you do. Robyn's utterance is true iff

P': There is some day d during which the utterance occurred, and Robyn and Fred were neighbors on d.

Suppose we also didn't tell you who answered the door. Then you know that the utterance is true iff

P'': There is a day d and a person y such that Robyn was talking to y at the time of the utterance, and Robyn and y were neighbors on that day.

Note that P' and P'' put conditions on the utterance itself: we call them *reflexive* or *utterance-bound* truth-conditions. In contrast, P puts conditions only on the items referred to by the utterance. P gives the *referential* truth-conditions of the utterance. P could be true if the utterance had never been made. But not P' and P'.

These three propositions are different and independent. But they are consistent. P' follows from P'' when we add the fact that the door answerer was Fred. P follows from P' when we give the date.

Having different propositions, classifying different and incremental truth-conditions, is useful for many things. To begin with, of course, it gives a comprehensive account of what needs to be the case for a particular utterance to be true and of the several layers included in what is said by it. With this explanation at hand, it is quite easy to deal with puzzles in philosophy of language, such as the puzzles mentioned above involving names. Let us look at a couple more examples, to see how it works.

Bob puts a big platter of kale before his young children and says: "You will love this kale." He knows his children have never seen this ugly vegetable before. But he thinks they will learn the name for this vegetable from his utterance. They will realize that his utterance is true iff there is some stuff Bob is referring to with "this kale" and they will love it. They realize that "kale," in the singular phrase "this kale," is most likely a name of the kind of stuff he is pointing at. That is, they know how English works. They do not know this in the way people who have taken a linguistics or a philosophy of language class know it. They may not know what an utterance is, or what referring is, or what a singular term is. But they are *attuned* to these facts about English and are capable of making inferences from them, without being able to articulate the premises of their reasoning. What explains their inference is an utterance-bound content of Bob's utterance, given the meaning of the sentence and the fact, conveyed by glance and gesture, that he was referring to the green stuff on the platter. Given all that *what else* had to be the case for Bob's utterance to be true? That "kale" is a name for the ugly green stuff. Note that in this case Bob succeeds in teaching his children something, that "kale" names kale, even though what he *says* is almost certainly false.

John tells Frenchie he is going to San Sebastian in the Basque Country for a week. She looks at the map of the Basque Country in John's office for "San Sebastian" but cannot find it. He says, "San Sebastian is Donostia." Frenchie finds "Donostia" on the map, points to it, and says, "That's where you are going?" and John says "yes." John has conveyed to Frenchie that "Donostia" and "San Sebastian" are names for the same city. But what he said was simply that San Sebastian was Donostia, a necessary truth, which is the same thing he would have said with "San Sebastian is San Sebastian" and

"Donostia is Donostia," if what is said is always to be identified with referential content. But those utterances would not have been helpful. A philosophical rule of thumb should be that utterances of identity sentences can almost never be understood simply in terms of their referential content. If you insist on doing that, you will be lucky to get much of anything right.

The reflexive-referential theory not only accepts and accommodates the intrusion of the theory of action into the philosophy of language but also takes the theory of action as fundamental to understand how language works. We claim that a theory like this, with utterances at the center and considering them as episodes, that is, as cognitive acts with a variety of contents, is better equipped to deal with the context-sensitivity of language than theories that take (one single) content to be a property of sentences plus contexts.

5 Utterance versus Sentence-in-Context

Kaplan discusses utterances to motivate his theory, but he does not bring them into his theory as such; they are replaced by, or perhaps modeled as, pairs of expressions and contexts: "expressions-in-context." Kaplan's main interest was developing a logic of demonstratives and indexicals. For this purpose he regarded utterances as an unnecessary complication. For one thing, a pair of context and expression can have a content, even if the speaker of the context does not utter the expression at the time and place of the context in the world under consideration. More importantly, utterances take time; the validity of an argument with one hundred steps might depend on the context being the same for all of them, but we can't talk or write that fast. So, for logical purposes, utterances can get in the way.

From the point of view of understanding the relations between the contents of states and their causal roles, however, it is very helpful to have episodes that have contents, have causes, and have effects. So, in a theory of language framed in a theory of action, episodes and, in particular, utterances are too important to ignore, in spite of the complications they pose for logic.

For this purpose, we consider the elements of Kaplan's contexts to simply be properties of utterances, which objects fill the roles of speaker-of, time-of, and location-of. The fact that utterances have speakers and occur in locations at times clearly inspired Kaplan's concepts of context and character. We promote these inspiring episodes to first-class status. The chief advantage of this view is simply that it accounts for—and makes use of—the fact that utterances have many other properties, in addition to having speakers, locations, and times, that can be relevant to understanding their cognitive significance.

Consider Gricean intentions, which are basically intentions to produce concrete utterances in order to achieve certain effects on the hearer by the recognition of those intentions. The meaning of the sentence and expressions uttered, the content uttered, and the elements of Kaplan's context all contribute to that goal. But they are not enough. Conversations, linguistic transactions, fundamentally involve a speaker, who intends to do something and achieve certain effects by uttering a sentence or an expression, and a hearer, who perceives an event (or a token of such event) and needs to reason about the intentions behind it. Properties associated with meaning and content are key to guessing intentions, but not only. On many occasions, the hearer has to interpret what the speaker is trying to do by producing an utterance, and not only what she says. The hearer, that is, needs to know if the speaker intends to command something, amuse, impress, mislead, etc.

One way to handle these, while sticking with Kaplan's approach, is to add more members to the context set, or to introduce additional sets. The latter is more or less the approach of Jon Barwise and John Perry in *Situations and Attitudes* (1983 [1999]). On their "relational theory of meaning," the meaning of a sentence is taken to be a relation among various situations connected to an utterance, although the utterance itself is, as in Kaplan's theory, only modeled and not introduced directly into the theory. The basic relation is between the utterance situation, which determines the speaker, location, and time, and, in lieu of propositions, described situations. But various other situations are added to the range of the relation, to deal with names, descriptions, ambiguity, and other phenomena.

On the reflexive-referential account, however, the treatment of such factors is simpler and more straightforward. They are all properties of the utterance, recognized as necessary to handle various phenomena. The reflexive-referential theory inherits a key insight of Kaplan's theory—and Perry's earlier views—but the inclusion of utterances gives it, at least, one important advantage.[12] The inherited key insight is the distinction between different ways in which information can be discovered, believed, and asserted.

The advantage is, briefly, that the cognitive significance of an utterance for different hearers can depend on the perceptual and causal relations the hearer has to the utterance, which reference-determining facts they know, and how they think of them. To account for this, we need to bring in additional properties of the utterance and, in particular, causal properties. These are not modeled by Kaplan's expressions-in-context. This advantage is particularly relevant for us here, since it offers a solution to the cognitive significance problem without having to renounce to the referentialist insights.

---

[12] There is second important advantage, which concerns Prior's well-known root-canal example and his utterance of "Thank goodness that's over!" See Chapter 13, for a discussion of both advantages.

6 Cognitive Significance

Consider a classical puzzle in semantics. In his important essay "Has Semantics Rested on a Mistake?" (1986), Howard Wettstein pointed out that whatever virtues of what he called the "Kaplan–Perry" account has in explaining cognitive significance of cases involving indexicals, it does not handle Frege's *Begriffsschrift* (1879 [1967]) problem, the origin of worries about cognitive significance, which involves proper names. "Hesperus is Hesperus" and "Hesperus is Phosphorus" clearly have different cognitive significance; one learns from the second that the names co-refer, but not from the first. On a directly referential account of proper names, which is more or less what Frege had in the *Begriffsschrift*, this is hard to account for. On Kaplan's account, the character of a proper name is a constant function, from any context to the bearer of the name. The two sentences have the same content, a singular proposition to the effect that Venus is Venus. So, whatever the virtues of the Kaplan–Perry thesis for cases involving indexicals, it does not help with proper names.

In response to Wettstein's essay, Perry (1988) introduced the concept of the proposition created by an utterance, in contrast with the proposition expressed by an utterance, which was basically the distinction between reflexive and referential content.

On the reflexive-referential account, the two utterances have different reflexive truth-conditions. The first is true if and only if there is an object named by "Hesperus" which is self-identical. The second is true if and only if there is such an object, and there is also an object named by "Phosphorus," and the objects are identical. So, even though the referential truth-conditions of the two utterances are the same, they differ in cognitive significance, in virtue of their different reflexive truth-conditions.[13]

Consider now a puzzle involving reference to time. This puzzle involves dates, which are akin to names, and temporal indexicals, such as "today" or "tomorrow." It is quite common, at least for some of us, not to know the day one lives in. In this case, however, we certainly know when we live; we know that what is happening is happening *now* or *today*, even though we do not know what time is "now" or what day is "today." Also, it is relatively common to be wrong about the date one lives in. One can be in a dateless haze without knowing it; that is, one can be quite certain about the date, but be wrong. In such a case, it is natural to think, in retrospect, that one might have been correct; even that one's false belief was justified. This provides another advantage for the reflexive-referential theory with respect to Kaplan's.

---

[13] See also Corazza and Korta, 2015.

Suppose John and Dan are planning to go to the Giants game on August 22, 2021. The day before, John types out a reminder: "The Giants game is tomorrow. Don't forget." But he forgets to hit the "send" button. He notices that the message has not been sent just before retiring and hits the button. But he doesn't notice that it is already after midnight.

Dan, a dateless-hazer, sees the reminder, "The Giants game is tomorrow," when he wakes up on August 22, and sees that date on the email heading. He knows that the game is on August 22, and reasons, given John's notorious reliability, "Today must be August 21." He then immerses himself in linguistic esoterica until late in the evening, when John calls and says, "You missed the game!"

Dan thought, on August 22, that it was August 21. He had good reason for this belief. The game was scheduled for August 22. John said, in an email this morning, that the game was tomorrow. John is very reliable. Therefore, today must be August 21.

Could Dan have been right? It seems not, because for his belief to be true, August 22 would have to be August 21, which is not possible. Surely had Dan said,

(4) August 22 is August 21.

we could diagnose some kind of irrationality (or assume he is making some subtle linguistic point). But if he just says, as he did:

(5) Today is August 21.

on August 22, this does not seem like the right diagnosis.

There is a way in which way Dan's utterance could have been true: If it had occurred on August 21 rather than August 22. In other words, if the role of time-of for the utterance of "today" had been filled by some moment occurring on August 21, the utterance would have been true.

On the expression-in-context approach, this does not seem like an option. Since the pair of expression and context is individuated by its members, we would not have the same pair if the time of the context was August 21. So, we have another advantage for the reflexive-referential theory and for granting utterances first-class status in the semantics of tense and indexicals.

There is a possible objection to our strategy, as Richard Vallée has pointed out.[14] One theory of events is that they are individuated by the time at which they occur, by where they occur, and by which object and properties

---

[14] Personal communication.

involved. If we accept this account of event individuation, the reflexive-referential account is no better off than the expressions-in-context account.

But we reject this account of the individuation of events. In our opinion, it is a plausible account of the individuation of facts, but not of events. Being a fact is a property of whatever one takes to serve as possibilities, be it circumstances, state of affairs, or whatever. We will not here develop an account of events, which we regard as very basic elements of reality. But we think an adequate account must allow for counterfactuals of the form, "if the election had occurred two weeks earlier, Clinton would have won," or, to follow with our example, "if Dan's utterance had occurred on August 21, he would not had missed the Giant's game." It is a fact that he missed it and that he made his utterance on August 22. Nothing can change that. But the episodes involved, Dan's belief and Dan's utterance "Today is August 21" could have been true, had they occurred on August 21.

In his paper "Frege on Demonstratives" (1977), Perry introduced the example of Heimson, who thought he was David Hume. Let's suppose instead that Heimson thought he was Bob Dylan, which will make it easier to make a case for his rationality. Here is the background story. Heimson falls, hits his head, and has amnesia as a result. He does not know who he is. He carries no identification. He awakes in a hospital where no one has any idea who he is. Heimson decides to figure out who he is. Heimson's amnesia is of a rather peculiar sort; he retains "third-person" memories about lots of people, he simply does not remember which of them he is. He assumes he is one of the people about whom he knows a great deal. He notices that he knows all of Bob Dylan's songs by heart, the date of every concert where he performed, and loads of other things. He also knows a lot about a fellow named "Heimson," but not nearly as much as he knows about Dylan. He decides he is Dylan, and thinks, with some confidence, "I am Bob Dylan."

His thought cannot be true. Indeed, it seems necessarily false. But it might be rational. And we think it does get at a possibility, even if a rather remote one. The possibility is found at the reflexive level. Call his thought—the event of thinking, the episode, not its content—T. If Bob Dylan had the thought T, rather than Heimson, T would be true. This is the possibility that Heimson's sifting of the evidence available to him led him to think this was the case.

David Lewis (1979), considering Perry's original example, comes to the opposite conclusion. In "Frege on Demonstratives," Perry advocated a version of the Kaplan–Perry view, that he called the two-tiered view. In a nutshell, to deal with the attitudes we need to recognize two levels of content for beliefs. What is believed is a proposition, often a singular proposition. How it is believed corresponds to character (Kaplan) or role (Perry)

Lewis had nice things to say about this account but thought that the level corresponding to character or role could serve as what is believed, and the upper tier could be jettisoned. Lewis noted that a character, a function from contexts to propositions, could be regarded as a property: The property an agent has at a time iff the character, applied to that agent and time, yields a true proposition. So, when JP says, "I am sitting," he "self-ascribes" the property $P_{sitting}$:

$P_{sitting}$ = the property x has iff the character of "I am sitting," with arguments x and t, yields a true proposition, that is, the property someone x has at time t, iff x is sitting at t.

On Lewis's view, properties, rather than propositions, are the true "objects" of beliefs. A belief consists of an agent at a time self-ascribing a property.

Lewis's view, like the Kaplan–Perry approach, does not involve episodes. We have agents, times, the relation of self-ascription, and properties. Lewis (1979, footnote 16) regards singular propositions and "de re" beliefs as unnecessary intrusions into the theory of the attitudes based on preoccupation with the analysis of our customs for reporting beliefs.

Lewis's view incorporates much of the traditional picture that belief is a relation between an agent at a time and a proposition. His innovation is to replace propositions with properties. But we think the idea of objects of beliefs in this sense is a mistake. A belief consists in an agent at a time being in a mental state, an episode. This episode has truth-conditions, which can be characterized by propositions, many different propositions, depending on what is taken as given. But neither propositions, nor characters, nor characters construed as properties, are objects of belief in the sense that belief consists of a relation to them. Propositions, in our sense, are tools we use to characterize and keep track of the truth-conditions of the episode.

Lewis's account, like the Kaplan–Perry account, does not have episodes, utterances or beliefs, as elements. So, on Lewis's view, Heimson's belief, whether he thinks he is Hume or thinks he is Dylan, cannot be true in the strong sense that there is no possible way it could be true. On his view, the belief consists of Heimson, the relevant time, and the attitude of self-ascription to the property of being Hume/being Bob Dylan. Since there is no possibility that Heimson at the time has that property, there is no way the belief can be true. Heimson is irrational in all possible circumstances.

7 Conclusion

In this essay, we have offered a brief and undoubtedly partial account of the ways an account of language as a human activity intruded in the philosophy of language during the past century, focusing, in particular, on the discussion of singular reference. As a way of confronting the need to embrace this intrusion, we presented and defended the reflexive-referential account, and we discussed an example of the beneficial impact of action theory on the philosophy of language.

The conception of language as action inaugurated by Austin, Grice, Strawson, and others not only brought new pragmatic theories of language and novel theoretical tools, such as the distinction between locutionary, illocutionary, and perlocutionary aspects of utterances or the systematic study of nonliteral speech via the notion of implicature, but inspired new philosophical theories, like the reflexive-referential theory or critical pragmatics, to deal with classic puzzles in the philosophy of language like reference and cognitive significance.[15]

---

[15] We are grateful to the members of the Zoom group of philosophical discussion for their constant inspiration. The first two authors acknowledge two grants, one by the Spanish Government (Grant PID2019-106078GB-I00 funded by MCIN/ AEI/ 10.13039/501100011033) and another from the Basque Government (IT1612-22). We are also grateful to an anonymous referee for their helpful comments. But most of all, the three of us thank the editor Jesús Romero-Trillo for his kind invitation and immense patience.

17

Critical Pragmatics: Nine Misconceptions

María de Ponte, Kepa Korta and John Perry

1 Introduction

It is now almost twelve years that *Critical Pragmatics* was published. It is some years more since it was conceived. Korta and Perry published their first joint article, "Three demonstrations and a funeral," in 2006 (Chapter 1), and, given that it was the product of some years work, it is now almost twenty years or so that they started thinking together about issues concerning language, mind, action and the world. In the last few years, a new member has joined the authors' team, María de Ponte, and new papers have been added to the *oeuvres* of Critical Pragmatics.[1] Some philosophers and linguists have adopted the framework to deal with this or that philosophical or linguistic issue. They have been exciting and satisfying years for us, no doubt.

In this paper, we are not concerned with celebrating our achievements; we focus on some misconceptions detected during these years about—and around—Critical Pragmatics, what it is, what it assumes and what it proposes. Doubtless, some of these misconceptions are due to clumsy writing on our part; perhaps others are due to inattentive reading. And some may be due to an effort to shield us from the apparent implausibility of what we said—and in fact meant. It does not matter much. We focus on those misunderstandings that most matter to us, either because, by repetition, they have ended up being annoying, even if they are not, perhaps, that important; or, because they are substantial enough to represent a distortion of the basic picture of Critical Pragmatics and its theoretical foundations, namely, Critical Referentialism—

---

[1] Other than the essays included in this volume, see also Korta & Ponte, 2014, 2015, and de Ponte & Korta, 2023.

also known as the Reflexive-referential Theory—and, more generally, Perry's fundamental views on meaning and content(s).

Critical Pragmatics is a natural development of the approach developed by Perry in *Reference and Reflexivity* (2001 [2012]), which, in turn, has its roots in his seminal papers "Frege and demonstratives" (1977) and "The problem of the essential indexical" (1979). Arguably, the origin of some of the misunderstandings can be traced back to those early papers, perhaps not so much by action but by omission. Most of the examples given by Perry on those papers are well-remembered—Hume/Heimson, Rudolf Lingens, the messy shopper, the tardy professor, the lost hiker...— but his positive claims have been often distorted, and often overlooked.

A central thesis defended by Perry that has been largely ignored is his rejection of the doctrine of propositions, and, in particular, his rejection of the view according to which beliefs—and "propositional" attitudes in general—[2] consist in a relation between an agent and a proposition. Perry forcefully argued against this in his earlier papers—one might even say, with Falk, that the rejection of the doctrine of propositions is actually the main revolutionary idea of those papers (Falk, 2015). Many people, however, seem to have either misunderstood, or simply forgotten this.[3] Otherwise, it would not be easy to understand how they can attribute to Perry's Critical Referentialism, or to Critical Pragmatics, the thesis that beliefs consist in a relation between an agent and multiple propositions. Without the rejection of the doctrine of propositions, Critical Pragmatics cannot be understood.

Some of the misconceptions, then, have a relatively long history, but some emerged later, either associated to the publication of *Reference and Reflexivity* (2001 [2012]), or to the series of papers that started with "Three demonstrations and a funeral" (Chapter 1 of this volume) and led to *Critical Pragmatics* (2011). Then again, some of the misconceptions might have to do, in part, with the title of the latter book, which is also (one of) the label(s) we use for our approach. We start discussing those.

2 Misconceptions Due to the Title

The term "pragmatics" in the title refers to the third level of semiotics according to Charles W. Morris in "Foundations of the Theory of Signs" (1938). Roughly, syntax is about the way words going together makes phrases and

---

[2] The reasons for the scare quotes in "propositional" are made clearer below, but let us anticipate that, following Critical Pragmatics, we take it to be a bad terminological choice, product of a bad philosophical view that takes intentional mental states to consist in attitudes towards propositions.

[3] See Perry, 2019b.

sentences; semantics is about meaning, and pragmatics deals with the use of language. Morris was a pragmatist, in the tradition of Peirce and James. But our use is not meant to suggest any particular connection with that movement.

We didn't realize at the time that there were terms like "critical pragmatism" out there, that pointed to various critical takes on Dewey's pragmatism, or a sort of synthesis between discourse analysis and critical theory, or to illustrate "a new critical relevance of pragmatist reflection for science and ethics" (Ulrich, 2007), among other things.[4] Our term has nothing to do with any approach like that. Thinking that it does is the first misconception, perhaps a natural one for readers with broader knowledge of all that is going on in philosophy than the authors had (or have).

Misconception One: *Critical Pragmatics (CP) is related to Critical Pragmatism.*

Our approach started as a natural development of the application to issues of pragmatics of Perry's *Reflexive-referential Theory* or *Critical Referentialism*. These two terms are used in his *Reference and Reflexivity* to refer to the theory there. Critical Referentialism accepts the main thesis of referentialism, as developed by Donnellan, Kaplan, Kripke and others: That utterances of sentences with names, indexicals, and demonstratives express singular propositions with the references of those terms as constituents.

Straightforward referentialism is well-argued for, and plausible as far as it goes. But utterances involving indexicals, proper names, and the like seem to convey more than what is captured by singular propositions. To suppose that the singular proposition exhausts the content is to commit to what Perry called "the subject matter fallacy."[5] This is clearest in the case of identity statements. One might utter "Donostia is San Sebastian" not to convey the information that the city is self-identical, but that the two names refer to the same city. This might be dismissed as "mere pragmatics,"— i.e., a matter of Gricean conversational implicatures—, but Perry thought that if we are more critical about the role that propositions play in semantics, there is a better explanation.[6] If we shift our attention to truth-conditions, we see that the truth

---

[4] For a more exhaustive description of the various uses of the term "Critical Pragmatics," see Ulrich, 2007.

[5] See Perry, 2003 [2019c], for a short and relatively simple explanation of the key ideas.

[6] The borders between semantics and pragmatics are, of course, a matter of dispute. We address this topic in *Critical Pragmatics* (2011), as well as in Korta and Perry, 2006b, and in Chapter 2 of this volume. We have a "contextualist" conception of pragmatics, which admits its "intrusion" in the truth-conditional content of utterances, and a radically minimalist view of semantics which delivers their reflexive truth-conditions. Sometimes, however, we have adopted more

of "Donostia is San Sebastian" requires a bit more of the world that the truth of "Donostia is Donostia." He argued that by introducing "reflexive" truth-conditions or, more generally, contents, we can explain the cases where the singular proposition doesn't capture all of the information that an utterance can be used to convey, without giving up the central insights behind referentialism. Hence the word "critical."

But that doesn't mean that pragmatics drops out of the picture. Critical Referentialism takes some of the pressure off pragmatics, while at the same time offering it some new tools. Perry was working in the second and expanded edition of *Reference and Reflexivity* at more or less the same time that he and Korta were completing *Critical Pragmatics*. It just seemed natural to use "Critical Pragmatics" to refer to the approach to pragmatics that incorporated Critical Referentialism, especially for two authors ignorant of the uses to which the phrase had already been put. Also, they were being critical about some basic theses assumed by the contemporary pragmatic theories they were familiar with. In particular, they thought that pragmatic theories didn't fully assume the theoretical consequences of adopting Austin's and Grice's lessons on language as action; that they were mostly focused on the hearer's understanding rather than the speaker production of linguistic utterances; and that they committed the fallacy of the unique truth-conditional content of utterances.

Critical Pragmatics was critical with other theories and offered an alternative. That was another reason for the adjective in the title. Also, Korta and Perry think that pragmatics is critical in the study of language, in the sense of being *crucial*. The title was intended to exploit the ambiguity of "critical," which provided several things they advocate.

Korta and Perry said something along those lines in the book, but apparently not very explicitly, since, during this dozen years, they have received multiple messages asking about the reasons for the title. We have also found some citations to our work in papers that have apparently little to do with our framework.[7] So apologies are due, in this case, for using a possibly misleading label. It is probably too late to rectify, and a bit of an overstatement to call this a "misconception," but we thought we should clarify things.

An important theme in *CP* is our distinction between the truth-conditions of an utterance or a belief and the proposition that is expressed or believed. The next six misconceptions are all connected with various ways of grasping what we are getting at with this distinction.

---

traditional terminology to engage in discussions with other views, as in *Reference and Reflexivity* (2001 [2012]), where Perry uses "Semantics" in a wider more traditional sense.

[7] See, for instance, Al-Hindawi and Al-Khazali, 2021; Chen, 2020; Du, 2022; Huang, 2020; and Talmy, 2010.

Misconception Two: *CP might better be called "Multi-propositionalism" or "Pluri-propositionalism."*

Perry's views on *Reference and Reflexivity* were a development of his *rejection*, in "The problem of the essential indexical" (1979), of what he called "the doctrine of propositions." This is basically the view that propositions are the objects of the "propositional" attitudes, and that belief, for example, consists in a relation to a proposition.

CP incorporates the rejection of the doctrine of propositions, and explores further its implications. Beliefs and other so-called intentional states *do not consist* of minds standing in relations with propositions. Beliefs, desires, intentions and the like are states of the brain/mind that are typically caused by objects that play various roles in our lives: objects seen, heard, touched, tasted, remembered, and so forth. Combinations of such states typically cause actions that affect these objects and other that are related to them. For example, the belief that there is a cookie in front of one and the desire to eat a cookie typically causes one to pick up a cookie and eat it. It is these states, and combinations of them, that have typical causes and effects. (See Armstrong, 1968; Lewis, 1972).

The working theory of attitudes, sometimes called "folk-psychology," is available to most humans, who can't see brains and know relatively little about them in other ways. It developed long before people were aware of the importance of brains. What Armstrong (1968) calls "The causal theory of mind" classifies mental states in terms of their typical causal roles.[8] An important part of the theory is assigning truth-conditions to beliefs, satisfaction-conditions to desires, etc. This is what propositions are for. They are abstract objects that we use to classify attitudes in terms of truth- and satisfaction-conditions. Utterances are intentional activities, motivated by beliefs, desires and intentional states, and inherit the feature of being usefully classified with propositions.

These truth- and satisfaction-conditions arise from the typical causes and effects of a given intentional state. Centrally and roughly, beliefs have truth-conditions and desires have satisfaction-conditions, and the combination of a belief and a desire will motivate actions the results of which will satisfy the desires if the beliefs are true. Such truth- and satisfaction-conditions can be represented by propositions, but intentional states do not consist in having relations to such propositions. The truth-conditions of utterances derive from

---

[8] We think this is compatible with our concepts of intentional states also being connected with "what it is like" to be in the relevant states. See Perry, 2001, *Knowledge, Possibility and Consciousness*.

the truth-conditions of the intentional states that motivate them, or the truth-conditions of intentional states in others the speaker desires to cause. This is all oversimplified, of course, but we hope it clarifies the role we think propositions have in talking about mind and action, as opposed to the picture that underlies "the doctrine of propositions."

Looked at in this way, different propositions may be useful in classifying the same attitudes. For example, if Kepa's utterance **u** is of the sentence "I am a Basque," we can characterize **u**'s truth-conditions with the proposition that the speaker of **u** is a Basque, or that Kepa is a Basque, and in various other ways. It is natural to call this account "multi-propositionalism," since there are multiple propositions that can do a classification job, depending on interest, what is given, and so forth. But the phrase "multi-propositionalism" is a bit misleading. In keeping the focus on propositions, it suggests to many that our view is simply a *modified* doctrine of propositions where the relation between intentional state and proposition is "one-many" instead of "one-one," a simple step from *mono*-propositionalism to *multi*-propositionalism.

Actually, we have used this misleading terminology at times. Korta (2007), for instance, argued against mono-propositionalism, emphasizing the virtues of a *multi*-propositionalist approach, closely connected to the Reflexive-Referential Theory or Critical Referentialism. Jesus M. Larrazabal told him that he should use "pluri-" instead of "multi-," because, while the former prefix means a possibly austere *several, more than one*, the latter means *many* and can suggest a multitude of propositions populating the space around an utterance or intentional attitude. "Pluri-propositionalism" was the term chosen then, and it made its way to *Critical Pragmatics* (on pages 92, 94, 138; "mono-propositionalism" appears on pages xii, 158 and 160).

Since then, and after realizing the potential confusions that it might provoke, we have tried to avoid these terms altogether. Apparently, however, "pluri-propositionalism" and "multi-propositionalism" are catchier than "Critical Pragmatics" or its predecessors "Reflexive-Referential Theory" and "Critical Referentialism," because their use is quite common. These terms are regularly used, for instance, by brilliant philosophers like Eros Corazza (2012), Carlo Penco (2010), and Richard Vallée (2018), who like our view.[9]

But whatever their virtues, we think now we should discard the terms "multi-" or "pluri-propositionalism" for designating our view, and use "Critical Referentialism" (*CR*) or "Critical Pragmatics (*CP*)" to avoid confusion. So, to emphasize, *CP* does not endorse the doctrine of propositions. Intentional attitudes do not consist in a relation, neither to one proposition nor to many of them.

---

[9] See also Stainton and Sullivan (eds.), 2002, and articles therein.

3 The Expression of Propositions

Actually, one of the most common misconceptions about *CP*, possibly invited by the use of the mentioned misleading tags, is the following:

Misconception Three: *An utterance expresses multiple propositions.*

The verb "express" is part of ordinary language and we use it regularly in different ways. We talk about expressing ideas, opinions, feelings, and even expressing oneself. But it is very problematic when it is used to talk about the relation between a belief or an utterance, and a proposition. As we see it, in philosophical conversations, at least, the default use of "express" is for a relation between an utterance and its referential content, clearly suggesting that this relation is constitutive of saying or believing, rather than an important fact about an assertion or belief. When used in this way, we are likely to fall into the "doctrine of propositions": Saying that so-and-so *consists in* expressing the proposition that so-and-so.

If, however, by "expressing a proposition" one simply means saying something that has certain truth-conditions, which are captured by a given proposition, that's fine. But this is not the usual meaning of that phrase. It seems pretty clear to us that, in its uses in philosophy of language, the phrase "express a proposition" has been co-opted by the traditional doctrine of propositions.

This being so, saying that, according to *CP*, an utterance expresses several propositions, is at best very confusing and, at worst, wrong. For instance, despite his highly interesting applications of *CP* to a number of important linguistic phenomena, Vallée has sometimes attributed to Perry a "Multiple Proposition View," which "introduces a suggestion according to which an utterance of a sentence expresses many propositions for semantic, rather than syntactic, reasons" (Vallée, 2005 [2018], 60); or a "Manifold View of Propositions," according to which "an utterance of a sentence expresses many propositions."(Vallée, 2008 [2018], 105.)[10]

CP assigns to the referential content of an utterance or belief an important role—*CP* incorporates *Critical Referentialism*, after all. It is the default for the content of beliefs, utterances, and the like, and it is usually what the

---

[10] Rejection of the idea that an utterance expresses several propositions is an important difference between *CP* and other views also labelled as "multi-propositionalists," which "countenance counterexamples to the widespread implicit assumption that a simple indicative sentence (relative to a context of utterance) semantically expresses at most one proposition" (Sullivan, 2013, 2773). On the one hand, *CP* focuses on utterances, and not on sentences (in context). On the other hand, leaving aside our qualms with the phrase "express a proposition," *CP* assumes that utterances express one proposition, which captures what is said; not many.

speaker intends the hearer to come to believe. We could use the term "express" for the relation between a belief or an utterance and its referential content. And the term can be used in other cases for other contents. But, to emphasize, if we take "expresses" to be the relation between an attitude and its propositional object, in the spirit of the doctrine of propositions, this is wrong.

What *CP* has repeatedly asserted is that the referential content of a statement is what corresponds by default to what referentialist philosophers call "what is said" or "the proposition expressed." But *CP* has also repeatedly asserted that this is not always the case. When making identity statements, for instance, we've claimed that what the speaker says is not the referential content, but some utterance-bound or "hybrid" content. This is what *else* has to be the case, given not only the utterance, but also some additional facts, though not enough to yield referential contents. And likewise for what the speaker says via the that-clause in an attitude report. Often times it is not the referential content but some hybrid content which better explains what the speaker is talking about. In the case above the person who says "Donostia is San Sebastian" intends to convey the reflexive content of the utterance with the reference of "is (the same city as)" fixed, but not the reference of the names. Furthermore, as we have discussed more than once, there are various roles the notion of "what is said" is supposed to play, which sometimes leads to replacing it with other notions like the "locutionary content."[11]

Given all this, it might be advisable to talk about the *belief* expressed rather than the *proposition* expressed by a statement. On our view, a speaker does not express abstract theoretical entities. Rather, she expresses particular mental states: She expresses beliefs—with statements; intentions—with promises; desires—with requests; and so on. These mental states play crucial causal roles in the production of a statement or other sorts of utterance. A causal role that propositions, or any other abstract theoretical entity, cannot play. In a paradigmatic communicative situation, for example, with a statement, a speaker expresses a belief with the same referential content as her statement; a belief she holds, if she is being sincere; a belief she does not hold, if she is being insincere, but a belief about which she is publicly committing to, as for its truth.[12]

A speaker, however, does not express multiple beliefs with a statement, or other type of utterance. Paradigmatically, with a statement, the speaker expresses one belief, and only one belief. So, once again, *CP* does not claim that a single statement expresses many propositions, and it doesn't claim that one single statement expresses multiple beliefs either. What *CP* claims is that the belief expressed has more than one kind of truth-conditions. In particular,

---

[11] See Chapter 3 of this volume, and Korta and Perry, 2011, Ch. 10.

[12] Roughly, this corresponds to the sincerity conditions of a speech act (Searle, 1969).

that it has reflexive, referential, and hybrid truth-conditions. But we should be careful, because this last part of our claim has sometimes been misunderstood, leading to the following two misconceptions about *CP*.

Misconception Four: *A statement and the belief expressed in making it have exactly the same truth-conditions.*

It is a common assumption that the statement and the belief expressed by the speaker when/by/in making it share the same content, that is, that they have the same truth-conditions. According to *CP* this is true, but with important qualifications. Suppose Perry uttters **u**: "Korta is a Basque." His belief and the statement it motivates have the same referential truth-conditions, that Korta is a Basque. But the reflexive truth-conditions of the motivating belief and of the utterance are not the same. The reflexive truth-conditions of the motivating belief **b** will have **b** as a constituent, and not **u**. The reflexive content of the utterance **u** will have **u** as a constituent, and not **b**.

In other words, different statements and beliefs can, and often do share their *referential* truth-conditions. But they do not share their *reflexive* truth-conditions. Statements have *statement-bound* truth-conditions—truth-conditions with the statement itself as a constituent. Beliefs have *belief- bound* truth-conditions—truth-conditions with the belief itself as a constituent. The belief-bound truth-conditions of the belief expressed by a statement, which when dealing with singular terms are what we sometimes call *notion-bound* truth-conditions, are relevant to explain issues like the cognitive significance of statements, but it is important to keep in mind that they are contents of the belief motivating the statement, not of the statement itself.[13]

Another thesis on beliefs and other propositional attitudes that has been (wrongly) attributed to us, often to then argue (correctly) against it, is the following one:

Misconception Five: *A belief state involves believing multiple propositions.*

Beliefs—or cognitions, as Perry sometimes calls the mental states under discussion in *Reference and Reflexivity*—have several layers of truth-conditions or contents—from reflexive to notion-bound to referential. But this does not mean that, being in a belief state, an agent believes multiple propositions. Any reader of the first few pages of *CP* will likely come to believe that Kepa Korta is Basque. They will believe this via their notion of Kepa Korta, which will be part of their belief-state. According to *CP*, for that belief to be true,

---

[13] For the "architectural" connection between the reflexive contents of statements and beliefs, see Perry, 2001 [2012], section 5.7.

their Kepa Korta notion will have to be *of* Kepa Korta, the person their belief is *about*; i.e. the person who is part of the referential content of the belief. But the agent, the reader in our case, may not believe this is the case, at least not in the ordinary sense of "believe." For one, they may not know what a notion is. After doing the reading, they will be *attuned* to the fact that this is so, that their notion is *of* Kepa Korta. But people are attuned to many facts, about which they don't have the concepts necessary to believe, in the ordinary sense.

If the reader masters the whole book, acquires the necessary concepts, and is convinced of the approach, they will believe, not only that Kepa Korta is Basque, but also that the person their Kepa Korta-notion is *of* is Basque. However, if this reader finds the theses of the book unconvincing, they may still not believe this. According to us, they would still be attuned to it.

The distinction between belief and attunement can be illustrated by John Searle. He uses proper names competently, indeed his language is usually quite elegant. That means that he is attuned to the way proper names work— that an utterance of a proper names refers to the object to which the utterance has a rather complex historical connection (in our humble opinion). But he doesn't believe that; in fact, he has denied it vigorously. Philosophers are typically attuned to many truths they deny. No doubt including us.

Misconception Six: *Believing consists in a relation between a subject and multiple propositions.*

To quote ourselves from a recent paper:

> Saying, believing, hoping, and other "propositional attitudes" do not consist in relations of a speaker or thinker to propositions, although they induce such relations. One of the authors is 79 years old. This fact puts him into a relation to the number 79 and the numeral "79" because they are the number and numeral used to classify and refer to his age. But being 79 years old doesn't consist in having these relations to numbers and numerals. It involves living for a long time, however we measure or refer to lengths of time. Similarly, having the belief that the Canary Islands are beautiful induces a relation to the proposition *that the Canary Islands are beautiful*. The belief induces the relation to a proposition, just as a person's height induces the relation to the number assigned to that height by some system of measurement. But the belief does not consist in the relation to this abstract object. It consists in having memories and images of the Canary Islands and a concept of beauty that these memories and images fit.
> (Chapter 15, 249)

Taking into consideration this and the previous misconceptions, it might be a good healthy measure to stop using the term "proposition" altogether when doing *CP* or Critical Referentialism. Not only because it leads to confusions about the name of the theory. Innocent talk about propositions expressed easily and usually leads to talking of propositions asserted, believed or grasped, and of abstracts objects being the bearers of truth-values and holding causal relations.

Using this jargon, we tend to forget that it is particular cognitive episodes, such as utterances and beliefs, which are true or false, satisfied or unsatisfied, and so on. Also, we might forget that these cognitive episodes are the ones that are causally efficient, the ones that have causes and effects. This is important to incorporate our theory about language and communication with both folk psychology and speech act theory; i.e. our best theories about human action and communication. Cognitive episodes, such as beliefs or desires, play an important causal role in our actions and, among those, in our linguistic actions—me wanting a cookie, and believing that the small round object in front of you is a cookie, will normally cause me to either move my body in appropriate ways to get the cookie or to say "please, give me a cookie." Cognitive episodes such as utterances are usually part of the cause of others doing things—my utterance of the sentence "please, give me a cookie" will normally, assuming there are cookies around and the hearer is a nice person, cause the hearer to give me a cookie.

Sticking with the use of "propositions," and with phrases like "expressing propositions," "grasping propositions," "believing propositions," or the like, we either end up embracing the old doctrine of (one) proposition, rejected by Perry in the 70's, or embracing the newer doctrine of multiple propositions, rejected by *CP*. Therefore, we think it is best to leave proposition-talk aside for the moment.[14]

4 Two Levels

Despite the labels sometimes used to refer to *CP* that involve a plurality or a multiplicity of truth-conditions, several people take *CP* as a variant of a two-dimensionalism of sorts. According to this view, *CP* essentially postulates *two*—and only *two*—kinds of content, or truth-conditions: reflexive and referential.

---

[14] This is not a novel proposal, of course. Perry has already suggested or tried, more or less explicitly, avoiding the term "proposition" whenever it was possible. Its use, however, is ubiquitous in the philosophy of language literature, so it is, actually, a difficult practice to maintain. "Early on, I avoided the term 'proposition'; in the later papers, I use it freely" (Perry, 1993 [2000], xi. Preface to the First Edition). From our present perspective, Perry should have kept his earliest policy.

Misconception Seven: *There are only two kinds of truth-conditions: reflexive and referential.*

Accompanying this claim, it is assumed that each of these two levels would account for problems of its own. For instance, the reflexive level would account for epistemological phenomena like learning from hearing utterances, while the referential level would be the level relevant for issues involving metaphysics (Clapp and Lavalle Terrón, 2019). Consider Frege's puzzle about identity statements. On the one hand, "Hesperus is Phosphorus" is a necessarily true statement, as much as "Hesperus is Hesperus." At the referential level, we have the self-identity of a single planet, Venus. The apparent contingency of "Hesperus is Phosphorus" is just epistemic: It is possible for a competent speaker to believe that it is false. It is a truth known *a posteriori*, and this fact is reflected in its reflexive truth-conditions.

Once again, this is not entirely correct. According to *CP*, there are more than just two kinds of truth-conditions, and it is not right to assign issues of metaphysical and epistemic modality (or semantic versus cognitive issues) to referential and reflexive truth-conditions, respectively. Similarly, it is not always correct to identify the referential content with what the speaker states. Often times, other kinds of hybrid truth-conditions turn out to be the relevant ones to account for these and related issues. So, it is not right to reduce the array of levels of truth-conditions to just two, or to identify *CP* with a two-dimensionalism of sorts.

There might be, however, some historical reason for this wrong association between *CP* and two-dimensionalism. At an early stage of his reflexive-referential theory, Perry (1988) formulated a twofold distinction between

- the proposition expressed by an utterance; and
- the proposition that the truth-conditions of the utterance are satisfied;

adding that the former—the proposition expressed—could be true if the utterance had never occurred, and that, since the other has the utterance itself as a constituent, its existence is contingent: it is, in a sense, a proposition *created* by the utterance.

> Both can be regarded as singular propositions ...But ...we should equate the cognitive significance [i.e. cognitive content] with the proposition created by an utterance, not the proposition the utterance expresses (Perry, 1988 [2000], 197).

Interpreted literally, one could say, not only that issues regarding cognitive significance should be accounted for appealing to reflexive truth-conditions, but even that, according to Perry, the cognitive significance should be *equated* with them.

We won't say much about this, we believe it is pretty clear, both in other works by Perry and in *CP*, that this is not the intended interpretation. But it is worth making some remarks, to clarify the quote above:

1. Perry's distinction between these two kinds of propositions is framed, among other things, by the discussion of Wettstein's important essay "Has semantics rested on a mistake?" (1986) and his distinctions there. In this context, there are various notions of "cognitive significance" at stake. Wettstein's notion is not Kaplan's notion, for example. In that paper, Perry uses "cognitive significance" in Wettstein's sense as something like the cognitive *content* that could be characterized, or even equated with a proposition:

> It seemed to me that the way Wettstein used the term ["cognitive significance"] and its close cousins like "cognitive content" in discussing his examples required that a cognitive significance be a proposition, that having one be a property of utterances, and that the cognitive significance of an utterance be something a competent speaker recognizes. Given those requirements, I think the concept I develop in this paper does pretty well. But the concept that meets these requirements will not be the right object to individuate thoughts by their psychological role. (Perry, 1988 [2000], 205 (Afterword)).[15]

2. With the development of *CP*, it should be clear that there is not just *one* reflexive "utterance-created" propositional content, but rather several. Also, that *they* are all used to resolve *problems of cognitive significance*, and that we do not, and cannot, equate one single content with the cognitive significance of the utterance.

CP assumes an array of *hybrid* contents between reflexive and referential—and, also, *beyond* referential content, as it is the case with *designational* (Perry 2001[2012]) or *referential** (Korta and Perry 2011) contents—, which are the result of incrementally taking on board—from the theorist's perspective—facts about the utterance—related to the sentence used, the circumstances of the utterance, and the speaker's plan. It can be concluded that the two dimensions of two-dimensionalism are included among the layers of

---

[15] See also that afterword for Perry's remarks about the non-existence of a Perry/Kaplan view on cognitive significance as character and the history of the term "cognitive significance."

truth-conditions of *CP*, but reducing the latter to the former is a reductive misconception.

5   Metalinguistic Truth-Conditions

In logic and linguistics, a metalanguage is a language used to describe another language, often called the object language. The idea is that one can speak and understand a language without having the capacity to use a meta-language, so it is implausible to suppose that the contents of our utterances at any level are metalinguistic.

In discussions, we have often heard that the use of reflexive contents in understanding the pragmatic reasoning is dubious, since these contents are "meta-linguistic." But pragmatic reasoning does not require meta-linguistic beliefs or knowledge. This wrong attribution can also be found in some interpretations of *CP* or of Perry's views.

Marga Reimer (2002) says, about Perry's account of proper names in *Reference and Reflexivity*:

> Perry's reflexive content (...) captures the insights of meta-linguistic accounts of proper names promoted (at one time or another) by Frege, Russell, and even Mill himself. But is Perry's "cognitive significance" what Frege was so worked up about in the opening paragraph of "On sense and reference"? (...) Frege's cognitive significance is not explicable by appealing to meta-linguistic considerations of the sort Perry appeals to via his reflexive content.

Ray Elugardo (2013), discussing Korta and Perry's (2011) account of sub-sentential utterances, claims that "reflexive content is problematic insofar as it meant to be a meta-linguistic, truth-conditional, content of sub-sentential utterances" (Elugardo, 2013, 106). More recently Botterell and Stainton (2017) follow the same thread.

In a nutshell, they misunderstood us: Our reflexive truth- conditions are not metalinguistic. This is the eighth misconception in our list:

Misconception Eight: *Reflexive contents are metalinguistic.*

Consider the statement, "Donostia is a city." The referential content of the statement is the singular proposition that Donostia is a city; it is about Donostia, not about the name "Donostia" or the other words in the sentence. It is true, so it states a fact, a *geographical fact*. The utterance uses language, but it does not state a *linguistic* fact. But consider,

"Donostia" is a name.

Quotes are used to indicate that a name is being mentioned rather than used; they are meta-linguistic devices. The utterance uses metalinguistic devices to refer to the bit of language it is about, the name "Donostia." But the fact stated is a linguistic fact, not a meta-linguistic one (whatever that might mean exactly). We use quotes as metalinguistic devices to refer to names and other expressions which are constituents of reflexive and hybrid contents. But that does not make the contents metalinguistic rather than linguistic, any more that the fact that we use words to refer to cities makes it a linguistic fact, rather than a geographical one—i.e. that San Sebastian is a city.

Suppose María tells Kepa, who is looking for his copy of *Critical Pragmatics*:

(**u**) It is on the top shelf.

Following *CP*, and simplifying a bit, the reflexive truth- conditions of (**u**) are

($\mathbf{u}_{rx}$) That there is an object x that the speaker of (**u**) is referring to and x is on the top shelf.

According to Elugardo, and other interpreters, the fact that the reflexive truth-conditions are about (**u**) itself make them meta-linguistic. But (**u**) is not a piece of language; it is *an act* that involves a piece of language. In other words, ($\mathbf{u}_{rx}$) are not truth-conditions of a sentence, not even a sentence in a context, but an utterance, an act that might or might not involve a complete sentence. They can involve sub-sentences or no sentence at all—in *CP*, we use "utterance" à la Grice, in a broad sense, including non-linguistic communicative acts.[16]

---

[16] A related confusion considers the reflexive contents as second-order, since they are taken to be conditions *on* the utterance: "... they are second-order contents, having these utterances as their subject matter ..." (Bozickovic, 2021, 32); "In the indexical case, the truth conditions are, in Perry's view, also provided by the relevant identifying condition playing such a dual role, but within the second-order reflexive content; i.e. as the *reflexive* truth conditions *on* the utterance of the sentence" (Bozickovic 2021, 34. His italics). Bozickovic claims, further, that because they are second-order, they cannot be used to account for the differences in cognitive significance. But, once again, reflexive truth-conditions are neither utterances of utterances, nor truth-conditions of truth-conditions, so they are not second-order in any sensible meaning of the term.

6 Metaphysics versus Epistemology

Adding to his remark about the metalinguistic nature of reflexive contents, Elugardo notes that

> Very young English-speaking children do not have difficulty understanding utterances of "on the top shelf," but it is unlikely that they possess the requisite meta-linguistic concepts needed for understanding utterances of (5.13) [(5.4)].[17] So, just on empirical grounds alone, it is doubtful that the language faculty generates anything like complex reflexive contents as outputs.
> (Elugardo, 2013, 101, fn 17.)

We think that there is another misconception of *CP* here. One that has to do with taking reflexive truth-conditions to be a representation of the linguistic meaning of an utterance; a representation that would constitute the first step of what the hearer has in mind in his utterance comprehension process. Once again, this is not right.

To begin with, the theoretical notions and concepts we use to characterize the various levels of truth-conditions of an utterance *are not* restricted to those that are typically supposed to be known by competent users of the language.

They are the concepts and notions that the theory uses to make explicit the truth-conditions that competent speakers and communicators, including very young ones, are attuned to. The apparent complexity of reflexive truth-conditions is due to the complexity of our formulation of the truth-conditions, but these are not representations in the hearer's mind.[18]

---

[17] In Elugardo's paper, (5.13) does not refer to an utterance but a reflexive content of an utterance, namely:

(5.13) **u** is true if and only if the speaker of **u** referred to some object x such that x is on the top shelf. (Elugardo, 2013, 12.)

That is surely an error on his part. It just does not make sense to talk about utterances *of* truth-conditions, be them reflexive or not. So, we take it he means (5.4), "On the top shelf," instead of (5.13).

[18] Botterell and Stainton conclude, on similar premises, that reflexive truth-considerations are somewhat absurd:

> Our point is: there is no reason to think that the alleged reflexive truth conditions, if such there be, are in fact part of the literal linguistic meaning of utterances of "Jane smokes cigars." (...) All the same, it's absurd to build information of this kind into what an utterance of "You like small dogs and cats" semantically encodes in English. In short, we don't actually have any good reason for building reflexive truth conditions into the linguistic content of utterances of unembedded words and phrases. (Botterell and Stainton, 2017, 509)

We do not take reflexive truth-conditions to be part of the *linguistic* content of utterances. That might be absurd, or might not. But *CP* does not do it.

The possible source of this sort of misunderstanding is the conflation of the *metaphysics* of meaning and the *epistemology* of interpretation, (See Devitt, 2013, 2019; Korta and Perry, 2019a, b). In fact, Elugardo, among others, has taken *CP* to be a theory about the epistemology of utterance comprehension, such that the various levels of truth-conditions represent the hearer's inferential steps in that process. That is another misconception.

Misconception Nine: *The variety of contents of an utterance reflect the series of steps in the utterance comprehension process.*

The hierarchy of contents we supply, from reflexive contents through hybrid contents to referential contents, is not a theory of the steps involved in understanding an utterance. No doubt, the various levels of contents play a role in the hearer's understanding process, but we do not give a precise account of that process as a serial inferential process. Actually, *CP* may be compatible with various theories. In Chapter 11 of *Critical Pragmatics*, we show its compatibility with relevance theory, but it might be compatible with others. It is important to keep in mind, in any case, that the hierarchy of contents should not be considered as a hierarchy of language-of-thought sentences in the speakers-hearers minds.

In conversation, we often start by identifying the referential content without much thinking. We consider lower levels when we try to figure out why the speaker said in a particular way. And sometimes, when we can narrow down the referential content possibilities, it is helpful to consider what they imply about the lower levels. In speaking with people who mumble, for example, we often grasp the likely referential content intended, and then use it to figure out which words were used. And sometimes there is a back and forth to come up with the likeliest hypothesis.

For example, Paul Grice once came up to Perry after Perry gave a talk at an APA meeting and said, "That was really an ex-mumble-mumble talk." Perry thought he intended to say either that it was an excellent talk or that it was an excrement of a talk. Perry decided he meant that it was excellent, because he had a pleasant expression and why would he walk all the way to the podium to say that it was an excrement of a talk? Also, the thought expressed by the latter would not require such a crude term; "lousy" would be fine. So Perry's reasoning went from likely referential contents to likely reflexive contents, and back.

Perry, of course, may have been wrong. And he did not *think* these contents; nor did he consciously make inferences from one content to another. His reasoning was pretty automatic, and it involved many different observations and previous beliefs, from Grice's facial expression, to his believe that Grice was a nice person, not prone to rudeness or unnecessary cruelty.

The variety of truth-conditions of an utterance is a theoretical tool, aiming at encapsulating the different levels of truth-conditions that are relevant on each case. A means to reconstruct, theoretically, what is said by an utterance, how is said and, perhaps, what is understood, which is compatible with various neo- and post-Gricean theories of communication and theories about what happens in the speaker-hearers's minds in speech production and comprehension.

7 Conclusion

We are certain that there are many valid criticisms to be made of Critical Pragmatics, understood just as we meant it. Philosophers need to have somewhat conflicting attitudes towards the theories they put forward. They have to believe what they are saying is correct, otherwise they lose the motivation to write and explain what they think. But, at least as we conceive it, the history of philosophy consists of brilliant people putting forward ideas that turn out to be not quite right, and in many cases dramatically wrong. What are the chances of a team of not-so-brilliant philosophers coming up with ideas that have everything—or even most things—right?

We try to explain what we believe to be true, at one level, as best we can. At the same time, or at least later in the day when we go out to get a drink, we have no doubt that we don't have everything right, and hope that we have at least put forward some ideas that will add to the understanding of the phenomena we discuss.

So we are happy when others confront our ideas and explore how they measure up to their own concerns and insights. Most times, these confrontations turn into fruitful debates and exciting new philosophical challenges, either because they show us new aspects of our theory we had not thought of—new applications or new implications—or because, oftentimes, they bring about new limitations that need to be overcome.

The point of this paper is to help clarifying some aspects of Critical Pragmatics, focusing on those that have been most often misunderstood. We also incorporate some of the insights we've gained in discussion with other philosophers and linguists during the last decades. The focus, however, is put on clear misinterpretations of the theory, in the hope this helps avoiding criticisms to things we didn't mean.[19]

---

[19] A first version of this paper was written with occasion of the Workshop on *Ten Years of Critical Pragmatics* (ILCLI, December 2021). Thanks to the organizers of that workshop and to

the editors of this issue for their work in putting all this together. This work has been partially supported by grants of the Department of Education, Universities and Research of the Basque Government (IT1612-22) and the Ministry of Science and Innovation of the Spanish Government (PID2019-106078GB-I00; MCI/AEI/FEDER, UE).

References

Al-Hindawi, Fareed Hameed and Alaa Baji Jebur Al-Khazali. 2021. A Theoretical Survey on Critical Pragmatics. *Kufa Journal of Arts* 2 (50): 559–570.

Anscombe, G. Elizabeth M. 1957 [2000]. *Intention*. Cambridge, MA: Harvard University Press.

Angelelli, Ignacio. 1967. *Studies on Gottlob Frege and Traditional Philosophy*. Dordrecht: D. Reidel.

Armstrong, David M. 1968. *A Materialist theory of Mind*. London: Routledge.

Austin, John L. 1961. *How to Do Things with Words*. Oxford: Oxford University Press.

Bach, Kent. 1994a. Conversational Impliciture. *Mind & Language* 9: 124–162.

Bach, Kent. 1994b. Semantic Slack: What is Said and More. *Foundations of Speech Act Theory: Philosophical and Linguistic Perspectives*, ed. S. Tsohatzidis, 267–291. London: Routledge.

Bach, Kent. 1999. The Myth of Conventional Implicature. *Linguistics and Philosophy* 22: 327–66.

Bach, Kent. 2000. Quantification, Qualification, and Context: a Reply to Stanley and Szabo. *Mind & Language* 15: 262–83.

Bach, Kent. 2006. The Excluded Middle: Semantic Minimalism without Minimal Propositions. *Philosophy and Phenomenological Research* LXXIII (2): 435–442.

Bach, Kent. 2011. Review of *Truth-Conditional Pragmatics* (François Recanati). *Notre Dame Philosophical Reviews*. http://ndpr.nd.edu/news/25657-truth-conditional-pragmatics-2/. Accessed 26 Sept 2011.

Bar-Elli, Gilead. 2006. Identity in Frege's *Begriffsschrift*: where both Thau-Caplan and Heck are Wrong. *Canadian Journal of Philosophy* 36 (3): 355–370.

Barcan Marcus, Ruth 1961 Modalities and Intensional Languages *Synthese* 13(4): 303–322.

Barwise, Jon and John Perry 1983 [1999] *Situations and Attitudes*. Publications. Cambridge: MIT Press. Second expanded edition. Stanford: CSLI, 1999.

Beaney, Michael. 1996. *Frege: Making Sense*. London: Duckworth.

Beaney, Michael (ed.). 1997. *The Frege Reader*. Oxford: Blackwell.

Beard, Mary. 2015. *SPQR: A History of Ancient Rome.* Liveright: New York.

Bezuidenhout, Anne and J. Cooper Cutting. 2002. Literal Meaning, Minimal Propositions, and Pragmatic Processing. *Journal of Pragmatics* 34: 433–456.

Borg, Emma. 2004. *Minimalist Semantics.* Oxford: Oxford University Press.

Borg, Emma. 2006. Review *Literal Meaning* by F. Recanati. *Mind* 115 (458): 461–465.

Botterell Andrew and Robert J. Stainton. 2017. Logical Form and the Vernacular Revisited. *Mind and Language* 32(4): 495–522.

Bozickovic, Vojislav. 2021. *The Indexical Point of View. On Cognitive Significance and Cognitive Dynamics.* New York: Routledge & Kegan Paul.

Bratman, Michael. 1987. *Intention, Plans, and Practical Reason.* Cambridge, MA: Harvard University Press.

Broncano-Berrocal, Fernando. 2015. Luck as Risk and the Lack of Control Account of Luck. *Metaphilosophy* 46(1): 1–25.

Capone, Alessandro. 2006. On Grice's Circle (a Theory-internal Problem in Linguistic Theories of the Gricean Type). *Journal of Pragmatics* 38: 645–669.

Cappelen, Herman, and Ernest Lepore. 2005. *Insensitive Semantics. A Defense of Semantic Minimalism and Speech Act pluralism.* Oxford: Blackwell.

Carston, Robyn. 1988. Implicature, Explicature, and Truth-Theoretic Semantics. *Mental Representations: The Interface between Language and Reality,* ed. R. Kempson, 155–81. Cambridge: Cambridge University Press.

Carston, Robyn. 2002. *Thoughts and Utterances: The Pragmatics of Explicit Communication.* Oxford: Blackwell.

Carston, Robyn. 2007. How many Pragmatic Systems are There? *Saying, Meaning, and Referring: Essays on François Recanati's Philosophy of Language,* ed. M. J. Frápolli, 18–48. Houndmills: Palgrave.

Chastain, Charles. 1975. Reference and Content. *Minnesota Studies in the Philosophy of Science, Vol VII: Language, Mind and Knowledge*, ed. K. Gunderson, 194–269. Minneapolis: University of Minnesota Press.

Chen, Xinren. 2020. *Critical Pragmatic Studies on Chinese Public Discourse.* Routledge, New York

Clapp, Lenny and Armando Lavalle Terrón. 2019. Multipropositionalism and Necessary a Posteriori Identity Statements. *Pacific Philosophical Quarterly* 100 (4): 902–934.

Clark, Herbert H. 1992. *Arenas of Language Use.* Chicago: University of Chicago Press.

Clark, Herbert H. 1996. Clark, Herbert H, 1996, *Using Language.* Cambridge: Cambridge University Press.

Clark, Herbert and Richard J. Gerrig. 1984. On the Pretense Theory of Irony. *Journal of Experimental Psychology: General* 113: 121–126.

Conan Doyle, Arthur. 1887 [2010]. A study in Scarlet. *The Complete Sherlock Holmes*, 1–54. Lexington: The Sherlock Holmes Collection.

Corazza, Eros. 2011. Unenriched Subsentential Illocutions. *Philosophy and Phenomenological Research* 83(3): 560–82.

Corazza, Eros. 2012. Same-Saying, Pluri-Propositionalism, and Implicatures. *Mind & Language* 27 (5): 546–569.

Corazza, Eros. 2017. Proper Names: Gender, Context-Sensitivity, and Conversational Implicatures. *Reference and Representation in Thought and Language,* eds. M. Ponte and K. Korta, 20–45. Oxford University Press, Oxford.

Corazza, Eros and Kepa Korta. 2010. Minimalism, Contextualism, and Contentualism. *Philosophy of Language and Linguistics. Vol. 2: The Philosophical Turn,* ed. P. Stalmaszczyk, 9–39. Frankfurt: Ontos-Verlag.

Corazza, Eros and Kepa Korta. 2015. Frege on Subject Matter and Identity Statements. *Analysis,* 75(4): 562–65.

Corazza, Eros and Mark Whitsey. 2003. Indexicals, Fictions and Ficta. *Dialectica* 57(2): 121–136.

Crimmins, Mark. 1992. *Talk About Beliefs.* Cambridge, MA: MIT Press.

Crimmins, Mark and John Perry. 1989. The Prince and the Phone Booth: Reporting Puzzling Beliefs. *Journal of Philosophy* 86: 685–711. Reprinted in Perry 2000, 207–232.

Curcó, Carmen. 2013. From Pragmatic Processes to Pragmatic Processing: Consciousness, Propositionality, and Linguistic Mandatoriness. Talk at the *Second ILCLI-IFF Workshop on Language, Cognition and Logic.* Mexico, January 2013.

Davidson, Donald. 1980 [2001]. *Essays on Actions and Events.* Oxford: Clarendon Press.

de Ponte, María. 2017. Promises, the Present and "Now": Lessons from Austin, Prior and Kamp. *Journal of Pragmatics* 112: 33–43.

de Ponte, María and Kepa Korta. 2017a. New Thoughts about Old Facts: On Prior's Root Canal. In M. de Ponte and K. Korta (eds.) 2017b, 163–178. [Chapter 11 of this volume.]

de Ponte, María and Kepa Korta (eds.). 2017b. *Reference and Representation in Thought and Language.* Oxford: Oxford University Press.

de Ponte, María and Kepa Korta. 2023. Frege y sus Circunstancias: Una Interpretación de la Teoría Fregeana del Significado. *Análisis filosófico, 43*(1), 5-40.

de Ponte María, Kepa Korta, and John Perry. 2020a. Truth without Reference. The Use of Fictional Names. *Topoi* 39: 389–99. [Chapter 12 of this volume.]

de Ponte María, Kepa Korta, and John Perry. 2020b. Utterance and Context. *The architecture of context and context-sensitivity,* ed. T. Ciecierski and P. Grabarczyk, 15–28. Springer, Cham. [Chapter 13 of this volume.]

de Ponte María, Kepa Korta, and John Perry. 2021. Four Puzzling Paragraphs. Frege on '≡' and '='. *Semiotica* 240:75–95. [Chapter 14 of this volume.]

de Ponte María, Kepa Korta, and John Perry. 2023a. Language and Luck. *Linguistic luck. Essays in anti-luck semantics,* eds. A. Fairweather and C. Montemayor, 15–35. Oxford: Oxford University Press. [Chapter 15 of this volume] de Ponte María, Kepa Korta, and John Perry. 2023b. Philosophy of Language and Action Theory. *The Cambridge Handbook of Language in Context,* ed. J. Romero-Trillo, 95–115. Cambridge: Cambridge University Press. [Chapter 16 of this volume.]

de Ponte María, Kepa Korta, and John Perry. 2023c. Critical Pragmatics: Nine Misconceptions. *A Critical Eye on Critical Pragmatics: Issues at the Frontier of Semantics and Pragmatics,* eds. C. Genovesi and E. Garmendia-Mujika. *Topoi* 42: 913–923. [Chapter 17 of this volume]

Devitt, Michael. 2013. Three Methodological Flaws of Linguistic Pragmatism. *What is said and what is not. The Semantics/Pragmatics Interface,* eds. C. Penco and F. Domaneschi, 285-300. Stanford: CSLI Publications.

Devitt, Michael. 2019. A Methodological Flaw? A Reply to Korta and Perry. *Journal of Pragmatics* 139:180–82

Dickie, Imogen. 2008. Informative Identities in the *Begriffsschrift* and "On Sense and Denotation." *Canadian Journal of Philosophy,* 38(2): 269–288.

Donnellan, Keith. 1966. Reference and definite descriptions, *Philosophical Review* 75: 281–304.

Donnellan, Keith, 1970, Proper Names and Identifying Descriptions. *Synthese* 21: 335–358.

Donnellan, Keith. 1974. Speaking of Nothing. *Philosophical Review* LXXXIII: 3–31.

Donnellan, Keith. 1978. Speaker Reference, Descriptions, and Anaphora. *Syntax and Semantics, Voi. 9. Pragmatics,* ed. P. Cole, 47–68.

Dretske, Fred. 1981 [2000]. *Knowledge and the Flow of Information.* Stanford: CSLI. Original edition: Cambridge: Bradford/MIT, 1981.

Du, Yao. 2022. Adopting Critical-Pragmatic Pedagogy to Address Plagiarism in a Chinese Context: an Action Research. *Journal of English for Academic Purposes* 57(2):101–112.

Dummett, Michael A.E. 1981a. *Frege: Philosophy of Language.* 2nd ed. Cambridge, MA: Harvard University Press.

Dummett, Michael A.E. 1981b. *The Interpretation of Frege's Philosophy.* Cambridge, MA: Harvard University Press.

Elugardo, Reinaldo. 2013. Sub-Sentential Speech Acts, Reflexive Content, and Pragmatic Enrichment. *Brevity,* ed. L. Goldstein, 91–106. Oxford: Oxford University Press.

Evans, Gareth. 1973. The Causal Theory of Names. *Proceedings of the Aristotelian Society, Supplementary Volume* 47: 187–208.

Falk, Arthur. 2015. Hermann Cappelen and Josh Dever. The Inessential Indexical: on the Philosophical Significance of Perspective and the First Person. *Journal of Indian Council of Philosophical Research* 32 (3): 425–430.

Føllesdal, Dagfinn. 1966 [2004]. *Referential Opacity and Modal Logic.* New York and London: Routledge.

Forguson, L. W. 1973. Locutionary and Illocutionary Acts. *Essays on J. L. Austin*, eds. Berlin et al., 160–85. Oxford: Oxford University Press.

Frege, Gottlob, 1879 [1967], *Begriffsschrift, eine der Arithmetischen Nachgebildete Formelsprache des Reinen Denkens*. Halle: Verlag von Louis Nebert. Translated by Stefan Bauer-Mengelberg. 1967. Begriffsschrift, a Formula Language, Modeled upon that of Arithmetic, for Pure Thought. *From Frege to Gödel: A Source Book in Mathematical Logic*. 1879–1931, ed. J. van Heijenoort. Cambridge, MA: Harvard University Press.

Frege, Gottlob, 1892 [1997]. Über Sinn and Bedeutung. *Zeitschrift fü Philosophische Kritik*, 100: 25–50. Translated by Max Black. 1952. On Sense and Reference, *Translations from the Philosophical Writings of Gottlob Frege*, eds. P. Geach and M. Black, 56–78. Oxford: Basil Blackwell. Also in Beaney (ed.). 1997, 151–171.

Frege, Gottlob. 1892-5 [1997]. Comments on *Sinn* and *Bedeutung*. In Beaney (ed.). 1997, 172–80.

Frege, Gottlob. 1897 [1997]. Logic. Translated by P. Long and R. White. *Posthumous Writings*, eds. H. Hermes, F. Kambartel, and F Kaulbach, 126–151, 1979. The University of Chicago Press, Chicago. Also in Beaney (ed.). 1997, 225–254.

Frege, Gottlob. 1893, 1903 (1952). *Grundgesetze der Arithmetik*. Band I, 1893. Band II, 1903. Jena: Verlag Hermann Pohle. Translations of parts of it by P.E.B. Jourdain and J. Stachelroth. In Geach and Black (eds.) 1952, 137–159.

Frege, Gottlob. 1918 [1967]. Der Gedanke: Eine Logische Untersuchung. Translated by A. Quinton and M. Quinton, The Thought: A Logical Inquiry. *Beitra ̈gezur Philosophie des deutschen Idealismus*, I (1918–1919), 58–77. Reprinted in Strawson 1967, 17–38.

Friend, Stacie. 2014. Notions of Nothing. *Empty Representations: Reference and Non-Existence*, eds. M. García-Carpintero and G. Martí, 307–332. Oxford: Oxford University Press.

Friend, Stacie. 2017. The Real Foundation of Fictional Worlds. *Australasian Journal of Philosophy* 95 (1): 29–42.

Garmendia, Joana. 2010. Irony is Critical. *Pragmatics & Cognition* 18(2): 397–421.

Garmendia, Joana. 2011. She's (Not) a Fine Friend: "Saying" and Criticism in Irony. *Intercultural Pragmatics* 8(1): 41–65.

Gazdar, Gerald. 1979. *Pragmatics: Implicature, Presupposition, and Logical Form*, New York: Academic Press.

Geach, Peter T. 1950. Russell's Theory of Descriptions. *Analysis*, 10(4), 84–88.

Geach, Peter T. 1965. Assertion. *Philosophical Review* 74: 449–65.

Geach, Peter T. and Max Black (eds.). 1952. *Translations from the Philosophical Writings of Gottlob Frege*, 2nd ed., 1960. Oxford: Basil Blackwell.

Godfrey-Smith, William. 1979. Special Relativity and the Present. *Philosophical Studies*, 36: 233–244.

Goldfarb, Warren. 2010. Frege's Conception of Logic. *Cambridge Companion to Frege,* ed. T. Ricketts, 63–86. Cambridge: Cambridge University Press.

Goldman, Alvin I. 1970. *A theory of Human Action.* Princeton, NJ: Princeton University Press.

Grice, H. Paul. 1967a [1989]. Logic and Conversation. *The Logic of Grammar,* eds. D. Davidson and G. Harman, 64–75, 1975. Encino: Dickenson. Also published in *Syntax and Semantics 3: Speech Acts,* eds. P. Cole and J. L. Morgan, 41–58, 1975. New York: Academic Press. Reprinted in in Grice 1989, 22–40.

Grice, H. Paul. 1967b [1989]. Further Notes on Logic and Conversation. *Syntax and Semantics 9: Pragmatics,* ed. P. Cole, 183–197, 1978. New York: Academic Press, 1978. Reprinted in Grice 1989, 41–57.

Grice, H. Paul. 1969. Vacuous Names. *Words and Objections,* eds. D. Davidson and J. Hintikka, 118–145. Dordrecht: Reidel.

Grice, H. Paul. 1971. Intention and Uncertainty. *Proceedings of the British Academy,* 57, 263–279.

Grice, H. Paul. 1989. *Studies in the Way of Words.* Cambridge, MA: Harvard University Press.

Hales, Stephen D. 2016. Why Every Theory of Luck is Wrong. *Noûs,* 50(3), 490–508.

Heck, Richard. 2003. Frege on Identity and Identity-Statements: A Reply to Thau and Caplan. *Canadian Journal of Philosophy,* 33 (1): 83–102.

Huang, Yan. 2012. *The Oxford Dictionary of Pragmatics.* Oxford: Oxford University Press.

Huang, Siyun. 2020. Identity Construction of Female Consumers in Chinese and American Cosmetics Advertisements: a Critical Pragmatic Study. *International Linguistic Research* 4(3):131–141.

Israel, David and John Perry. 1990. What is Information? *Information, Language and Cognition,* ed. P. Hanson, 1–19. Vancouver: University of British Columbia Press.

Israel, David and John Perry. 1991. Information and Architecture. *Situation Theory and Its Applications, vol. 2,* eds. J. Barwise, J. M. Gawron, G. Plotkin and S. Tutiya, 147–60. Stanford: Stanford University: Center for the Study of Language and Information.

Israel, David, John Perry, and Syun Tutiya. 1993. Executions, Motivations and Accomplishments. *Philosophical Review* 102: 515–540.

Jackson, Frank. 1986. What Mary didn't Know. *Journal of Philosophy* 83: 291–295.

Kaplan, David. 1975. Dthat. *Syntax and Semantics,* 9: 383–99.

Kaplan, David. 1979. On the Logic of Demonstratives. *Syntax and Semantics, Vol. 9: Pragmatics,* ed. P. Cole, 221–243. New York: Academic Press. Reprinted in P. Yourgrau (ed.). 1990. *Demonstratives.* Oxford: Oxford University Press, 11–33.

Kaplan, David. 1989a. Demonstratives. *Themes from Kaplan,* eds. J. Almog, J. Perry, and H. Wettstein, 481–563. New York: Oxford University Press.

Kaplan, David. 1989b. Afterthoughts. *Themes from Kaplan*, eds. J. Almog, J. Perry, and H. Wettstein, 565–614. New York: Oxford University Press.

Kiernan-Lewis, Delmas. 1991. Not over Yet: Prior's "Thank Goodness" Argument. *Philosophy*, vol. 66, 256: 241-243.

Korta, Kepa. 1997. Implicitures: Cancelability and Non-Detachability. Report ILCLI-97-LIC-6, Donostia: ILCLI (Revised version in Spanish: De lo Dicho y otros Aspectos de la Comunicación. *Palabras: Víctor Sánchez de Zavala in Memoriam*, eds. K. Korta and F. García-Murga, 201–218. Bilbao: UPV-EHU.)

Korta, Kepa. 2007. Acerca del Monoproposicionalismo Imperante en Semántica y Pragmática. *Revista de Filosofía* 32(2):37–55.

Korta, Kepa. 2008. Malinowski and Pragmatics: Claim Making in the History of Linguistics. *Journal of Pragmatics* 40: 1645–1660.

Korta, Kepa. 2013. Grice's Requirements on What is Said. *What is Said and What is Not*, eds. C. Penco and F. Domaneschi, 209–224. Stanford: CSLI Publications.

Korta, Kepa and John Perry. 2006a. Three Demonstrations and a Funeral. *Mind and Language* 21/2: 166–86. [Chapter 1 of this volume]

Korta, Kepa and John Perry. 2006b. Pragmatics. *The Stanford Encyclopedia of Philosophy (Revised summer 2024)*, ed. E. N. Zalta. http://plato.stanford.edu/entries/pragmatics/.

Korta, Kepa and John Perry. 2007a. Radical Minimalism, Moderate Contextualism. *Context-Sensitivity and Semantic Minimalism: Essays on Semantics and Pragmatics*, ed. G. Preyer and G. Peter, 94–111. Oxford: Oxford University Press. [Chapter 2 of this volume]

Korta, Kepa and John Perry. 2007b. How to Say Things with Words. *John Searle's Philosophy of Language: Force, Meaning, and* Thought, ed. S. L. Tsohatzidis, 169–189. Cambridge: Cambridge University Press. [Chapter 3 of this volume]

Korta, Kepa and John Perry. 2007c. Varieties of Minimalist Semantics. *Philosophy and Phenomenological Research* 73(2): 451–59.

Korta, Kepa and John Perry. 2008. The pragmatic Circle. *Synthese* 165(3): 347–357. Reprinted in Asa Kasher (ed.) 2011, *Pragmatics II (Critical Concepts in Linguistics)*. London: Routledge. [Chapter 4 of this volume]

Korta, Kepa and John Perry. 2009. Reference: A New Paradigm. *Meaning, Content and Argument*, eds. J. M. Larrazabal and L. Zubeldia, 73-88. Bilbao: UPV-EHU. [Chapter 5 of this volume]

Korta, Kepa and John Perry. 2010a. Intentions to Refer. *Meaning and Context*, eds. L. Baptista and E. Rast, 161-186. Bern: Peter Lang. [Chapter 6 of this volume]

Korta, Kepa and John Perry. 2010b. What is Said. *Context-Dependence, Perspective and Relativity*, eds. F. Recanati, I. Stojanovic, and N. Villanueva, 51–67. Berlin: Mouton De Gruyter. [Chapter 7 of this volume]

Korta, Kepa and John Perry. 2011. *Critical Pragmatics. An Inquiry into Reference and Communication.* Cambridge: Cambridge University Press.

Korta, Kepa and John Perry. 2013a. Highlights of *Critical Pragmatics*: Reference and the Contents of the Utterance. *Intercultural Pragmatics* 10 (1): 161–182. [Chapter 8 of this volume]

Korta, Kepa and John Perry. 2013b. Squaring the Circle. *Perspectives in Pragmatics and Philosophy*, eds. A. Capone, F. Lo Piparo, and M. Carapezza, 291-302. Springer. [Chapter 9 of this volume]

Korta, Kepa and John Perry. 2017. Full but not Saturated: The Myth of Mandatory Primary Pragmatic Processes. *Meaning, Context, and Methodology,* eds. Sarah-Jane Conrad and Klaus Petrus, 31–49. Mouton de Gruyter. [Chapter 10 of this volume]

Korta Kepa and John Perry. 2019a. Our Alleged Methodological Flaw. *Journal of Pragmatics,* 139:175–179.

Korta Kepa and John Perry. 2019b. Our Response to Devitt. *Journal of Pragmatics,* 139:183–184.

Korta, Kepa and María Ponte. 2014. On Times and Contents. *Cognitive and Pragmatic Perspectives on Speech Actions,* ed. I. Witczak-Plisiecka, 13–34. Berlin: Peter Lang.

Korta, Kepa and María Ponte. 2015. Tenses, Dates and Times. *Research in Language*, Vol. 12, 4, 301–317.

Kremer, Michael. 2010. Sense and Reference: The Origins and Development of the Distinction. *Cambridge Companion to Frege*, ed. T. Ricketts, 220–293. Cambridge: Cambridge University Press.

Kripke, Saul. 1977. Speaker Reference and Semantic Reference. *Midwest Studies in Philosophy* 2: 255–276.

Kripke, Saul. 1980. *Naming and Necessity.* Cambridge, MA: Harvard University Press.

Kripke, Saul. 2013. *Reference and Existence: The John Locke Lectures.* Oxford University Press, Oxford.

Le Poidevin, Robin (ed.). 1998. *Questions of Time and Tense.* Oxford: Oxford University Press.

Levinson, Stephen. 2000. *Presumptive Meanings.* Cambridge, Mass: MIT Press/Bradford Books.

Lewis, David K. 1972. Psychophysical and Theoretical Identifications. *Australasian Journal of Philosophy* 50: 249–258.

Lewis, David K. 1979, Attitudes De Dicto and De Se. *Philosophical Review* 88: 513–543.

Loar, Brian. 1976. The Semantics of Singular Rerms. *Philosophical Studies: An International Journal for Philosophy in the Analytic Tradition*, 30(6), 353–377.

Maclaurin, James and Heather Dyke. 2002. "Thank Goodness that's Over": The Evolutionary Story. *Ratio* vol 13, 3: 276-292.

Markosian, Ned. 2014. Time. *The Stanford Encyclopedia of Philosophy* (Spring 2014 Edition), E. N. Zalta (ed.), URL = <http://plato.stanford.edu/archives/spr2014/entries/time/>.

Martí, Genoveva. 1995. The Essence of Genuine Reference. *Journal of Philosophical Logic* 11: 1–16.

May, Robert. 2001. Frege on Identity Statements. *Semantic Interfaces: Reference, Anaphora and Aspect,* eds. C. Cecchetto, G. Chierchia, and M.T. Guasti, 1–62. Stanford: CSLI Publications.

May, Robert. 2012. What Frege's Theory of Identity is Not. *Thought: A Journal of Philosophy,* 1 (1): 41–48.

McTaggart, John M.E. 1908. The Unreality of Time. *Mind,* 17: 457–73

Mellor, D. Hugh. 1998. *Real Time II.* London: Routledge.

Mendelsohn, Richard L. 1982. Frege's *Begriffsschrift* Theory of Identity. *Journal of the History of Philosophy,* 20 (3): 279–299.

Morris, Charles, W. 1946. *Signs, Language and Behavior.* Englewood Cliffs, NJ: Prentice-Hall.

Morris, Charles W. 1938. Foundations of the Theory of Signs. *International Encyclopedia of United Science, Vol. I.,* eds. O. Neurath, R. Carnap, and C. Morris, 1–59. Chicago: Chicago University Press.

Neale, Stephen. 1999. Coloring and Composition. *Philosophy and Linguistics,* eds. K. Murasugi and R. Stainton, 35–82. Boulder, CO: Westview.

Nida-Rümelin, Martine. 2015. Qualia: the Knowledge Argument. *The Stanford Encyclopedia of Philosophy* (Summer 2015 Edition), E. N. Zalta (ed.), URL = <http://plato.stanford.edu/archives/sum2015/entries/qualia-knowledge/>.

Oaklander, L. Nathan. 1992. Thank Goodness It's Over. *Philosophy,* Vol. 67, 260: 256-258.

Oaklander, L. Nathan. 1994. A Defense of a New Tenseless Theory of Time. *The New Theory of Time,* eds. L. N. Oaklander and Q. Smith, 57–68. New Haven: Yale University Press.

Peet, Andrew. 2017. Referential Intentions and Communicative Luck. *Australasian Journal of Philosophy,* 95(2), 379–384.

Peirce, Charles S. 1931–1958. *Collected Papers of Charles Sanders Peirce.* Cambridge, MA: Harvard University Press.

Penco, Carlo. 2010. Essentially Incomplete Descriptions. *European Journal of Analytic Philosophy,* 6(2):47–66.

Perry, John. 1977. Frege on Demonstratives. *Philosophical Review* 86 (4): 474–497. Reprinted in Perry 1993 [2000], Chapter 1.

Perry, John. 1979. The Problem of the Essential Indexical. *Noûs* 13 (1): 3–21. Reprinted in Perry 1993 [2000], Chapter 2.

Perry, John. 1986. Thought without Representation. *Proceedings of the Aristotelian Society Supplementary Volumes* 60: 263–283. Reprinted in Perry 1993 [2000], Chapter 10.

Perry, John. 1988. Cognitive Significance and New Theories of Reference. *Noûs* 22: 1–18. Reprinted in Perry 1993 [2000], Chapter 11.

Perry, John. 1993 [2000]. *The Problem of the Essential Indexical and Other Essays.* New York: Oxford University Press. 2nd expanded edition, Stanford: CSLI Publications, 2000.

Perry, John. 2001. *Knowledge, Possibility and Consciousness.* Cambridge: MIT Press.

Perry, John. 2001 [2012]. *Reference and Reflexivity.* Stanford: CSLI Publications. 2nd expanded edition, 2012.

Perry, John. 2002. *Identity, Personal Identity and the Self.* Indianapolis: Hackett Publications.

Perry, John. 2003. Predelli's Threatening note: Contexts, Utterances, and Tokens in the Philosophy of Language. *Journal of Pragmatics* 35: 373–387.

Perry, John. 2003 [2019c]. The Subject Matter Fallacy. *Journal of Applied Logic* 1: 93–105. Reprinted in Perry 2019c, chapter 15.

Perry, John. 2012a. Donnellan's Blocks. *Having in Mind: The Philosophy of Keith Donnellan*, eds. J. Almog and P. Leonardi, 30–52. Oxford: Oxford University Press.

Perry, John. 2012b. *The Art of Procrastination: A Guide to Effective Dawdling, Lollygagging and Postponing.* New York: Workman.

Perry, John. 2017. Indexicals and Undexicals. In M. de Ponte and K. Korta (eds.) 2017b, 46–56.

Perry, John. 2019a. *Frege's Detour.* Oxford: Oxford University Press.

Perry, John. 2019b. *Revisiting the Essential Indexical.* Stanford: CSLI Publications.

Perry, John. 2019c. *Studies in Language and Information.* Stanford: CSLI Publications.

Ponte, María and Margarita Vázquez. 2012. Tense and Temporal Reference: Hybrid Temporal Logic. *Logique et Analyse* 220: 555–578.

Predelli, Stefano. 1998. I am not Here Now. *Analysis* 58: 107–112.

Predelli, Stefano. 2011. I am Still not Here Now. *Erkenntnis* 74: 289–303.

Prior, Arthur N. 1959. Thank Goodness that's Over. *Philosophy* 34:12–17.

Prior, Arthur N. 1970. The Notion of the Present. *Stadium Generale*, 23: 245–248.

Recanati, François. 1989. The Pragmatics of What is Said. *Mind and Language* 4: 295–329.

Recanati, François. 2004. *Literal Meaning.* Cambridge: Cambridge University Press.

Recanati, François. 2006. Predelli and Garcia-Carpintero on *Literal Meaning. Crítica*, 38 (112): 69–79.

Recanati, François. 2010. *Truth-Conditional Pragmatics.* Oxford: Oxford University Press.

Recanati, François. 2012. *Mental Files.* Oxford: Oxford University Press.

Reichenbach, Hans. 1947. *Elements of Symbolic Logic.* New York: The Free Press.

Reimer, Marga. 2002. Review of *Reference and Reflexivity* (John Perry). *Notre Dame Philosophical Reviews*. https://ndpr.nd.edu/reviews/reference-and-reflexivity/. Accessed October 14 2021.

Russell, Bertrand. 1905. On Denoting. *Mind* 14: 479–493.

Russell, Bertrand. 1948. *Human Knowledge: Its Scope and Limits*. New York: Simon and Schuster.

Russell, Bertrand. 1957. Mr. Strawson on Referring. *Mind*, 66(263), 385–389.

Salmon, Nathan. 1986. *Frege's Puzzle*. Cambridge, MA: Harvard University Press.

Saussure, Ferdinand de. 1916 [1977]. *Cours de Linguistique Générale*, ed. C. Bally and A. Sechehaye, with the collaboration of A. Riedlinger and Payot. Translated. by W. Baskin. 1977. *Course in General Linguistics*. Glasgow: Fontana/Collins.

Searle, John R. 1968. Austin on Locutionary and Illocutionary Acts. *Philosophical Review* 57(4). Reprinted in I. Berlin et al.(eds.) 1973. *Essays on J. L. Austin*, 141–159. Oxford: Oxford University Press.

Searle, John R. 1969. *Speech Acts: An Essay in the Philosophy of Language*. Cambridge: Cambridge University Press.

Searle, John R. 1975. The Logical Status of Fictional Discourse. *New Literary History* 6(2):319–332

Searle, John R. 1980. The Background of Meaning. *Speech Act Theory and Pragmatics*, eds. J. Searle, F. Keifer and M. Bierwisch, 221–32. Dordrecht: Reidel.

Searle, John R. 1989. How Performatives Work. *Linguistics and Philosophy*. 12: 535–58.

Sluga, Hans. 1980. *Gottlob Frege*. Boston: Routledge & Kegan Paul.

Sperber, Dan, and Deirdre Wilson. 1986. *Relevance: Communication and Cognition*. Oxford: Blackwell; 2nd rev. edn., 1995.

Sperber, Dan & Deirdre Wilson. 2002. Pragmatics, Modularity and Mind-Reading. *Mind and Language* 17 (1/2): 3–23.

Stainton, Robert J. and Arthur Sullivan (eds.). 2022. *Varieties of Context-Sensitivity in a Pluri-Propositionalist Reflexive Semantic Framework, Disputatio* 14 (66) (Special Issue).

Stalnaker, Robert. 1970. Pragmatics. *Synthese*, 22, 272–289.

Stanley, Jason and Szabo, Zoltan G. 2000. On Quantifier Domain Restriction. *Mind & Language* 15: 219–61.

Stojanovic, Isidora. 2007. What is Said as Lexical Meaning. *Cuadernos de Filosofía*, 21: 7–42.

Strawson, Peter F. 1950. On Referring. *Mind* 59: 320–344.

Strawson, Peter F. 1967. *Philosophical Logic*. London: Oxford University Press.

Strawson, Peter F. 1973. Austin and "Locutionary Meaning." *Essays on J. L. Austin*, eds. I. Berlin et al., 46–68. Oxford: Oxford University Press.

Sullivan, Arthur. 2013. Multiple Propositions, Contextual Variability, and the Semantics/Pragmatics Interface. *Synthese* 190 (14): 2773–2800.

Talmy Steven. 2010. Achieving Distinction Through Mock ESL: a Critical Pragmatics Analysis of Classroom Talk in a High School. *Pragmatics and Language Learning* 12: 215–254.

Taylor, Kenneth. 2001. Sex, Breakfast, and Descriptus Interruptus. *Synthese* 128: 45–61.

Thau, Michael and Ben Caplan. 2001. What is Puzzling Gottlob Frege? *Canadian Journal of Philosophy.* 31(2): 159–200.

Travis, Charles. 1997. Pragmatics. *A Companion to the Philosophy of Language*, eds. B. Hale and C. Wright, 87–107. Oxford: Blackwell.

Ulrich, Werner. 2007. The Greening of Pragmatism (iii): the Way Ahead. https://wulrich.com/publications. Accessed November 2 2021.

Vallée, Richard. 2005 [2018]. Complex Demonstratives, Articulation and Overarticulation. *Dialogue* 44 (1): 97–121. Reprinted in Vallée 2018, 45–68.

Vallée, Richard. 2008 [2018]. Conventional Implicature Revisited. *Journal of Pragmatics* 40 (3): 407–30. Reprinted in Vallée 2018, 95–124.

Vallée, Richard. 2012. On Local Bars and Imported Beer. *Pragmatics and Cognition* 20(1): 62–87.

Vallée, Richard. 2014. Slurring and Common Knowledge of Ordinary Language. *Journal of Pragmatics* 61:78–90.

Vallée, Richard. 2018. Fictional Names and Truth. *Organon F*, 25 (1).

Vallée, Richard, 2018, *Words and Contents*. Stanford: CSLI Publications.

Wettstein, Howard. 1986. Has Semantics Rested on a Mistake? *The Journal of Philosophy* 83: 185–209.

Wettstein, Howard. 1991. *Has Semantics Rested on a Mistake?* Stanford; Stanford University Press.

Wilson, Deirdre and Dan Sperber. 2012. *Meaning and Relevance.* Cambridge: Cambridge University Press.

Zimmerman, Dan. 2008. The Privileged Present: Defending an "A-theory" of Time. *Contemporary Debates in Metaphysics*, eds. T. Sider, J. Hawthorne and D. W. Zimmerman, 211–225. Oxford: Basil Blackwell.

Zubeldia, Larraitz. 2010. *"Omen" Partikularen Azterketa Semantikoa eta Pragmatikoa/Semantic and Pragmatic Analysis of the Basque Particle "Omen".* Doctoral Dissertation, University of the Basque Country.

Index

accomplishment, 46, 47, 51, 79, 126
act, 51, 52, 79, 80, 90, 95, 105, 124–126, 131, 135, 140, 141, 153, 162, 163, 199n, 204, 269, 273, 275, 279, 301
   communicative, xiv, 87, 88, 130, 167
   illocutionary, xiv, 43, 45, 47, 123, 207, 265
   intentional, 1, 10, 22, 60, 63, 219
   locutionary, 43–46, 49, 50, 53, 55, 56, 64, 123, 265
   perlocutionary, 43, 47, 123, 265
   referential, 88, 94, 96, 106, 203
action, xv, 5, 6, 17, 22, 45, 46, 51, 59, 63, 79, 80, 83, 86–88, 97, 99, 100, 102, 105, 115, 120, 123–125, 141, 168, 170, 177n, 186–188, 196, 248, 256, 261, 266–268, 273n, 274, 275, 285, 287, 288, 290–292, 297
action theory, xvii, 123, 125, 265, 268, 273, 279, 285
agent, xvi, 27, 29, 46, 63, 76, 77, 79, 89, 90, 92–94, 105, 112, 114, 123, 125–127, 162, 177, 187, 188, 199, 223, 245–247, 273, 284, 288, 295, 296
ambiguity, 33, 64, 69, 125, 149n, 169, 175n, 215, 280, 290
Anscombe, Elizabeth, 268
Aphrodite, 192, 193
Aristotle, 37, 50, 51, 65, 197n, 257, 258
Armstrong, David, 291
attitude report, 110–116, 120, 223, 245, 284, 294
Austin, John L., xvii, 26, 43, 45, 51, 55, 56, 64, 70, 86, 123, 265, 266n, 267, 268, 275, 276, 285, 290

Bach, Kent, 23n, 25, 144n, 147, 155, 160, 166, 169
Bain, Shannon, xviii
Barcan Marcus, Ruth, 181, 271
Barceló, Axel, 171n
Barwise, Jon, 124n, 147, 214, 280
Batman, 204n
Beckham, David, 6
Binoche, Juliette, 85
Black, Max, 236n, 268
Bobonich, Chris, 257
Botterell, Andrew, 300, 302n
Broncano-Berrocal, Fernando, 248n

buffer, 93, 126–129, 136
Bush, George, 95, 128–130, 257

Calado, Eduarda, xviii
Canary Islands, xv, 249, 297
Caplan, Ben, 243, 244
Capone, Alessandro, 154n
Cappelen, Herman, 25, 64, 66, 69, 72, 147, 151, 152, 155, 156, 166n, 169
Carnap, Rudolf, 131, 132, 267n
Carston, Robyn, 25, 34, 40, 147, 151, 155n, 156–158, 159n, 166, 169, 171
character, 2, 27, 29, 44, 76, 77, 89, 109, 128, 133, 146, 149, 168, 193, 194–198, 206, 209, 211, 213, 214, 219, 220, 223, 258, 273, 279, 281, 283, 284, 299n
Ciecierski, Tadeusz, 210, 244
Clapp, Lenny, xviii
Clark, Herbert, 95, 96, 101
Clemens, Samuel, 270
Clinton, Bill, 87
Clinton, Hillary, 222, 283
coco-refer, 135, 137, 138, 195, 200–202, 206, 209
cognitive episode, xvii, 211, 213–216, 220–224, 248, 249, 252, 261, 275, 276, 279, 283, 284, 297
cognitive fix, xv, 88, 90, 93, 96–99, 101–103, 105, 127–131, 133, 135, 136, 139, 203, 218
cognitive value, 235, 237–239
completion, xv, 20, 71, 160, 161
condition
  existential, 199, 202, 205–208
  identifying, xiv, 44, 60, 62, 75–77, 85, 89, 93, 108, 108, 139, 163, 193, 271

reference, 199, 202, 205–208
satisfaction, xiv, xv, 199, 202, 205–208, 249, 276, 291
content (see also *truth-conditions*)
  hybrid, xiv, 251, 252, 254, 294, 299, 301, 303
  locutionary, 26, 27, 29, 32, 34–37, 42–45, 47–54, 55n, 56–59, 64, 72, 294
  pluralism, xiii, 35, 37, 40, 140, 141, 170
  referential, xiv, 26, 31, 37, 44, 47, 48, 54, 56, 59, 61, 62, 66, 71, 73, 99, 109, 114, 116, 117, 119, 121, 142, 153, 164, 166, 170, 217, 219, 251, 252, 254, 255, 258–261, 279, 281, 293, 294, 296, 298–300, 303
  reflexive, xiv, 31, 35, 44, 48, 53, 54, 56, 58, 59, 62, 66–68, 70–73, 158, 164, 165, 218, 294, 295, 300–303
  semantic, xv, 25, 26, 32, 33, 35, 41, 42, 64, 66, 69, 73, 144, 145, 148, 149, 153, 170, 171
context, xvi, 6, 8, 21, 27, 29, 30, 32, 36, 38–40, 43, 44, 47n, 53–55, 62, 63, 66, 72, 74, 76, 77, 90, 108, 111, 114–116, 128, 134, 144n, 146, 147, 157, 160, 161, 165, 170, 182, 211, 213, 214, 219, 220, 222–224, 227, 228, 273–275, 279-282, 284, 293, 301
contextualism, xiii, 34, 65, 66, 140n, 146, 170, 171
Corazza, Eros, xviii, 142, 154n, 171n, 189n, 292

co-refer, 135, 138, 195, 200, 202, 220, 238, 241, 281
CSLI, ix, 47, 52, 62n, 142n, 189n, 210n, 224n
Curcó, Carmen, 157, 158, 171n

Davis, Wayne, 171n
Dedekind, Richard, 267
demonstrative, xiv, xv, xvii, 3, 4, 15–18, 41, 42, 44, 46, 64, 76, 80–82, 88, 89, 99, 103, 105, 120, 128n, 129–132, 134, 136, 139, 141, 152, 156, 161, 165, 170, 181, 183, 186, 196n, 199, 203, 211, 213, 214, 217, 255, 258, 259n, 260, 262, 274, 275, 279, 289
description
   definite, 3, 75, 84, 86, 88, 89, 99, 105, 138, 139, 181n, 205, 268, 270–272, 274
   utterance-bound, 7, 18, 32, 34, 35, 70
Diamond XX Phil. Institute, 23n, 42n, 210n, 224n
Díaz Legaspe, Justina, 171n
Dole, Bob, 87, 98, 99
domain of quantification, 4, 18–20, 72, 146
Donnellan, Keith, 37, 39, 77, 89, 90, 107, 125, 127, 135, 138, 139, 181, 201, 202, 268, 271, 289
Donostia, ix, 16, 17, 19, 37, 110–115, 133, 134, 253–255, 278, 279, 289, 290, 294, 300, 301
Doyle, Arthur Conan, xvi, 193, 195–198, 204, 208
Dummett, Michael, xv, 226n, 231n, 235n
Dylan, Bob, 222–224, 283, 284

Elugardo, Ray, 300–303
emotion, 174–177, 179, 188, 189
enrichment, 3, 19, 151, 158, 160, 169
equality, 229n, 230n, 235, 236
Esnaola, Beñat, xviii
Etchemendy, John, ix, 147
Etchemendy, Nancy, ix
execution, 46, 79, 125,
explicature, 34, 35, 41, 64, 73, 151, 158, 159, 169
Ezcurdia, Maite, 171n

Fairweather, Abrol, 263
file, 51, 58, 125, 126, 127, 202, 256, 258
Føllesdal, Dagfinn, 271
Franco, Francisco, 270
Frege, Gottlob, xii, xvi, xvii, 48, 88, 125, 192, 196, 199n, 205, 220, 225–244, 249, 255, 257, 259, 263, 265–267, 270–272, 275, 276, 281, 298, 300
Friend, Stacie, xviii, 197n

García-Ramírez, Eduardo, 171n
Garmendia, Ekain, xviii
Garmendia, Joana, xviii, 55, 62n, 142, 154n
Geach, Peter, 48, 227, 236n, 268, 269
Genovesi, Chris, xviii
Gödel, Kurt, 232, 242
Goldfarb, Warren, 231
Goodman, Ellen, 87, 98
Grice, H. Paul, xii, xiv, xv, xvii, 1–6, 8, 13–16, 21–23, 26, 28, 33, 35, 37, 42, 44, 45, 47, 48, 64, 66, 70, 71, 86, 94, 95, 107, 121, 124, 135n, 143–146, 149, 151-153, 158, 159, 168, 169, 265–

268, 275, 276, 285, 290, 301, 303, 304
Grice's (pragmatic) circle, xiv, xv, 65–67, 69, 74, 142, 143n, 144, 145, 147, 152, 153

Hales, Stephen, 247, 248n, 252
Harris, Kamala, 256
Heck, Richard, 243
Heimson, 222–224, 283, 284, 288
Holmes, Sherlock, 191, 193–198, 204, 206–210
Homer, 192
Hondarribia, 110
Horn, Jacob, 191–193, 201, 203, 204, 206
Horn, Jakob, 201
Horn, Larry, 171n
Horn, William, 192, 201
Huang, Yan, 169, 171n
Hume, David, xv, 222, 224, 283, 284, 288
Hung, Jenny, xviii

identity, xvi, xvii, 4n, 38, 73, 74, 105, 120, 147, 164, 185–187, 204n, 225, 226, 228, 229, 230n, 235, 241, 242–244, 252, 260, 262, 270
identity of content, xvii, 225, 227–229, 230n, 231, 233, 237, 243, 244
identity statement, 26, 53, 58, 166, 174, 184, 186, 226, 238, 239, 243, 244, 255, 279, 289, 294, 298
ILCLI, ix, 62n, 121n, 142n, 154n, 171n, 210n, 224n, 304n
illocutionary point, 57–59, 70, 71
implicature, xiii, xiv, 1, 2, 4, 12–22, 28, 29, 34, 35, 40, 41, 44, 47, 59, 65, 66, 69–71, 74, 88, 107, 109, 118–121, 125, 128, 135n, 140, 141, 143, 144, 146, 147, 151–153, 159, 168–170, 266, 275, 285, 289
incompletism, 155, 157, 158, 161, 164, 165, 170, 171
indexical, xiv–xvii, 3, 4, 9, 15, 19, 21, 32, 42, 44, 46, 53, 58, 62, 64, 65, 76, 77, 80–83, 85, 88–90, 93, 99, 105, 120, 127, 129, 130, 132–134, 136, 141, 144, 146–148, 156, 161, 162, 165, 170, 174, 175, 177n, 181–183, 187, 199, 203, 211, 213, 214, 220, 222, 258, 260, 266, 268, 272–275, 279, 281, 282, 289, 301n
intention (see also *referential plan*)
auxiliary, xiv, 87, 99, 100, 128, 130
communicative, 2, 62, 124, 272
directing, xiv, 87, 99, 101, 103, 128–132, 138
grammatical, xiv, 87, 99–101, 130
path, xiv, 87, 99, 100, 102, 103, 128, 130, 132, 133, 138
referential, 88, 103, 105, 130, 131
speaker, 4, 15, 139, 274
target, xiv, 87, 99, 100, 102, 103, 128, 130, 131, 133, 136, 138, 139
Israel, David, 23, 32, 61, 62, 95, 124n, 126

Jack the Ripper, xvii, 247, 248, 252–254, 260
Jackson, Frank, 174, 177–180, 183

INDEX / 323

James, William, 289
Jesus Christ, 8
Joel, Billy, 224

Kant, Immanuel, 232, 235
Kaplan, David, xiv, xvi, 26, 27, 29, 32, 37, 44, 63, 67n, 75–77, 89, 90, 107–109, 111n, 119, 128n, 131, 133, 134, 146, 181, 211, 213, 214, 216, 218, 220, 223, 224, 266, 269, 271, 273–275, 279–281, 283, 284, 289, 299
Karagueuzian, Dikran, ix, 189
Kecskes, Istvan, 142n
Kennedy, Jackie, 50
Kennedy, John F., 61
Kiernan-Lewis, Delmas, 178

Larrazabal, Jesus M., ix, 23n, 292
Lavalle Terrón, Armando, xviii
Lepore, Ernie, xiii, 25, 64, 66, 69, 72, 147, 151, 152, 155, 156, 166n, 169
Le Verrier, Urbain, 205, 206
Lewis, David, 223, 224, 283, 284
literalism, 64, 65, 71
Loar, Brian, xvii, 246, 255, 258–260, 263
Lodwick, Michelle, 189n
Lo Guercio, Nicolás, 171n
London, xvii, 191, 195, 16, 197n, 206–208, 247, 250, 253
Losada, Alfonso, 171n

Malcolm, Norman, 266n, 268
Malinowski, Bronislaw, 123n
McAlary, Davis, 166, 167, 170
McTaggart, John M. E., 173, 212
Martí, Genoveva, xviii, 62n

Mellor, D. Hugh, 180n
Mercury, 191, 205, 206
minimalism, 2, 29, 30, 31, 33, 35, 40, 41, 64, 140n, 147, 161, 170, 171
mode of presentation, 17, 19, 93, 237, 257
Moloch, 204n
Montemayor, Carlos, 263n
Morris, Charles W., 265, 288, 289

nambiguity, 46, 61, 62, 257
necessity, xvii, 170, 246–248, 252–254
Neptune, 205
Nida-Rümelin, Martine, 179,
notion, xvi, xvii, 9, 83, 84, 97–99, 102, 104, 111–116, 120, 126–129, 131, 135, 136, 138, 164, 194, 200, 201–205, 207–210, 256–263, 295, 296

Oaklander, L. Nathan, 180n
Odysseus, 191,192
Onassis, Aristotle, 50, 65
Orlando, Eleonora, xviii

Palo Alto, 119, 275
Pease, Emma, 189
Peirce, Charles, 265, 289
Penco, Carlo, xviii, 292
Perini Santos, Ernesto, xviii
Perry, Frenchie, ix, 254, 255, 278
physicalism, 174, 177–180, 184
plan
  communicative, 87, 129, 168
  speaker, 1, 71
Polakof, Ana Clara, xviii
possibility, 28, 103, 116, 147, 188n, 223, 253, 283

possible world, 11, 36, 63, 75, 220, 248, 250, 253, 271, 273, 277
Potts, Chris, 189n
pragmatic process, xiv, xv, 7, 20, 21, 40, 41, 144, 151, 153, 155, 157–159, 171
pragmatics
  far-side, xiv, 64, 65, 68, 70, 72–74, 145, 159, 168, 275, 276n
  near-side, xiv, 36, 64, 65, 68, 69, 74, 144, 145, 149, 151, 153, 158, 168, 275, 276n
Preyer, Gerhard, xiii, 26
Princeton, 107–109, 115–120
Prior, Arthur, xv, xvi, 173–183, 185, 187–189, 212, 213, 216–220, 280n
proper name, xi, xiv, 4, 7, 20, 33, 37, 41, 42, 44–47, 50, 54, 55, 58, 61, 64, 65, 75–77, 81–85, 88–90, 92, 93, 98, 99, 102, 104, 105, 110–113, 120, 127, 129, 130, 133–139, 141, 146, 147, 162, 164, 181, 183, 191, 198–204, 215, 220, 226, 227, 229, 231, 233–241, 243, 244, 254, 255, 257, 258, 260, 263, 266, 268–272, 274, 280, 281, 289, 294, 296, 300, 301
  empty, 191, 192, 194, 197, 202–206, 208
  fictional, xvi, 191–198, 200n, 204, 206–209
proposition, xv, 6, 11, 27, 36–39, 42, 48, 50, 51, 56, 57, 60–62, 66–69, 74, 76, 83, 92, 110, 114, 117, 125, 148–150, 155, 160–165, 169, 170, 174, 175, 177, 180, 183, 185, 214, 224, 245, 248–250, 255, 262, 267, 269, 276–278, 280, 284, 288, 292, 295, 296–299
  expressed, xii, xiv, 2, 5, 8–10, 12, 13, 17, 18, 20, 21, 25, 26, 30–32, 34, 35, 41, 44, 45, 58, 59, 62, 64, 67, 69–73, 75–77, 85, 105, 107, 108, 117, 120, 121, 123, 133–135, 137, 138, 140, 143–147, 151–153, 156–159, 163, 180–182, 184, 187, 199, 205, 211–213, 219, 220, 251, 265, 274, 293, 294, 298
  reflexive, 66, 165, 166
  singular, xii, xiv, 4, 66, 85, 99, 108, 109, 116, 120, 121, 135, 139, 165, 167, 181, 193, 198, 204n, 220, 223, 241, 258, 271, 281, 283, 284, 289, 290, 292, 298, 300
propositional attitude, 105, 245, 249, 295, 296
propositionalism, 158, 161
  mono-, xv, 105, 124, 140, 170, 292
  multi-, 291-293
  pluri-, 276, 291, 292

Recanati, François, 3, 25, 41, 64–66, 71, 74, 83, 84, 155–160, 165, 166, 169
reference, xii, xiv–xvii, 3n, 9, 15, 18, 26, 33, 37, 41, 42, 46, 51, 55, 63, 64, 68, 69, 75–77, 81, 84–90, 94–97, 99–101, 103, 105, 116, 121, 123, 125, 127–132, 140, 142, 144, 146, 147, 151, 153, 158, 160, 169, 175–177, 181, 184, 191, 194n, 199n, 200, 202, 203, 209, 212, 215, 216, 241, 244, 250, 251, 254, 256–

261, 263, 266–277, 280, 281, 285, 294
referential plan, xiv, 87, 97, 99, 100, 103, 128, 130
  GDTPA structure of, 87, 88, 99, 100, 105, 128
Reimer, Marga, 300
relevance theory, 141, 142, 169, 303
Roberts, Julia, 81–85, 97, 98
role, 80, 91, 126
  -coordination, xiv, 80–85
  epistemic, 91, 93, 94, 101, 131, 132, 174, 126
  -linking, 78, 80, 83, 84, 136
  -management, 90, 97, 99, 105, 128, 135, 136, 138, 140
  -nesting, 78
  pragmatic, 91, 93, 101, 131, 132
  speaker-relative, 85, 91
  -transferring, 78, 103
  utterance-relative, 82, 89–91, 126, 127, 136, 219
Romero-Trillo, Jesús, 285
Ronaldo, 6
Russell, Bertrand, 88, 125, 129, 137, 138, 192, 205, 266–269, 271–273, 275, 276, 300
Ryle, Gilbert, 266n

Sag, Ivan, 110–115
San Francisco, 277
  Bay, 218
San Sebastian, 37, 110–114, 254, 255, 278, 289, 290, 294, 301
saturation, 19, 20, 66, 74, 157, 159n, 160, 161, 164, 165, 170
Saussure, Ferdinand de, 265n

Searle, John R., xiii, xiv, 8, 41, 43, 45, 51, 55–59, 64, 70, 71, 140, 197n, 207, 265, 274, 296
self,
  self-identity, 37, 298
  self-knowledge, 186, 189, 275
  self-notion, 132, 133
speech act, xiv, 25, 40, 57, 66, 72, 88, 145, 161, 271, 294n
  pluralism 26, 34, 35, 38
  theory, 43, 44, 59, 64, 70, 71, 140, 141, 265, 275, 297
Sperber, Dan, 25, 40, 141, 155–159, 166n
Stainton, Robert, 302n
Stanley, Jason, 156n
Stojanovic, Isidora, 74n
Strawson, Peter F., xvii, 55n, 125, 199, 205, 266n, 267–269, 272–274, 285
Szabo, Zoltan, 156n

Tarski, Alfred, 232, 242
Taylor, Ken, 23n, 155n
Tenerife, xv
Thau, Michael, 243, 244
thought, xvi, 6, 12, 86, 102, 158, 174, 175, 181, 184, 214, 223, 224, 226, 227, 238–241, 243, 244, 248, 249, 272, 276, 283, 299, 303
  A-thought, 176, 177, 179, 180, 182, 185, 187–189
  B-thought, 176, 177, 179, 180, 182, 185, 186–187
Thunderbold, Ignatius P., 193
time
  A-properties, 173, 174, 176, 177n, 179, 180, 183, 187, 189, 212
  A-series, 173

B-relations, 173, 174, 176, 179
B-series, 212
future, 57, 59, 70, 71, 141, 173, 175, 176, 179, 182, 183, 188, 212
past, 59, 75, 127, 173, 174, 176–179, 182, 183, 188, 212, 285
present, 3, 12, 156, 173, 175, 176, 179, 182, 183, 187, 188, 195, 212, 259, 269, 272, 273, 297n
Travis, Charles, 41, 156
truth
truth-conditions (see also *content*), xiii, xv, 2, 11, 21–23, 27, 50, 59, 60, 62, 67, 71, 88, 114–118, 120, 121, 132, 140, 143, 149, 150, 157, 158, 161, 162n, 163, 199, 204, 205, 207–209, 212, 223, 224, 242, 249, 253, 258, 270, 272–274, 276, 277, 284, 289, 290–294, 300, 304
designational, 139, 152n, 299
hybrid, xii, xiv, 218, 251, 252, 254, 294, 295, 298, 299, 301, 303
incremental, 52, 62, 135n, 219, 278
network-bound, 130, 137, 138, 152n, 164, 170
notion-bound, xvi, 256, 258, 259, 262, 295
referential, xii, xvi, 10, 46, 52, 58, 124, 134, 135n, 138, 151, 164, 206n, 215–218, 281, 295 297, 298
referential*, 139, 140, 299
reflexive, xi, xii, 9, 10, 12, 16, 18, 33, 46, 47, 52, 54, 56, 57, 68, 72, 117, 124, 137, 153, 215–218, 220, 221, 278, 281, 289n, 295, 297–299, 301, 302
speaker-bound, 69, 137, 138, 141, 152n, 164, 170
utterance-bound, 9, 32–36, 117, 134–136, 138, 151–153, 164, 218, 219, 250, 251, 278
truth-value, xvi, 30, 31, 39, 117, 155, 192, 193, 197, 205, 239, 240, 242, 267, 273, 297
Tsohatzidis, Savas L., xiii, 62n,
Tutiya, Syun, 126
Twain, Mark, 9, 10, 12, 270, 271

unarticulated constituent, 3, 19, 21, 34, 113, 139, 140, 142, 146, 160, 164, 199
underdeterminacy, 18, 21, 148, 158, 161
Uranus, 205
Urmson, James O., 268

Vallée, Richard, xviii, 142, 222, 282, 292, 293
Vagueness, 30, 32, 42, 65, 69, 93, 169
Vulcan, 191, 192, 194, 204–207

Washington, George, 245, 246
Watson, John H., 194, 195, 208
what is said, xiii, xiv, 1–10, 12–15, 17–23, 25, 26, 29, 34–45, 47, 49, 51, 53, 54, 59, 62, 64, 65, 67, 70–72, 105, 107–110, 114, 117, 119–121, 135n, 137, 140, 143–153, 157–160, 165–171, 206n, 253–255, 258, 259, 266, 278, 279, 293n, 294, 304
Wayne, Bruce, 204
Wettstein, Howard, 89, 93, 127, 213n, 218n, 220, 281, 299

Whitehead, Alfred N., 267
Wilson, Deirdre, 25, 40, 48, 141, 155–159, 166, 171
Wilson, Harold, 3n, 4–6, 12–14, 16
Wittgenstein, Ludwig, 86, 123n, 266n, 268

Zeus, 191–193
Zubeldia, Larraitz, xviii, 142, 154